Medieval Thought

The Western Intellectual Tradition from Antiquity to the
Thirteenth Century

Medieval Thought

The Western Intellectual Tradition from
Antiquity to the Thirteenth Century

Second edition

MICHAEL HAREN

University of Toronto Press
Toronto and Buffalo

For Elspeth, Sarah and Andrea

First edition 1985

Second edition first published in North America by
UNIVERSITY OF TORONTO PRESS INCORPORATED 1992

ISBN 0–8020–2868–3 (cloth)
ISBN 0–8020–7758–7 (paper)

Second edition published in Great Britain by
THE MACMILLAN PRESS LTD 1992

Canadian Cataloguing in Publication Data
Haren, Michael
Medieval thought: the Western intellectual
tradition from antiquity to the thirteenth century
2nd ed.
Includes bibliographical references and index.
ISBN 0–8020–2868–3 (bound)   ISBN 0–8020–7758–7 (pbk.)
1. Philosophy, Medieval.   2. Philosophy, Ancient.
I. Title.
B721. H37   1992   189   C92–094449–3

Printed in Hong Kong

Contents

List of Plates

1. Genesis initial, showing the creation (thirteenth century)
2. Socrates and Plato (thirteenth century)
3. Fortune's Wheel (fourteenth century)
4. Monk writing (twelfth century)
5. Monastic school, probably representing that of St Victor (thirteenth century)
6. A scholar's hand of the thirteenth century – considered to be that of Thomas Aquinas

Acknowledgements

The cover illustration (Ms.Auct. F. 6. 5, fol. 7ᵛ), Plate 2 (Ms. Ashmole 304, fol. 31ᵛ) and Plate 5 (Ms. Laud Misc. 409, fol. 3ᵛ) are reproduced by permission of the Bodleian Library, Oxford. Plate 1 (Ms. Burney 3, fol. 5ᵛ) is reproduced by permission of the British Library. Plate 3 (Corpus Christi College, Cambridge, Ms. 66, page 66) is reproduced by permission of the Master and Fellows of Corpus Christi College, Cambridge and the Conway Library, Courtauld Institute of Art. Plate 4 (CUL, Ms. Ii.4.26, fol. 63ᵛ) is reproduced by permission of the Syndics of Cambridge University Library. The author and publisher are grateful to Aberdeen University Photographic Department for supplying the print for Plate 6, taken from F. Steffens, *Lateinische Paläographie* (Trier, 1909), Plate 95.

Preface to the First Edition

IT is agreeable to recall the help which I have received and the debts which I have incurred while engaged on this book. The late Denis Bethell was responsible for suggesting it to me and he encouraged my earliest progress in it. I am deeply conscious of the stimulus which he afforded. Maurice Keen, as general editor, has helped me greatly by his judicious comments and suggestions and his characteristic courtesy has added much to the pleasure of writing. Leslie Macfarlane read a large part of the work in draft and Michael Richter the whole. From both I derived valuable insights. I also profited from a reading of the first chapter by William Charlton and from discussing my ideas at a formative stage with Jeremy Catto. To all I am grateful. I hope they will feel that some of the seed of their good advice bore fruit. For such as fell on stony ground I apologise.

My wife, Elspeth, has been a constant counsel and critic, whose lively interest in the classical period and clear judgements helped me over many difficulties of formulation and expression. My sister-in-law, Anne, took from me a large part of the burden of making a clean typescript. I am grateful to the publishers for patiently awaiting completion and for their assistance throughout.

One debt is old and of peculiar status. It is that which I owe for my interest in medieval thought. I acknowledge it in the dedication.

Dublin   MICHAEL HAREN
June 1984

Preface to the Second Edition

IN this second edition I have included a Supplementary Bibliography recording, as far as relates to the principal themes of the book, the considerable wealth of scholarship on medieval thought that has appeared since it was written. A new annotated Epilogue surveys the implications of recent research, while the original epilogue is now incorporated as a chapter in its own right. The publisher has, moreover, allowed me to make some line changes both to the

original text and to its notes. I hope that with these additions the
book will provide into a new decade an up-to-date account of the
state of the question in a subject whose current vitality testifies to its
continuing importance.

I am most grateful to the readers by whose comments on the first
edition I have been prompted to fresh thinking, not all of it as yet
elaborated. They include those who had a formal role as academic
reviewers and those scholarly friends who have informally and
generously given me the much valued benefit of their advice and
encouragement. Among the latter I think particularly of Leslie
Macfarlane, to whom, in inadequate acknowledgement of an intellectual debt, the first edition was dedicated. I am conscious too of
the special contribution of my students in University College Dublin
who over the years have been at first the guinea-pigs and, latterly,
among the shrewdest assessors of my experiment in communicating
medieval thought — 'unwitting guinea-pigs' I was to say, though
since, as Chaucer has it, students 'ben ful subtile and ful queynte',
this may be my illusion. One of the lessons I have learned from them
is the verisimilitude of those references by medieval teachers to
intellectual departures that had their origin in the classroom.

Sophie Lillington of Macmillan suggested that I write the new
piece on recent research and I acknowledge a stimulus without
which, amid other preoccupations, I would not have collected my
thoughts. Anne Neville as copy editor made most helpful suggestions regarding presentation.

The women in my life give me so much support and put up with
so much disruption that some token of recompense is due. I dedicate
the second edition to them.

Dublin   M. H.
Autumn 1991

Abbreviations

AHDLMA	*Archives d'Histoire Doctrinale et Littéraire du Moyen Age*
BGPMA	*Beiträge zur Geschichte der Philosophie [und Theologie] des Mittelalters*
Chart. Univ. Par.	*Chartularium Universitatis Parisiensis*
CHLGEMP	*The Cambridge History of Later Greek and Early Medieval Philosophy*, ed. A. H. Armstrong (Cambridge, 1970)
CSEL	*Corpus Scriptorum Ecclesiasticorum Latinorum*
JEH	*Journal of Ecclesiastical History*
MS	*Mediaeval Studies*
PL	*Patrologia Latina*, ed. J. P. Migne
RB	*Revue Bénédictine*
RSPT	*Revue des Sciences Philosophiques et Théologiques*
RTAM	*Recherches de Théologie Ancienne et Médiévale*
SM	*Studi Medievali*
STGM	*Studien und Texte zur Geistesgeschichte des Mittelalters*

Introduction

THIS book in some respects defies its title. Important areas of the intellectual composition of the middle ages have been consciously omitted. Broadly speaking, theology is not considered, to the extent at least that it derived from scripture rather than from philosophical reflection, though exceptions have been admitted where necessary in order to illuminate particular aspects of a thinker's method. Nor do I deal with literature as such, music, art, architecture or law, except for passing references – as, for instance, to their place within the programme of study or to how, in the case of law, it was affected by evolving techniques of criticism. The emphasis is on speculative thought, not however considered in the abstract but as manifesting the continuing vitality of an aspect of classical culture in the medieval world.

Medieval thought stemmed from the confluence of the speculative legacy of antiquity with a powerful new religious orientation and changed structures of society. Once again in the history of culture 'captive Greece' demonstrated its power to take captive. In the course of doing so its ideas too were changed and given new application. The process was not without its turbulent episodes and these are a part of the theme. But the result was an outlook and a critical approach of immense depth and sophistication. The systems of thought thus generated were the products of the greatest minds of western Europe within the period surveyed: Augustine, Scotus Eriugena, Anselm, Abelard, Aquinas, Bonaventure, to name only the most outstanding. A study of their methods and conclusions is indispensable for an understanding of medieval civilisation and of the subsequent intellectual history of Europe.

Of the several foundations and components of medieval thought, the review pays most attention to the classical legacy. This is because it is an aspect with which students in the English-speaking world are progressively less acquainted. Little is said within by way of introducing specifically Christian concepts, though the more technical points are explained as the need arises. However, the same degree of familiarity with the Christian background as heretofore can no longer be assumed and some preliminary remarks seem called for.

Christianity began as a messianic movement within Judaism. Soon

1

after the death of Jesus its message was carried into the Gentile world chiefly through the mission of Paul. Paul's letters or 'Epistles' are its earliest writings. The principal source for Jesus' life and teaching are the four Gospels, compiled on the basis of earlier material and traditions between *c.* AD 70, the probable date of the first, that of Mark, and *c.* 110, the probable date of the last, that of John. Paul's letters were written before Christianity began to be persecuted by the Roman authorities. This and the fact that Paul himself, though a Jew, was a Roman citizen, explains his positive attitude towards temporal power, which he regarded as having divine sanction. As will be seen, this aspect of his teaching had an important influence. A quite different view was taken by the *Book of Revelation*, written probably in the reign of the emperor Domitian (81–96). This saw Rome as one of the great enemies of Christianity and prophesied the imminent overthrow of the empire and the ushering in of Christ's kingdom. Apart from its own scriptures (the New Testament), Christianity accepted the canonical books of Judaism (the Old Testament), seeing itself as the fulfilment of prophecies which they contained.

In its initial phase Christianity owed nothing to speculative philosophy and shows little evidence of contact with it. An exception to this may be the prologue to the Fourth Gospel (the Gospel of John), which presents Christ as the eternal Logos, a term current in contemporary thought. There are possibly echoes of Stoicism in Paul but he was generally dismissive of worldly wisdom. His letters are not philosophical in inspiration; they are rather an urgent statement of the divine purpose in history. As Christianity met the classical systems, points of special sensitivity and even of incompatibility were identified between the Christian and pagan perspectives. One such was the doctrine of the creation of the world, described in the Old Testament Book of Genesis as a deliberate act of God and as accomplished over a period of six days. Moreover, Christianity saw the world as subject to providential care and God as intervening in it. On these points it was at odds with the Aristotelian and Neoplatonist analyses. Another sensitive matter, debated between Christianity and Neoplatonism, was the Christian doctrine that the bodies of the dead would be resurrected at Christ's second coming. The way in which this would take place was subject to varying interpretations within Christianity itself but it was particularly problematical for those Neoplatonists who saw flesh and spirit as radically foreign to each other. When Neoplatonist apologetic ceased, this debate lost its topicality but aspects of the resurrection of the body featured as a minor issue in the reception of Aristotle's philosophical works during the thirteenth century.

Close contact between Christianity and classical philosophy is evident from about the middle of the second century. Justin Martyr (d. 162–8), a Greek Samarian who had studied philosophy at Ephesus before converting to Christianity, was open in his appreciation of all wisdom and had an especially high regard for Plato, despite errors which he considered him to have made. His attitude was both representative of and influential on a strand of contemporary Christianity, mainly though not exclusively in the east. A similar outlook is found in Clement of Alexandria (d. *c.* 215), who valued logic in particular as a tool of the theologian and philosophy as a preparation for theology. The same acceptance of logic and philosophy but with a marked loftiness of tone appears in Clement's younger contemporary at Alexandria, Origen (184–*c.* 254). He had studied philosophy perhaps under the same teacher as Plotinus, the Neoplatonist. With appropriate emendations from a Christian perspective, Origen took large elements of philosophy, especially of Stoicism and Platonism, as a matter of course, and relied on it to answer the attacks of pagan philosophical apologetic. His account of the soul corresponds to aspects of contemporary Platonism, particularly the idea that souls inhabit bodies as a result of a Fall and are destined to recover their true state upon their achieving release from material attachment. Origen held that no part of creation was to be considered permanently alienated from its source and that all rational creatures could eventually, through purgation, return to their Creator, though they might be subject to recurring Falls. His doctrine that even the devil could be saved was condemned at Alexandria and he withdrew to Palestine where he spent about the last twenty years of his life. Despite the distrust in which he was held by many, his influence in the east was great. In the next century, it affected the Cappadocian Fathers – St Basil of Caesarea (*c.* 330–79), Basil's friend, St Gregory Nazianzen (*c.* 329–*c.* 390), and above all, Basil's brother, St Gregory of Nyssa (d. 394), all of whom and particularly Gregory of Nyssa were also heavily and directly indebted to Neoplatonism.

The continuous subject of the present study begins in Chapter 2 with the thought of St Augustine, the greatest of the Latin Fathers and the major theological authority of western Christendom during the middle ages. Chapter 1 is an introductory survey of the Greek systems whose impact on Christian thinkers is the main theme of the book. There are distinct advantages in approaching medieval thought by way of a preliminary review of the classical background. First, it is a convenient introduction to terminology and preoccupations which will become current in the middle ages and is an economical point of reference when classical ideas are explored by later writers. Similarly, it is a point of reference by which to measure modifications and elaborations of the original ideas. Secondly, it provides a criterion by which to estimate the progress of the movement by which the middle ages gradually recovered large parts of the ancient heritage. In particular, it gives substance to the distinction between the logical and the philosophical phases of Aristotelianism from the eleventh to the thirteenth century. This distinction is an important feature of a history of medieval thought. From being first known to the middle ages in his own right as a logician, Aristotle became in the course of a century of fervid activity between 1150 and 1250 a challenging and provocative expounder of the natural order. The broad shape of the book is thus that it begins with an account of a body of ideas and ends at a point where they have been reabsorbed into the western Latin tradition.

The term tradition itself is an aspect of the book's title which requires some definition, since it might give a misleading impression of homogeneity. In fact, there are several traditions or, better, several strands within the tradition. First, there is the Platonist strand. This was transmitted to the west principally in the works of Augustine and in the theological tractates and the *Consolation of Philosophy* by Boethius but was augmented by the pseudo-Dionysius and the other translations and independent work of John Scotus Eriugena. It is the dominant feature of Chapter 2. Then there is the Aristotelian strand, at first, as has been indicated, an education in method – the principal theme of Chapter 3 – and then in the substance of scientific thought. Between the reception of the Aristotelian logical and philosophical systems there has to be considered another strand in which too various perspectives were comprised. This is the Arabic philosophical tradition, the subject of the first part of Chapter 4. It was based on the Greek authorities but contained its own interpretations and insights, some of which were to be congenial, others devastatingly unsettling to the Christian world. The rest of Chapter 4 describes how the Latins' corpus of philosophical texts was expanded by the translation movements of the twelfth and thirteenth centuries and how at approximately the same time, but independently, new educational structures were being evolved in the rise of the universities. Chapter 5 considers the early period of the reception of Aristotle's philosophy in the west, c. 1210–50, a time when its implications and the implications of some of the Arabic elaborations of it were only partly understood. Chapter 6 considers an even shorter period, c. 1250–77, one of intense activity. This is the period of Bonaventure, Albert and Thomas Aquinas, whose approaches and contributions are examined in turn. It is also a period during which Aristotle was being studied in the major arts faculty of Europe, in a formal, exegetical fashion, divorced from the wider theological considerations with which it was soon to be confronted. This confrontation with radical teaching in the arts faculty at Paris was a dramatic manifestation of the intellectual tensions felt at the time. However, the underlying problems were not confined to the arts faculty. They were problems attendant on the meeting of diverse perspectives. The intellectual crisis of the thirteenth century derived from the fact that Aristotle was both an authority who could not be long ignored and an authority who in major respects sat most uneasily within a Christian outlook, especially since that outlook had been deeply influenced at an early stage by an approach which Aristotle's surviving works were in part aimed to demolish.

This outline has perhaps already signalled two aspects of my treatment for which a final word of explanation is required. In the first place, my approach is more thematic than chronological, though I have tried to present my themes firmly within a chronological framework. Inevitably, however, there is some chronological overlap between my chapters. In the second place, the reader will notice a marked imbalance towards the later period, with between a quarter and a third of the book devoted to the thirteenth century. This seems to me a just reflection of the greatly heightened level of activity at that time.

This is a book for historians seeking an introduction to a subject whose technical aspects can be initially forbidding. It is a description of a tradition – the transmission of ideas and their interpretation. There is no attempt to evaluate the ideas themselves by modern critical standards. Attention is paid throughout to the stages in the evolution of the tradition, the sources on which it depended, the discrepancy which existed from time to time between the availability of texts and their actual circulation and use, the institutions which fostered intellectual developments and the general historical background. I have not tried to be encyclopaedic in my approach. In so rich and complex a subject selection was necessary. The criterion adopted was that the treatment should serve as a foundation for direct reading of the texts of the major thinkers within the period surveyed and as a starting point for study of later developments. I have assumed that a majority of my readers are unlikely to know classical languages. I have therefore always quoted in translation in the text, from the most accessible satisfactory version where such existed. I have however given sufficient reference to permit the reader to consult the original or to find the passage in another translation. Where there was no satisfactory or readily accessible translation I have made my own. I have also normally used translated titles, while giving the standard titles as necessary to provide a recognised frame of reference. In some cases, where either the translated title was more cumbersome or the original sufficiently familiar, I have used the latter, while providing a translation on the first occurrence at least.

1. Masters of Those Who Know – Plato, Aristotle and the Neoplatonists

'MASTER of those who know' was Dante's tribute to Aristotle whom in the *Divine Comedy* he saw accorded a place of honour in the highest state to which the unbaptised could aspire.[1] It was a proper recognition of Aristotle's pre-eminent influence on the intellectual life of the late thirteenth and early fourteenth centuries. But Plato was to be found in the next room[2] and had Dante been fully aware of his contribution to the medieval heritage he would doubtless have allowed of their closer association. With the benefit of a historian's perspective, he might have extended the title not only to Aristotle's own master but to their common disciples, the Neoplatonists, who were the principal channel of Platonism to the middle ages and who so profoundly influenced the formulation of Christian ideas in the patristic age. In a history of medieval thought the dominating contribution of these giants among ancient philosophers is a more obvious feature than the primacy of any one. They are conveniently treated together, for despite the differences between their systems they are linked in a direct line of intellectual descent.

In a book of this kind a survey of Greek speculation is inevitably ancillary to the main theme. The object is to review those aspects of the classical background which are indispensable to an understanding of later developments. This dictates the emphases of the present chapter. Stoicism and Epicureanism, so important in their own right, are mentioned only incidentally, though there will later be occasion to notice certain contributions of Stoicism. With the exception of part of the *Timaeus* and later of the *Meno* and *Phaedo*, Plato's dialogues were not directly known in the medieval west. In particular, a whole dimension of his thought, on political and social organisation, was forgotten since this was an area ignored by Neoplatonism. It is therefore omitted here. All that is aimed at is an indication within the space available of the metaphysical problems which he posed and the nature of the solution which he offered. Aristotle's is a different case. His logical works were early translated and by the later middle ages his system was known in its full range. A summary of his thought is insufficient. The student must familiarise himself with at least the principal texts through which it was expounded. An attempt is

therefore made to introduce them in the course of the discussion.
Similar considerations of utility affect the presentation of Neoplatonist doctrine.

Plato: the Background to his Thought

Plato's predecessors have only a remote significance for medieval
thought, through the direction which they gave to philosophical
inquiry. Their influence on Plato himself was profound. It may be
briefly stated under three main heads. From the school of Pythagoras
(*fl.* 530 BC) he derived the doctrine of the permanence of the soul,
which the Pythagoreans had expressed in terms of transmigration.
His idea that order in the universe could be reduced to mathematical
formulae was possibly also borrowed, with modifications, from them.
The theory underlies his description of the composition of bodies, in
the *Timaeus*, and another application of it will be noted later. His
second principal debt was to earlier speculations on the nature of
reality. These had been dominated by the problem of interpreting
change. Heraclitus (*fl.* 500 BC) had taught that change was the
natural condition of reality and had emphasised the relativity of
things as we experience them. But he had also held that the
divergences were aspects of the same reality and that accordingly
reality was one. His thought can therefore be seen as aiming at a
resolution of the antithesis between the Many – the plurality of the
world as experienced – and the One, the point at which differences are
ignored in favour of a judgement of similarity or cohesion. This was
certainly a feature of the thought of Parmenides (*fl.* 475 BC), the
founder of the Eleatic school, called after his birthplace. He had
begun, however, with the opposite emphasis. To notice change and
plurality was to be deceived by appearances; reality as perceived by
reason was one – constant Being. Such a monolithic concept of Being
forbade change. If a thing did not exist (was not already Being) it
could not change and if it did exist it was Being before and after
'change'. One's impression of change, derived from sense experience,
must therefore be corrected by an intellectual judgement which
dismissed it. The solution was more logical than satisfying. However,
its central tenet, that behind the facade of impermanence lay a
continuity, was capable of more sophisticated development – either in
the direction of materialism or of idealism. The former was the path
chosen by the early atomists who saw reality as composed of

indestructible particles. The latter was the direction taken by Plato's thought. It implied a narrow interpretation of reality, its identification with the universal truths discerned by the mind.

The third major influence upon Plato was an emerging philosophy of man, above all as elaborated by Socrates (c. 470–399 BC). Although the earliest phases of Greek thought had been biased towards cosmology – analysis of the structure of the world – there was a natural overflow from this to ethics. An understanding of the physical universe had implications for man's concept of his own role within it and a close association between the two studies long continued as a feature of classical thought, notably in the Stoic and Epicurean systems and in Neoplatonism. Socrates seems to have inherited both interests but he abandoned cosmology early to concentrate on man himself. In this he resembled his contemporaries, the Sophists. Where he differed from the latter, at least as they are represented in the Socratic tradition, was in his retention of the spirit of abstract inquiry. They meanwhile gained a reputation for being concerned more with practical pursuits, such as rhetoric, than with raising the level of human consciousness. Socrates devoted his life to this aim. Not only that but his stubborn acquiescence in his own execution was intended as an example of right conduct – the observance in accordance with the civic laws of an unjust judgement on the charge that he was an atheist and corruptor of youth.

In the case of Socrates the connection between speculation and ethics derived from his identification of virtue with knowledge of the Good, knowledge being understood in this context as conviction rather than simple recognition of fact. On the supposition that all men act in pursuit of an object which they consider beneficial, the fact that they do evil may be attributed to their imperfect understanding of what they seek to obtain. From this stemmed the disciplined search which Socrates conducted for the Good through criticism of the various interpretations which may be offered of it.

Plato: Knowledge and Being

The figure of Socrates dominates Plato's writings but it is generally agreed that the latter's doctrines, at least in their advanced form, are his own construction even when attributed to Socrates as a character in the dialogues. Plato gave a much wider dimension to the search for standards, extending it beyond morality to the whole of knowledge. It was in the course of doing so that he tacitly developed a theory of knowledge (or 'epistemology') and a theory of being (or 'ontology'). These are the central features of his thought, encapsulating vital philosophical questions which were to preoccupy all later thinkers.

The conclusion of Parmenides that there was no change superseded the information conveyed by sense experience while even that of Heraclitus, that there was more to reality than change, implied that the senses were an inadequate guide to knowledge. Plato's thought was deeply affected by this tendency to divorce the sensual and the intellectual. It was also deeply affected by the first proposition in Heraclitus' analysis, that the physical world was one of constant flux, a state of becoming rather than of being. His own solution was to accept the fact of change in the world experienced by the senses but to deny that the latter was a proper object of knowledge or that its entities were fully real. This refusal to ascribe reality to the individual objects of experience was not a reflection of scepticism about their actual existence; they were real enough as stimulants to the senses. It was an intellectual judgement on their character. Being subject to change they were always in transit from one mode of existence to another and this was true even of things which were comparatively stable. Therefore they did not lend themselves to definition in that they could not be said to be completely one thing rather than another. The problem was particularly acute in the case of evaluations based upon experience. These were always relative, for what appeared beautiful, good, true or just in one context might appear to disadvantage in different circumstances or upon comparison. In any case, the search for definitions could not be satisfied by the discovery of particular instances of beauty, goodness, truth or justice – however true to type they might be considered in the light of such a definition – for they did not, like the latter, state a general law. Plato's argument was that knowledge in its full sense must be of something constant and that it must be certain and of general application. Knowledge of this kind was an understanding of principles or, as they are usually referred to in accounts of Plato's theory, of 'Forms'.[3] When Diogenes the Cynic attempted to ridicule the notion of 'Forms' by protesting that he could see the cup but not 'cupness', Plato attributed this to his having eyes but no intellect.[4] So far as concerned the values to which Socrates' inquiries had been directed, knowledge consisted of being able to state what constituted justice and so on. In regard to material objects it consisted equally in being able to state what their essential feature was – what aspect of their reality caused the mind to classify them as one type of being rather than another.

The Forms are being at its most intelligible level. What is their exact status? It is quite basic to Plato's position that they are principles which are discovered rather than invented by the knowing mind. They are objective principles. In what sense are they said to be so? At this point Plato's theory becomes notoriously difficult to interpret. He speaks of the Forms as having an existence independent of the world of sense experience in which they are represented. There is an obvious sense in which principles or standards are prior to the objects of experience, for the former are the criteria by which the latter are classified and judged. But Plato's account envisages a still more transcendent status for these principles. Firstly, it is asserted that the human soul (in this sense, mind) is peculiarly equipped to discover them because it has known them in an earlier, disembodied, existence. The doctrine of the soul's pre-existence and of its recollection of the Forms is an aspect of the religious element in Plato's thought (Socrates in the *Meno* attributes it to men wise in religious matters and to inspired poets[5]) and is probably due to Pythagorean influence. Secondly, Plato's cosmology is founded upon the transcendence of the Forms. The dialogue in which this is chiefly expounded is the *Timaeus*. It too contains religious presuppositions and it is noteworthy that its eponymous disputant is a Pythagorean. Its central theme is a creation myth in which the Craftsman or Father of the visible world with his mind on the patterns of the Forms moulds the chaotic elementary material of the universe. It is debatable how far Plato intended either his account of Recollection (*anamnesis*) or of the Craftsman to be taken literally. At the very least however both are graphic representations of the doctrine that standards are absolute and are outside of the process of change and becoming. The myth of the Craftsman is more. It is a statement that the world is the product of intelligent and consequently of intelligible design and the best embodiment which can be achieved of eternal principles. These were Plato's characteristic contributions to the history of thought and the power and fascination of his interpretation of reality ensured its survival in the face of the sharp challenge which it was offered almost as soon as it had been formulated.

Plato's search for a rational account of reality did not end with the discovery of the Forms. He became concerned with the relation of the Forms to one another and the need to posit a principle which would represent a common bond between them. Such a principle he refers to variously as the Good or Absolute Beauty though it is more readily recognisable as Being. From accounts of what Plato taught in lectures it appears that his later thought was devoted to showing that the Forms were in fact mathematical principles. This became the mechanism for imparting to them the unity which he had been seeking. In this construction, all order resulted from the interaction between two ultimate terms, the One – an ideal number – seen as the principle of order and specification, and the Dyad or Indefinite Duality, the principle by which the One is multiplied and fragmented. This rather esoteric line of thought continued after Plato's death and in Neoplatonism 'the One' finally replaces terms such as 'the Good' or 'Absolute Beauty' as an expression of ultimate cohesion.

Aristotle: Life and Works

A notable feature of Plato's activity as a philosopher is that he established an institution devoted to intellectual inquiry. This was the Academy, founded at Athens in 388 BC, whose name is used by historians to refer to various phases of Platonist thought. Plato's most famous pupil, Aristotle (384/3–322/1 BC),[6] was a member of the Academy from the age of about seventeen until shortly after Plato's death. He subsequently spent about five years in Asia Minor and the Aegean conducting those observations into biology – particularly marine biology – which were to leave such a heavy imprint upon his philosophy; later he acted for a few years as tutor to the son of Philip of Macedon, the future Alexander the Great. In about 335 BC he returned to Athens and founded there his own institute of study, the Lyceum, in competition with the Academy.[7]

Whereas the surviving corpus of Plato's works are those composed for publication, his lectures being known only in small part and indirectly, the opposite is the case with Aristotle. Except for fragments, what survive are in effect his lectures at the Lyceum, organised as we know them not by himself but in the edition of Andronicus of Rhodes, head of the Lyceum c. 60–50 BC, by which they first became widely known. While his published works were Platonic in form and content, being mostly products of his period at the Academy and soon after, the extant treatises represent his independent thought, much of it elaborated in friendly reaction against the theories of his master. At best they are notoriously pedagogical in style and are often so compressed as to be difficult to follow. Although they are by a highly systematic thinker, they are not of a piece but reflect the development of Aristotle's mind over several decades. This point, which is of great importance for a critical reading, was established by modern scholarship[8] and was not appreciated by earlier interpreters.

The most important of Aristotle's writings intrinsically and in terms of their influence on medieval thought may be listed under four headings: (i) the logical works; (ii) the works on the structure of the universe. Among these chief place must be accorded to the *Physics* and to the series of treatises grouped under the title, *Metaphysics*, a term which was probably not originally intended to describe their content but merely to indicate their position 'after the Physics' in the corpus of his works; (iii) treatises on psychology, most important of which is the great work, *De Anima* ('On the Soul'); (iv) the social treatises, most important of which are the *Nicomachean Ethics* and the *Politics*.

Aristotle: Logic

The logical treatises of Aristotle have been known collectively since the sixth century AD as the *Organon* or 'Instrument'. The term was originally given currency by Neoplatonist philosophers of the third century AD as a description simply of the discipline of logic. Its later, restricted, use is a compliment to Aristotle's outstanding contribution in the field. Both in its own right and as a title for the Aristotelian corpus it neatly implies the propaedeutic function of logic, its role as an ancillary subject for the philosopher. This is wholly in keeping with Aristotle's own view. He distinguished three types of knowledge or 'science', theoretical, practical and productive. The first is defined as encompassing mathematics, physics and metaphysics, the second is concerned with human conduct and the third with manufacture of the useful or beautiful. Logic is not for him a branch of knowledge but a constituent of it and a necessary preparation for its acquisition. It is subordinate to the philosopher's purpose, as conceived by Aristotle, which is the attainment of truth. Yet it is intimately connected with his search. In his approach to logic Aristotle is therefore a metaphysician as well as a logician. Not only are the two aspects of his system congruent but much of his logic has an ontological import. On the one hand, it is not a treatment of reality; on the other, it is not, considered as a whole, an analysis of thought patterns as self-contained. It is an examination of thought about reality and of thought as a reflection of reality, reality itself being the subject of his 'scientific' treatises. For that reason, in an abstract presentation of Aristotle, there is much to be said for dealing with his logic last. In a survey of medieval thought, however, it is the first aspect of his system to demand attention since it was, for long, all that educated men in western Europe knew of his work at first hand.

The *Organon* consists of six treatises. The first of these, the *Categories*, is devoted to the meanings of words considered in isolation from the propositions where they are combined. Although elsewhere there are minor differences in Aristotle's listing of them, here the 'categories' or ways in which we think about things are given as ten: substance; quantity (e.g. length); quality (e.g. colour); relation (that is, as expressed by relative terms or terms of comparison); location; time; posture; state (e.g. 'shod', 'armed'); activity; passivity. Of these terms, 'substance' is the most complex and the most important for understanding Aristotle's thought. In its primary sense, substance is an individual thing. The other categories are predicates of substance and substance is regarded as being distinct from the amalgamation of predicates. In this primary sense, substance is not itself a predicate. However, the *Categories* admits of the term's extension in a secondary sense to include the universal concepts of species and genus into which substances in the primary sense are classified. In doing so it reveals the continuing influence of Plato's realism. By allowing for the secondary sense of substance it is affirming that these universal concepts are not simply products of the mind's activity but have an extra-mental status or justification.

While the *Categories* considers how individual words describe reality, the *De Interpretatione* ('On Interpretation') is an examination of words combined as propositions. It is in their combination only that words are capable of conveying truth or falsehood. In its analysis of the grammatical form of propositions and particularly in its identification of the range of meanings conveyed by universal and particular, affirmative and negative statements, the *De Interpretatione* lays the foundation for a study of the syllogism. This is the subject of the third treatise of the *Organon*, the *Prior Analytics*.

The syllogism was Aristotle's great contribution to formal logic. It is an argument consisting of two premisses, called the major and the minor, and a conclusion. The major premiss is so called because it contains the term known as major – that which is predicated in the conclusion – the minor premiss contains the minor term – that which is the subject of the conclusion. The premisses share a term, called the middle term, the varying functions of which determine the 'figure' of the syllogism. Aristotle distinguished three figures: the first has the middle term as the subject in one premiss and the predicate in the other; the second has the middle term as predicate in both premisses; the third has the middle term as subject in both premisses. Of these figures, the first is the most important as Aristotle goes on to show that the others can be reduced to it. An example of a syllogism of the first figure would be:

All men are rational.
All philosophers are men.
Therefore: all philosophers are rational.

The principles discovered by Aristotle's analysis were taken over and elaborated by medieval logicians who identified the range of valid syllogisms by artificial Latin names in which the vowels 'A', 'E', 'I' and 'O' represented the universal affirmative, the universal negative, the particular affirmative and the particular negative propositions respectively. So, for example, the four syllogisms of the first figure were known as 'Barbara', 'Celarent', 'Darii', and 'Ferio'. Combined in mnemonic rhymes, these names showed at a glance what kind of conclusion could be drawn from a set of premisses. The system is esoteric but to those who were rigorously trained in it, it became second nature.

As an exposition of deduction through the mechanics of the syllogism the *Prior Analytics* had an unparalleled influence on the method of philosophy. The *Posterior Analytics* is less purely formal in content. Book I consists of a treatment of demonstration as an application of the principles of the syllogism to scientific reasoning. But Aristotle makes clear that he does not consider all knowledge to depend on demonstration, the starting point of which must be based elsewhere. The question is resolved at the end of Book II, where he shows that induction – inference from the particular, which is the subject of sense knowledge, to the general, which is the product of abstractive knowledge – supplies the first premisses from which all deduction derives. Though the subject is very scantily dealt with, here is the characteristic Aristotelian approach to epistemology.

The last two treatises of the *Organon* are of little importance for an exposition of Aristotle's mature thought. The *Topics* is an early work which precedes the composition of the *Analytics*. It considers the art of argument as a general dialectical exercise, though even at this stage in his development Aristotle has in mind its use for scientific knowledge. The *De Sophisticis Elenchis* ('On Sophistical Refutations') is an appendix to the *Topics*. It is a study of fallacy and its title reflects the Socratic antipathy to the Sophists as anti-philosophers, mystifying their hearers by tricks of reasoning. In fact, while some of the fallacies which Aristotle reviews amount to mere quibbling, others are more subtle traps into which the incautious philosopher might himself fall. The *De Sophisticis Elenchis* is therefore a useful *via negativa* or deterrent inculcation of the principles of valid argument.

Aristotle: Knowledge and Being

The reader of the *Organon* would already have been introduced to the doctrine on which Aristotle's theories of knowledge and being rest. This is 'substance' – the first of the categories – a concept of central importance in his thought. It was through it that he directed the search for understanding to the concrete world of individuals. Plato had contrasted the intelligible and fully real status of the Forms with the objects of experience. The latter, relative, unstable, in a continual state of becoming something else, lent themselves in his view only to an imperfect degree of knowledge. Aristotle contradicted him. In the order of being or reality he insisted on the primacy of the individual thing – substance in its first sense, as defined in the *Categories*. The corollary is his emphasis on the primacy of sense experience, contact with the individual thing, in the generation of knowledge. When he said that it was only in a secondary and derived sense that the term 'substance' could be applied to the universal concept he was implicitly rejecting the theory that the elements of intelligibility in things were in some way separate from them. In the *Metaphysics* he is more explicit. There he repeatedly criticises the notion of subsistent Forms as uneconomical and vague. For him, 'substance' is the bridge between things as we experience them and things as we understand them. By observing individual beings – substance in the primary sense – the philosopher isolates essential characteristics and knows substance in the secondary sense. It is only by this process of abstraction from reality as he experiences it that he arrives at an understanding of the natures of things, the principles by which they are classified, and at a general concept of undifferentiated being.

It is obvious that such a theory of knowledge required an answer to the problem of change, that apparent instability in things which had vexed earlier thinkers including Plato himself. The most general solution which Aristotle propounds is the distinction, advanced mainly in Book 9 (Θ) of the *Metaphysics*, between potentiality and actuality. It is an attempt to render all change intelligible by denying that it is catastrophic. According to this analysis, before the change took place the subject had the capacity to change in that way and therefore already was potentially what it was to be actually. To the modern reader this seems a platitude. But Aristotle was confronting a tradition in Greek thought which emphasised the stability of what exists to the point of excluding change as logically impossible and hence illusory. Moreover, his assertion that change is the realisation or actualisation of a potentiality did not merely serve as a counter to the static view. In its own right it offered a highly optimistic interpretation of change as development, the fulfilment of capacity. It was a piece also with his wider philosophy and played a part in his explanation of cosmology, psychology and ethics.

The basis of a related but more particular account of change was supplied by the doctrine of substance. In this context, Aristotle made a distinction between two types of change. The more easily resolved is what he broadly calls 'alteration'.[9] This is better known as 'accidental' change, from the terminology developed in the *Topics*,[10] where he differentiates between predicates which state the essence or comprise the definition of a thing and those – accidental predicates – which signify an attribute not relevant to the definition. In this case, the subject of the change does not need to be redefined as a result of it. In Aristotle's terms, there is continuity of substance. The second type of change, 'substantial' change, what Aristotle calls 'coming to be and passing away',[11] requires precisely such a redefinition. Here the original substance disappears to be replaced by a new one. The discontinuity is apparently complete. But Aristotle insisted that in this process too there is an element of constancy as well as an element of change. Accordingly he distinguished two corresponding features in all being which undergoes substantial change,[12] matter and form.

These two features are only notionally distinct in that there is no experience of matter in this sense neither does it exist apart from form. Conversely, form does not exist apart from matter, at least in the terrestrial world. (It will be seen later that the 'prime mover' or 'movers' of Aristotle's system is a special case.) Form represents the discontinuity in substantial change. It is the principle by which the new substance is determined or constituted as something – a being of a certain class – just as it is the principle by which the old substance was determined as a being of a different class. Matter represents the element of continuity, expressing the relationship which we judge to exist between old substance and new. It is a difficult term to use because of its association.[13] Matter – referred to by the Aristotelians of the middle ages as 'first matter' (*materia prima*) – is not something material. In Aristotle's analysis the material something is substance – the composite of matter and form. Matter in the metaphysical sense does however retain one of the nuances of 'material' in its everyday usage. It implies the capacity of things to exist with extension, to occupy a certain spatial position. It does not itself constitute their extension, of course, as is implied by matter in its everyday sense. Only as considered in combination with form can it be said actually to have this or any other characteristic. This aspect of matter, though, explains why the heavenly bodies of Aristotle's universe – otherwise quite unlike other material substances in that they are exempt from all change except local motion – should be considered as composite substances. If they were pure form, they could have no local motion.

To say that matter represents the element of continuity in substantial change is to describe it from the point of view of change which has occurred. It can also be viewed as the capacity of a thing to undergo change – a complex of changes in the case of terrestrial substances, a strictly limited change in the case of the heavenly bodies. Stated in this way it corresponds to the concept of potentiality. Similarly, form corresponds to actuality. However, 'matter and form' do not simply repeat the point made in the distinction between potentiality and actuality. They are an important amplification of the notion of substance and they led Aristotle to a fuller elaboration of his theory of knowledge. 'Hylomorphism', as the doctrine of matter and form is known,[14] served him well in establishing that the universal element or principle of classification is immanent in the thing. Form immanent in substance is his answer to Plato's transcendent form. At the same time it served him well in retaining the objectivity of form. On this point he is in agreement with Plato. Both thinkers locate the basis of classification in the character of external reality rather than in the mental structure of the observer. For both, the universal concept is a recognition by the mind of an order which really exists, not an imposition of order by the mind. It is in this sense that both their philosophies are said to be 'realist'. This fundamental similarity between them can easily be lost sight of in view of the critical and highly apologetic approach which Aristotle adopts towards his master and in view of the different ways in which they state the objective reality of the universal. The similarity becomes more apparent as Aristotle explores the implications of his refinement on the concept of substance. In his analysis, the principle of individuation – the element in the composition of substance to which its individual characteristics are attributed – can only be matter. Form is the universal element by which a thing is constituted and rendered recognisable as a member of a certain class. Yet matter, as indeterminate, is the aspect of reality which is impervious to the intellect. There is therefore the paradox in his thought that the fully real is not fully knowable or is unknowable precisely at the point – its individuality – at which it is said to be fully real. The difficulty is probably best understood as a relic of Platonism. Aristotle's failure to resolve it may be partly due to the fact that as a working biologist his preoccupation was with the species rather than with the individual. However, as it stands, the harmony of his theory of knowledge and being is seriously marred by the discrepancy.

Aristotle: Causation and Cosmology

Aristotle refers to matter and form as two of the four 'causes' of change. This is an unfamiliar use of the term 'cause'. Matter and form are more easily thought of as philosophical conditions or aspects of the philosophical explanation of the phenomenon. The other two factors which he identifies are the final and the efficient or moving causes.[15] The 'final cause' represents change as intelligible from its effects. Considered from this aspect, the process of substantial change is seen to be directed, *de facto* and unconsciously, towards the production of new form. The new form is therefore, viewed in retrospect, the terminus and in that sense the purpose or 'final cause' of the activity. Accidental change, considered as a stage in the full realisation of form – such as growth to maturity – can also be seen to be directed towards a final cause. Both accidental and substantial change must also normally be explained by reference to an efficient cause. This is cause in its familiar sense – the agency by which a process is instigated and completed. Aristotle's account of the mechanism of efficient causation is an aspect of his wider cosmological doctrine.

The universe as Aristotle conceives it is divided into two regions – the superlunary and the sublunary – governed by different laws. The superlunary region is constituted of a single element, 'ether', which tends to circular movement. The sublunary region by contrast is constituted of four elements – fire, air, water and earth – which tend to rectilinear movement, the first two upwards and the second two downwards. This is the physical basis of the distinction between the continuous, unvaried patterns which seemed to be the condition of the heavenly bodies and the state of change and decay which obtains below. The four elements are the material cause of change and decay,[16] in the case of the complex organisms which they combine to form and which disintegrate on their dissociation. They too are being continually transformed into one another. The efficient cause of both processes of interaction is the varying influence of the sun through the changing seasons.

In Aristotle's theory, this seasonal effect of the sun is due to its annual movement as observed from the earth. The earth itself, spherical in shape, lies at rest in the centre of the universe. The astronomical appearances produced by its daily rotation and annual orbit of the sun, as well as the particular courses of the planets, are attributed to the movement round it of an elaborate system of concentric spheres in which the heavenly bodies are embedded. The outermost of these spheres is that of the fixed stars and the innermost that of the moon. Their arrangement and number Aristotle based, with modifications of his own, on the conclusions of the near-contemporary astronomers, Eudoxus and Callippus, from whom he borrowed the idea of a geo-centric universe composed of spheres.

The annual approach and retreat of the sun thus establishes a link between the continuity of manifold change in the sublunary world and the continuity of the simple 'accidental' change – regular local motion – to which alone the superlunary world is subject. But physics does not constitute a self-contained explanation of activity in Aristotle's universe. The main argument which he presents for the existence of a source of cosmic activity is the need to avoid an infinite regress of objects that are moved. This requirement, combined with his theory that everything which is in motion is moved by something, demanded a source of motion that was itself motionless. And since motion is the actualisation of a potentiality, the concept of an ultimate source of motion translated readily into the doctrine of potentiality and actuality. Expressed in these terms, the 'unmoved mover' is the prime agent in the reduction of potentiality to actuality and is defined as actuality without potentiality. Furthermore, since matter is identified with potentiality the purely actual must be immaterial. This is an important line of thought for it led Aristotle to fuse cosmology with theology.

The existence of the unmoved mover is postulated in Book VII of the *Physics*[17] and established in Book VIII.[18] Its nature and operation are developed mainly in Book Λ of the *Metaphysics*.[19] The fixed stars, comprising the first sphere, are apparently regarded as living beings, which desire to achieve the perfection of motionlessness exhibited by the unmoved mover. Unable to do so, they imitate it as closely as possible by the circular motion natural to their element. This is the primary cosmic movement, a revolution from east to west. Transmitted through the inner spheres it becomes the common movement of the planets. The effect is produced only indirectly by the unmoved mover, which acts as the final and only thus as the efficient cause of movement in the first sphere. Its own integrity is therefore preserved complete. Although Aristotle refers to this unmoved mover as God and portrays a being with an intellectual life it is not a God who could be the object of religious worship or who might be thought of as a creator. Indeed it is quite unaware of anything outside itself and its sole activity consists in consciousness of its own perfection. Nor is it a unique principle. The various courses of the planets, which Aristotle supposed to be governed by as many as fifty-five spheres, some of them moving in opposite directions, cannot derive from a single source. Accordingly, he was forced to allow a plurality of unmoved movers – one for each particular motion. This conclusion seems to have been a development in his thought from an initial preference for a simple model. He saw the difficulty of explaining the plurality philosophically[20] and that and the relationship between the unmoved movers remains a problem in the interpretation of his theory. But the fact that he was prepared to make the adjustment to meet the astronomical evidence emphasises the bond between his theology and his cosmology. His 'unmoved mover', one or many, is merely the eternal explanation of eternal motion in an eternal universe, an ultimate term which must be posited if an infinite series is to be avoided. Quite detached from the effects which it accidentally generates it stands in as sharp contrast to the Craftsman of Plato's *Timaeus* as to the God of *Genesis*, epitomising the mechanical nature of Aristotle's account of reality.

Aristotle: Psychology

Aristotle's psychology or 'theory of soul' is best approached after his *Physics* and *Metaphysics* for it involves a special application of the general principles discovered there. While the *Physics* discusses nature as a whole, the *De Anima* ('On the Soul') deals with one aspect – living things. In it, soul is defined as 'the first actuality of a natural body which has life potentially'.[21] What Aristotle means is that in all living substances which come into being and pass away one must admit the same distinction between potentiality and actuality or matter and form on which he bases his wider explanation of substantial change. In their case, the corresponding distinction is between body and soul. Soul is the form or actuality of the substance, by which it exists and is defined as a member of a species; body is that which has a potentiality for changing. As in the general application of the hylomorphic doctrine, the distinction between the two aspects is a notional one. Substance is never to be envisaged as first a body requiring only the addition of a soul to be a live body, any more than as first a disembodied soul and then an embodied one. Plato had presented just such an *a priori* view of soul and Aristotle's doctrine is a rejection of it. 'Body' as an aspect of substance is equivalent to 'live body'; it is an organism with a unity. Dead body, by contrast, lacks unity; it is simply a collection of a variety of substances in the course of dissociation from one another.

Having thus defined his subject, Aristotle distinguishes between three types of soul – vegetative, sensitive and intellective, in ascending order of refinement. The vegetative soul is characterised by the basic functions of nutrition and reproduction, necessary for the main- tenance of life. The sensitive soul is characterised in addition by sense perception, more or less complex depending on the species of animal life. This includes, in the case of animals with multiple sense faculties, the capacity to integrate the information derived from the various organs of sense – eyes, ears, touch, nose and taste – so that, for instance, noise may be related to an object seen. This synthetic faculty, which Aristotle refers to as the 'common sense', is fallible, unlike the operations of the special senses. The latter, being directly stimulated by their object, he considers to be incapable of deceiving. Also represented as an extension of sensation are the faculties of imagination and memory. 'Imagination' – the rendering of Aristotle's *phantasia* – consists of the production of images in response to sensual stimuli. It seems to be a faculty which is possessed in rudimentary fashion by all animal life since Aristotle argues that desire, which is the cause of movement in animals, presupposes imagination.[22] But it is chiefly considered and is most easily appreciated as a faculty of higher animals. Memory is the retention of images and is to be distinguished from recollection – deliberate and spontaneous recall – which is a feature of the intellective soul alone.[23]

The analysis of this last, the highest type of soul, is one of the most obscure aspects of Aristotle's thought, the obscurity being compounded by the probability that the principal text for it is corrupt. The passage, in Book III, Chapter 5 of the *De Anima*, reads as follows:

And . . . mind as we have described it is what it is by virtue of becoming all things, while there is another which is what it is by virtue of making all things: this is a sort of positive state like light; for in a sense light makes potential colours into actual colours. Mind in this sense of it is separable, impassible, unmixed, since it is in its essential nature activity (for always the active is superior to the passive factor, the originating force to the matter which it forms). Actual knowledge is identical with its object: in the individual, potential knowledge is in time prior to actual knowledge, but in the universe as a whole it is not prior even in time. Mind is not at one time knowing and at another not. When mind is set free from its present conditions it appears as just what it is and nothing more: this alone is immortal and eternal (we do not, however, remember its former activity because, while mind in this sense is impassible, mind as passive is destructible), and without it nothing thinks.[24]

Aristotle justifies his distinction of these two aspects of mind by reference to his general doctrine of potentiality and actuality in the operations of nature. On this model the passive intellect is a potentiality for acquiring the abstracted form of a new reality and the actualisation of its potentiality is, as elsewhere in Aristotle's metaphysics, due to the operation of a principle already active – in this case the 'active intellect'. However, his argument on the point is very brief and he need not perhaps be taken to have regarded it as definitive. A point of some importance which emerges from what he says is that mind is, in one respect at least, an active principle. The conclusion would seem to invite consideration of the part which mind itself might play in shaping our view of the world. Aristotle neither tackles this nor shows any consciousness of a difficulty. It may therefore be supposed that he does not attribute to the 'active intellect' a definite character such as would impede the correspondence between mental concept and external reality upon which his philosophy rests.

The direction in which he does pursue the implications of this feature of mind suggests that his treatment of the topic may have been designed as an answer to the Platonic theory of anamnesis as an explanation of the *a priori* element in thought and to the associated doctrine of the soul's immortality. It is true that no reference is made to the Platonists at this point but in what he goes on to say he can hardly have been oblivious of the rival doctrine of the soul which he had himself at one time championed.[25] Mind, he proposes, considered as an active principle not undergoing change, 'alone is immortal and eternal'. This is a sudden twist given to what has until now been a consistent view of soul, that it is a simple actualisation and that it is only notionally a distinct feature of being. What is now apparently envisaged is not indeed that the soul but that an aspect of the soul is capable of separate and eternal existence. Since this enigmatic statement is difficult to reconcile with Aristotle's general outlook it is impossible to offer a confident interpretation of it. Possibly in making it he had no clearly developed view on the questions which were to vex later commentators. The immortal 'active intellect' has been understood in various ways: it has been identified with Aristotle's God, particularly in the Neoplatonist tradition; it has been thought of on the one hand as a feature of the individual and on the other as being identical within members of the species. The last interpretation seems the least problematical. It is difficult to see how the active intellect which is not affected by the individual's experience and which transcends bodily function could be thought of as having distinguishing features even during the life of the individual. This is all the more so after his death when, on Aristotle's own principle, memory ceases. But the question of its status remains. Is it an intellectual substance? The only example of such explicitly recognised in Aristotle's universe is the unmoved mover or movers. If it is conceived to be a substance it will either be identified with the unmoved mover or distinguished from it on a basis which is quite unclear. If it is not a substance it has in Aristotelian theory no separate existence. Perhaps Aristotle's reference to immortality is simply an assertion that in his highest activity man – briefly as an individual, eternally as a species – approximates to the divine life. The question is intractable but judged against the Pythagorean–Platonic doctrine with which he was quite familiar his own accommodation of immortality is remarkably spare. His brief account was to prove the single most controversial aspect of his thought in the medieval context.

Aristotle: Political Science

Aristotle's definition of political science is wider than ours. He includes under it what we should call ethics. The particular and general aspects of his topic are treated separately. The *Nicomachean Ethics* considers the nature of the good life for man. It is the more complete and is probably the later version of his teaching on this subject.[26] The *Politics*, a collection of several originally independent works, considers how man may organise in society to achieve the good life. The two treatises are intended to be complementary and together they constitute a study of human conduct, without formal distinction between private and public. It should be clear at once therefore that Aristotle does not subscribe to a dual standard of morality. When he distinguishes, as he occasionally does, between a good citizen and a good man[27] he is not conceding a moral autonomy to the former. He is merely recognising the fact that not all constitutions are sufficiently demanding to allow of an equation between conformity to law and the whole of the virtuous life. Another, technical, reason for the distinction is that the good man possesses the virtue of practical wisdom which is not necessarily part of the condition of being a good citizen. But coincidence, at least on the level of behaviour, between the two categories is the ideal and is the mark of a good constitution. This does not at all mean that he makes individual morality subject to public interest. Quite the reverse is true. The state exists to facilitate and promote man's progress in virtue and there is a perfect harmony between the public and private good.

The analysis of political science so defined rests on general philosophical principles, most important being the teleological bias, the preoccupation with explaining things in terms of their purpose, which is the characteristic feature of Aristotle's thought. However, as is equally characteristic of his method, there is constant reference throughout to how men actually behave and this observational dimension is generally successful in inhibiting the adoption of arbitrary standards. So in the *Ethics* we continually find such remarks as 'All men have not the same views about what is to be feared',[28] 'With regard to desires, they would seem to fall into two classes',[29] 'Men who know nothing of the theory of their subject sometimes practise it with greater success than others who know it'[30] and so on. By the same token, the *Politics* incorporates the results of an ambitious comparative study of political institutions.

From the beginning of the *Ethics* Aristotle accepts as a working hypothesis that the good is that at which all things aim.[31] This teleological criterion then becomes the means to a more precise definition of the good for man. Wealth, for instance, is not the good for it merely serves to get something else.[32] Similarly, honour, pleasure, intelligence and other advantages, while chosen for their own sake as worth having, are also chosen as contributing to the good life which is what Aristotle implies by the word generally translated as 'happiness'.[33] In accordance with the concept of actuality which runs through his philosophy, this happiness is conceived as a state of activity with its own dynamic; and since rationality is the distinctive feature of man, full human happiness is an activity of the reason. The consideration leads to a view of the ethical life as directed towards a very specialised and intellectual end – the contemplation of philosophical truths, in which man finds his highest fulfilment and resembles the divine.

In this sense, Aristotle's political science assumes the propaedeutic character of his logic. The normal approach to happiness is a programme of training designed both to free the subject from those dispositions which would impede his progress and to promote those which will aid him. This is the foundation for Aristotle's detailed consideration of the virtues, to which most of the *Ethics* is devoted. His general concept of virtue is of a trait which can be cultivated to the point where it becomes a deeply ingrained part of the personality. Considered in detail, the virtues are of two kinds, intellectual – wisdom, intelligence (or insight) and prudence – and moral, such as liberality and temperance.[34] The intellectual virtues are acquired through education, the moral through practice or habit. The link between the two orders is forged by the intellectual virtue of prudence or 'practical wisdom' which represents the guiding role of reason in determining correct behaviour and is one of the central concepts of his moral theory. Not that Aristotle accepts that knowledge of the good or of virtue necessitates action in conformity. He insists that virtue and vice are equally matters of choice and he attacks the Socratic axiom that 'nobody acts in opposition to what is best' and that one can only do wrong out of ignorance,[35] as providing a possible excuse for dereliction. But he admits the force of the argument properly understood[36] and his own treatment vacillates between attributing perverse conduct on the one hand to lack of conviction about the good and on the other to the force of passion or other irrationality.

The central importance of 'practical wisdom' emerges from Aristotle's definition of virtue. This is 'a disposition of the soul in which, when it has to choose among actions and feelings, it observes the mean relative to us, this being determined by such a rule or principle as would take shape in the mind of a man of sense or practical reason'.[37] What Aristotle is saying is that it is impossible to define for example justice *a priori*, outside of the circumstances in which a just act is to be performed. However, justice is not subjective or a matter of whim. Practical wisdom, which is reason applied to moral action, recognises the justice inherent in the situation and in accordance with it dictates the course to be followed. It is an approach which very much limits what may usefully be said about the virtues on the general level. His lengthy review of justice, which occupies Book 5 of the *Ethics* and is of considerable importance for its wider relevance, illustrates this point. Aristotle recognises two senses of 'justice': a general or universal, which refers to the observance of law, and a special or particular, which refers to fair dealing. The second is further subdivided into distributive justice, which is the allocation of the community's possessions in accordance with desert, corrective justice, which remedies grievances between parties, and justice of exchange, which is the reciprocity governing trade. The first sense of the term was prompted by a nuance in the Greek word for justice, implying conformity to law, and Aristotle's acknowledgement of it is simply a clearing of the way to a consideration of justice in its particular aspects. The whole, with its specific reference to the political dimension[38] and its influential addendum on equity,[39] amounts to a masterly description of the social and legal context of justice rather than the statement of a unifying principle. In his discussion of the other moral virtues Aristotle is at pains to show that each is a mean between extremes of conduct. The device is in fact specious as a definition, being rather a broad guideline to determining virtue and an observation on how it appears when it has been determined. In the final analysis virtue consists in doing that which a reasoning man would approve.

Books 8 and 9 of the *Ethics* are devoted to friendship as an ingredient of happiness. In the course of his treatment Aristotle makes, not for the first time, the famous point that 'Man is a social animal' observing that 'the need for company is in his blood'.[40] Among the other reasons for having friends is that 'association with virtuous persons may form in a way a training in virtue'.[41] We have therefore here an adumbration of the wider social environment in which the Aristotelian life of virtue is to be led. Throughout the *Ethics* the habitual nature of moral virtue has been emphasised and the corollary is an emphasis on the importance of the social context. Hence the intimate relationship which obtains between the ethical and political aspects of Aristotle's theory of conduct.

It is by presenting the state as the culmination of primitive forms of association – the family, the village and so on – that Aristotle justifies his contention in the *Politics*[42] that it is a natural society. While the less complex groupings are designed to preserve life, the state serves the purpose of the sufficient life. It has an educative role of which a detailed examination is undertaken in the last two books of the treatise. This positive attitude to the state is the foundation of Aristotle's social theory. Some political association is necessary for man if he is to fulfil his potential for happiness as defined in the *Ethics*. (Aristotle supposes that there may be individuals who are so bestial or so god-like that they can dispense with it[43] but they are by definition abnormal.) There is however no 'natural' form of government. Aristotle was well aware that the state could be successfully organised in different ways. These are classified as rule by the one, by the few and by the many – corresponding to monarchy, aristocracy and what he normally calls 'polity'. Each of them is legitimised by an orientation towards the common good and it is this criterion which distinguishes them from their deviant counterparts, tyranny, oligarchy and democracy. Although in theory monarchy of the virtuous man is the best government, in practice polity is recommended. This is a balance of sectional interests – government by the many but not by the mass of have-nots. Though not his own invention it seems a typically Aristotelian compromise between extremes. It was perfectly in accord with the mainstream of medieval views on political organisation at the time the *Politics* was received in the west. For their part, the theses, lost for many centuries, that the state is a natural organ and that citizenship is a craft with its own authenticity and integrity, were to revolutionise political theory.

From Plato to Neoplatonism

While Plato's Academy remained active in Athens into the Christian era, as a school of thought it went through several transformations. Faced with challenge by the schools of Stoicism and Epicureanism – whose founders, the Cypriot Zeno and the Athenian Epicurus, belonged to the next generation after Plato – the original Academy retreated into a position of scepticism or philosophical agnosticism. This phase is known to historians of ancient thought as the Middle or Second Academy. The attitude lasted for over a century and a half during which the chief activity of the Academy was the refutation of rival theories. This cultivated suspension of judgement was modified by the mid-second-century thinker, Carneades of Cyrene, founder of the so-called New Academy, into an acceptance of a formal theory of probability as the guide to life and action. Though of relatively slight intrinsic importance, the position has a wider interest in that it was adopted and propagated by the Latin writer, Cicero (106–43 BC). His philosophical influence was small compared to his immense literary stature but no student of medieval thought can ignore its significance for the early development of St Augustine.[44]

At this point the Academy had no more than a historical connection with Plato. Its temper was anything but denominational. Indeed, an outstanding feature of the reversion towards a positive philosophy in the century which straddles the beginning of the Christian era and in the two centuries following is its receptivity to a variety of ideas. In favour were not only the doctrines of Plato and Aristotle, whom commentators of the period tended to reconcile, but of Stoicism and revived Pythagoreanism. This return to dogmatism is known by the transitional title, Middle Platonism. The term covers an assortment of thinkers – at Athens, at the other major Greek cultural centre, Alexandria, and elsewhere – within the period *c*. 80 BC–AD 220 and includes a wide range of interpretations. It is therefore impossible to summarise but its most notable features can be stated briefly. The first principle from which all reality derived was generally conceived to be 'Mind'. This concept is characteristic of the contemporary reconciliation of Plato and Aristotle for it was a combination of the idea of the Good and the Unmoved Mover. Middle Platonism tended to represent the Forms as thoughts of Mind, thus giving them a definite status which they had lacked in the classic version. There was an increasing stress, moreover, on the transcendence of Mind – a point chiefly owed perhaps to the Pythagorean influence – and its relation to the material world only through intermediaries, such as the Second Mind or Logos (Word) and the World Soul.

The interest of Middle Platonism from the medieval standpoint is on several levels. Firstly, it represents the most important ingredient of the Greek philosophical outlook during the first two centuries of Christianity. The effects of its terminology, whether absorbed directly or, as is more likely, through Hellenic influences on Judaism, are apparent in the prologue to the Johannine gospel. It had already, in the thought of Philo of Alexandria (*c.* 20 BC–*c.* AD 40), made inroads into Jewish theology and it deeply affected the thought of the early Christian theologians Clement of Alexandria (*c.* 150–215) and Origen (184–254). Secondly, its scholarship made some direct contribution to the sources of medieval thought. The influential commentary by Chalcidius on the *Timaeus* – the only one of Plato's dialogues known to the Latin west until the twelfth century – seems to relate to Middle Platonism rather than to later developments, despite the fact that it was written probably in the middle of the fourth century.[45] Thirdly and most importantly it was the indispensable preliminary to Neoplatonism. The latter was to have an unrivalled influence on Christian thought in the early medieval centuries, was effectively to constitute the medieval view of Platonism and was even to bulk large in the process by which Aristotle was received in the west.

Neoplatonism

'Neoplatonism' refers primarily to the system constructed by the Greek writer Plotinus (AD 204/5–270) and to reworkings of his thought by his immediate disciples and by schools in several parts of the Greek world until about the sixth century. Plotinus was born in Egypt and received his philosophical training at Alexandria. He himself taught at Rome, from *c.* 244 almost until his death, and there established a coterie which included his literary executor and biographer, Porphyry. Porphyry was responsible for editing the master's writings as a collection of six groups of nine treatises known accordingly as the *Enneads* (literally 'nines'). Although Porphyry knew and carefully listed the approximate chronology of the treatises, he decided to arrange them by subject matter. The first three Enneads form a group dealing mainly with the world: the first Ennead is on man and ethics, the second on the physical world and the third on philosophical problems concerning the world, such as fate, providence, eternity and time. The fourth Ennead deals with Soul, the fifth mainly with Mind and the sixth with Being and the One.

Plotinus' thought revolves round two principal topics, the origin of reality and its destiny. It is a description of descent from unity and perfection to multiplicity and of a reversionary process of ascent. The tendency of Middle Platonism to explain reality by a transcendent principle was taken by Plotinus to its logical conclusion. 'Mind' seemed an inadequate final term, being a complex where thought and the object of thought were distinguishable. Plotinus posited instead a principle, the One, which represented the ultimate simplicity. Its simplicity and transcendence is such that it surpasses all categories and is incapable of being the subject of predication. This is a formidable barrier indeed to philosophical discussion. Most of his thought about the One is inevitably therefore an examination of its effects and implications rather than an attempt to explore its nature. However, despite the handicap, Plotinus' concept of the One is not devoid of positive content. Central to his account of reality is the doctrine that good, of which the One is the absolute type, is necessarily productive. Thus the One, without effect upon itself and without deliberation or intent, generates the first being according to our categories. This process of generation, or emanation as it is usually called, is explained in its first and subsequent stages in Aristotelian hylomorphic terms. From the One derives a potentiality for being – the matter of intelligent life – which is attracted to contemplate its source and thereby receives as its form and according to its potentiality the image of the One. This first being, Mind, is the nearest approximation to the simplicity of the One but it is itself less than a unity. Its intellectual life consists of a direct and eternal apprehension of all that is intelligible – that is the forms of reality including, in Plotinus' analysis, the forms of individual beings. (The attribution of individuating characteristic to form was not accepted by all Neoplatonist thinkers but it was a development of great importance for medieval thought.) It is to be noted that Mind does not produce the forms by thinking them. They are in fact the nature of Mind and in knowing them Mind knows itself, in accordance with the Aristotelian principle that thought and its object are identical. In this way Plotinus retains the objectivity of the forms while managing to incorporate them into the system of emanation. He also accords to the forms a coherence and an interpenetration which they lacked in the original Platonic theory, though it will be remembered that Plato in his later thought had searched for just such a unified relationship between them. This unity in plurality is the best realisation which Mind, by contemplating the One, can achieve of the simple unity exhibited there.

The creative effusiveness of goodness is not yet exhausted. As Mind is produced by emanation from the One it in turn generates the principle called Soul. A borrowing from the *Timaeus*, it is the bridge between the intellectual and the sensible worlds. Precisely because it is a bridge, Soul is conceived as having two parts, the second of which is sometimes presented by Plotinus as a separate principle, Nature. In its higher part, Soul remains intent on contemplating Mind; in its lower part it is the principle of order in the material world and reproduces there by emanation the forms contained in the thought of Mind, reflections of which are contained in Soul at both levels. The forms of corporeal beings are individual souls which have the bi-partite character of universal Soul and are never therefore completely incorporated. While they have a function of organising matter, they are linked in a chain of emanation to the highest realities. They are capable by contemplation of retracing their descent from Mind and of becoming alive to the knowledge of reality which is their birthright.

The outer limit of the Plotinian universe in terms of ontological gradation is matter. This is the opposite pole of indeterminacy from the One, of which it is the weakest reflection. Whereas lack of form is ascribed to the One because of the inadequacy of thought to conceive its richness, the indeterminacy of matter is its complete emptiness. It is the point at which emanation from the One and therefore intelligibility and order ceases. Strictly considered matter is a pure potentiality for being formed, a necessary factor in the universe. In this statement the concept is recognisably Aristotelian. But Plotinus also takes a more hostile view of matter. The relation between the individual soul and the matter which it informs is not the close and easy bond of Aristotelian hylomorphism. In his account of the composition of bodies there is a dualism which belies the Aristotelian terminology and proclaims the true affinity of his thought with the Pythagorean–Platonic tradition. Matter is regarded with suspicion as a seductive and contaminating indeterminacy, contact with which has a stultifying effect upon the soul. It obscures its true character and brings it, at the lowest level of material being, almost though not quite to the point of extinction.

This equivocation on the status of matter is symptomatic of a general tension, frequently noted by commentators on Plotinus' thought, between two opposing perceptions. On the one hand there is the optimistic view of Soul's descent according to which it enters matter through 'a desire of elaborating order on the model of what it has seen in Mind'.[46] (Desire must be understood metaphorically, for the process is an automatic and necessary one, a stage in the self-diffusion of good.) On the other hand there is the pessimistic view, derived from Plato himself and reinforced perhaps by the ideology of the contemporary mystery cults, that the incarnation of Soul is a regrettable degeneracy. The emphasis as between these two approaches varies depending on whether Plotinus is analysing creation or developing its moral implications. He himself was a mystic and this dimension of his experience is a major influence upon his theorising. Release from material entanglements is a prerequisite for the soul's effecting its cosmic return. More than this, the reunion of Mind with the One which is inaccessible to intellect can be achieved only in ecstasy, the goal of the purified soul. Porphyry reports Plotinus' death-bed confidence in the return of the divine in man to the divine in the All.[47] His system is the most profound and complete example in Greek philosophy of the close association between cosmology and religious outlook. Their mutual interplay constitutes the richness and is essential to an understanding of his thought.

Porphyry's edition of Plotinus' writings was undoubtedly his greatest service to Neoplatonism but several of his own works were influential. His *Isagoge* or 'Introduction' to the *Categories* of Aristotle is one of the most important examples of the scholastic activity of the period. It became a standard accompaniment to the *Organon* and was indirectly to be the starting point for the early medieval debate over the status of universals. In addition, some of his philosophical writing, now for the most part lost, was known to St Augustine and was frequently referred to by him as typifying the Neoplatonist position. So far as can be established Porphyry seems to have presented on several points a simplified version of Plotinus' thought, though it must be said that Plotinus was not always internally consistent and was capable of giving rise to differences of interpretation. In particular, Porphyry tended to reduce the distinction between Mind and the various levels of Soul and to emphasise the dualism between soul and matter. He also contributed heavily to the polemics of Neoplatonism. It is not certain that Plotinus knew Christianity though he was a relentless critic of the gnosticism with which it was widely associated. Porphryry however attacked Christianity directly. This and the attempt to align with pagan religion in a common front is a feature of the later history of the movement. Iamblichus, a pupil of Porphyry and the leading figure of the Syrian school, incorporated the pagan gods into the Plotinian system and otherwise expanded and complicated its hierarchy. More important than this however is the change of ethos which becomes apparent in Neoplatonism at this time. Plotinian mysticism was supplemented and partially overshadowed by the mechanics of theurgy, a kind of cosmic acupuncture by which it was considered possible to reach out to the divine beings by a manipulation of material objects associated with them. This element of Neoplatonism had an influence, particularly in the Renaissance, quite disproportionate to its value in the system. Although a bizarre notion it did however rest on a philosophical point of some importance: a definite approbation of matter as a feature of the universe, in contrast to the equivocal stance of Plotinus on the subject.

It was the strand of Neoplatonism associated with Iamblichus which was adopted by the Platonic Academy at Athens. Ironically, its conquest of the latter was not effected until the early fifth century from which time it continued to dominate its ancestral home until in 529 the emperor Justinian closed the school there as inimical to Christianity. Its most important figure was Proclus (412–85). His *Elements of Theology* consisted of 211 propositions which presented Neoplatonism in textbook fashion, eliminating many of the tensions and discrepancies found in the *Enneads* and integrating the contributions of Iamblichus, modified on some points, with the thought of Plotinus. Although a derivative thinker, Proclus eventually rivalled Plotinus as a source of western knowledge of Neoplatonism. The works of the pseudo-Denis (*c.* 500), the fountain-head of mystical theology in the middle ages, drew heavily on the Athenian school and probably on Proclus himself. A version of the *Elements* circulated among the Arabs as a work of Aristotle and thence passed into the Latin west where it was known as the *Liber de Causis* (*Book of Causes*). Other works by Proclus, on providence and the status of evil, were also known there by the mid-thirteenth century.

The final chapter of Neoplatonism which is relevant to this background survey is its progress at Alexandria. There it was largely free of the pagan polemical associations which it had acquired elsewhere. The chief activity of the Alexandrian school was the continuance of the tradition of scholarship and commentary on the texts of Plato and Aristotle, with special emphasis on Aristotle's logical works.

In this brief statement of the later history of Neoplatonism, the concern has been less with variation of doctrine than with the identification of centres and channels of influence. Within the broad limits of a spiritual interpretation of reality, a hierarchical structuring of the universe and the reference of all that exists to a unitary principle, there was considerable range of expression and interest among the several thinkers and schools. The differences of emphasis are crucial to the specialist in tracing the pedigree of individual authors. The general reader is more impressed with how completely Neoplatonism in one form or another constituted the intellectual diet of Europe in the early middle ages. The reason for this was partly its inherent attractions, despite certain problems, for Christian thinkers and partly the absence of a rival. The linguistic gulf which opened in late antiquity between the Greek world and the Latin threatened to cut the latter off from all that has been the subject of this chapter. What material was at first available for philosophical study was scanty in the extreme. Much of the intellectual history of Europe for over a thousand years is an account of the process by which Greeks spoke to Latins. Neoplatonism as the dominant philosophical system of the late classical world was in occupation of the lines of communication. Its impact was felt first.

2. From Ancient World to Middle Ages: Adaptation and Transmission

SCHOLARS now generally agree that the term 'Dark Ages' will not serve as a judgement on the period from the fall of Rome to the Carolingian 'renaissance'. Yet it is not clear what if anything should replace it. The truth is that this like most periods of history is an obvious blend of darkness and light, of death and birth. Although far from being a golden age of intense creativity, neither is it a time of obscurantist indifference, let alone hostility to learning. One of the great contributions of St Augustine to Latin Christianity was his justification of the role of secular learning for the theologian. His own world view, which he bequeathed to the early middle ages, as well as his spiritual progress towards Christian belief were heavily indebted to ancient philosophy. Boethius saw himself as retrieving the treasures of Greek thought for a world losing contact with them. His younger contemporary, Cassiodorus, and other contributors to the encyclopaedic tradition more modestly performed a similar role for the liberal arts and for a wide range of ancient lore. The theme of adaptation and transmission lends whatever coherence the intellectual history of western Europe may be said to possess in this transitional period. The coherence should not be exaggerated. Activity was sporadic and, like its subject matter, piecemeal.

Politically, the period begins and ends with instability and fragmentation. The short-lived though impressive Carolingian empire and its patronage of the arts is the background to the work of the last thinker in this chapter, John Scotus Eriugena. He lived indeed when the revived empire was already being partitioned and repartitioned among Charlemagne's heirs but his career is unthinkable without the cultural stimulus which it had afforded. The fragmentation was never again successfully repaired, though imperial unity remained as a potent ideal both for theorists and practitioners of politics. In an important respect, from the viewpoint of the intellectual historian, the fragmentation of Europe had never been overcome even by Carolingian power at its fullest. The Greek world remained apart. The close ecclesiastical contacts which had been fostered between Rome and Constantinople in the century before 750 proved not to be of lasting significance.[1] Charlemagne's acclamation as emperor by spontaneous action of the pope on Christmas Day 800 symbolises a changed orientation in both ecclesiastical and political terms. In this respect, the political and intellectual histories of Europe in the period 400–1000 are in tandem. The gulf between east and west, already evident on the level of language and thence of thought at the beginning of our period, is politically solidified. Intellectually, Scotus Eriugena stands as an exception to this generalised picture but only as an exception proving the rule. It was the very unfamiliarity of the Greek material on which he worked that gave a radical flavour to his thought when read in a Latin context.

I St Augustine: a Philosophy of the Christian in Society

The Historical Background to St Augustine's Thought

Historians study movements of speculative and political thought against their cultural background. In the case of no medieval thinker is this more necessary or more rewarding than in St Augustine's. His career illustrates many of the most important intellectual trends of the late empire and reflects its chronic political problems. Born in Latin Africa in 354 to a pagan father and a Christian mother, St Monica, he received the Latin rhetorical education which despite its pagan content was prized by Christians everywhere as an avenue to social advancement. His youthful religious opinions demonstrate the attraction of Gnostic sects, of which Manicheism was only one. His conversion to Christian faith is one of several testimonials to the spiritual power of Neoplatonism in the Milan of St Ambrose. As a bishop he combined a respect for and pride in North African tradition with an adherence to catholicism as it was emerging in contradistinction to the exclusivity of rigourist, local churches. His greatest work, the *City of God*, grew into an interpretation of history and an analysis of the relationship between religion and society at a time when the Roman empire was dissolving.

The reign of Diocletian (284–305) is a convenient point at which to begin surveying the history of the Roman world in so far as it bears on St Augustine's life and writings. Under Diocletian commenced the last great persecution of Christianity. In its incidental consequences this was to leave a mark on North African religious life for over three hundred years. Diocletian had divided his empire into a western half, which became the responsibility of his co-emperor, Maximian, and an eastern, which he ruled himself with the aid of a deputy. The campaign against Christianity began in the east and lasted longer there. In 303–4 edicts were issued closing churches, requiring that copies of the Scriptures should be surrendered for burning and ordering the arrest of clergy and compliance with general sacrifice. In 305 both emperors abdicated and persecution in the western provinces ceased. The suffering was relatively severe in North Africa, where Christianity had uncharacteristically spread amongst the peasantry.

Diocletian's persecution was followed after a brief interlude by the reign of Constantine (312–37) under whom Christianity was officially tolerated and lavishly patronised. If Constantine expected religion to be a unifying bond in his empire he was disappointed. His attention was quickly drawn to the fundamentalist claims of the North African church as it had emerged from the persecution. Here a schism had developed, formally from a dispute between two rival claimants to the see of Carthage. These were Caecilian, a representative of that party in the church which had bowed before the storm by allowing books to be surrendered for burning, and Donatus, whose name has become identified with the rigourist movement. The issue was not confined to past behaviour for the Donatists stigmatised as invalid the acts of bishops who had in any way compromised with the secular authorities. Constantine made a number of efforts to resolve the schism but without success. Donatism was to surface as a major topic of controversy during St Augustine's episcopacy. The other great religious issue during Constantine's reign was the division in the eastern church over the views of Arius, a priest of Alexandria. Influenced by Neoplatonist emphasis on the indivisibility and transcendence of the One, Arius insisted that in the Trinity, the Son must be inferior to the Father. The dispute provided a classic example of imperial intrusion into theological discussion. The council of Nicaea in 325 at the behest of the emperor accepted a western formula, defining the relationship between Father and Son as *homoousion* or identity of substance. The rift was patched over rather than healed, for large sections of the eastern church, Arians and non-Arians, regarded this dogma as heretical. However, Arianism itself gradually dwindled in importance, being confined in the end mainly to those barbarian tribes who received Christianity early – the Visigoths, Ostrogoths, Vandals, Burgundians and Lombards.

The conversion of Constantine was a decisive event for the triumph

of Christianity. His deliberate preference for Christians was calculated to influence the educated and upper classes on whom the new
religion had made only a limited impression. The policy was
continued under his sons, who had been reared as Christians. In 360,
however, the last surviving son, Constantius II, emperor in east and
west, died and was succeeded by his nephew, Julian. A sincere,
ascetic pagan and devoted admirer of Greek civilisation, Julian
initiated not a persecution of Christians but a reversal of Constantine's policy of patronage. His aim of encouraging a return to
paganism through public incentives was frustrated by his death, on
campaign in Persia in 363. Julian's object had been by no means a
forlorn hope. The contest in 386 between St Ambrose and Symmachus, prefect of the city of Rome and a champion of the pagan
cause, over the removal of the altar of Victory from the Senate House
was a further indication of the strength which paganism derived from
its roots in Roman tradition.[2] The destruction of so many temples in
the reign of Theodosius I (379–95) is as much a sign of anxiety that
they might be reinstated as of the emperor's determination to
establish Christianity officially. This lingering uncertainty but more
especially the rearguard polemical action which pagan intellectuals
continued to mount explains the detailed and sometimes tiresome
apologetic of the early books of the *City of God*.

While these great internal changes were taking place, the northern
and eastern frontiers of the empire were crumbling under the pressure
of migrating barbarian tribes. Theodosius I had some success in
dislodging the Ostrogoths from the Danube region, where they had
settled in large numbers, but the Visigoths remained as an
entrenched enclave there and in the Balkans. The decade and a half
after Theodosius' death was dominated by a contest between Alaric,
leader of the Visigoths, and Stilicho, the Vandal general whom the
Romans – long dependent on barbarian troops – had commissioned
for the defence of the west. Stilicho defeated an attempt by the
Visigoths to invade Italy in 401. However, relations between him and
the Romans deteriorated; a mutiny was fomented among his troops
and he was executed. Military obstacles to Alaric were now reduced
and on 24 August 410 he took and sacked Rome itself. The city had
not been entered since the Gaulish siege of 391 BC and the psychological effect on pagans and Christians throughout the empire was very
great. Strategically, the event was of less significance. In the following

year Alaric died and his successor led the Visigoths to new pickings in Gaul.

In addition to being threatened in this way from the east, Gaul and later Spain were also subjected to the southward drive of Vandals, Alans, Sueves and Burgundians who had crossed the frozen Rhine in the winter of 406. A Roman revival, aided by treaties with the Visigoths, achieved a large measure of pacification in Spain for the next decade and the Vandals were confined to the north-western province of Galicia. In 429, however, encouraged by the disorder of Roman Africa, they crossed the straits of Gibraltar and established themselves there. One of the questions with which St Augustine was preoccupied in the last year of his life was the poignant one, whether the clergy should flee with other refugees or remain to the last to offer what comfort they could to the victims of invasion.[3] As he lay dying in 430 his episcopal city of Hippo, to the west of Carthage, was under siege and nine years later Carthage too fell.

St Augustine's Early Life

Augustine's early life is one of the best known intellectual odysseys in literature.[4] In several important respects his youthful experience had a marked influence on his mature thought, not least in his abiding consciousness of how precarious was the quest for wisdom and how apparently arbitrary was the divine purpose in regard to individuals. The principal source for it is his autobiographical *Confessions*. This book, cast in the form of a long, reflective prayer, was composed in 397, about ten years after the last events described there. By then, Augustine was forty-three and had been a bishop for two years. Although the *Confessions* is a document of great frankness and of a degree of minute psychological observation unparalleled in the ancient world, its author is a man severely critical of what he regards as a mis-spent youth. The perspective has to be remembered in evaluating his judgements upon it. This said, the *Confessions*, supplemented by the more explicitly philosophical *Soliloquies* (written at Cassiciacum in the winter of 386–7), are an invaluable and easy introduction to Augustine's mind and the influences which helped to form it.

The *Confessions* provides evidence of two sorts of influence on the young Augustine: personal and intellectual. Of the personal relationships mentioned there, three groups stand out. First, there is his mother, Monica, whose concern for his welfare he undoubtedly found oppressive at the time but who emerges from his later account as a model of Christian constancy. Second, there is the long liaison with an unnamed mistress by whom, in 372, he had a son, Adeodatus ('the gift of God'). Augustine writes glowingly in the *Confessions* of Adeodatus' intellectual prowess.[5] He was present at the discussion recorded in *On the Happy Life* (written in the autumn of 386) and participates with his father in the dialogue on epistemology, *The Teacher* (written in 389, the year of Adeodatus' death). Third, there is society with his friends, not all of them named. Friendship, among the most highly regarded of the classical virtues, remained as an important element of Augustine's life after his conversion, though he was careful to emphasise its subordination in his new vision of the hierarchy of goods.[6] His first decision after conversion was to retire to Cassiciacum, north of Milan, in the company of his friends. Their discussions there are the basis of his earliest extant writings – *Against the Academics* (*Contra Academicos*), *On the Happy Life* (*De Beata Vita*) and *On Order* (*De Ordine*).[7] As a bishop, he lived among his own monastic community – the model of the Augustinian canons of the middle ages – whose members helped to spread his reforming influence among contemporaries.

It is the intellectual influences, however, which are the more obviously and directly relevant to an understanding of Augustine's thought. By citizenship and cultural orientation he was a Roman. His formal education was as a Latin rhetorician: he studied first in Thagaste, his native town, to the south-west of Carthage, then in neighbouring Madauros and finally in Carthage itself. Later he taught rhetoric in Thagaste, Carthage, Rome and Milan. The training centred on the arts of effective speaking and writing and was an alternative to the less practical pursuit of philosophy. In the *Confessions*, Augustine often dwells on the antithesis between form and content, epitomised in this distinction between the disciplines, and identifies his sensitivity to form as an impediment to his spiritual progress. He was first drawn to philosophy through an exhortatory essay on the subject by Cicero, the great model of the rhetoricians. This work, the *Hortensius*, is now lost and even the work on which it was based, Aristotle's *Protrepticus*, is known only in fragments. It is significant for this one episode. Even so there is an irony, for as has been noted Cicero advocated a sceptical approach to philosophical questions. Augustine was later to argue against this agnosticism but not until it had rendered him a final service.

The tributes which Augustine pays to the effect of the *Hortensius* on him, at eighteen or nineteen, are warm.[8] Though not baptised, he was familiar with the tenets of Christianity from his mother. Stimulated by the *Hortensius* to search for wisdom, he turned to the Scriptures. His reaction was that of the rhetorician: 'To me they seemed quite unworthy of comparison with the stately prose of Cicero.'[9] But rebarbative style was neither the only nor the most serious of his objections. At this time he began his association with Manicheism, an illegal but influential sect named after the Babylonian prophet, Mani (*c.* AD 216–77).

Manicheism derived partly from Christianity, which it regarded as an incomplete revelation. A powerful element in its teaching was a critique of the Gospels as reliable narrative and a rejection of the image of God as presented in the Old Testament. However, its characteristic doctrine was dualism. It explained the universe as a compound of two eternally conflicting principles, Light and Darkness or Good and Evil, each of which was conceived as being limited and material. The struggle between them was at its most acute in man, who was a particle of light imprisoned in a body. This analysis dictated the Manichees' arcane programme of salvation – discrimination between foods containing light and dark particles and, for the higher orders, sexual abstinence, based on a refusal to procreate and thus extend the realm of evil.

In the *Confessions*, Augustine is contemptuous of Manicheism. Yet it had held his attention for some ten years. Not only did it offer a solution to the perennial philosophical problem of the nature and origin of evil but it explained the experiences of spiritual struggle and lapse as due to an agency foreign to man's true nature. Augustine's earliest objections to its teaching stemmed from dissatisfaction with its spurious scientific and astronomical observations. The first refuge in his disenchantment was Ciceronian scepticism which he embraced with fervour as a relief from Manichean dogmatics.[10] In this state he was exposed to the attractions of Neoplatonism. Now resident at Milan, he found in the preaching of St Ambrose and in his contacts with other Christian intellectuals there a philosophical exposition of Christianity which he was later to amplify by a close reading of the Pauline epistles. He was also introduced to copies of Neoplatonist works.[11] These were Latin translations made by Marius Victorinus (d. *c.* 362), himself a convert to Christianity and an African. Augustine did not then know enough Greek to read them in the original and was probably never sufficiently competent to do so extensively.[12] It is not certain what were the treatises which made so profound an impression on him at this time,[13] but it seems probable that they included sections of Plotinus' *Enneads* and some of Porphyry. His initial enthusiasm for the vision of a spiritual reality which they presented was complete. Only gradually did he become conscious of the technical difficulties of Neoplatonism for the Christian. At the time, its effect was to dispel the lingering problems of Manicheism and to leave the way open for his acceptance of Christianity.[14]

The Character of St Augustine's Thought

Almost all that Augustine wrote – some 105 extant books, not counting his letters, several of which circulated as treatises in their own right[15] – dates from after his conversion to Christianity in August 386. All of these works are informed by a conviction of the truth of Christianity. He was aware of the formal distinction between conclusions based on revelation and those derivable from philosophising, in a modern sense, but he would not have regarded as a useful exercise the attempt by a Christian thinker to preserve it. Nor, in neglecting to do so, was he offending against the philosophical norms of the ancient world. His conception of philosophy as an answer to the quest for human fulfilment would have agreed with that of Varro, whom he cites as having listed 288 opinions on the subject.[16] It is in this sense that he thinks of Christianity as philosophy. Though the verdict would not have been approved by a Neoplatonist of Porphyry's bent, their modes of thought were not so different. It has been convincingly shown that Augustine's readiness to interpret the Scriptures as oracles which have been realised[17] is a direct counter to Porphyry's attempt to enlist the pagan revelatory utterances in the service of Neoplatonism.[18] Augustine was not the first to recognise the susceptibility of Scripture to this kind of exposition. Philo of Alexandria had sometimes presented the Old Testament in such a light, in response to a similar though less explicit stimulus.[19] The importance of the technique in Augustine's case is that it is at once symptomatic of the integral character of his thought, in which philosophy – in the modern sense – at its best complements Scripture, and of the intellectual climate in which he wrote. The difference in emphasis as between 'rational' and mystical or revelatory truths in Augustine and Neoplatonism, even of the Porphyrian strand, is quite clear. For Augustine, Scripture is always the primary datum and philosophising a useful tool for expounding and understanding it.[20] For pagan Neoplatonists, rational reflection must be the starting point and central feature of their system, if only because of the dearth of alternatives. But the gulf between philosophy and theology – as they would now be understood – was not so marked nor did the transition from one to the other involve such a wrench as the modern reader might be inclined to suppose. Not only is this consideration necessary for understanding the character of Augustine's writings. It helps to explain both his own intellectual progression at the time of his conversion, and that of others such as Marius Victorinus who had trodden a similar path and by whose example he had been inspired.[21]

The essential difference between rational philosophy and Christianity to Augustine's mind is that the one is fallible and the other certain. This is the brunt of his apologetic against the Platonists as against all the pagan schools. Where he felt that a justification of his method was required it was not against the philosophers but against the tradition in Christianity itself, particularly marked in sections of the North African church, which would dispense with philosophising altogether. The attitude is epitomised in a famous outburst by Tertullian (c. 160–c. 220): 'What has Athens to do with Jerusalem? What concord is there between the Academy and the Church? What between heretics and Christians? . . . Away with all attempts to produce a mottled Christianity of Stoic, Platonic and dialectic composition. We want no curious disputation after possessing Christ Jesus, no inquisition after enjoying the gospel.'[22] Against this way of thinking, Augustine argued explicitly in his treatise *On Christian Doctrine* (*De Doctrina Christiana*). The considerations which he adduces are, appropriately and typically, drawn directly from Scripture, figuratively interpreted:

If those who are called philosophers, especially the Platonists, have said things which are indeed true and are well accommodated to our faith, they should not be feared; rather, what they have said should be taken from them as from unjust possessors and converted to our use. Just as the Egyptians had not only idols and grave burdens which the people of Israel detested and avoided, so also they had vases and ornaments of gold and silver clothing which the Israelites took with them secretly when they fled, as if to put them to better use. They did not do this on their own authority but at

God's commandment, while the Egyptians unwittingly supplied them with things which they themselves did not use well. In the same way all the teachings of the pagans contain not only simulated and superstitious imaginings and grave burdens of unnecessary labour, which each one of us leaving the society of pagans under the leadership of Christ ought to abominate and avoid, but also liberal disciplines more suited to the use of truth, and some most useful precepts concerning morals. Even some truths concerning the worship of one God are discovered among them. These are, as it were, their gold and silver, which they did not institute themselves but dug up from certain mines of divine Providence. . . . When the Christian separates himself in spirit from their miserable society, he should take this treasure with him for the just use of teaching the gospel. And their clothing, which is made up of those human institutions which are accommodated to human society and necessary to the conduct of life, should be seized and held to be converted to Christian uses.[23]

Begun about the time he became bishop, *On Christian Doctrine* offers the key to his subsequent massive output in support and defence of his view of Christianity. It laid the foundations, moreover, of that learned Christianity which was to reach its finest expression in the 'humanism' of the fifteenth century but which had a worthy tradition throughout the middle ages.[24]

The supercilious tone of these references to the Platonists in *On Christian Doctrine* may be attributed to the nature of the case which Augustine was making there. Elsewhere, he could be more open in his appreciation of what they had to contribute.[25] There has been much debate over the extent of Augustine's direct knowledge of Platonism and the sources on which he relied. The questions have proved difficult to resolve. It is easier to suggest in general terms what he owed to the Platonist – and particularly the Neoplatonist – analysis. Four propositions are of outstanding significance. Firstly, as we have seen, it impressed him at a critical stage with a perception of the universe as derived from a unitary and non-material principle. To the importance of this, his own acknowledgements are ample testimony and he relied upon it heavily in his controversies with the Manichees. Secondly, Neoplatonism presented him with a universe in which there was an objective and intelligible order. The concepts of order and disorder are recurring features of his thought. Thirdly, he took over the Neoplatonist view of soul as a dynamic principle, a substance ruling a body. It led him to think of soul as identical with personality and afforded him the basis of a moral theory which in the last resort always insists on man's responsibility for his actions. The fourth point of indebtedness is the least technical and the most far reaching. Augustine's philosophy like Plato's is one not of argument but of vision and his vision has a distinctly Platonist quality. Though imperfectly read in the literature of Platonism, he had penetrated to its essential feature, the recognition that perfection like all the absolutes is of the transcendent not of the mundane. It is an insight which affected more than his epistemology. It had most profound implications for his moral theory, his ecclesiology and his concept of the place of the Christian in society at large.

As a final comment on the character of Augustine's thought, it is well to note that much of it was elaborated in response to rival theories. The earliest writings are devoted to a resolution of the problems associated with his own recent intellectual positions – the brief period of scepticism and the more formidable Manichean dualism. His ecclesiology was largely developed in argument with the rigourist thesis of the Donatists. His moral theory, expounded in defence of freedom of the will against the Manichees, again became an urgent topic when, from 411 onwards, Pelagius and his followers advanced their voluntarist doctrine of human perfectibility and appealed to Augustine's own earlier views to refute his theology of predestinating grace. The chief source for his views on the relationship between Christianity and secular society is the *City of God* (*De Civitate Dei*), begun as a defence against pagan apologetic. It is not possible here to follow these successive discussions in detail. Their significance can, however, be appreciated by considering three central features of Augustine's thought – his theories on knowing and willing, on the relationship between God and creatures and on the organisation and implications of the Christian life.

St Augustine: Knowing and Willing

Augustine's refutation of scepticism takes several forms. Least important is the dialectical and rather crude attempt, in *Against the Academics*, to demonstrate the insufficiency of the theory of probability as a guide to action.[26] The strongest formal argument is what is sometimes called the Augustinian 'Cogito' – by analogy with the formulation 'Cogito ergo sum' ('I think, therefore I am'), of the seventeenth-century French philosopher, Descartes. The very act of doubting conveys at least one certainty – that the doubting agent exists. This appears in an undeveloped form in the first work to be completed by Augustine after his conversion, *On the Happy Life* (*De Beata Vita*), written between Books I and II of *Against the Academics*. It is used with more confidence in several of his later works.[27] Its importance for the character of his thought is that it is symptomatic of his Platonist conviction that certainty is attained from abstract reflection rather than by reference to sensible reality.

Augustine's account of sensation follows closely from his view of the nature of the soul. In *On the Quantity of the Soul* (*De Quantitate Animae*), written in 388, he defined soul as a 'rational substance adapted to ruling a body'.[28] Although he later reduced the dualism implicit in this statement by defining man as a composite – a 'rational substance made up of soul and body'[29] – he continued to take an *a priori* view of soul,[30] regarding it as a principle in its own right, superior to body, and incapable of being acted upon by it. This conception of the primacy and ruling function of soul led him to think of sensation as proceeding from the soul. Sensation, for Augustine, is the soul's responses to the circumstances arising from its union with a body. Even though sensation has the material as its object, it presupposes, in his view, a spiritual principle transcending and assessing the material.[31]

For Augustine as for Plato, the points of reference for the assessment of the world of sense experience are the absolute standards or archetypal Forms, which in accordance with the Neoplatonist tradition he locates in the divine mind and regards as the exemplars of creation. Knowledge of them is not based on experience of sensible reality but comes from within the soul itself. However, where Plato had invoked 'reminiscence' to explain the mind's access to universal ideas, Augustine preferred 'divine illumination'.[32] God, the 'inner teacher', provides the conditions under which it is possible for man to glimpse eternal truths of which God is the foundation and which, as Augustine held, constitute a proof of his existence. The notion of illumination itself derives ultimately from Plato's conception that the Form of the Good reveals the whole of the intelligible world like a sun.[33] Its exact epistemological function in Augustine's theory is far from clear.[34] In fact, its point there is only partly epistemological. Like so much else in his thought, the need for divine illumination serves to emphasise man's essential dependence, a dependence which extends even to the exercise of that capacity – rationality – by which the human species is defined.

This process of knowing reveals one aspect of soul's operations. Another aspect, which had great significance for Augustine's early thought, is its implications for moral theory. The connection is best studied in *On Free Will* (*De Libero Arbitrio*), a treatise, mostly in dialogue form, which Augustine began in 388 but which he did not complete until some eight years later. Its fundamental arguments are aimed at the Manichees: the soul rules the body in virtue of the subordination of lower reality to higher. There is no external force capable of binding the soul to evil action. Therefore, evil action is due to its own will or free choice. But the interest of the treatise is by no means confined to its application against Manicheism. There is also laid the foundation of much of Augustine's later thought. How is it, he asks, that if all men will and choose happiness and the will is an efficacious agent, not all obtain happiness?[35] It is the Socratic question and it is answered, in what will become typical Augustinian terms, by distinguishing between the orders of the objectives at which the will aims. 'It is . . . manifest that some men are lovers of (that is, will to achieve) eternal things, others of temporal things.'[36] The security of their happiness is determined accordingly. Here is adumbrated an argument which will be a central thesis of the *City of God*.

Because of the nature of its apologetic, *On Free Will* is a highly optimistic statement of Augustine's theory of moral choice. It contained much to which the Pelagians could later appeal as seeming to corroborate their views. However, read as a whole it cannot be said to be formally inconsistent with Augustine's later pessimistic statements on the subject, in his controversy with the Pelagians over the necessity of grace for human perfection. The differences are largely of emphasis and perspective. The last part of *On Free Will* may date from as late as 396. This would make it close in time to the treatise *To Simplician, On Various Questions*, in the second book of which the Epistle to the Romans is expounded along rigorously predestinatory lines.[37] For that reason, it is not at all surprising to find towards the end of *On Free Will* what is surely the key to understanding Augustine's doctrine of the effect of the grace of election upon the will.

The will is not enticed to do anything except by something that has been perceived. It is in man's power to take or reject this or that, but it is not in man's power to control the things which will affect him when they are perceived. We must admit therefore, that the mind is affected by perceptions both of superior things and of inferior things. Thus the rational creature may take from either what it will, and, according to its deserts in making the choice, it obtains as a consequence either misery or happiness.[38]

Election is to the will what illumination is to the mind. It is the grant of a conviction as to the true nature of happiness sufficient to produce free conduct directed towards its attainment. In so far as this is simply a recognition of the bond between insight and action, Augustine is fully in accord with the Socratic tradition. But his theory departs radically from it in allowing for the inscrutable and irreproachably arbitrary act of God which supplies the conditions of varying motivation.

St Augustine: God and Creatures

Augustine's treatment of moral choice is simply a particular application of a general principle in his thought, that God is the ultimate source of all good – including, that is, man's virtuous acts. The more general application of the principle can be followed in his account of the origin of reality. His *Literal Commentary on Genesis* (*De Genesi ad Litteram*), written in the period 401–14, contains a detailed analysis of the work of creation in which the biblical narrative is amplified by the use of philosophical material. A prime example is his application of the Stoic theory of 'seminal reasons' to show that creation included, latently at least, all the causes of subsequent developments in the physical order. Although God rested from his labours on the seventh day, he had already established germinally in the perfected condition of his creation a dynamism sufficient to account for what followed.[39] This idea would play an important part in the defence of God's unique creativity mounted by some thirteenth-century theologians against the challenge of the naturalistic Aristotelian theory.

A more explicitly philosophical summary of the origin of reality is found in *On the Nature of the Good* (*De Natura Boni*), written in 404. God is the supreme good and alone is unchangeable. All that exists is created by him. (This is to deny any independent, co-eternal substratum from which reality might be brought into being, on the model of Plato's *Timaeus*. Augustine did not reject the idea of such a substratum or prime matter but insisted that it too must owe to God whatever being it may be said to have.) Everything that exists apart from God – all created spiritual and all corporeal reality – is essentially mutable. (This, and the point made at the beginning of the treatise, that while things have their origin from God they are not part of him, is a rebuttal of the Manichean view that the highest aspect of man derives from the divine substance. Mutability epitomises the gulf between God and creatures, mirroring the Platonic distinction between the absolute and the relative.) No creature is absolutely good but all are relatively good. There is no such thing as evil, only degrees of good. 'All things are good; better in proportion as they are better measured, formed and ordered, less good where there is less of measure, form and order.'[40] Where there is no measure, form and order, there is no goodness but that is to say that there is nothing. Evil is defined in relation to goodness, of which it is a corruption, being evil only in so far as it is corrupt. Similarly, the very notion of corruptibility implies a degree of goodness, that which can be corrupted. Only rational beings are capable of happiness or its opposite and their happiness consists in exercising the power which they have not to be corrupted. It is at this point alone in the universe that disorder is possible, for 'terrestrial things', that is infra-rational beings, 'have peace with celestial things, being as it were submissive to things which are more excellent than they are'.[41] Even this capacity for disorder, however, is part of the cosmic order and its consequences become part of the order of justice.[42]

It can be readily seen from this exposition how much Augustine's cosmology owed to the classical outlook, especially Neoplatonism. Where he departed from it, it was in response to the demands of Judaeo-Christian revelation. Several of these divergences, such as his Trinitarian doctrine and his insistence on a resurrection of the body,[43] for all their importance theologically, had little general effect upon the character of his thought. One difference however is of profound significance: his infusion of the Judaeo-Christian concept of a free and deliberate creation to replace the Neoplatonist structure of mechanical and necessary emanation. Not that he regarded this as a controversial point. He was familiar with the doctrine of the *Timaeus* and considered it to be so close to Genesis as to suggest that Plato might have been influenced by Judaism.[44] However, the effect of attributing all that exists to a free act of the creator was not only to break the chain of necessity in the process of outgoing but also in that of cosmic return. Augustine's view of the relation of creatures to creator is one of total dependence and contingency, unmitigated by any necessity, whether in the analysis of origin or of destiny. The question only became critical in regard to the destiny of man himself, but it is precisely the relationship between man and God which is the core of Augustine's thought. Here there was the complication of what Augustine saw as man's vitiated nature. The story of man's primal disobedience and its consequences was understood by him as a breach of cosmic harmony. Though perfect in its origin, man's nature seemed manifestly imperfect. There is, in Augustine, a rift between man and his origin which defies his own powers to transcend. This is a concept quite foreign to the pagan Neoplatonist account. It is the point at which Augustinian theology is most sharply distinguished from the classical philosophical tradition.

St Augustine: Christian Life

So far as Augustine may be said to have a political or social theory, it is rooted in a particular view of the history and destiny of mankind. His interpretation of history is noteworthy on several counts. It is another point on which he is distinguished sharply from the pagan philosophical tradition; to some extent also it distinguishes him from the Latin Christian tradition in which he wrote. In the first place, against the Neoplatonist theory of cosmic cycles, developed from the Stoics, according to which universes succeed one another indefinitely and souls transmigrate, he offered a linear view of history. He thus safeguarded the unique character of the divine interventions in human affairs which constituted Judaeo-Christian revelation, and preserved the value of the individual lives on the basis of which men are eternally established as elect or reprobate. Secondly, he relied on Scripture for an interpretation of the past which could not be attained by philosophical reflection alone. It is an excellent example of the priority and indispensability of revelation in Augustine's system. Thirdly, in his mature thought, he refused to speculate on the detailed course of the relationship between God and man after the conclusion of this revealed or 'sacred' history. His diffidence contrasts with the earlier, chiliastic outlook of Christianity. This had lasted longer in the west than in the Greek church where it had been effectively discouraged by the theology of the Alexandrian school. According to Augustine, the sixth day of the world began with Christ's nativity and its length is unknown.[45] It is followed by the seventh day, when eternal rest begins. His stance on this subject was important. Even his authority did not quell millenarian expectation, which continued sporadically throughout the middle ages, receiving its fullest intellectual expression in the works of Joachim of Fiore (c. 1145–1202), but it ensured that it would be a minority attitude set against an official and standard view formed by his account.[46]

The success of Augustine's analysis of the Christian life is largely due to the fact that he thus accepted a framework in which the end of the world might be indefinitely delayed, and that in accepting it he laid down principles applicable to all times. He retained the sense of Christian detachment from the world, typified by chiliasm, but adapted it to a new environment. Where hostility to Christianity was no longer generally overt and where it was being officially patronised by the state which had once persecuted it, the distinction between spiritual and secular values was less marked. Augustine devoted much thought to maintaining that distinction in circumstances where the Christian was called upon to take an active part in society.

Detachment or other-worldliness is the dominant theme of Augustine's description of the Christian life. The classic expression of this detachment and of its opposite, worldliness, is found in the *City of God*, on which he was engaged from 413 to c. 427. In his *Retractations*, completed in 427, in which he surveys and frequently corrects his writings, and in the course of the work itself, Augustine shows that he thought of the *City of God* as falling into two parts. Its first ten books are an attack on polytheism, whether inspired by the desire for earthly or for eternal happiness (Books I–V and VI–X, respectively). They contain much that is of interest for assessing his knowledge and appreciation of classical culture. This is particularly true as regards classical philosophy and in the arguments of Books VI–X he has the Neoplatonists chiefly in mind. But the subject of the second part of the work, comprising its remaining twelve books, is of more universal significance. It is the origin, history and destiny of two 'cities' or mystical societies – the City of God and the earthly city, or as he sometimes calls it, the City of Man, or of the Devil – which between them encompass all created rational beings. Augustine's account of them, written comparatively late in his life, contains directly or by implication many of his most important perceptions.

The very definition of the two 'cities' derives from Augustine's basic insight: the relationship between happiness and right ordering of the affections. He had long before observed how 'Some men are lovers of eternal things, others of temporal things'. The *City of God* is an analysis of the logic of these diverse orientations. Two loves create two societies[47] and these societies are as different as the goals by which they are attracted and defined. In terms of its remote ancestry, much of Augustine's psychological and social doctrine can be read as an adaptation of the Platonic theory of *eros* (love), particularly the distinction which Plato had made in the *Symposium* and in the *Phaedrus*, between physical and heavenly eros.[48] Love, for Augustine, is the motive force of the will.[49] 'My love is my weight', he remarks in the *Confessions*:[50] that is, I gravitate towards the object of my affections. But the love of higher things – summed up in the idea of love of God – he regarded as being beyond the capacity of man's debased nature. Where it exists in man it must be attributed to the grace of election. A statement of the membership of the city of God involves the use both of the concepts of spontaneous love of God and of love of God generated by grace. Thus, it includes the good angels of Christian biblical exegesis and that part of the human race – Augustine tends to think of them as a minority – who have been elected by grace to eternal salvation and, by virtue of the conviction which they have been granted, choose the heavenly goal. The rest of mankind and the fallen angels are members of the earthly city.

The human membership of these cities is known only eschatologically – at the Last Judgement. In the course of expounding Revelation 20. 2–3, Augustine interprets the reference there to the devil's confinement under seal, as follows: 'And the addition of "set a seal upon him" seems to me to mean that it was designed to keep it a secret who belonged to the devil's party and who did not. For in this world this is a secret, for we cannot tell whether even the man who seems to stand shall fall, or whether he who seems to lie shall rise again.'[51] Accordingly, there is no visible society either of the unregenerate or of the elect, though there is of course in the case of the elect a community of minds devoted to the same perfect object, just as there is, with less unity of purpose, a tacit agreement among the unregenerate on the priority of what are objectively lesser goods. The church itself is a mixed society, as Augustine had vigorously maintained against the Donatists. The concept which he held of the church and the triumph of which he did much to ensure was an expansive one, capable of including all within its membership. This meant, as he realised, that some church members would be Christian only in the formal or external sense.[52] By accepting this and at the same time defining true Christianity in terms as rigorously exclusive as those of Donatism, he managed to combine two divergent approaches to ecclesiology. The achievement of the perfect society, which was the Donatist aim, was transferred by Augustine from the mundane to the transcendent order.[53]

The state too is a mixed society. Augustine's attitude towards it is never hostile, though taken as a whole it is reserved. He would have accepted Aristotle's dictum that man is a social animal but the political ordering of society he regarded as a consequence of human nature only in the sense that human nature was debased.[54] This is by no means to disparage the state's legitimacy. He followed St Paul (Romans, 13) in regarding government as part of the providential decree, and his tendency is to emphasise the coercive function of the state as imposing an order upon men who are for the most part incapable of generating their own good order. In his combination of pessimism and authoritarianism he has been well compared to Hobbes.[55] His lively regard for the blessings of peace no doubt reflects an apprehension born of an unstable world. It must be one reason for his ready acceptance of government as divinely ordained. There is also, however, the fact that he was writing when the catholic position was immune from persecution. Several of his firmest statements on deference to authority are made with the Donatists in mind.[56] It should not be assumed that had circumstances been otherwise he would have found it impossible to make the same transition as sixteenth-century Calvinists from the doctrine of non-resistance, which characterised the early phase, to the justified rebellion held by Knox and the Huguenots. Augustine was neither a systematic nor a wholly consistent thinker. However, as it was elaborated, the trend of his thought on this point is clear. It exalts the legitimacy of temporal authority and emphasises the duty of obedience, except where there is conflict with divine law. Even then, the duty to refuse obedience is not developed into a right of resistance and it would appear that the subject's only alternative is to follow the lead of the martyrs.[57]

For the most part, Augustine's view of the state is as of something peripheral – a context, largely neutral, in which the Christian lives according to his own principles. His theory is a minimalist one. He rejected Cicero's definition of a republic as 'a multitude joined together by agreement on law (or right) and by community of interest'.[58] In doing so he was rejecting the classical concept of the state. There was no consensus as to law or right considered absolutely. Among the multitude embraced by the secular framework were the citizens of the heavenly city for whom law meant the law of God and right an absolute principle. The extent of their agreement with their secular fellows must be more modestly stated than in the classical formula. But they did have basic interests in common, and this community of interest is for Augustine what defines the state.[59] The state has a law and a resulting peace which is to be used but not mistaken for the goal.[60]

This resignation to the disparity between heavenly and earthly standards helps to explain the narrow elaboration of Augustine's 'political thought' and in particular his lack of interest in prescribing for the reformation of earthly society. His general reticence on the point is well illustrated by his treatment of one important aspect of justice – ownership of property:

If we look carefully at what is written: 'The whole world is the wealth of the faithful man, but the unfaithful one has not a penny,' (Proverbs 17.6) do we not prove that those who seem to rejoice in lawfully acquired gains, and do not know how to use them, are really in possession of other men's property? Certainly, what is lawfully possessed is not another's property, but 'lawfully' means justly and justly means rightly. He who uses his wealth badly possesses it wrongfully, and wrongful possession means that it is another's property. You see, then, how many there are who ought to make restitution of another's goods, although those to whom restitution is due may be few; wherever they are, their claim to just possession is in proportion to their indifference to wealth. Obviously, no one possesses justice unlawfully: whoever does not love it does not have it; but money is wrongly possessed by bad men while good men who love it least have the best right to it. In this life the wrong of evil possessors is endured and among them certain laws are established which are called civil laws, not because they bring men to make a good use of their wealth, but because those who make a bad use of it become thereby less injurious. This comes about either because some of them become faithful and fervent – and these have a right to all things – or because those who live among them are not hampered by their evil deeds, but are tested until they come to that City where they are heirs to eternity, where the just alone have a place, the wise alone leadership, and those who are there possess what is truly their own.[61]

On the level of strict theory, only the just have a true title to ownership, but Augustine does not advocate its application. The perfect and imperfect, ideal and mundane, remain sharply differentiated and effectively separate.[62] However, although this is Augustine's approach, his line of argument here has a wider significance. It was taken over and developed by a series of thinkers in the later middle ages, notably Giles of Rome, Richard FitzRalph and John Wyclif, and was to be a fertile source of radical reforming theory.

Augustine's chief preoccupation in defining the role of the state is with ensuring that the Christian can never allow his horizons to be limited by inferior standards. He is constantly concerned to maintain the distinction between the two dimensions, absolute and relative. While doing so, however, he does not oppose the Christian's participation in affairs of state. Indeed he is careful to show that there is no incompatibility between the spiritual vocation and the discharge of public responsibility. He was conscious of the need to reassure opinion within the African church on this point:

We find now the citizen of Jerusalem, citizen of the kingdom of heaven, involved in earthly administration, as for instance, wearing the purple, being a magistrate, an aedile, proconsul, emperor, governing the earthly republic; but he has his heart above if he is a Christian, if he is of the faithful, of the devout, if he sets slight value on where he is at present and places his hopes on where he is not yet. . . . Let us not despair therefore of citizens of the kingdom of heaven when we see them engaged in some of Babylon's affairs or on something earthly in the earthly republic.

(The converse is that the exercise of ecclesiastical office is no guarantee of election.)[63] He was also conscious of the need to silence a strand of pagan apologetic which associated Christianity with the decline of Roman power. He replied specifically to charges that the gospel precepts against rendering evil for evil and requiring the turning of the cheek were incompatible with the duties of citizenship. The precepts, he says, refer to internal disposition rather than to external action.[64] In particular, he allowed of the 'just war' – that fought in defence or to redress an injury – and did not forbid the Christian to take part in it, any more than to exercise other offices within the state.[65] His intention should be to effect a salutary remedy and he should be without rancour. As always for Augustine, it is preservation of personal or moral integrity, in a way reminiscent of Stoic ethics but here associated with the pursuit of higher aims, which marks the Christian, even in secular activity, and distinguishes him from his non-Christian fellow.

The strict tenor of Augustine's thought on the nature of the two cities, as summarised here, would seem to demonstrate the futility of secular intervention in spiritual matters, and the superfluity of any theocracy. There is however the paradox that in combating first the Donatists and then the Pelagians he was prepared both to condone and to invoke the use of coercion against them by the imperial authorities. It is possible that in no small part this dark side of Augustine's episcopal career was a pragmatic reaction which he then sought to justify on the theoretical level. But the attitude is not entirely out of keeping with some of his general perceptions.[66] He was aware from his own experience of the force of external stimuli in the achievement of conversion, even allowing for the fact that divine predestination was both a prerequisite for conversion and in itself an effective direction towards it. It is the dilemma which faces all who believe in an inexorable process – whether to aid it or simply await it. Having once allowed, in contrast to the Donatists, for a church that was mixed, the theoretical obstacle to secular coercion was much reduced. Augustine did not promote a union of church and state. If this was because he considered it fantastic and impractical within the contemporary context, he showed a discernment which lesser thinkers in the Augustinian tradition sometimes lacked. Nor does his thought, on the whole, envisage the fusion of secular and spiritual ends, even in a hierarchical relationship: quite the reverse. However, it is undeniable that his theorising, elaborated over a long period and in response to a variety of problems, contained the germs of such a high ecclesiastical doctrine. His medieval commentators who developed that position were not perhaps thereby doing violence to classic Augustinianism. Given Augustine's own capacity to develop his views in reaction to changed circumstances, they might be said to have merely updated him in a manner of which he would perhaps have approved. But a development it was. In the last analysis, the relationship of state to church in Augustine's own writings cannot be neatly stated. They contain as much to justify a theory of radical dissociation as of partnership.

II   Boethius: Executor of Antiquity

The Historical Background to Boethius' Work

In the half century following St Augustine's death, the barbarian tribes consolidated their occupation of most of the western part of the Roman empire. By the late fifth century, Britain was lost to the Angles and Saxons – though the Britons continued to mount a resistance – while the Vandals had secured control of Roman North Africa. Most of Spain became a Visigothic kingdom and Gaul a Frankish kingdom under Clovis. In Spain at least and to an extent also in Africa, the invaders retained the Roman administrative system, while replacing the military structure. The process of change was therefore less sudden than might be thought. As may be expected, the continuity was greatest in Italy. The deposition in 476 of the last Roman emperor in the west, the ironically named Romulus Augustulus, by Odoacer, king of the East German federates, is not regarded by modern scholars as the significant event that it appeared to historians of the older school. Nor was it regarded by contemporaries as the demise of Roman authority in Italy. In theory, this authority was now resumed by the Eastern emperors. To it, the barbarians who now ruled Italy looked for the titles which would justify and clothe with legality their jurisdiction over Roman citizens. Through the agency of the senate, Odoacer negotiated with the emperor, Zeno, for the style of patrician and though the emperor refused it, he was forced to accept the *de facto* regime. There was a weakness in this situation from Odoacer's viewpoint, as he was vulnerable to attack by rival forces acting with the emperor's connivance. The threat materialised in 488 when Zeno, to rid himself of the Ostrogoth king, Theoderic, who was ravaging Thrace, commissioned him to expel Odoacer from Italy. In 493 Theoderic killed Odoacer, occupied Ravenna, the seat of his rule, and took his place as unofficial regent. As such, he retained the ancient forms. The senate remained, as an institution of prestige, and the civil administration was for the most part exercised by Romans, holding the traditional offices. As the Ostrogoths were Arians there was a religious difference between the two peoples. Theoderic's policy however was one of toleration, unlike Vandal rule in Africa under which catholicism was remorselessly persecuted. 'We cannot give orders as to religious belief,' he is reported as saying, 'since no one can be compelled to believe against his will.'[67]

The career of the aristocrat, Anicius Manlius Severinus Boethius, is itself an illustration of the administrative continuity. He was born probably about 480. His father had been prefect and consul under Odoacer. Symmachus, his guardian after his father's death and later his father-in-law, was leader of the senate.[68] Nothing is known of Boethius' earliest relations with the new king but in 510 he became consul, an appointment in Theoderic's hands. The nomination of his sons, Boethius and Symmachus, as joint consuls in 522 was a signal compliment to him. In the same year, he became Master of Offices, at the head of the civil government. The turn in his fortune, which was the occasion of the *Consolation of Philosophy*, was as dramatic as Job's. In 523 Theoderic suspected a plot on behalf of the emperor or, as is more likely, on behalf of the emperor's nephew, Justinian, the power behind the throne. He arrested the pro-consul, Albinus, whose letters had been intercepted. When Boethius intervened for the defence, he too was arrested on a charge of treason. It was during his imprisonment at Pavia, awaiting execution, that the *Consolation* was written. Albinus and he were not the only notable casualties of the purge. In the following year Symmachus also was executed.

Boethius the Logician

These distinguished figures, Symmachus and Boethius, combined an active part in public life with a lively interest in scholarship. It is an indication of the growing rift between the Greek and Latin worlds as well as of his own intellectual bent that Boethius proposed to translate the complete works of Plato and Aristotle, with a commentary harmonising their differences.[69] A synthetic treatment of the two philosophers was not at all an original project. As has already been noted, it was characteristic of Middle Platonism and remained a salient feature of Neoplatonism. Nor did Boethius feel rigidly bound by the programme.[70] In the event, he seems not to have got beyond Aristotle's logic. His contribution here, however, was of momentous importance. Working in a scrupulously literal fashion, he translated all of the *Organon*, though his version of the *Posterior Analytics* has not survived. He also translated the *Isagoge* or *Introduction* which Porphyry had written as an accompaniment to Aristotle's *Categories*, and produced two editions of a commentary upon it. The first edition of his commentary he based on a Latin paraphrase of the *Isagoge* by Marius Victorinus which continued to be influential in the middle ages. Having subsequently made his own translation, he issued the second and fuller edition of his commentary. A point of great interest for the middle ages about these expositions of the *Isagoge* was that they contained an explicit discussion of the status of universal concepts. As for the Aristotelian works themselves, commentaries by Boethius on the *Categories* and on the *De Interpretatione* (the latter in two editions, one avowedly for beginners and the other for advanced students) were to have wide circulation. Less important was his commentary on Cicero's *Topics*, a reworking by the great Latin rhetorician of Aristotle's treatise of the same name. Boethius compiled too a number of independent treatises on special aspects of logic, namely the syllogism (three treatises, entitled 'Introduction to the Categorical Syllogism', 'On the Categorical Syllogism' – in two books, of which the first broadly parallels the 'Introduction' – and 'On the Hypothetical Syllogism'), 'division' (that is, analytical method) and 'topical differences' (the technique of argument in logic and rhetoric).

Boethius' knowledge of late classical scholarship may not have been so extensive as was once thought. It is possible that much of the material on which he based his logical commentaries and independent treatises came from scholiastic notes in contemporary editions of the *Organon*,[71] though it need not be assumed that he was wholly dependent on such aids since it is at least as likely that he had direct access to the authorities on which they were based. Certainly, he is a writer whose influence far exceeded his originality. Moreover, in assessing his influence on logical study some qualification is necessary. He was not the only source for a knowledge of ancient logic in the early middle ages. Much of the doctrine of the *Categories*, some of the *De Interpretatione* and a compressed treatment of the syllogism was provided by Book IV of the immensely influential *Marriage of Philology and Mercury* (*De Nuptiis Mercurii et Philologiae*) by Martianus Capella. The evidence of surviving manuscripts clearly indicates the important part played by Martianus' treatise in the tenth-century revival of logic.[72] As for a text of the *Categories*, the most influential version during the Carolingian renaissance was a paraphrase dating probably from the second half of the fourth century and wrongly attributed to St Augustine. It was not until the eleventh century that Boethius' translation supplanted this as the standard source. For the *De*

Interpretatione, a Latin work known as *Perihermeneias* – a transliteration of the Greek title – attributed to the second-century writer Apuleius was used in the middle ages, as will be noted later. However, when all is said, Boethius remains the pivotal figure in the history of medieval logic. Without his translations and explanatory treatises, the history not only of logic but of philosophical debate in the early middle ages would have been different and the progress towards a recovery of the ancient expertise slower and more painful.

Boethius the Christian Theologian

Boethius is now generally accepted as the author of four theological treatises. Three of these (i, ii and v in the manuscript order) relate to contemporary concern with the formulation of doctrine on the Divine Trinity. A fourth (iii in the manuscript order) is in fact a purely philosophical essay on being and goodness. The authorship of a fifth treatise (iv in the manuscript order), with the late title *De Fide Catholica*, which is also attributed to him, has been much debated but now seems probable.[73] This theological writing has a twofold interest. In the first place, Boethius' elaboration of the doctrine of the Trinity presages the philosophical approach to theology which will be so prominent a feature of the intellectual history of the high middle ages. His 'sacred treatises', especially the *De Trinitate* ('On the Trinity') were a source and model of much later work. He was not, of course, the earliest exponent of the method in the Latin church. Besides the highly philosophical content of much of St Augustine's work, to which Boethius acknowledged his indebtedness, there is the example of Marius Victorinus' Neoplatonist defence of the Nicene creed.[74] But Boethius is noteworthy for having explicitly advocated the disciplined reconciliation of reason and faith and for the confidence with which he wrote to that end. Secondly, and with more immediate point, his theological writing is significant for an interpretation of the *Consolation of Philosophy*. It may also have had a bearing on the circumstances surrounding his fall from favour with Theoderic.

The fact that the *Consolation of Philosophy* is devoid of Christian reference led critics in the eighteenth and nineteenth centuries to challenge the medieval tradition that Boethius had been a martyr and to question whether he had been a Christian at all. However, his formal religious position at least was established by a fragment of Cassiodorus published in 1877 and known after its discoverer as the

Anecdoton Holderi. This credited Boethius with having written 'a book on the Holy Trinity, certain doctrinal articles and a book against Nestorius'.[75] Nestorius, a fifth-century archbishop of Constantinople, had held that there were two persons as well as two natures in Christ, against the more generally accepted doctrine that there were two natures but one person. Nestorius' views in turn had evoked an extremist reaction, the Monophysitism of Eutyches, who insisted that there was only one nature in Christ, the divine nature. The formula 'two natures and one person' was sanctioned by the council of Chalcedon in 451. Nestorius was condemned and Nestorianism rapidly dwindled in the Greek world, though it spread through Persia and as far as India and China. Monophysitism, however, endured as an obstacle to the religious unity of the Greek empire. When Boethius wrote his Trinitarian essays (*c.* 512–22) strenuous efforts were being made by the court of Constantinople to resolve the issue. Theopaschism, a version of the catholic position, advanced by a group of Latin-speaking Scythian monks to the effect that 'one of the Trinity suffered in the flesh', was promoted as a possible compromise. It has been plausibly argued that Boethius' treatment, particularly his tract *Contra Eutychen et Nestorium* ('Against Eutyches and Nestorius'), should be interpreted as a contribution specifically to this quest for a settlement.[76] Albinus is known to have been interested in the Theopaschite debate and it is probable that Symmachus too was involved in the contacts over it. Theological unity would have been a notable advantage to Justinian in his aim of political unity throughout the empire. In such circumstances, Boethius' involvement in the theological debate may well have aggravated Theoderic's suspicions. His denial of the charges against him might simply indicate that he did not regard any association with imperial policy as treason. It is not therefore incompatible with this interpretation of his theological activity or with the philosophical integrity which readers of the *Consolation* would wish to attribute to him.

The Consolation of Philosophy

The central themes of the *Consolation* are not at all original. They are variation of fortune (Books II–III), the nature of evil (Books III–IV) and the compatibility of providence with freedom of choice (Book V). In his treatment of them, moreover, Boethius has been shown to draw heavily on the Greek tradition.[77] But the book is not simply a mosaic of doctrine from the various schools. The circumstances in which Boethius poses these time-honoured problems removes them from a purely speculative plane and the urgency which they acquire gives his treatment of them a unique character. The *Consolation* demands reading both as a record of the philosopher's reaction to personal crisis and as evidence of the intellectual climate of the time. The two aspects are closely linked. The intellectual historian is interested in the problems which are tabled for discussion, though in large part they may be supposed to derive from Boethius' predicament; he is interested still more in the materials which were available or which were chosen for their solution. The distinction between what was available and what was chosen leads in particular to questions regarding the depth of Boethius' Christianity. Assuming him to have been indeed the author of the theological tractates attributed to him, he was, in western terms, an orthodox Christian. Did he, as has been emphatically argued, abandon Christianity and turn to philosophy as the sole consolation?[78] Or did he tacitly set out to keep separate the dictates of faith and reason and thereby merit the title which has been accorded him of being the first scholastic?[79] The problem which the reader sees in accepting the second interpretation is that it injects an element of artificiality into the work, reducing the realistic description of the prisoner's dejection and gradual rationalisation of his plight to literary verisimilitude. The victim of the mental depression portrayed in Book I may only with difficulty be supposed capable of spontaneously excluding one of his sources of support. That is not to say that the *Consolation* is devoid of artifice. The sufferings of the prisoner and the effect on him of Philosophy's appearance are described in a highly technical, almost stilted, fashion.[80] But it seems best to take the order of progression in the *Consolation* at face value. Boethius may be assumed to have been a Christian, in the sense of a believer in a personal God and in a providential ordering of the universe. These two fundamental doctrines, easily reconciled with prosperity, were put under the severest pressure and perhaps even shattered by the reversal of his fortunes. It should be remembered what alternative interpretation of man's cosmic role presented itself. A prominent strand of the classical culture in which Boethius was steeped was that man is either the plaything of chance or the pawn of an inexorable Fate. In this context the *Consolation* exhibits a real development. There is a psychological progress from a point where the possibility of providence requires detailed explanation to a position where it is considered reconciled or at least reconcilable with the inequity of the world's order as man experiences it.

The form of the *Consolation* is five books of alternating prose and metrical verse passages. The combination of prose and verse derives ultimately from the satires of the Greek Cynic philosopher Menippus (third century BC) but the technique had been imitated in Latin by Varro and had also been used by Martianus Capella in his *Marriage of Philology and Mercury*. Not only is Boethius' poetry highly accomplished; it discharges a function similar to that of the myth in Plato's dialogues, by encapsulating the point at issue and advancing it rather more freely than is possible in prose.

Book I is largely autobiographical. It describes the prisoner's account of his career and high intentions to his visitor, the Lady Philosophy, whose disciple he has long been. These passages are of great interest in providing hints of the circumstances of Boethius' downfall and offering historical insights into the character of Theoderic's regime. This is particularly true of Chapter 4, where Boethius is shown restraining excesses among Gothic officials in Italy and enjoying the king's support in doing so. But the theme of principal concern to the work as a whole is the puzzle posed by the prosperity of the wicked, succinctly stated in metric 5:

> For why should slippery chance
> Rule all things with such doubtful governance?
> Or why should punishments,
> Due to the guilty, light on innocents?[81]

This leads directly to an examination of the fickleness of Fortune, which is the subject of Book II. Fortune gives, Fortune takes away and will suffer no rebuke for doing so, justifying herself in an image which becomes part of the stock in trade of medieval moralists:

> I may boldly affirm that if those things which you complain have been taken from you had been your own, you should never have lost them. Must I only be forbidden to exercise my right? It is lawful for heaven to bring forth fair days and to hide them again in darksome nights. It is lawful for the year sometimes to compass the face of the earth with flowers and fruits and sometimes to cover it with clouds and cold. . . . And shall the insatiable desire of men tie me to constancy, so contrary to my custom? This is my bent, this is the

sport in which I continually indulge. I rotate my wheel with speed and take a pleasure in turning things upside down. Ascend, if you will, but with this condition, that you think it not an injury to descend when the course of my sport so requires.[82]

Philosophy then proceeds to rationalise this state of affairs, in what is undoubtedly the most successful part of the *Consolation*. What is presented, tacitly, is the Stoic doctrine: man's happiness is not or should not be dependent on the accidental gifts of Fortune but consists in his own integrity. Furthermore, loss of Fortune is a valuable lesson which the philosopher should be glad to learn.

Book III extends this consideration of true happiness. By expounding the Socratic doctrine that the purpose of men's actions is the good as they see it, Philosophy faces up to the apparent prosperity of the wicked in their designs. Their accomplishment of their purposes, given that these are misguided, is in fact a greater evil than their failure to accomplish them. They have sought the good without having properly discerned in what it consists and therefore obtain only the shadow of it. The argument is continued in the first four chapters of Book IV. These rest ultimately for their substance on Plato's *Gorgias*, the dialogue in which Socrates smartly quashes the contention that might is right. Wicked men too desire the good but are powerless to obtain it. They are therefore unhappy when they attain their desire and particularly so when they remain unpunished. Those who commit wrong are more to be pitied than those who suffer it.

The prisoner is now in quite a different mental state to that of Book I. The nominal purpose of the *Consolation* has been achieved, though some of its most important arguments as it stands are yet to come. The remainder of Book IV considers how the existence of evil is compatible with the idea of divine governance of the world.[83] A basic and explicit conception underlies the discussion: since God, though omnipotent, is incapable of doing evil, evil is not a positive factor but a deprivation or absence of good. It is the same definition as that arrived at by St Augustine and it comes from the same, Neoplatonist, philosophical tradition. The solution offered is that all that appears wickedly done is part of the providential dispensation – of which Fate is the cosmic agent – and tends towards a beneficial result.

Book V examines an implication of this doctrine of providential disposition, querying how it can be compatible in the first place with chance and in the second with human freedom. On the first point, it is suggested that chance, in the sense of an uncaused event, does not exist. There is what readers of Horace Walpole would recognise as Serendipity, a fortunate concurrence of circumstances, which is also part of the providential ordinance. The resolution of the second point depends on a precise definition of the sphere in which Providence operates – an extension of the distinction between Providence and Fate made in Book IV. This introduces, not for the first time in Boethius' writing,[84] a concept of eternity different in quality from that of perpetuity. The two orders, of eternity and of time – even considered as indefinitely prolonged – are distinct. The eternal does not impinge on the order of time and eternal awareness of an event no more determines it than the detached observation of events in the temporal order influences them. The treatment is subtle, draws heavily on Aristotelian logic and is important for having provided a terminology for the discussion of the problem. But it is essentially a limited exercise on a technical topic. Its conclusion, that the nature of divine awareness, abscinded from time, does not affect the quality of what to man are future events, became the standard medieval opinion on the subject.

Boethius and the Liberal Arts Tradition

Boethius' logical corpus and the ever popular *Consolation of Philosophy*, which attracted a long line of translators and commentators,[85] are his most important achievements for the history of thought. However, he also stands with a number of other authors as having made a more general contribution to the educational syllabus of the middle ages. The classical Roman curriculum of the liberal arts, as defined by Marcus Terentius Varro (116–27 BC), had consisted of nine subjects – grammar, logic, rhetoric, geometry, arithmetic, astronomy, music, medicine and architecture. In the middle ages, medicine eventually became a university subject, while architecture was a craft learnt in apprenticeship and practice rather than in school. The other seven liberal arts continued to be studied, at least nominally, throughout the middle ages, though the actual content of the teaching varied in intensity, becoming more thorough in the twelfth century and reaching a height of professionalism in the arts courses of the universities. At an early stage, the programme became formally divided into a first and second phase, the trivium and quadrivium.[86] The trivium – grammar, logic and rhetoric – dealt with techniques of discussion. The quadrivium – geometry, arithmetic, astronomy and music – constituted a 'scientific' syllabus, summarising the principles of order in the physical world. The most convenient single source available for these subjects was the allegorical treatment given them in Martianus Capella's *Marriage of Philology and Mercury*. Martianus wrote in Roman North Africa in the early fifth century. The first two books of his treatise are a fanciful allegory on the betrothal and marriage of the maiden Philology to Mercury, the god of eloquence. They describe Philology's ascent to heaven, with some cosmological detail on the relationship of the planets, and portray the pagan heavenly court. The remaining seven books allow the attendants whom Mercury has brought for his bride to introduce themselves. They are the seven liberal arts in the order (Books III to IX respectively), Grammar, Dialectic, Rhetoric, Geometry, Arithmetic, Astronomy, Music. Martianus' work was probably based in large part on Varro's nine-volume treatise on the disciplines which was lost early in the post-classical period. It therefore constituted a direct link with the classical Latin encyclopaedia. If Boethius' logical works are more particularly inspired by his philosophical interests, they also follow, with his contributions to the quadrivium, in this line of didactic writing. His 'scientific' works in fact antedate his logical ones. They originally consisted of three treatises, one each on geometry, arithmetic and music, that on music being an account of harmonic theory. The first of these has left no trace – a pseudo-Boethian work on the same subject has survived – but his accounts of arithmetic and music were widely used as textbooks in the middle ages.

The same concern with the conservation and transmission of learning, though with a specifically Christian bias, is evident in the career of Boethius' contemporary Cassiodorus. Born around 485 to a Calabrian family, he became quaestor and secretary to Theoderic and later, like Boethius, consul and master of offices. He is another example of the scholar and intellectual actively involved in the Gothic administration. His political career survived the crisis of 523 but ended with the Byzantine invasion of Italy when Justinian succeeded (536–63) in restoring direct imperial government. Having failed in his first project of establishing a school of theology in Rome, Cassiodorus took refuge in the monastic life, centred on his villa of Vivarium in southern Italy. Here he set his monks to study and copy patristic and secular authors. Although his monastery probably foundered immediately upon his death, it is significant in foreshadowing the future of learning in Europe until the rise of the cathedral schools. However, Cassiodorus is important for more than having established a model of intellectual monasticism.[87] His own *Institutions of Divine and Human Readings*, written *c.* 562, is in its inspiration the Christian counterpart to the pagan encyclopaedia of the arts. The first book details the theological treatises necessary for monastic reading. The second details the disciplines necessary for a comprehension of the Scriptures. These are the seven liberal arts, to which the *Institutions* provides a bibliography. Cassiodorus thus presents the arts as ancillary to scriptural study. In the event, the two books of his *Institutions* frequently or indeed usually circulated apart.[88]

The compilations of Martianus Capella and Cassiodorus were favourite textbooks of the early middle ages. As representatives of the encyclopaedic tradition they were joined in the early seventh century by the *Etymologies* of Isidore of Seville. This impressive if unevenly erudite work is an attempt to organise the whole of knowledge through an explanation of the meanings of words. Besides the seven liberal arts, which occupy its first sections, the *Etymologies* covers the terminology of a host of subjects, including medicine, law, chronology, the bible, theology, ecclesiology, geography, geology, and a range of ordinary human activity. Its influence would be difficult to exaggerate. It became the standard work of reference in monastic and cathedral libraries throughout Latin Christendom and is one of the first sources to be consulted in the search for the intellectual pedigree of subsequent writers in the next four centuries.[89]

Education and Culture in a Period of Transition

The education system of late antiquity was organised on a mixture of public funding and private fee-paying. Elementary schooling in reading, writing and arithmetic was not supported by the authorities. It was provided either within the household, as usually in the case of the aristocracy, or by schoolmasters charging per pupil. A higher education in grammar and rhetoric was available at most principal towns, where professorships were frequently established at municipal or in the most important centres at imperial expense. It will be obvious that this level of the structure was especially vulnerable to the disruption caused by the invasions. However, as with political and administrative institutions, ancient education had a lingering continuity under the barbarians. It faded out gradually rather than disappearing at once. Again, the degree of continuity varied between regions. The amount of information available to historians for a reconstruction of the picture also varies. For the most part it is meagre indeed. What can be pieced together has mainly to be inferred from the records of those whose outlook and level of attainment is known and from standards of administration. One general point needs to be remembered. Although some philosophy had been taught in the west, notably at Rome, the great philosophical centres of antiquity had always been in the east, at Athens and Alexandria especially. It is not clear at which of these centres Boethius had received his advanced training but his was the last generation in the west to enjoy this benefit. Despite Justinian's closure of the school of Athens in 529, the teaching of philosophy continued in the Greek world. The fact would be of great significance for Latin culture in the high middle ages from the transmission of texts to the Arabs, a process which will be examined in due course. As far as concerns this early period, however, when one speaks of a limited survival of classical culture and teaching in the west what is involved is learning at a much humbler level than that enjoyed by Boethius and his distinguished contemporaries. In effect, it is the liberal arts programme – or rather, parts of it – with perhaps medicine and Roman law too continuing to be taught for a time.[90]

In Rome, the liberal arts were still being taught *c*. 550 when Gregory the Great was a youth, though as he was an aristocrat his accomplishments cannot be taken to prove what was available generally. There is also evidence of teaching in Ravenna at this time. Justinian's temporary and partial reconquest of the west had some significance for education. In his Pragmatic Sanction (554) he made provision for the maintenance of masters in grammar, rhetoric, medicine and law, with the declared purpose of ensuring a supply of trained people. It is not certain, though, how far or whether the measure was implemented; probably it was insufficient to repair the havoc wreaked by the war of reconquest. In any case, there was soon (568) a new invasion of northern and shortly after of central Italy, by the Lombards. Byzantine rule was now much reduced, being confined to the coastal region round Ravenna and a narrow corridor between centre and north. It seems that by the end of the sixth century the classical schools had generally been lost. Now what education there was centred on the church and was concerned primarily with maintaining church services and training clerics. This appears to be the case even in Rome which remained under Byzantine control during the seventh century. Rome at this time had resources which impressed visitors from northern Europe. The Lateran library which had received some part of the collection at Vivarium served as a source of texts and there are several instances of borrowings from it by northerners. However, the intellectual climate of the city was defensive and its impact very limited. Later, there would be an expansion of education in northern and central Italy, favoured by the more settled conditions of the late seventh and early eighth centuries and the easier relations which accompanied the conversion of the Lombards from Arianism to catholicism. Later still, towards the end of the tenth century and during the eleventh, secular education in grammar, rhetoric and most characteristically in law would emerge as a vigorous feature of the life of the northern cities.

Conditions in Gaul after the Frankish conquest of the first half of the sixth century varied markedly between north and south. In Aquitaine, Provence and Burgundy, Roman culture remained strong and continued so for another century. The municipal schools did not survive beyond the late fifth or early sixth century but after their demise aristocratic families continued to provide an education in the home. However, this seems to have ceased or its products cease to be evident by about the middle of the seventh century. In North Africa, the Vandals had initially been at best uninterested in Latin culture. Gradually they began to make concessions to it. Schools revived in the late fifth century and when Justinian reinvaded he found them still in being. Roman education was still being maintained in Carthage up to the Arab conquest in 698. This fact was of some importance for the European scene, as it has been shown that the culture of Spanish monasteries was influenced by continuity of relations with North Africa. Even if there were no other evidence, the work of Isidore of Seville would be enough to suggest that Spain was an especially strong centre in the seventh century. Medicine, law and letters remained alive. The old aristocracy had retained their culture and by the beginning of the seventh century contacts with their Visigothic counterparts began to draw the latter to imitate them. During the century, the Visigothic court at Toledo actively patronised learning. But the chief institutional strength lay in the monasteries adjacent to large towns like Seville, Toledo and Saragossa. Devotion to learning was by no means the only element in the Spanish monastic outlook; there was also an ascetic strand, inimical to secular culture, and this strand came to dominate. However, the greater monasteries were cultural centres. Not only were they important in their own right but their members when appointed to bishoprics helped to maintain educational standards outside. It was to this intellectual monasticism that Isidore of Seville owed his training and the resources on which he drew.

III   John Scotus Eriugena: a Cosmic Analysis

The Background to Eriugena's Work

The Visigothic culture which had produced Isidore of Seville was submerged in the Islamic invasion which swamped the Spanish peninsula – with the exception of the Basque land and the adjoining coastal region – in 711. From then until the Carolingian renaissance, some seventy years later, the focus on intellectual developments moves to the north-western periphery of Europe. Ireland had never been part of the Roman empire but Christianity had brought with it a Latin culture which continued, at least as far as grammar and rhetoric were concerned, in Irish monasticism during the sixth century. Columbanus in particular was widely read in classical poetry and was himself a fine metric poet and rhetorician. He was the greatest of the Irish missionaries to Europe (*c.* 591–615) and the founder of Bobbio, later to become a major centre. Northern England, where Irish and Roman Christianity met somewhat stormily in the mid-seventh century, proved an especially fruitful area of cultural exchange. The Northumbrian, Benedict Biscop, founder of monasteries at Wearmouth and Jarrow, knew Greek as well as Latin. He had studied on the continent and visited it often. He was also for a time an associate of Archbishop Theodore of Tarsus, the Greek monk who was appointed to Canterbury in 669, and of Theodore's companion, Abbot Hadrian, a monk of African extraction imbued with the Greek culture of southern Italy. The fusion of these various influences produced at Wearmouth and Jarrow an outstanding scholar in the Venerable Bede (673–735). A little later they produced Alcuin, at York, the centre of a thriving school and library. It was with Alcuin (*c.* 730–804) that the northern learning came to be formally transplanted into the Carolingian empire. In 782, Alcuin accepted an invitation from Charlemagne to become head of the king's palace school at Aix-la-Chapelle.

The history of general learning and literary activity during this period lies beyond the scope of the present survey. Charlemagne's policy was aimed at raising the level of basic education, especially in the church. Through the work of teachers like Alcuin and the latter's pupil, the encyclopaedist, Rhabanus Maurus (c. 776–856), who became archbishop of Mainz in 847, and through the establishment of monastic and capitular schools, he promoted an expanding knowledge of the liberal arts. The 'renaissance' was not directly concerned with furthering speculative thought. However there are some suggestions of philosophical interests. Alcuin was not an original thinker but his writings show an understanding of the philosophical content of ancient texts – those of the Fathers, especially St Augustine, and of Boethius. He was keenly interested in logic and promoted the study of it both through his own textbook on the subject, *De Dialectica*, and through the copying of texts, notably the pseudo-Augustinian *Categoriae Decem* ("Ten Categories'). Moreover, evidence of the philosophical activity of Alcuin and his circle has been augmented by the case for the provenance of a number of texts from the period, preserved most fully in a Munich manuscript and referred to accordingly as the 'Munich passages'.[91] One of these passages, the *Dicta Albini* ('Sayings of Albinus'), may probably be taken to be by Alcuin himself. The remaining fourteen seem to have been written or collected by his friend and pupil, the Anglo-Saxon monk, Candidus. These texts raise such questions as the soul's capacity to know, the nature of existence, the existence of God and the implications of his creation of man in his 'image'. They also provide evidence of contemporary assimilation of the doctrine of the *Categories* and preoccupation with the technique of argument. Although greatly indebted for their starting points to St Augustine's *De Trinitate* ('On the Trinity'), among other works of late antiquity, they reveal considerable sophistication of interest and of treatment. Candidus may also have written several sermons of philosophical import, in which, among other matters, the topics of 'being', 'potentiality' and 'volition' are examined.[92] He was probably the author too of a treatise on the beatific vision.[93] All in all, he emerges as a figure of considerable importance for his period. Certainly, the material with which he is associated is an important demonstration of the concerns of his milieu.

To the evidence of the 'Munich passages' and related material may be added the work of another pupil of Alcuin, Fredegisus of Tours (d. 834). His letter *On Nothing and Darkness* (*De Nihilo et Tenebris*) treats nothingness as substantial – as being something. From a letter written *c*. 830 by Agobard, bishop of Lyons, to refute his views, it appears that he subscribed to a Platonic theory of the pre-existence of the soul which may have had some currency in Alcuin's circle.[94]

Further documentation of a philosophical outlook, contemporary with the century's greatest thinker, comes from the controversy over the soul between Ratramnus of Corbie, writing probably before 864, and an unnamed monk.[95] The discussion here started from St Augustine's analysis of soul in *On the Quantity of the Soul*. Augustine had set out three approaches to the subject without a firm decision in favour of any: that all souls are one – a statement of their specific and generic unity; that individual souls are quite separate – a statement of the opposite perspective; and the synthesis that they are both one and many, a position which he seems to have found absurd. In his treatment, Ratramnus was at pains to show that genera and species were mental constructs abstracted from individuals. In this he relied on Boethius, particularly on the first commentary on the *Isagoge*, but his bias was unequivocally towards the absolute priority of indi- viduals. His opponent, by contrast, seems to have insisted on the reality of genera and species at the expense of allowing for real individuating difference. The unnamed monk attributed his views to his master, an Irishman, Macarius, who is not otherwise known.

Apart from their intrinsic interest, the discussions and views which we have been considering of Alcuin, Candidus, Macarius, his pupil and Ratramnus are important for another reason. They help to place in context the work of the Irishman, John Scotus Eriugena. This is particularly so of the controversy over the soul. It supplies a record, though meagre and somewhat tenuous, of ultra-realist teaching on the part of another Irish master, Macarius. Its interest is the more in view of the contacts which Irishmen on the continent at this time are known to have maintained with one another.[96] Eriugena remains a towering figure in his originality and genius but it is now more apparent than formerly that there existed among his immediate predecessors and contemporaries a certain level of philosophical literacy which gives his work the greater point.

Eriugena's Career and Writings

Eriugena's biography is very imperfectly known. Since he was writing up to 875, an approximate date of 810 has been arrived at for his birth. He was called 'Scottus' – or 'Irishman' – by his contemporaries and the best manuscript tradition of his works preserves the tautology, 'Eriugena', 'of the Irish race', as part of his name. In addition, the contemporary writer Prudentius of Troyes testifies to his Irish provenance. Apart from these references, however, he appears to history only as a continental figure. Professor Bieler has pointed out that the Irish exiles in the Gaul of Charlemagne and his successors were a different historical phenomenon from the missions of the seventh and early eighth centuries.[97] They were attracted both by the intellectual life of the Carolingian court and the episcopal sees and by the security which Gaul afforded them at a time when Irish monasteries were being subjected to the Viking raids. The question whether Eriugena could have obtained his knowledge of Greek, which was by no means perfect, and his generally advanced training in Ireland is a controversial one. In reaction to exaggerated earlier accounts of what the Irish had to offer to the continent, Dom Cappuyns was dismissive; his views have been challenged by Professor O'Meara.[98]

A point more susceptible of definitive statement is Eriugena's acquaintance with his main Greek authority, Dionysius the pseudo-Areopagite. This was reputedly the convert made by St Paul at Athens; hence the great reverence accorded him by Eriugena and the later mystics. In reality, he was a fifth- or early sixth-century Christian writer who may have been a Syrian monk. Due to a further confusion between the pseudo-Areopagite and the undated Parisian martyr, Bishop Denis, who became France's patron saint, his works were of peculiar local interest. In 827, the Greek emperor, Michael II, had presented Louis the Pious, Charlemagne's son and successor, with the Greek text. An earlier attempt to translate them had resulted in an unsatisfactory version and in 860 Charles the Bald commissioned Eriugena to do the work.

The treatises of the pseudo-Dionysius comprise the *Celestial Hierarchy*, the *Ecclesiastical Hierarchy*, the *Mystical Theology* and the *Divine Names*, as well as ten separate *Epistles*. The *Mystical Theology* and the *Divine Names* were the most influential. Besides their general Neoplatonist content, their central theses are the inadequacy of the common attributes, just, good and so on, as names for God and, as an extension of this point, the distinction of three levels of theology. These are the affirmative (cataphatic), by which an attribution is made, the negative (apophatic), by which it is at once denied, and the superlative, which is both affirmative and negative, in that it uses attributes in a transcendent sense while denying that predicates derived from knowledge of finite things can apply to God. Eriugena translated the Dionysian corpus and commented on part of it. He also translated a Greek commentary upon it, the *Ambigua* of Maximus the Confessor (580–662). Maximus had modified the doctrines in the light of his special expertise in Aristotelian logic and had related them to a Christological pattern. According to this, Christ was the Logos or Word through whom the ideas or archetypes of creation were realised and through whom the Neoplatonist return of all things to their source was to be effected. In addition, Eriugena translated *On the Creation of Man*, a work of St Gregory of Nyssa (d. 394). Its Christianised account of the Neoplatonist descent and return of the soul heavily influenced his own treatment of this topic in the *Periphyseon*.

Eriugena's precise indebtedness to Greek authors may be summarised by recalling the important point made by Professor Sheldon-Williams.[99] It is that apart from his dialectical doctrine of the fourfold division of nature, which seems to come directly from Alexandrian logical theory, he had no first-hand knowledge of the pagan philosophers. Even of Aristotle his knowledge is confined to Boethius' commentary on the *De Interpretatione* and to the pseudo-Augustinian paraphrase of the *De Categoriis*. His Greek sources therefore are Christian and his Neoplatonism largely the product of the pseudo-Dionysius, Maximus the Confessor and Gregory of Nyssa.

Because the *Periphyseon*, written c. 864–6, is so heavily indebted to the pseudo-Dionysian corpus it is difficult to imagine what form Eriugena's ideas would have taken had he not come into contact with it. There are, however, some indications of the direction in which he would have tended. According to Prudentius of Troyes, he had already embarked on a radical line of cosmological speculation before his discovery of the pseudo-Dionysius. The source for it was said to be Martianus Capella's *Marriage of Philology and Mercury*, on which Eriugena was writing a commentary in 859–60. It could have provided the basis for reflection on the soul's journey through the planetary spheres and on the impossibility of a local hell, since there was no space outside the cosmos.[100] Another possible source was the Commentary on the 'Dream of Scipio' (*Somnium Scipionis*), by the early fifth-century author, Macrobius. The 'Dream of Scipio' was an extract from the *Republic* of Cicero and contained a statement of the Platonic doctrine of the soul. It became influential as a school text in the early middle ages. Eriugena shows some evidence of having read Macrobius.[101] On the theological level, Eriugena's preference for a naturalistic, quasi-Pelagian approach to human perfectibility is detectable as early as 850 in his treatise *On Predestination*.[102] This was directed against the extreme Augustinianism of Gottschalk, whose doctrine of double predestination, that is of the damned as well as of the elect, had been condemned two years before by the Council of Mainz. Eriugena's defence of free will, his criticism of the concepts of predestination and prescience as applied to God, his insistence on the unreality of evil and his denial that it is a proper object of divine knowledge made a sufficiently disturbing package for his own treatise in turn to be condemned at two local synods. Finally, like all Christians, he had in the Fourth Gospel a stimulus to philosophical interpretation of salvation history. It is significant that after the completion of the *Periphyseon* he was drawn to write both a homily on the Prologue to that Gospel and a commentary on the Gospel itself.

These various pointers combine to suggest that the broad lines of Eriugena's thought as elaborated in the *Periphyseon* may have developed before he began his translations. In particular, the general structures round which the work is built must have been deeply laid in his outlook. They are dialectical method and confidence in the power and role of reason. The two are complementary. Eriugena's rationalism has a metaphysical basis. For him, reason is the natural impulse of the soul towards its source. It is a part of the divine creation and its object is the theophanies or manifestations of God in his progress from unity to multiplicity.[103] Eriugena's definition of nature too relates it closely with the One, so that philosophy extends to a consideration of the 'divine, eternal and immutable'. This is the explanation of his astonishing observation in the commentary on Martianus Capella that 'no one can enter heaven except by philosophy'.[104] The high value set upon reason emerges even more explicitly from a passage in the *Periphyseon* where Eriugena expounds the difference between reason and authority. The 'Master' of the dialogue has made the Dionysian point that the nature of God is ineffable and that names are inadequate. The 'Disciple' requests that the argument be supported by references to the Fathers. But the Master urges that this would be to imply a false priority, 'For authority proceeds from true reason but reason certainly does not proceed from authority. For every authority which is not upheld by true reason is seen to be weak, whereas true reason is kept firm and immutable by her own powers and does not require to be confirmed by the assent of any authority.'[105] The dialectical method is an unavoidable corollary to this. For Eriugena there is no question of dialectic's being an order imposed on reality by the mind. It is an order rooted in the nature of things: 'The art of dialectic, which divides genera into species and resolves species into genera, was not fashioned by human devices, but created in the nature of things by the Author of all arts that are truly arts; and discovered by wise men and, by skilful research, adapted to use.'[106] Theology and analysis of the universe are inextricably connected and dialectic is the method appropriate to both.

Eriugena: the Periphyseon

The *Periphyseon* or *On the Division of Nature*[107] comprises five books in dialogue form between a master and his disciple. In the first chapter of Book I a twofold scheme of the division of nature is proposed. The first scheme is the more fundamental and defines Eriugena's concept of nature. It is a startling comprehensive term: 'The first and fundamental division of all things which either can be grasped by the mind or lie beyond its grasp is into those that are and those that are not. Nature is the general name for all things, for those that are and those that are not.'[108] In other words, every object of thought is embraced in the term nature. Idealism can go no further.

Later, five modes of interpretation are distinguished in this primary division, 'this basic difference which separates all things'. In the first place, being or non-being is considered according to perceptibility – that is according to whether or not it can be predicated by intellect or sense. God is not perceived in this way and according to this mode shall be said not to exist. Secondly, being and non-being is determined according to its place in the Neoplatonist concept of the hierarchy linking creator with the lowest creation and vice versa. In this, the intellectual power is highest. To the extent that being is predicated of a creature of a higher order it is denied of a lower and vice versa. This is what constitutes the difference in things. Thirdly, it is considered according to actualisation, a mode which recalls the Aristotelian distinction between potentiality and actuality. Fourthly, it is considered according to the faculty of perception. This is really a subdivision of the first mode. If a thing is perceptible to the intellect it is said truly to be, if perceptible to the senses it is said not truly to be, in accordance with the Platonic doctrine that it is the intelligible which is fully real. Fifthly, there is a mode pertaining to man only, as having in Eriugena's system freedom of will. This is the mode 'according to the realisation of God's image': to the extent that a man is removed from similarity to God, he is said not to be.

The second scheme of the division of nature is introduced between the statement of the first scheme and its elaboration. It is less radical though it is better known as a feature of Eriugena's thought. The scheme is a fourfold division between: (i) that which creates but is not created – that is God, the source of creation; (ii) that which is created and creates. This concept, which is the subject of Book II, is a fusion of Neoplatonist and Christian idioms. The Neoplatonist Logos – the expression of the divine mind and the eternal embodiment of the archetypes of creation – is identified with the second person of the Trinity; (iii) that which is created but does not create – that is, the created universe which is the subject of Book III; (iv) that which does not create and is not created – the subject of Books IV and V. This is God considered as the end of the universe in a Neoplatonist reversion up the hierarchy, of bodies to souls, of souls to causes and of causes to God, who will be all in all.

Eriugena's analysis, which can only be briefly outlined here, raises a number of problems in the context of Christian theology. The first problem is peculiarly one for a tradition where the authority of St Augustine was paramount. He considered Augustine to be a major support for his position and cites him more frequently than any other single writer. But it is Augustine as interpreted in the light of the pseudo-Dionysius when there is any conflict between the two.[109] In particular, Eriugena's endorsement of the Neoplatonist return of all things to their source is an implicit statement of a theology of man's perfectibility which is radically different from that of St Augustine. He upholds the role and efficacy of grace but it is a grace which is given to the elect to proceed beyond the state of original, primordial perfection which all are considered capable of achieving. The special status accorded to the elect is referred to as 'deification', which is 'the passing of the saints into God not only in soul but in body, so that they are one in Him and with Him when nothing animal, corporeal, human or natural remains in them'.[110] The term is highly contentious, as Eriugena was well aware. However, despite the language in which the process is described, it is clear that he wished to safeguard the continued distinct existence of the individual soul.[111] In this respect the claims of Christianity and of Neoplatonist mysticism agreed.

The second problem is whether Eriugena's notion of nature, particularly as regards the cosmic return, is a pantheistic one. He was certainly conscious that his scheme might be interpreted in that sense and was anxious to disavow the doctrine, which was in any case incompatible with a Neoplatonist regard for the transcendence of the One. Yet the insinuation of pantheism is at some points very strong and indeed the *Periphyseon* was to be condemned on this count by Honorius III in 1225.

The third problem is related to the first. What is the place of evil in Eriugena's system? He followed the Platonist tradition and Augustine closely in ascribing the origin of evil to the will. But what becomes of evil in the cosmic return? Since it is not part of God's creation it cannot be subsumed and if it cannot be subsumed it cannot exist in the final condition of nature when God is all in all. Is it possible therefore to have eternal damnation? Eriugena goes to considerable lengths in fact to reconcile the scriptural datum with his Neoplatonist system. There is no localised hell but the wicked are eternally punished, despite their having regained the state of pristine perfection. Their unhappiness consists in a continuing attachment to the memory of their former temporal state. It is a subtle solution, similar to the psychological doctrine of hell propounded by Origen.[112] One feels, however, that the Disciple is justified in his puzzlement over the apparent permanence of tension in a nature which has been purified. One feels also that Eriugena would have been happier to have followed the doctrine to its logical, Origenist conclusion and to have regarded hell as an incomplete state, capable of remedy. That he did not do so illustrates how a philosopher's bias can be restrained by overriding considerations – in this case, the force of established theology.

Eriugena: the Subsequent Tradition

The sources for assessing Eriugena's influence are scattered and fragmentary. Recent important research into it has drawn skilfully on two pieces of evidence: a set of contemporary notes and glosses which have been variously taken to have been written by Eriugena himself but which it is now argued are in the hands of two of his closest circle, and the manuscript witness to an evolution in the text of the *Periphyseon*.[113] The evidence shows both that he had associates who read him attentively and that he in turn was conscious of his readership. Among id' 'tifiable figures connected with him is his friend, Wulfad, a mor .t the court of Charles the Bald, who is known to have possessed his translations of pseudo-Dionysius and Maximus as well as the *Periphyseon*.[114] The Irishman, Martin of Laon, master of the cathedral school there, can be shown to have read the *Periphyseon* at an early stage though he was not expert enough to have been much influenced by it.[115] Moreover, a body of glosses on Boethius' sacred treatises, on Martianus Capella's *Marriage of Philology and Mercury* and, most importantly, on the pseudo-Augustinian paraphrase of the *Categories* (*Categoriae Decem*) bear the influence of his thought. In particular, Heiric, master of the monastic school of St Germain at Auxerre *c*. 865, drew on Eriugena in writing his glosses on the *Categoriae Decem* and Eriugena's influence is also apparent in the work of Heiric's pupil, Remigius of Auxerre. Remigius wrote commentaries on a range of classroom texts – Scripture, the grammatical authors, Donat and Priscian, Boethius' *Consolation of Philosophy* and Martianus Capella. He taught probably first at Auxerre, then at the cathedral school of Reims in the last decade of the ninth century and perhaps afterwards at Paris.

    While it is clear therefore that Eriugena's readership in his own time and in the next generation was greater than has usually been recognised, his influence when viewed in longer perspective was much less than he deserved. St Anselm of Bec's follower, Honorius Augustodunensis, made substantial borrowings from the *Periphyseon* and there are other indications that it had some currency in northern France in the twelfth century. The Latin corpus of the pseudo-Dionysius did carry a small part of the *Periphyseon* in the form of a gloss[116] and further work in the history of mysticism may reveal as yet undiscovered disciples of its doctrine. But its effects so far known are trifling for a system of such power and challenge. Even before the pronouncement of Honorius III, which followed use of it by the heretic Amaury of Bène, Eriugena's reputation was tarnished. Berengar of Tours appealed, mistakenly, to his authority against the possibility of transubstantiation and suffered condemnation at the

Council of Rome (1050). If the legend that Eriugena was stabbed to death by the pens of his students is apocryphal it contains perhaps an element of truth. At all events, the relative obscurity into which his synthesis fell was a misfortune for western thought. It had opened a window on a parallel view of the universe, that of the Greek patristic tradition. Latin Christendom had lost contact with this other vision and on the whole it was to remain uncomprehending, even hostile, towards it.

Eriugena was the last systematic thinker before St Anselm of Bec in the late eleventh century, and St Anselm springs from a different tradition. In the interval between them activity was more humdrum though it was ultimately to be fruitful for the speculative movement. The kind of explanatory writing which has been noted in the case of Heiric and Remigius of Auxerre was continued. It produced new glosses, reworkings of already existing glosses and, occasionally, independent treatises. Martianus and Boethius continued to be read. In particular, metric 9 of Book III of the *Consolation of Philosophy* – a passage inspired by Plato's *Timaeus* – called on all the philosophical reserves which contemporary scholars owned. Gradually there came more direct contact with the *Timaeus*, through increasing use of Chalcidius. Macrobius' commentary on the *Dream of Scipio* also gradually became better known. By the eleventh century Chalcidius and Macrobius had joined the syllabus as standard authors.[117] This is one area in which the ninth-century achievement was continued and augmented. Scholarship on Boethius, on Martianus, on Chalcidius and on Macrobius would eventually reach its peak in the cosmological writing of the twelfth century. Another area is the development and expansion of logical expertise. Extension of the logical programme was the foundation of the major speculative endeavours of the eleventh and twelfth centuries. It is only by following its course that they can be understood.

3. The Central Middle Ages – Logic, Theology and Cosmology

The Character and Context of Thought in the Central Middle Ages

VIEWED from the perspective of the ancient philosophical tradition, the history of thought in the period *c.* 1000 to *c.* 1150 comprises two main strands. First, there is the Aristotelian contribution, which may be fairly said to be the more distinctive. Nothing is so characteristic of the thought of the eleventh and early twelfth centuries as the way in which Aristotle's logic at once stimulated a desire for intellectual order and was grasped as the means to achieve it. Secondly, there is the Platonist contribution. Directly and indirectly it exercised important influences on the intellectual life of the time. Its most direct influence was on the cosmological speculations of the twelfth century. Some note has already been taken of the Platonist sources on which these rested and more will be said in due course. Of the indirect influences of Platonism, two stand out. The twelfth century sees the revival of a philosophical mysticism based on the Neoplatonist tradition as known especially through the works of the pseudo-Denis. It is associated principally with the school of St Victor at Paris, most notably with Hugh and Richard of St Victor. The second indirect influence of Platonism at this time is the most pervasive of all. It derived from the recognition accorded to St Augustine as the greatest of the Latin fathers. From what has already been said about St Augustine's philosophical outlook it will be clear that this was a modified Platonism. However, taken with the general bias of Boethius, it largely explains the fact that at the beginning of the period the prevailing assumptions, epistemological and ontological, were ultra-realist in character.

In assessing the importance of Aristotelian logic to the intellectual life of the early middle ages it is important to remember the intimate connection which obtained in much of the *Organon* between the method and the subject of philosophical discussion. A substantial part of it was not a purely formal logic but was logic with a philosophical dimension. This was particularly true of the *Categories*, which was known early. Only by keeping the wider issues in mind can one understand the intensity of debate which technical problems excited. The use made by Boethius of Aristotelian terms in his sacred treatises further encouraged movement between the logical and ontological levels. His review of the categories in *On the Trinity* was an influential source of philosophical logic. St Augustine's work of the same title supplied other leads. As a result, questions such as the nature of universal concepts, the relationship between genus, species and individual or the meaning and reference of the term 'substance' were not thought of as purely logical. They had metaphysical and theological implications which rendered them potentially controversial. So, for instance, underlying St Anselm's debate with Roscelin over the Trinitarian doctrine that three persons shared one nature was the logical issue of the status of universal concepts. What reality did the concept 'nature' have, set against distinctness of person?[1] Even on the level of terminology logic could thus have proved a disturbing and challenging subject. It was bound to be especially so when applied directly as a method of theological inquiry. In their reverence for the authority of the past, men were apt to forget that traditional belief had itself been cast in a logical and philosophical mould. The re-examination of doctrinal formulations remained a delicate issue throughout the period – as indeed, in varying degrees, for the whole of the middle ages and beyond.

As a final comment on the general character of thought in the period, a point may be noted which strikes the reader as soon as he approaches the works of St Anselm or Peter Abelard, to take the most important exponents of the dialectical method. These reveal the same conflation of theology and philosophy into a single perception of truth as was found in the case of St Augustine. The two components may be unravelled in the search for influences and the theological writing of the eleventh and twelfth centuries provides much material from which the philosophical and logical capacity of contemporaries can be judged. It should not be forgotten however that the separation of the purely philosophical or logical content of such writing results in an artificial construct. The preservation of boundaries between the data of revealed religion and rational enquiry was a response to the rediscovery of the complete Aristotelian philosophical system and is not a feature of this earlier period.

Apart from the stimulus of particular sources and literary influences, the nature and pace of intellectual development in the period was closely bound up with the institutional context. In the ninth century, Christian Europe had been subjected to three separate waves of invasion – from Vikings in the north, Moslems in the south and Magyars in the east. The effects of these external threats would probably not have been sufficiently deleterious in themselves to halt the intellectual progress which Charlemagne had nurtured. Indeed, by favouring a concentration at the centre, as at the court of Charles the Bald, such conditions could indirectly be fruitful, at least for a time. More significant in the long term was the internal political fragmentation which followed on the divisions and subdivisions of the Frankish empire among Charlemagne's successors. Scholarship lost the determined patronage which it had briefly enjoyed and the relative security and ease of communications which might have been fostered by centralised rule. Particularism is the most evident feature of the political and social life of the later ninth and of the tenth centuries. The bonds of society were those local and personal relationships into which men entered for their greater protection and from which the feudal system emerged in north-western Europe.[2] The results were by no means wholly inimical to intellectual development. Local lords could be generous in their foundation and endowment of monasteries and it was the monasteries that provided the strongest initial impetus to a revival in study. However, this revival lay in the future. Meantime, learning often remained latent in the monasteries, apart from those practical studies, such as grammar, chronology, music and penmanship, which were essential to the organisation of Benedictine monasticism. The most important function which the monasteries performed in the interval until the later part of the tenth century was simply the preservation of texts on which the later recovery was based. They thus provided the necessary framework for the transmission of ideas, even when they were making no original contribution themselves.

Monasteries were not the only institutions with libraries and schools. Cathedrals offered another source of intellectual revival. An impressive example of an early cathedral library is provided by the reconstructed list of books known to have been collected at Laon between the middle of the ninth century and about the end of the first quarter of the tenth. It numbers around three hundred items, excluding minor hagiographical and liturgical material, and contains patristic and exegetical works, historical and chronological authorities, texts of medicine and law and some of the products of the Carolingian renaissance.[3] There was not, at least in northern Europe, a continuous and widespread tradition of study in the cathedral cloisters to match that cultivated under the rule of Benedict. But cathedrals were a potential focus of resurgence and at Reims, during the teaching of Gerbert of Aurillac, there was a brilliant instance of the contribution they could make. Gerbert began his career as a Benedictine monk of the Cluniac reform – a movement founded in 910, about thirty years before his birth – and ended it as Pope Sylvester II (999–1003). His reputation for scholarship he made at Reims.[4] As master of the cathedral school there, from 972 to 989, with a brief intermission, he expounded the trivium and quadrivium, introducing students to a breadth of disciplines not elsewhere available in the Latin west. He throws into relief several of the most important trends of the time. More than anyone else, he established Boethius as the master of philosophical technique for a world which knew no Greek. He himself lacked the single-minded attachment to logic which was to be the principal feature of philosophical method in the next century and a half, but his very range of interests pointed the way to the main areas of intellectual activity in northern Europe in the eleventh and twelfth centuries – logic, Latin literature and scientific study. His contributions to this last were mainly in the areas of mathematics and astronomy. Some of his familiarity with these subjects he may have owed to contacts, probably indirect, with Moslem learning. He had studied in Spain and is known to have been supplied later with textbooks on arithmetic and astronomy by friends whom he had made there. In one respect, though, his stay in Spain was unproductive. He does not appear to have known anything of the corpus of Aristotle's philosophical works, which would later be discovered in part through that channel. However, the fact that he was sent to Spain by his abbot for instruction implies a recognition of this source of learning and is a harbinger of future developments. Lastly, Gerbert's career momentarily draws together both the monastic and the cathedral dimensions and suggests the future integration of the strands of scholarship.

Monasteries and cathedrals provided an institutional framework for the revival of learning in northern Europe. In Italy, the autonomous urban schools were the dominant centres. As demand increased, however, and particularly as, in the course of the eleventh century, a training in logic came to be seen as the key to intellectual progress, there was considerable opportunity for individual freelance teachers. They claimed or were given the epithet 'peripatetic', in elegant allusion at once to their Aristotelian pedigree and to their mobility. Like the ancient Sophists, they purveyed a valued commodity to an eager market and their activities must have done much to advertise as well as to inculcate the new techniques. Peter Abelard, born in Brittany in 1079, recalled in his autobiography how he renounced the prospect of knighthood to travel about the provinces, 'disputing, like a true peripatetic', wherever he heard that there was keen interest in the art of dialectic.[5] But although he was indeed a wandering scholar, his career coincides with the growth of the permanent centre of higher teaching and illustrates its attraction. The story of his wanderings is in part that of the rise of the Paris schools to pre-eminence, at first in France and eventually, for the study of arts and theology, in Europe as a whole.

The gradual decline in importance of monastic as against non-monastic schools is a feature of the history of learning from the eleventh century onward. Several factors probably contributed to this. Although the scope which cathedral schools afforded could easily be exaggerated, they did have advantages over their monastic counterparts. Those which were located in important regional centres were well placed to benefit from a rapid growth of urban prosperity, fostered by an expanding economy and a consequent increase of trade in the period. Then, even against neighbouring monasteries, the regime of cathedrals imposed fewer demands to detract from scholarship and teaching, particularly as compared with the Cluniac system, under which elaborate liturgies and formal biblical reading vied with opportunities for study. For their part, the new and highly successful ideals of Augustinian and Cistercian monasticism represented in their different ways a diminution of the place of scholarship and teaching. The Cistercians deliberately removed themselves from centres of population. The Augustinians, while they established themselves in towns, did not usually concern themselves with providing external education, though the Augustinian abbey of St Victor in Paris which maintained a distinguished open school for at least thirty years after its foundation in 1110 is a notable exception.[6] The Benedictines continued to produce important authors of their own throughout the middle ages and even the Cistercians eventually succumbed to the attractions of academic study. However, after the eleventh century, monasteries as such generally ceased to be at the forefront of intellectual endeavour. In their turn, the cathedral schools north of the Alps, the urban schools in Italy and the independent schools of private masters were to give way to institutions exclusively devoted to the furtherance of learning within a professional and highly formalised structure. This, though, is a development outside the scope of the present chapter.

The Foundations of Logical Study

The most evident feature of logical studies in the period to *c.* 1250 is their complete dependence on the discoveries of the ancients. Aristotle had left by far the greatest literary legacy, in the six treatises of the *Organon*, and this fact alone was sufficient to establish the dominance of Aristotelian logic in the middle ages. In the ancient world, his approach was rivalled and partly supplemented by Stoic work. Recognising the interplay between thought and its expression, the Stoics had made logic a central part of their philosophy. By the same token, they had extended it to include an analysis of language and their contributions became incorporated in classical grammatical theory. As a result, some of the Stoics' linguistic approach to logic was transmitted to the west in the *Grammatical Institutions* of Priscian (*fl.* AD 491–518).[7] This became an immensely influential textbook of Latin grammar. Through it, Stoic logic must be counted a source of the sophisticated attention to the levels of meaning compressed within a term and of the careful, sometimes pedantic, analysis of statement which is common to the method of men as diverse as Berengar, Lanfranc, St Anselm and Peter Abelard.

The principal source of logical technique was however the Aristotelian corpus. Through more and better texts knowledge of it gradually extended. In the Carolingian period, the programme of logical study revolved around the *Categories* and the *De Interpretatione*. But the assimilation even of these treatises was imperfect. For a text of the *Categories*, scholars such as Alcuin and Eriugena were dependent on the pseudo-Augustinian paraphrase.[8] Although Boethius' literal translation had some currency in the early period, not until the eleventh century did it replace the paraphrase as the standard text.[9] As additional guidance, Porphyry's *Isagoge* was available in Boethius' translation and from the middle of the ninth century Boethius' two commentaries on Porphyry's work were known. A little later, towards the end of the ninth century or early in the tenth, Boethius' own commentary on the *Categories* began to be read. As for the *De Interpretatione*, it was known at first only indirectly, through Boethius' first commentary upon it, though some translated sections were preserved as lemmata in the transmission of the commentary. Boethius' commentary could be supplemented by Apuleius' *Periher-meneias*, which incorporated Stoic and Aristotelian theory. In the course of the ninth century, the full translation became available. Boethius' second commentary on the *De Interpretatione* came into circulation at about the same time as did his commentary on the *Categories*.

This original core of study was expanded in the period *c*. 970–1040 to include the independent logical works of Boethius: *On Division*, *On Topical Differences* and the three treatises on the syllogism. *On Topical Differences* served, with Cicero's *Topics*, as a substitute for the Aristotelian work at a time when the translation of this was still unknown. Similarly, two of the treatises on the syllogism – *On the Categorical Syllogism* and the *Introduction to the Categorical Syllogism* – deputised for the *Prior Analytics*. The third treatise, *On the Hypothetical Syllogism*, went beyond Aristotle's teaching to analyse the mechanics of conditional propositions. This neglected subject had been developed by the Stoics and their discoveries had passed into the Neoplatonist literature, from which Boethius had absorbed them.[10]

As may be expected, the expansion of the syllabus was gradual and uneven. An important, early part seems to have been played by the Cluniac monastic scriptorium. With the Cluniac house of St Benoît (or Fleury) sur Loire, near Orléans, is associated a manuscript dating from the late tenth or early eleventh century of most of the Boethian treatises – excluding the first commentary on Porphyry and the commentaries on the *De Interpretatione*. It derived from a codex made for a contemporary of the author himself.[11] The route by which this text was discovered is uncertain but the discovery was probably the product of a conscious search for better texts which was taking place at Fleury and elsewhere during this time.[12] Already, in the last quarter of the tenth century, Abbo, abbot of Fleury, had produced commentaries on Boethius' treatment of the categorical and hypothetical syllogism.[13] At approximately the same period, Gerbert was using these and the other treatises of Boethius in his teaching at Reims. However, it would be wrong to assume from this remarkable concentration of activity that the extended programme rapidly became commonplace. Even by late in the following century, at Norman Bec, it may well be that St Anselm had missed all contact with it. It has been pointed out that for all his powerful expertise, his technical logical learning may have been based on the old core of the

Categories and *De Interpretatione*.[14] Abelard, by contrast, was familiar with the whole range of Boethius' treatises and their importance to him cannot be missed.[15] Abelard in fact stands at a new turning point in the history of Aristotelian logic. From the second decade of the twelfth century more texts of the *Organon* began to circulate. The *De Sophisticis Elenchis*, hitherto quite unknown, became available, as did the *Topics* and the *Prior Analytics* – all in Boethius' translation. In the middle of the century, the translation by James of Venice of the *Posterior Analytics* supplied the Latin world with the last text of the *Organon* still unknown.[16] The rate at which knowledge was expanding in the leading circles can be plotted reasonably closely. Abelard, the greatest teacher of his age, did not know the text of the *Topics* or of the *Posterior Analytics* and was diffident on the subject of the *De Sophisticis Elenchis*. The Englishman, Adam of Balsham, called Adam Parvipontanus or Adam Petit-Pont from the location of his school at one of the bridges on the Seine, in his novel *Art of Discourse* (*Ars Disserendi*), written in 1132, shows contact both with the *Topics* and the *De Sophisticis Elenchis*.[17] The collection of texts in the *Heptateuchon* of Thierry of Chartres (d. after 1151) included the *Prior Analytics*, *Topics* and *De Sophisticis Elenchis* but not the *Posterior Analytics*. John of Salisbury, whose *Metalogicon* was completed in 1159, displays a familiarity with the whole of the *Organon* and conceives logic in its fullest Aristotelian terms.[18]

The Problem of Universals

Attention has already been drawn to the philosophical dimension underlying some early medieval logical discussions. This is well illustrated by what is called the problem of universals. Universals are the general terms used of a multiplicity of individuals – such as the words 'man' or 'humanity', applied to all men, or 'white' or 'black', applied to some. The problem which they raised could be variously stated. What was the genesis of such terms in the mind? What degree of reality did they possess? What was the relationship between general terms and the individuals of which they were used? In the literature of western philosophy, the issues had first emerged from Plato's search for objective standards. Following the trend of Socrates' investigations, Plato had begun by seeking to define the principles of conduct and evaluation and had ended by attempting to explain the basis of all intelligibility. When early medieval logicians discussed the nature of universal terms they were dealing with the same problem but in a more direct and abstract fashion. The preliminary, concrete stage of the inquiry was by-passed and the problem was posed in terms of the thought processes involved in classification. That it could be posed so directly was due to the existence of a *locus classicus* for treatment of the subject.

The fullest such source was a passage in Boethius' second commentary on Porphyry's *Isagoge*. It might be thought that Porphyry would have presented a highly Platonised version of Aristotle's *Categories*. In fact, the tendency of Neoplatonist logicians, conscious of the discrepancies between Plato and Aristotle and anxious to minimise them, was to strip Aristotle's logic of its philosophical framework and use it as a formal instrument.[19] So, Porphyry did no more than raise the problem of universals – or, more precisely, of the fundamental classes, genera and species – leaving aside the questions 'whether they subsist or are posited purely and simply in intellects alone and whether, [if] subsistent, they are corporeal or incorporeal, and whether they are separate or consist in and through the objects of sense experience' as matters requiring deeper consideration.[20] In his second commentary on the text, Boethius explained the problem, gave the differing interpretations of Plato and Aristotle and refused to judge between them, while offering the Aristotelian solution as the more appropriate in the present instance of an accompaniment to the *Categories*.[21]

Boethius' passage provided the starting point for the most success-ful treatment of the topic in the central period, that of Peter Abelard. When Abelard took up the problem it was already controversial. However, the details of earlier contemporary solutions are imper-fectly known. Roscelin (*c.* 1050–1125) was a canon of Compiègne and later a teacher at Loches near Vannes, where he may have had Abelard among his pupils. His ideas are known mainly from his opponents on the Trinitarian issue, who included St Anselm· and Abelard himself, and from a late reference in John of Salisbury's *Metalogicon*.[22] Roscelin's Trinitarian doctrine was taken as emphasis-ing the distinctness of Persons at the expense of divine unity. On the logical question he is identified with the assertion that universal terms are merely a 'sound' (*flatus vocis*). The view that universals are merely words or names is known as nominalism but the label is imprecise and to apply it to Roscelin is doubly hazardous as it is not clear how he understood the view ascribed to him. However, if he may be taken as typifying a minimalist theory of the significance of universal terms, William of Champeaux (1070–1121) represents the opposite perspective. It would be consonant with the individualism of the age as with the peripatetic and eclectic nature of study that proponents of one interpretation should have had masters of a different bent. William may have been a pupil of Roscelin, though this is not firmly established. The main sources for William's logical views are the criticisms of his own rebellious pupil, Abelard. William taught extreme realism; that is, he began not by asking how the concept of class could be reconciled with the existence of individuals but by accepting the priority of the universal concept and seeking to define individuals by reference to it. His first formulation of the matter was that the species, for instance humanity, existed entirely and identically in each individual, variation between individuals being due to accidental differences. Under attack from Abelard he modified his statement to an assertion that the species existed in a similar way or without difference, rather than identically, in its individual members. If William's teaching rested on the difficulty of finding a philosophical definition of the individual, he was making a valuable point. Abelard however treats him with scorn and says that his vacillation resulted in his being wholly discredited among his pupils.[23]

Abelard's own doctrine on the subject of universals is developed in his various logical works. Of these the most important are the *Dialectica* – in form, an original textbook – which went through several revisions in the period *c.* 1118–37, the *Logica* 'Ingredientibus', which consists of glosses on the *Isagoge*, the *Categories* and the *De Interpretatione* and was completed before 1120, and the *Logica* 'Nostrorum Petitioni Sociorum', an elaborated gloss on the *Isagoge*, completed *c.* 1124.[24] There are also insights to be derived from some of his theological writing.[25] In his analysis, understanding functions on the images which are retained by the mind after sense experience and which continue to exist independently of the objects which first gave rise to them. Here is the foundation of a psychological account of universals. However, the principal element in Abelard's approach is an examination not of the conceptual but of the verbal or significative aspects of classification. He considered the universal to be a word, though not in the sense attributed to Roscelin. In Abelard's fully developed usage there is a distinction, not however consistently maintained, between 'vox' or 'utterance', which describes the physical sound, and 'sermo' or 'expression'.[26] A universal 'expression' conveys an apprehension of the common 'status' characteristic of the individual members of a class. This 'status' is an objective reality, discovered rather than introduced by the mind, but it is not subsistent as in the crude interpretation of the Platonic theory.

The Aristotelian character of Abelard's treatment of the question is very apparent and this despite the fact that he criticises Aristotle for using the description 'universal' of things as well as words, whereas he himself is careful to ascribe universality to words only. In particular the way in which the mental concept is constructed recalls the Aristotelian theories of imagination and abstraction. Yet Abelard's direct knowledge of Aristotle did not extend beyond the logical works and did not even include the complete *Organon*. If he had had the *Posterior Analytics*, he would have found a short discussion there of the process of abstraction. The most likely sources for his reconstruction of an Aristotelian theory of cognition are the commentaries of Boethius, that on the *Topics* of Cicero, where Aristotelian and Stoic doctrines mix, as well as those on the *De Interpretatione* and on the *Isagoge*, the starting point of the discussion. Abelard's adroit analysis is a reminder both of how dependent thinkers were on Boethius' legacy and of how much that legacy contained.

The solution that universals are abstracted by the mind from experience of individual beings became generally accepted with Abelard and was to receive powerful reinforcement as more of Aristotle's works became known. The only significant further development of the topic by contemporaries is its treatment by Gilbert of Poitiers (Gilbert de la Porrée) (*c.* 1076–1154). He attempted to integrate the theory of abstracted universals with the Platonist doctrine, absorbed early into Christian thought, that the forms of creation were eternally located in the divine mind. Abelard too held this doctrine though it had no part in his theory of knowledge.[27] For Gilbert and some other masters it became the basis of a metaphysical interpretation of universals. Bernard of Chartres, called by John of Salisbury 'the foremost Platonist of our time',[28] taught that the 'ideas' were eternal, though posterior to God, and distinguished the ideas which are the patterns of creation from ideas embodied in matter.[29] The most likely sources of the terminology of his analysis are Boethius' *On the Trinity* and Chalcidius' commentary on the *Timaeus*. Gilbert, who had probably studied under Bernard, developed his own statement of the theory mainly in the course of commenting on this treatise of Boethius.[30] He identified universals with the 'native' (or generated) 'forms' (*native forme*); these were copies of the divine ideas or exemplars; they were concrete in created substances, to which they gave the property of being a determinate thing, and were abstracted from substances by the knowing mind. This theory was well known to John of Salisbury, who had studied under Gilbert and who gives a clear and concise account of it.[31]

Logic and Theology, an Eleventh-century Dilemma

Roscelin's contribution to the debate over universals has introduced another controversial facet of the logical revival, the application of logic to religious doctrine. The claims of the new logicians to analyse theological formulations were not admitted without a struggle and long continued to be a source of unease. Anti-intellectualism was a recurring theme in the medieval as in the early church. Its most important proponent in the eleventh century was the Italian regular hermit, reformer and cardinal, St Peter Damian (1007–72). A notable part of his opposition to what he regarded as the intrusion of logic into theology was his ridiculing of the principle of non-contradiction as applied to God. His stance is of interest not only in the context of his time but as foreshadowing the attack on 'rational theology' from quite a different quarter in the fourteenth century. His letter to his friend, Desiderius, abbot of Monte Cassino, written about 1067, was a trenchant defiance of those who seemed to curtail divine omnipotence by an appeal to logical arguments. God's power is not restricted even by past events, which he could cause not to have happened just as he could have prevented their ever having happened. Peter Damian was not simply opposed to learning. He distinguished between the pursuit of secular studies by monks, to which he was opposed, and its general utility for clerics, which he admitted. He was prepared, moreover, to allow a subordinate role to the arts in theological inquiry provided that the distinction of subject matter be always preserved: logic like rhetoric pertained to the human not the divine order.[32]

In fact, the defenders of orthodoxy had little choice but to meet the logicians on their own terms. Even the method of Peter Damian's letter concedes as much. The point emerges clearly from the controversy between Berengar and Lanfranc over eucharistic doctrine.[33] This raged in the early 1060s. Berengar (d. 1088) was, from at least 1032, master of the school at the collegiate church of St Martin at Tours. His intellectual pedigree was impeccable for he was a pupil of

Fulbert, bishop of Chartres (1006–28) and founder of the school there, who in his turn was a pupil of Gerbert of Aurillac. Berengar's eucharistic theory reflects several sources of influence. His interest in the subject was awakened by reading a treatise of the ninth-century writer, Ratramnus of Corbie, whom he understood as offering a purely symbolist interpretation of the sacrament. Ratramnus' treatise, mistakenly attributed to John Scotus Eriugena, supported Berengar in his conviction that his own analysis was the traditional and authoritative position. The other sources of his stance are methodological. He was firm in his assurance that logic was the means to truth and recognised no barriers to its use. Berengar's logical method, as evidenced by his arguments in this instance, was a combination of linguistic or grammatical scrutiny and an application of the Aristotelian concepts of substance and accidents.[34] Scrutiny of the exact form and literal meaning of texts was a recognised tool of contemporary biblical scholarship, to which Berengar was probably introduced by Fulbert.[35] Attention to the grammatical structure of the words of consecration led Berengar to argue that the pronoun 'this' in 'This is my body' implied continuity of the subject which it denoted, namely the bread. The same conclusion was dictated, he believed, by the permanence of the accidents, or physical appearances, of the bread and wine. The eucharist therefore did not involve a substantial change of bread and wine into body and blood but a symbolic or spiritual change. This view was the subject of a succession of condemnations, culminating in Berengar's grudging retraction at the Lateran council of 1079.

Lanfranc (c. 1010–89) was thoroughly familiar with the techniques on which Berengar drew. He had abandoned a career as a lawyer in his native Lombardy to pursue the study of grammar and logic in northern France and for a short time at least he attended Berengar's lectures at Tours. Having entered the abbey of Bec in Normandy, he made it an important centre of learning in the liberal arts and in theology, open to non-monastic as well as to internal students. Indeed, it was a large part of his offence in Berengar's eyes that in championing the cause of a real, substantial change in the eucharist he was debasing the skills which he possessed. The acrimony of the dispute tends to obscure the fact that despite the differences between the two protagonists, Lanfranc was closer intellectually to his opponent than he was to Peter Damian and others of the period who professed implacable hostility to the contamination of sacred with profane. Lanfranc was shy of Berengar's assertiveness in applying logic to doctrine but in controverting it he gave to the disputed topic a degree of logical and philosophical formality which it had lacked before, though his precise terminology was not adopted by the Lateran council and his own contribution to the formulation of eucharistic doctrine was slight. The effect of the controversy was to demonstrate the attractions of logical techniques for theology as much as its dangers. The attractions seem to have been felt more keenly than the dangers in Lanfranc's own monastery at Bec. There, shortly afterwards, St Anselm began to elaborate an argued theology which in originality and scope went beyond anything that either Lanfranc or Berengar had contemplated.

Logic and Theology – St Anselm

St Anselm was born in 1033 of a lesser noble family at Aosta, then within the kingdom of Burgundy. As a young man he crossed the Alps, probably for reasons of family connections rather than, as may have been the case with Lanfranc, from a resolve to pursue the logical and grammatical studies flourishing in the north.[36] In about 1059 he began to attend Lanfranc's school at Bec, first as a secular scholar, then, in 1060, as a monk of the community. In 1063 he succeeded Lanfranc as prior of Bec, on the latter's departure to the abbacy of Caen. In 1078 he became abbot of Bec and in 1093, much to his own discomfiture, succeeded Lanfranc in the see of Canterbury.

St Anselm's writing is of several types. It includes argued theological treatises, a teaching manual on an aspect of logic, entitled *De Grammatico* ('On Grammar'), devotional treatises, and letters, of which the text of nearly four hundred survives. The theological treatises are the principal source for his distinctive contribution to the intellectual tradition. As a body of thought they display two related features, systematic development of a number of basic ideas and a high level of internal consistency. This synoptic quality may be variously explained. In the first place, St Anselm inherited from Augustine a sense of hierarchical order in the universe. It was a perception which he received, as it were, ready made. He did not work towards it like Augustine in the face of competition from rival theories nor did he have to defend it or distinguish it against the claims of a near relation as Augustine had had to mark his own position from pagan Neoplatonism. Though the superstructure of Anselm's thought was his own and was designed and executed with originality and skill, it rested on the Christian Platonist foundation which Augustine had so firmly laid. This is a large part of the reason for its apparently effortless progress. Secondly, Anselm wrote in an atmosphere almost wholly free from contention. This contrasts not only with the context in which Augustine had written but with that in which Anselm's older and younger contemporaries, Berengar, Lanfranc and Peter Abelard made their contributions to dialectical theology. Except for the courteous exchange of views with Guanilo, the sharper encounter with Roscelin and a tract (written in 1102) on a doctrinal issue between the Latin and Greek churches, Anselm's writing is unmarked by controversy. The only evidence of pressure which it reveals is that of a readership eager for a considered statement of his views.[37] Thirdly, Anselm began to write comparatively late in life when his ideas on the issues which he first addressed had already been formed. The *Monologion*, the earliest of his major works, dates from *c.* 1076 and contains the material of discussions which he had been conducting with the brethren at Bec. The *Proslogion*, written in 1077-8, represented a new discovery but one wholly consonant with his general outlook. The *De Veritate* ('On Truth'), written between 1080 and 1085, begins from the same Platonist premise as the *Monologion*, that relative concepts and states require the postulation of an absolute. Later (1094-8), in the *Cur Deus Homo* ('Why did God become Man?'), he made a new departure, prompted by some of the implications of his recent debate with Roscelin over Trinitarian doctrine. Of these four treatises, the first three are eloquent testimony to the continuing power of Platonist philosophy, as mediated chiefly through Augustine; the last is a remarkable product of the application of contemporary logical method to a problem which was peculiar to Christian theology. Together, they provide a conspectus of Anselm's philosophical presuppositions and of his technique.

The title which Anselm originally gave the *Monologion* ('Soliloquy') – 'An Example of Meditating about the Rational Basis of Faith' – signals the approach which he was to adopt throughout his systematic work. What this 'example' comprised was an attempt to establish rationally the existence, creative activity and trinity of God. The Platonic character of the inquiry is clear from the outset: 'It is . . . easy for someone to ask himself the following question: Although the great variety of goods that we perceive through the senses or distinguish through the mind are so numerous, are we to believe that there is one thing through which all good things are good, or are we to believe that different goods are good through different things?'[38] The argument is that relative concepts require absolutes for their foundation: 'All other goods are good through something other than what they are and . . . this other alone is good through itself. But no good which is good through another is equal to or greater than that good which is good through itself. Hence, only that good which alone is good through itself is supremely good.'[39] The same logic is applied to the act of existing, from which it follows that 'there is something which – whether it is called a being, a substance or a nature – is the best and the greatest and the highest of all existing things'.[40] This being exists through itself and all else exists by virtue of it.

Then follows a discussion of how the relative world may be conceived to exist through this supreme being. The suggestion that there is a substratum of matter, having an existence independent of the supreme being, is rejected as implying an illogical plurality of absolute principles. The alternative, pantheistic theory, that the world is constructed from the matter of the supreme being, is dismissed on the grounds that it implies a change in what is perfect. There remains creation from nothing. The Judaeo-Christian doctrine thus stands on purely rational considerations.

Anselm next (Chapter 8) tackles the question what is meant by nothingness, countering an ultra-realist fallacy which would accord some degree of being to this concept. His insistence that 'nothing' signifies complete lack of being, like his rejection of an independent matter or substratum of the universe, was true to Augustine's own analysis of creation and may be thought to have been simply prompted by it. But the misconception of nothingness exemplified in the ninth-century treatise *On Nothing and Darkness* by Alcuin's pupil Fredigisus of Tours may still have had some currency and Anselm may here be confronting a genuine contemporary puzzle. The concept is explained again in Chapter 19, where it is shown that nothing existed before or will exist after the supreme being.[41]

The only existence which created reality had prior to its creation was as a thought in the mind of the creator, expressing the nature of the thing (Chapters 9–10). This thought (*ratio*) is the natural word or sign, the conception which precedes language (Chapter 10). To this extent, the creator resembles a craftsman, who knows in advance what he will make. But the craftsman's concepts are related in some way to objects of which he has experience and his execution of his concept depends on the materials available, whereas the creator's concepts are truly original and his execution is unfettered. Lastly on this theme, it is shown that the created world is dependent on the creator not only in its origin but for its continued conservation (Chapters 13–14).

The rest of the *Monologion* (Chapters 15–80) is almost entirely devoted to establishing what can be known of the nature of the supreme being and the necessity for human happiness of striving after such knowledge. The most interesting part of the discussion concerns the problem of making statements about the supreme being. Relational terms – such as the term 'supreme' itself – are inappropriate as they do not reveal the substance of the subject to which they are applied. Of non-relational terms, those may be used which indicate 'whatever in every respect it is better to be than not to be'.[42] Such terms are predicated substantively, to describe the essence of the supreme being; this follows from its absolute character, as established in the opening chapters of the treatise. Anselm then demonstrates, successively, that the supreme being is simple (Chapter 17), without beginning or end (Chapter 18), omnipresent (Chapter 20), unrestricted by place or time (Chapters 21–24) and immutable (Chapter 25). Discussion of this last aspect involves a distinction between substance and accidents and leads Anselm to consider the fundamental question in what sense the supreme being can be said to be a substance. As may be expected, the analysis is heavily indebted to Aristotle's *Categories*. Anselm recognises the two senses of substance – universal and individual. Neither sense, however, seems to apply to the supreme being, 'for neither is it common to many substances, nor does it have anything essentially in common with any other substance'.[43] This is the Neoplatonist point that the One transcends all the categories. Like Boethius before him, who had stressed that substance as applied to God was really super-substance, Anselm allows the force of the consideration. The supreme being, which is absolute, is radically different to the beings of which it is the cause. 'Hence, if it ever has some name in common with others, without doubt a very different signification must be understood in its case.'[44] However, Anselm is searching for a positive theology and is evidently reluctant to abandon the familiar terminology. His resolution of the dilemma is markedly diffident: 'Nevertheless, since it not only most certainly exists but even exists supremely, and since the being of any thing is usually called substance, surely if [the Supreme Being] can be acceptably called anything, there is no reason not to call it a substance.'[45] The problem of terminology recurs near the end of the treatise. By a long process of inference (Chapters 29–65), during which the guiding hand of faith is at its most evident, Anselm has elaborated an account of Trinitarian doctrine. He is at pains to point out the deficiencies of his explanation. It is an ineffable doctrine. Though capable of a degree of rationalisation it is incapable of being rendered comprehensible and ultimately must be accepted on faith. How to refer to this trinity? The only terms available are 'persons' and 'substances'. Anselm finds them well suited to signify a plurality in the supreme being, 'since the word "person" is predicated only of an individual rational nature' – an echo of Boethius' classic definition[46] – 'and since the word "substance" is predicated mainly of individual things, which mostly exist in plurality'.[47] How then to express the unity? Here 'substance' is the only possible term but it is to be understood as signifying simply 'being', in the sense that being is opposed to nothingness.[48]

The *Monologion* is an interesting source for testing the philosophical vocabulary of the eleventh century, as derived from St Augustine, particularly his treatise *On the Trinity*, the sacred treatises of Boethius and the *Categories* of Aristotle. Its chief claim to originality is not its content but the theological method which its author expressly adopts. It is an indication of the intellectual climate that the form of the exercise was determined by the request of the monks for whom Anselm wrote. As he records in the preface, they asked 'that nothing at all in the meditation would be argued on Scriptural authority, but that . . . rational necessity would tersely prove, and truth's clarity would openly manifest, whatever the conclusion of the distinct inquiries declared'.[49] In keeping with this ascetic prescription, Anselm omitted all citation of authorities from the work. The fact disturbed his former mentor, Lanfranc, to whom he sent it initially for approval. But despite the novelty of form, Anselm's conservatism and regard for authority is explicit. 'If in this investigation', he affirms in Chapter 1, 'I say something that a greater authority does not mention, then even if my statement is a necessary consequence of reasons which will seem [good] to me, I want the statement to be accepted as follows: It is not thereby said to be absolutely necessary but is only said to be able to appear necessary for the time being.'[50] His explanations of religious truths have the character of a hypothesis.[51] In the *Proslogion*, where he had no precedents on which to rely even had he wished, he made the clearest statement possible of the priority of faith in the attainment of a true understanding: 'I do not seek to understand in order to believe, but I believe in order to understand. For this too I believe, that "unless I believe, I shall not understand".'[52] The sentiment is borrowed from St Augustine and accords with his theory of knowledge. This programme, 'Credo ut intelligam' ('I believe in order to understand'), was neatly conveyed in the title which Anselm originally intended for the *Proslogion*, 'Fides quaerens intellectum' ('Faith in search of understanding').

The *Proslogion* ('An Address') is similar in spirit to the *Monologion*. It sets out Anselm's daring 'ontological argument' for the existence of God. 'The fool has said in his heart "There is no God".' (Ps. 13.1.) The statement, Anselm concluded, is in fact absurd. The concept 'God' is such that denial of his existence is a contradiction in terms. God is the being than which no greater can be thought. Such a being cannot exist in the understanding alone – and it does exist, according to Anselm, even in the understanding of the fool who makes the denial – for it can be thought of as existing also in extra-mental reality. Moreover, not only is it apparent on this reasoning that the being than which no greater can be thought has extra-mental existence, it alone has such existence necessarily in that it cannot be thought not to have it. This is the real achievement though probably not, as has been argued,[53] the real intention of Anselm's 'proof': it constitutes a definition of the concept of God as that of a necessarily existing being. The method by which the original concept is teased and amplified is characteristic of the period. In particular, it recalls Berengar's analysis of the language of the eucharistic formula.[54] However, while the form of Anselm's argument is logical its foundation is metaphysical. It derives from the realist's confidence that the idea in the mind and the extra-mental existence of the object of thought are linked in a common scale of being. It is not surprising to find that Anselm's argument is foreshadowed in St Augustine.[55] Since Anselm regarded the ontological proof as his own discovery he was probably unconscious of any model but it reflects a habit of thought which is thoroughly Augustinian.

The *Proslogion* was challenged shortly after it began to circulate. Guanilo, a monk of Marmoutier near Tours, pleaded two main contentions on behalf of the fool – a denial that the mind has more than a nominal concept of God and a denial that the existence of the concept in the mind would imply its existence in reality any more than to have a concept of an island excelling all others would make it impossible to doubt its actual existence. He also made an interesting use of the argument underlying the Augustinian 'Cogito':[56] if I am able to doubt my own existence, which I know most certainly, why should I be unable to doubt the existence of God? If, on the other hand, it is impossible for me genuinely to doubt my own existence, then the property of not being able to be thought not to exist does not belong uniquely to God. In his reply to Guanilo, Anselm restated his own case, jovially rejecting the appropriateness of the analogy between the concept at issue and that of the imaginary island.[57] The debate is an outstanding instance of the fascination which logical technique exercised for contemporaries. Anselm seems to have realised that it would be of perennial interest and ordered the preservation of Guanilo's criticisms and of his own reply as an addendum to the *Proslogion*.[58]

The *De Veritate* is a short dialogue between a master and his disciple aimed at exploring the concept of truth.[59] The fundamental insights are Platonic and Augustinian but the economical and controlled way in which the argument proceeds, through a careful employment of the Aristotelian technique of definition by successive division and subdivision, stamps it as of its time.[60] Truth is eternal, absolute and unified (Chapters 1, 10, 13); this absolute is the foundation of all aspects of truth – truth of statement and signification (Chapter 2), truth of thought (Chapter 3), truth of the will (Chapter 4) and of action (Chapter 5), and truth of the senses, which is not impaired even when the impressions derived from sense experience are erroneous (Chapter 6); all things depend for the truth of their being on 'supreme truth' (Chapter 7); the ordering of the world is therefore a right ordering despite the apparent anomaly and impropriety of evil (Chapter 8); justice and truth are synonymous with rightness; justice is rightness of the will motivated or 'preserved' by rightness itself (Chapter 12).

The *Cur Deus Homo*, a treatise in two books, also uses the dialogue form. Here the participants are Anselm himself and Boso, a monk of Bec whom Anselm had summoned to Canterbury. He seems to represent the demanding younger generation of monks who time and again called upon Anselm to expound burning issues of the day.[61] The *Cur Deus Homo* is supremely a work where faith seeks understanding. Whereas in the *Proslogion* Anselm had set out to demonstrate that God was a necessary being, he now set out to demonstrate that the

Incarnation was a necessary sequel to the Fall, required to repair a breach in the cosmic order. The main argument runs as follows: man was created by God for blessedness; by original disobedience this is forfeited; God's justice demands a satisfaction which is outside of man's capacity; the defect can be repaired only by the agency of a God–Man; repair of the defect is necessary if God's original purpose is not to be thwarted. In advancing this syllogistic theory of salvation (or 'soteriology') Anselm probably had two sets of potential critics in mind, whose challenges he attempted to meet.[62] The Incarnation needed to be justified against Jewish criticism that it represented a frivolous derogation from God's transcendence. Within a Christian perspective, Anselm's theory countered a contemporary version, known to have been current at the school of Laon. This presented the devil as an entity with legal rights; the Fall was an act of homage which made man the devil's vassal; the death of the God–Man was an unwarranted extension of the devil's claims, as a result of which he lost them totally. Anselm too used feudal imagery in his account but not as the foundation of it. Intellectually, his analysis was a considerable advance on the other view, though it did not succeed in ousting it. Nor did he solve all the problems which his own approach raised.

Anselm's influence on the next generation was much less than might be expected. He did have followers and imitators, among them Gilbert Crispin, abbot of Westminster, and Odo, bishop of Cambrai – both of whom shared his concern to defend Christian soteriology against Jewish criticism – and the prolific but superficial Honorius Augustodunensis.[63] This external evidence combines with internal indications that in his writings he was supplying a contemporary demand. However, he made little impact on the teaching of the cathedral schools, so important for the future of the dialectical movement. It is difficult to account for this failure to win a wider following but it seems that a difference of taste was involved. Although the concerns and activities of cathedral school theologians were varied, Anselm somehow slipped through the mesh of their interests. His synthetic approach to speculative theology, the careful, discreet elaboration of central themes, seems not to have caught the imagination. The method of much twelfth-century dialectical theology has a new flavour. The propositions of faith were, however reverentially, seen as material to be dissected, reduced to their components, analysed and reported on. It was a detached, formal inquiry, bound by its own rules of argument, and the test of its value was conformity to those rules. This highly professional, 'academic' quality contrasts with Anselm's style. Rather than more adventurous topics or more radical conclusions it marks the difference between cathedral school and monastic theology. It also helps to explain why the application of logic to theology should again have become controversial in the first half of the twelfth century.

Logic and Theology – Peter Abelard

Peter Abelard was born in 1079 at Le Pallet, near Nantes in Brittany, the son of a landed knight. As he shows no interest in the scientific subjects of the quadrivium, it may be assumed that his studies were confined to the trivium – grammar, rhetoric and logic. These he would have pursued in local schools, including, probably, that of Roscelin (c. 1095) at Loches. In about 1100 he transferred to the school of William of Champeaux at the cathedral church of Notre Dame in Paris. His attacks on William over the question of universals, begun while he was still his pupil, continued after he had set up his own school, first at Melun (1103) and then at Corbeil. Following William's entry into the regular life at the monastery of St Victor, Abelard taught for a short time at Notre Dame; then after an interval in Melun again, he opened his school in Paris itself, in the area of Mont Ste Geneviève, outside the city boundary, on the left bank of the Seine. Having established his reputation as a logician, at William's expense, he decided shortly after 1113 to apply himself to theology, under Anselm of Laon. Anselm's expertise as a scriptural exegete was held in high regard and has been confirmed by modern scholarship but Abelard soon grew impatient, commenting later that when Anselm lit his fire he gave out smoke rather than light. His disenchantment at first took the form of non-attendance at lectures but then he began to lecture himself, expounding the difficult and neglected text of the prophet Ezekiel. The success of this enterprise and the reaction to it of Anselm's supporters resulted in Abelard's returning to Paris (c. 1114) where he was invited to teach theology in the cathedral school. The sequel is well known: his love affair with Héloïse, niece of Canon Fulbert, their secret marriage, which barred him from ecclesiastical promotion, his mutilation by Fulbert's agency, Héloïse's retirement to the convent of Argenteuil and Abelard's own profession as a monk of St Denis (c. 1119). It was at

this period that he wrote his first theological treatise, 'On the Divine
Unity and Trinity' (also known as the *Theologia* 'Summi Boni').
Attacked by Alberic of Rheims and Lotulf of Novara, former pupils of
Anselm of Laon, it was condemned at the council of Soissons in 1121.
The set-back however was temporary. The next eighteen years,
during which Abelard is known to have taught at the Paraclete, a
hermitage which he established near Nogent-sur-Seine (*c.* 1121–9),
and again at Mont Ste Geneviève (*c.* 1135–6, 1139–40), were a period
of intense intellectual effort. The work condemned at Soissons was
revised and extended as the *Theologia Christiana*. It included in its
range of topics Trinitarian doctrine and the nature of creation,
especially the question whether God can do better than he does.
These were also part of the later unfinished *Theologia* 'Scholarium',
intended as a comprehensive textbook. The *Sic et Non*, an exercise in
the dialectical presentation of theological issues, was probably in
preparation from the mid-1120s. The *Commentary on the Epistle to the
Romans*, in which Abelard expounded his theory of grace and his
soteriology, and the *Ethics* 'Scito teipsum' ('Know thyself') date from
c. 1136. The *Dialogue between a Philosopher, a Jew and a Christian* is
another vehicle for the dialectical presentation of issues. It may be
from approximately 1136, though some scholars date it to the last
years of Abelard's life, 1140–2.[64]

Abelard's views as expressed in his various writings attracted the
attention of a battery of critics during his life, including Hugh of St
Victor, Walter of Mortagne, an associate of the circle of Laon, the
Cistercian William of St Thierry and, above all, St Bernard of
Clairvaux. It was mainly due to Bernard's determined prosecution,
based on information supplied to him by Abelard's other opponents,
that a list of propositions attributed to him was condemned by a
council at Sens in 1140 and a number of them transmitted for censure
by Pope Innocent II.[65] On his way to defend himself in Rome,
Abelard was invited by Peter the Venerable, abbot of Cluny, to retire
from the world. He died at a daughter house of Cluny in April 1142.

The controversies and censures which punctuated Abelard's life for
long misled historians in their assessment of his work. Modern
scholarship has discredited the portrayal of him as a sceptic and
freethinker and has restored him to his rightful place as a theologian
of serious purpose in the dialectical mould. In a letter to Héloïse
recorded by his supporter Berengar of Poitiers and written shortly
before or immediately after the council of Sens, Abelard protested the

sincerity of his faith: 'I do not wish to be a philosopher if it means conflicting with Paul nor to be an Aristotle if it cuts me off from Christ.'[66] It represents not a late change of mind but his consistent position except, indeed, in so far as it poses a dichotomy, untypical of his general perception of the relationship between reason and faith. This is characterised by a profound conviction of the unity of truth, an idea confidently expressed in one of his logical works where he defends the uses of dialectic for the Christian against the accusations of his critics that it 'destroys faith by the entanglements of its argumentation':

> But if they grant that an art militates against faith, without any doubt they are admitting that it is not knowledge. For knowledge is a comprehension of the truth of things; wisdom, in which faith consists, is a species of it. This (sc. wisdom) is the discernment of what is honourable or useful. But truth cannot be opposed to truth. Truth cannot be opposed to truth or good to good in the way that false can be found set against false or evil against evil; all things that are good are harmonious and congruent. All knowledge is good, even knowledge of evil, and cannot be lacking in the just man. For the just man to be on guard against evil it is necessary for him to have known in advance what evil is: he could not avoid it unless he knew what it was. . . . On these grounds therefore we prove that all knowledge, which is from God alone and proceeds from his gift, is good. Consequently it must be allowed too that the study of all knowledge is good . . . but study of that learning is especially to be undertaken in which greater truth is seen to be present. This however is dialectic, for to it all discernment of truth or falsehood is subject, in such a way that as the leader of the whole realm of learning it has all philosophy in its princely rule.[67]

Knowledge as the gift of God recalls St Augustine's theory of divine illumination. Abelard accepted the theory but as so often in his use of traditional terminology his adaptation revolutionised the perspective. For Augustine 'divine illumination' expressed distrust in the power of human reason. For Abelard it expressed assurance that human speculation, like human endeavour generally, was a gift of God and evoked a response from him. So, in his *Theologia* 'Summi Boni' and his *Theologia Christiana*, he was prepared to argue that Plato and other Gentile philosophers had been guided to an understanding both of the unicity and trinity of God. He was later to modify and finally to reject the idea that they had found the doctrine of the Trinity.[68] St Augustine had considered the same point seriously and was otherwise concerned to show that the philosophers might be considered friendly neighbours. His inclination, though, was to be defensive; if the Platonists had attained to truth, the explanation was that either they had borrowed from the Scriptures or they had enjoyed a separate revelation through a study of what God had made.[69] Abelard was assertive. The philosophers, by their high standards of morality, had shown themselves worthy of such a revelation.[70] The originality of Abelard's statement of the point should not be exaggerated. He was doing no more than to follow the trend of Augustine's optimistic pronouncements, while ignoring the restrictive, even pessimistic, vein of the saint's thought. However, it is this difference of tone, the unfailingly optimistic view of man's relationship with God, that is the core of Abelard's theology and, more than any single doctrine, lends it an air of novelty.

Abelard also adopted the Augustinian psychology, with its presuppositions of the superiority of the soul, its direction of the body and its moral agency and responsibility.[71] Although one of the principal effects of the Fall, in his account as in that of Augustine, is that the ruling function of soul is liable to misdirection and disruption, this is never such as to detract from man's accountability for his actions. Accountability is the subject of the *Ethics*, 'Scito teipsum'. The work was in two books, of which Book I and only a fragment of the second survives. Its title – 'Know thyself' – echoes the Delphic counsel to seekers of wisdom[72] but the treatise itself is wholly Christian in orientation, being an analysis of evil and goodness considered as disobedience and obedience to God. It ends with a treatment of confession as a means of obtaining remission of sin, a topic which received much elaboration in the course of the twelfth century. Abelard emphasises the interior disposition of the penitent. This is in keeping with his general approach. His chief contribution to moral theology in the *Ethics* is his definition of sin as a matter of consent, the thesis that action divorced from the intention which produces it is morally indifferent and the consequence that ignorance of the true nature of the action excuses from guilt. It is the intention that determines the morality of action and it is consent to what is known to be evil that, from the point of view of the agent, constitutes sin. The consideration led him to propose that the Jews were guiltless of

Christ's death and that given their convictions they would have sinned by failing to persecute him.

From this assertion of the internal character of morality it followed that neither virtue nor vice are augmented by the accomplishment of the agent's intention. The whole analysis was deeply disturbing to Abelard's critics.[73] In particular, the thesis that the actual execution of an intention is morally indifferent ran counter to a well established penitential tradition, the spiritual counterpart of the old Germanic laws governing redress of injuries, which required minute examination of the external content of the sinful act and established the degree of satisfaction accordingly.[74] What his critics failed to recognise was that Abelard was true to a strand of thought which in theological terms had its precedent in St Augustine's doctrine of moral integrity. In philosophical terms it went back further, to ancient Stoicism. In fact, the psychological account of morality was too powerful to be excluded.[75] It rapidly became absorbed into penitential discipline. Even then, however, the external dimension remained significant, for if the act did not contribute to the individual's guilt it might leave him entrammelled in a nexus of social obligations arising from it. This aspect, which was to become the province of the canon lawyer, was not part of Abelard's analysis. To that extent, his theory of sin might seem unbalanced and unsatisfactory even when the logic of his position was incontrovertible.

While the *Ethics* is undoubtedly Abelard's most original contribution to doctrine, the *Sic et Non* ('For and Against') is his most interesting exercise in dialectical method. It consists of 158 theological questions followed in each case by a collection of the often conflicting patristic solutions to them, generally without resolution of the dissension. It was a challenge 'such as may excite tender readers to the supreme endeavour of inquiring for truth and may render them sharper by their inquiry. For this is the definition of the first key of knowledge, namely assiduous or frequent questioning. . . . By calling into question (*dubitando*) we come to inquiry; by inquiring we reach the truth.'[76] The intention was not to bring patristic opinion into disrepute but to suggest the role which dialectic could play in clearing the ground:

Diligent discussion is also necessary when there are diverse pronouncements on the same matter, as to what is intended to have the force of precept, what to constitute an indulgent remission or what an exhortation of perfection, so that we may seek a remedy for contradiction by adverting to diversity of [authorial] intentions. If precept is in question, is it general or particular . . . ? Distinction has also to be made between the timing of and reasons for dispensations because often what is found allowed at one time is found forbidden at another, and what is generally commanded, as a rigorous standard, is sometimes tempered by dispensation. These are points over which it is especially necessary to make distinction in the enactment of ecclesiastical decrees or canons, for generally an easy solution to controversies will be found if we can establish that the same words are used in different senses by different authors. The careful reader will try in all these ways . . . to resolve contradictions in the writings of the saints. But if it happens that a contradiction is so explicit that by no argument can it be resolved, the authorities must be compared and that one retained in preference which is better testified and has greater corroboration.[77]

The juxtaposition of contraries was a technique practised in the schools and was not invented by Abelard. It was soon to bear fruit in canon law and theology respectively in the *Decretum* of Gratian (*post* 1139–*ante* 1155), the foundation of medieval canonical scholarship, and the four books of the *Sentences* of Peter Lombard (1150/4–7), the university textbook of the medieval theologian. It is not clear how far these seminal compilations were influenced by the method of the *Sic et Non* and how far they were independently conceived but between them the three works represent a triumph of productive criticism.

Among the controversial theological positions of Abelard were several doctrines concerning creation and salvation history. Influenced by the *Timaeus*, Abelard argued that God necessarily acts for the best and cannot be presumed capable of making the world better than he did. It was a question bristling with difficulties whatever the answer given to it. Abelard's line of thought evoked little argument from his critics but it readily lent itself to being interpreted as restrictive of divine freedom. He was aware of the hazard and sought to avoid it by stressing that the necessity was not an external constraint but an implication of God's nature, which is perfect goodness.[78]

The absence of external constraint on divine action is the foundation of Abelard's soteriology. Like St Anselm he rejected the theory that the Incarnation took place to redeem mankind from the devil's dominion. Despite the force of the *Cur Deus Homo*, the dominion theory was still being maintained in the school of Anselm of Laon and Abelard's review of the question, for which the main source is the *Commentary on the Epistle to the Romans*, may plausibly be seen as a direct challenge to his former associates there.[79] But if he himself had read the *Cur Deus Homo*, as seems likely, its satisfaction theory, with its emphasis on the claims of divine justice, found no favour with him. It began from the wrong pole of the relationship between man and God, implying that it was God's integrity which somehow needed to be restored rather than man's.[80] The sole reason for the Incarnation is the divine goodness which spontaneously seeks man out, liberates him from sin, reconciles him and enables him to turn to God.[81] The aspect of Christ's mission on which Abelard lays most stress is its exemplary quality by which man is shown the nature of perfect living.[82]

The spontaneity with which God approaches man is also the basis of Abelard's account of justification. For all the charges of Pelagianism brought against him by his critics, it is clear that he adhered to the Augustinian terminology of predestination[83] and was prepared to accept it as a mystery. However, he was anxious to emphasise that it is man's responsibility whether he reacts to grace with energy or with torpor and to this end he rejected the concept of successive enabling graces as a preliminary to meritorious acts. In fact, he cannot be said to have resolved the tension latent in this attempt to reconcile divine initiative with human responsibility. Not only can he not be convicted of having neglected divine initiative, in the very emphasis which he placed upon it he raised the problem whether it could be imputed to man as a fault that he did not accept the grace offered: 'Perhaps someone may say that it is his fault in that God has willed to give him that grace which he gave in equal measure to him and to the just but that he did not will to accept it when offered. To this I reply that it is impossible for him to accept it without the grace of God. Since God did not will to give him the grace to accept the gift offered and since he could not accept it without this grace, it is wrong to ascribe it to his fault that he did not accept the grace offered.'[84] The clarity with which he recognised the problem may suggest that he was uncomfortable with it. At least one of his sympathisers presented man's natural disposition to do good in a way that diminished the role of grace.[85] However, this was contrary to Abelard's stated position, which was to accept the primacy of grace with the difficulties which it entailed.

In his theology Abelard aimed to analyse the content of faith in such a way as to facilitate the intellectual conviction by which it was grasped. For him, to suppose that the act of faith involved less than an intellectual conviction was meaningless. This is also the view which he attributes to his students as the recipients of his treatise *On the Unity and Trinity*: 'They demanded something intelligible rather than mere words. In fact they said that words were useless if the intelligence could not follow them, that nothing could be believed unless it was first understood. . . .'[86] Lip-service to credal formulae was, he urged, not only inadequate but blasphemous.[87] The sentiment is the Christian counterpart to the ancient philosophical maxim that the unexamined life is not worthy of man. There is nothing artificial about Abelard's approach to theology, no attempt to exclude Christian dogma in order to work towards it from elementary principles. Quite the reverse, his standpoint is that of a believer bent on examining and expounding the nature of his commitment. In this sense, he conforms to the spirit of St Anselm and his method might as justly 'be described as 'faith in search of understanding'. But conservative minds, on guard for any suggestion that reason is the criterion of what should be believed, saw his efforts as radical and disturbing. They were confirmed in their suspicions by his earliest excursion into the most difficult area of patristic-conciliar theology, the doctrine of the Trinity. However, novelty of method or of conclusions is only a partial explanation of the antagonisms which he aroused. These stemmed in large measure from the context in which he moved and particularly from the existence of a well-established school at Laon with which he had taken issue and whose adherents were able to mount and promote an effective campaign against him.

Logic and Theology – the School of St Victor

The Augustinian abbey and school of St Victor in Paris was founded by William of Champeaux who gave up his archdeaconry at Notre Dame and retired there for a few years before becoming bishop of Châlons-sur-Marne in 1112–13. Its chief claim to a place in the intellectual history of the twelfth century, however, derives not from him but from two later members of the community, Hugh (d. 1140/1), who was possibly a native of Saxony, and Richard (d. 1173), who may have been a Scot.

Hugh of St Victor is best known for his *Didascalicon*, written in the late 1120s. Subtitled *On the Study of Reading*, it was intended as a guide for students at the abbey school, which was still at this period open to secular scholars. The work's nearest literary affinity is to the encyclopaedic tradition, especially as mediated by the *Institutions* of Cassiodorus, but it also breathes the spirit of Augustine's *On Christian Doctrine*, both in its appreciation of the role of secular learning in the pursuit of divine wisdom and in its strict subordination of one to the other.[88] To understand it correctly, it has to be remembered that the *Didascalicon* deals merely with the first stage in man's ascent to wisdom – reading; the subsequent stages are meditation, prayer, performance (action) and contemplation (the condition of the perfect).

Hugh describes the *Didascalicon* as comprising two parts, the first dealing with the secular arts, the second with scripture. Each part has three subdivisions. The first part is the more significant as a channel of ancient learning. It presents philosophy as divided into four branches, reflecting, with modification, Aristotle's treatment of the subject.[89] The four branches are theoretical (whose subject is wisdom), practical (whose subject is conduct), mechanical (containing various useful arts) and logical. The theoretical branch consists of theology, mathematics (understood as the quadrivium) and physics; the practical branch is subdivided into solitary (ethical), private (economic) and public (political); within the logical branch is distinguished a linguistic strand and a rational or argumentative one. This division was not exclusive to Hugh – it is found independently in his near contemporary, William of Conches[90] – but the popularity of the *Didascalicon* made it an important source of the idea. Familiarity with this detailed schema of knowledge was a valuable preparation for the reception and even the discovery of new texts of Aristotle, enabling them to be located readily within a general system.

Besides this review of the arts, Hugh also wrote a *Summa* of theology, *On the Sacraments* (*De Sacramentis Christianae Fidei*), the structure of which he sketched in Book 6, Chapter 4, of the *Didascalicon*. It is in two parts, beginning with the creation, proceeding through the institutions of the church and ending with the general resurrection and the final states of the wicked and of the just. Part I contains material closest to philosophical concerns. It deals among other topics with creation, divine knowledge, foreknowledge and providence, the divine nature, the Trinity, the divine will, spiritual substance, human free will and original sin.[91] While not a polemicist,

Hugh sought to counteract the tendency of Peter Abelard's thought concerning divine foreknowledge and immutability, especially the proposition that God cannot improve on what he does. That creation should be incapable of improvement would be to suppose either that it was supremely good – an attribute of God alone – or that it was irreparably flawed, the very implication that the 'optimistic' thesis sought to avoid.[92]

In the *De Sacramentis*, Hugh offered an explanation of the Trinity based on the distinction between intellectual power (*mens*), wisdom and love.[93] The quest for a satisfactory rational basis of the doctrine was a current preoccupation, already noted in the cases of Roscelin and Abelard and to be found also in William of Conches. After Hugh, in the school of St Victor, Achard, second abbot of the monastery (d. 1171), wrote on the topic, trying to state 'necessary reasons' behind the mystery.[94] This is the keynote of Richard of St Victor's treatise, *On the Trinity*. The work is in six books. The Prologue and the first chapter of Book I make clear that the programme is 'faith in search of understanding', although St Anselm's phrase is not explicitly recalled. There is a hint of Abelard's spirit in the sense of obligation with which Richard invests proceeding beyond faith to understanding. 'It ought to be insufficient for us . . . to hold on faith the truths of eternal realities, unless it be given to us also to establish by the witness of reason that which is held on faith. And let not that knowledge of eternal truths which is by faith only be sufficient for us, unless we may grasp also that knowledge which is by understanding, even if we are not yet capable of that which is by experience.'[95] Faith is the starting point for knowledge of 'eternal truths' since some of what we are enjoined to believe not only transcends reason but actually seems to contravene it 'unless, that is, these articles be discussed by a profound and most skilful inquiry or better still be made manifest by divine revelation'.[96] However, although the entry to such truths is by faith, one must not halt there but always press on to the inner and deeper recesses of understanding.[97]

The object of the treatise is, accordingly, to find necessary reasons for eternal truths and it is based on the conviction that 'for the explanation of any realities whose being is necessary there must be not only probable but necessary arguments, although for the time being it may be that they lie hidden from our efforts'.[98] The arguments for the existence of God hinge on the Platonist perception that the relative and contingent require an absolute.[99] The unique character and attributes of this absolute are established in turn, in the remainder of Book I and through Book II. This however is the less ambitious part of the inquiry. In Book III Richard proposes to show the rational justification of the doctrine of the Trinity. The argument here is from the character of perfect love. The necessity that perfect love be directed towards another requires that there be a second divine person and the necessary desire of these two persons to have a common object of love requires that there be a third. Book IV examines the concept of 'person' in order to show the compatibility of unity and trinity. Boethius' definition of 'person' – 'the individual substance of a rational nature' – is criticised: a divine person is 'an incommunicable existence of the divine nature'.[100] Book V is an account of the processions of the persons in the Trinity. Book VI explains the names of the persons by human analogies.

Not all the Victorines were well disposed to the investigation of the mysteries of faith. One member of the house, Walter, a contemporary of Richard, took the view that such investigation created a confused and dangerous maze.[101] He seems to represent an anti-intellectualist current there towards the end of the century, contrasting with the approach of Hugh and Richard and perhaps reflecting an inevitable tension within it.[102] Hugh and Richard express the earlier and general spirit of the school, which accepted dialectical theology as part of a progressive schema of knowledge. According to this, intellectual apprehension of eternal truths, attained under the guidance of faith, culminates by divine grace in direct experience. The last element is a reminder of the mystical dimension to St Victor. Both Hugh and Richard wrote treatises based on the pseudo-Denis and mediated his doctrine to the high and late middle ages. The way in which its two greatest figures underpin dialectical method with a sense of spiritual insight, pressing all three levels of human knowledge – faith, intellection and experience – into a single-minded and integrated quest, is the distinctive quality of the school in its time.

Twelfth-century Cosmology

The twelfth century saw an attempt on the part of a series of thinkers in northern France to combine the few strands of ancient scientific theory then available into a general understanding of the structure of the universe. The principal source for it was Chalcidius' partial translation of the *Timaeus* and his commentary on it. This was supplemented by the 'scientific' treatises of the quadrivium, notably Boethius' *On Arithmetic* and *On Music* and Martianus' *On the Marriage of Philology and Mercury*, by the account of the soul in Macrobius' commentary on the *Dream of Scipio* and by leads in Boethius' other writings, the theological treatises as well as the *Consolation of Philosophy*. Boethius' theological treatises were particularly valuable in providing a statement of Aristotelian hylomorphism, using the vocabulary of matter (*materia*) and form, while Chalcidius provided an alternative vocabulary for the same doctrine.[103] The related doctrine of actuality and potentiality was also reconstructed, from references in Aristotle's *De Interpretatione* and from Chalcidius' distinction between 'possibility' – lack of form – and effect. Thus, although twelfth-century cosmologists might think of themselves as a distinct group, 'lovers of Plato',[104] their Platonism was a hybrid. It could not be otherwise, given that their very scanty knowledge of Plato was derived from late classical sources, dating from the period when thinkers had been labouring to reconcile a variety of systems.

The literature of this strand of twelfth-century thought consists partly of glosses on the authorities and partly of 'original' treatises. Among the first class are glosses on Boethius' *On the Trinity* and on Genesis by Thierry the Breton (known as Thierry of Chartres from the fact that he became chancellor there *c.* 1142) and by his pupil, Clarembald of Arras, who wrote in the late 1150s and who also glossed another of Boethius' 'sacred treatises', on the concepts of substance and goodness.[105] Also in this class are glosses on the *Timaeus*, on Macrobius and on Boethius' *Consolation* by William of Conches (died *c.* 1154). Among the second class are a *Philosophy of the World* by William of Conches and a literary work, *Cosmographia*, by Bernard Silvestris (Bernard of Tours), written probably 1143–7, which presents its cosmology through an elaborate allegory and a mixture of verse and prose.[106]

As a systematic treatise, William's *Philosophy of the World* and its revised version, the *Dragmaticon*, provides a good summary of the scientific knowledge of the period and of its application in a Christian context. By philosophy William means 'the true comprehension of things which exist and are not seen and of things which exist and are seen'.[107] Thus, his subject is all reality. In Book I of the *Philosophy* he proceeds to discuss the possibility of knowledge of God in this life (we are not wholly ignorant – we know that he exists – but we do not know him perfectly). From this follows examination of the proofs for God's existence – the creation of the world and its rational ordering – and of aspects of Trinitarian doctrine. The most interesting discussion is of the nature of the World Soul, on which he cites three views: that it is the Holy Spirit; that it is 'a natural force (*vigorem*) implanted in things by God, in virtue of which some things have life only, others have life and feeling and discernment'; and that it is 'a certain incorporeal substance which is whole in individual bodies, although on account of the lethargy of some bodies it does not exercise the same effect in all'.[108] The remainder of Book I discusses angels and the elements which constitute the visible world. William's elements are atoms, which he is careful to distinguish from the four visible 'elements', earth, water, air and fire. For his source here William cites Constantine the African's *Pantechni*, an eleventh-century Latin version of the theoretical books of a comprehensive treatise on medicine by a tenth-century Arabic writer, Ali ben Abbas. This and other medical material from Arabic and Greek, including treatises by Galen (*c.* AD 130–201) and Nemesius of Emesa (*c.* AD 390), was now coming into circulation in the west. Its influence was not confined to the theory and practice of medicine but can be discerned, as here, in contemporary philosophical literature.[109]

The rest of the *Philosophy* surveys the physical universe. Book II deals with the ether and astronomy, Book III with air, meteorology and the final conflagration of the world – a notion derived from Stoic theory but compatible with Christian eschatology – and Book IV with earth as a constitutive 'element', geography and life on earth, including observations on human biology and anatomy.

The works of Thierry, of William of Conches, by extension and analogy of Clarembald of Arras and Bernard Silvestris, and of Gilbert of Poitiers were for long regarded by historians as the products of a single school – the school of Chartres – with a distinctive humanistic and scientific outlook. This view has been effectively challenged in terms both of the careers of the masters once thought to have comprised the school and the interpretation of their interests.[110] It can now be seen that theirs was not a localised perception but that of a generation steeped in common sources. The interests which they shared represent 'a phase in the continuous development of western studies and of medieval humanism'.[111] Their writings contain the fullest accumulation in the Latin west of the ancient teaching on the structure of the universe and man's place within it before the new access of Aristotelian science.

:lfth century represents an end and a beginning
ristotle. The logical corpus was now complete
vas being gradually assimilated. The recovery
l scientific system, on the other hand, was only
had been found was not yet part of the
e. The second phase of recovery and absorp-
century and proceeded along two routes, from
Direct translations from Greek were the most
t enduring source of new Aristotelian texts.
rculation and particular defects meant that a
ndirect versions, these could be no more than
he chief contribution of Arabic culture to the
n western Europe lay not so much in the
Aristotelian texts which it transmitted as in
philosophers and commentators gave to
he absorption of Aristotle's philosophy by
bly bound up with their discovery of Arabic
t of the western tradition finds that the path
nd Oxford leads through Baghdad and

nd Oxford introduces another theme of the
re this momentous extension of the sources
was complete new educational institutions were
appearing through which its effects could be realised. From the
thirteenth century onwards the reception of the new texts and the
debate over their implications took place mainly within the 'schools'
or universities. These were a development unique to western Europe.
They provided a structured and highly professional setting for the
propagation and continuance of the new programme of study. The
extent to which they were responsible for its massive impact on the
European outlook is one of several features of the western tradition
which are illuminated by a comparison with the Arabic world.

I   Arabic Thought

The Character and Context of Arabic Thought

The direct contribution which Arabic commentators and philosophers made to the understanding of Aristotle is the principal interest of their thought from the European perspective and will be the main subject here. There is however a secondary aspect which deserves notice. The speculative movement in Islam affords several interesting analogies to its Christian counterpart. There is ample evidence in Islam of the tension between reason and faith which is a recurrent feature of Christian thought. The tension is represented in Islam both by the differences between philosophers and theologians and by divergent approaches within theology. The divergence was especially marked between the Mu'tazilites, a school of speculative theology patronised by the Abbasid Caliphs of the ninth century, and the followers of Abu'l-Hasan al-Ashari (d. 935). A one-time adherent of the Mu'tazilite school, he departed from them and established a fundamentalism which came to dominate Islamic theology. The issues which divided the Mu'tazilites and the Asharites included their views on the nature of divine power, its scrutability or inscrutability, and the question whether the categories of good and evil were essentially rational or whether they depended simply on divine ordinance. The Mu'tazilites grounded themselves on the rationality and objective justice of divine action, emphasised the freedom of man's will and in general aimed at elaborating a coherent system of 'natural' or rational theology. For their part, the Asharites insisted on the absolute power of God, especially as regards his inscrutable predestination of man. In their view, this determined the particular acts of man's will, which were held to be a part of the divine creation and to have God as their eternal author. To the charge that predestination implied an injustice in God, they pleaded that by his absolute power God was above and exempt from all obligation and that it was therefore impossible for him to act unjustly. These differences of approach mirror divisions which were latent indeed in Christian theology too throughout the middle ages and which were to come to the fore in the later period.

However, while there were striking coincidences between the preoccupations of speculative theologians in Islam and Christianity, it would be wrong to ignore important differences between the two

intellectual contexts. Although questions posed by philosophy inevitably influenced Islamic theological discussion and although Moslem
philosophers in turn were conscious of the force of revealed theology,
the formal gap between theology and philosophy was much wider in
Islam than in Christianity. In the Islamic world the pursuit of
philosophy remained a private activity. It never attained the position
which it rapidly established in the western universities, where a
mastery of Aristotelian texts came to be a prerequisite for entry to the
advanced faculty of theology. The Moslem system of higher education centred on training in Islamic law and was relatively little
influenced by philosophical studies.[1] This lack of an institutional
framework was a serious handicap. It tends to be obscured by the
brilliance of what was achieved in the field by individual effort but it
largely explains the failure of philosophy to maintain itself in the long
term as an intellectual force in Islam.

The lack of an institutional framework is true of the teaching of
philosophy as distinct from the work of translation, scholarship on
texts and their conservation. For this essential preparatory work there
did exist at the crucial junctures facilities provided by official
patronage. The availability of these depended on the interests of
individual rulers. Before reviewing the history of the philosophical
movement it is therefore necessary to take some note of the political
structure of the Islamic world.

In 644, on the assassination of Omar, second successor of the
Prophet, the headship of Islam passed to the Ommayad caliphate,
though its position was not established until 661. The Ommayads
presided over the lightning expansion of the Arab empire from its
initial gains, which included Syria, Palestine, Egypt and parts of
Persia, under Omar. Eastwards, the Islamic conquest was pushed to
the Indus valley and the frontiers of China. Westwards, it extended
through north Africa and into Spain and Gaul. Here it was halted by
Charles Martel at the battle of Poitiers in 732 and shortly afterwards
was forced back to the Pyrenees. In 750, the Ommayad caliphate was
overthrown in the east and replaced by the Abbasid dynasty,
descendants of the Prophet's uncle. They championed the cause of
non-Arab Moslems and their advent saw an increasing Persian
influence in government and the transfer of the caliphate from
Damascus to Baghdad. Their rule lasted nominally until the Mongol
sack of Baghdad in 1258. From the late eighth and early ninth
centuries the Abbasids ceased to control north Africa, west of Egypt.

Their authority was never accepted in Spain. There, the continuance of the Ommayad dynasty had been secured by the escape of a sole survivor from the coup of 750.

Although the Abbasids purported to inaugurate a regime of strict adherence to Islam, it was under them that Greek thought first began to be absorbed into Moslem culture. For the most part, the Arabic corpus of Greek thought was received indirectly, from Syriac rather than from Greek. Translations into Syriac are known from about the middle of the fifth century, when the great debates over the person of Christ stimulated the search for a philosophical foundation to theology. After the repression of Nestorianism and the attempted repression of Monophysitism[2] several waves of refugees fled to the east, mainly to the Persian empire, and it was to this line of exiled Christian scholarship that the first Arabic versions were owed.[3] The work of translating afresh began at the Abbasid court of Baghdad in the middle of the eighth century and is associated with practitioners of medicine there under the Caliph al-Mansur (754–75). Among the treatises translated at this time were Aristotelian logical texts, for which there had been an early demand in Syriac as aids to scriptural exegesis. The movement continued under the Caliphs Harun al-Rashid (786–809) and Ma'mun (813–33) as well as at the instigation of wealthy private patrons who funded the search for texts and recruited translators. Now philosophical and scientific texts began to be rendered. The most systematic of the Arabic translators was Hunain ibn Ishaq (809–73), whose activities scholars designate as the second phase of the translation movement. With the cooperation of a number of colleagues, including his son and his nephew, he collated texts, revised earlier versions and extended the corpus, usually through translations first into Syriac and then freely into Arabic. His son, Ishaq, is credited with the translation of parts of the *Metaphysics* and *Ethics* of Aristotle, the latter's *De Generatione et Corruptione* ('On Coming to Be and Passing Away') and Plato's *Sophist* and some of the *Timaeus*. It seems that by the middle of the century most of the *Metaphysics* – known to Arabic readers as the 'Book of Letters', from its internal organisation – had been made available. The process of improving versions and adding new texts continued at Baghdad for another century and a half, until by the middle of the eleventh century Arabic thinkers had at their disposal all the works of Aristotle now extant, with the exception of the *Politics* and parts of the *Ethics*.

As a general comment, the syllabus of writings which passed into

Arabic reflects the dominant interests of the late classical schools. Aristotle figured largely but not exclusively. Plato too was known. Probably through paraphrases rather than in their integrity several of his dialogues were studied. These included the *Timaeus* and *Sophist*, already noted, the *Phaedo*, a source for Plato's doctrine on the soul, and the *Republic* and *Laws*, which in default of Aristotle's *Politics* were the Arabic source for Greek political theory. The Arabs also had Neoplatonist texts.[4] Most significant was the so-called *Theology of Aristotle*, an arrangement by an unknown author of Books iv–vi of Plotinus' *Enneads*. The *Theology* was the principal Arabic source for Neoplatonist emanationist theory. It coloured the interpretation of the genuine works of Aristotle by Arabic philosophers down to Ibn Rushd (Averroes), who rejected its implications. The *Liber de Causis* ('Book of Causes'), a version of Proclus' *Elements of Theology*, is another possible Arabic source of Neoplatonism at an early stage. However the date of its compilation is uncertain and its influence, if any, before the twelfth century is unknown.[5]

In addition to these works, the Arabs possessed an important body of late classical scholarship on Aristotle. Of particular significance was a strand of commentary developing his psychological doctrine. The enigmatic remarks in Book iii, Chapter 5 of the *De Anima* and an equally puzzling passage in *On the Generation of Animals*, where Aristotle referred to the intellect as coming 'from outside',[6] evoked a series of resolutions. Common to them was an analysis which required in the act of knowing a capacity for understanding, an object capable of being understood and an explanation for the fusion of the two poles. It was on the third aspect that the several interpretations varied significantly. The question was whether the active principle of intellection inferred from Aristotle's account – the agent intellect of the commentaries – was a faculty of the soul or something acting upon the soul from outside. Theophrastus, head of the Lyceum after Aristotle, seems to have considered the agent intellect to be both immanent and transcendent. Later commentators emphasised one or other of these features. Alexander of Aphrodisias (*fl. c.* AD 200) presented the agent intellect as something extrinsic to the soul and his discussion of it suggested its identification with the prime mover. Themistius (*fl. c.* AD 360) rejected this last point and held the agent intellect to be internal to the soul and to be a constitutive aspect of it. That this was Aristotle's sense seemed to him to be established by the assertion that the agent intellect alone was immortal and eternal. The statement would be untrue of the prime mover because there were other immortal movers in the Aristotelian universe. It made sense only if Aristotle were distinguishing one aspect of the soul from others. Themistius' analysis became very influential in the thirteenth century but among the Arabic philosophers Alexander's view prevailed, at least as regards the externalisation of the agent intellect. This had important consequences not only for the character of Arabic thought but also for the reception of Aristotle in the west.

The Development of Islamic Thought

The first systematic Arabic philosopher is generally considered to be Al Kindi (died c. 873). He lived mainly at Baghdad, where he served as court astrologer. Although much of his work is lost, he is known to have been a prolific writer in scientific, mathematical and philosophical subjects. In common with the Mu'tazilite movement, of which he is probably best considered a part, his philosophical interests included a range of theological matters, especially questions concerning the divine unity and justice, the character of divine agency, the absolute creation and end of the world, revelation, miracles and the resurrection of the body. On these he sought to vindicate Scripture against rival Greek theories, while remaining confident that there could be no essential disparity between revelation and the conclusions of rational inquiry.

Several of Al Kindi's scientific and logical treatises were translated into Latin in the twelfth century.[7] However, his chief interest from the western viewpoint lies in his exposition of Aristotle's theory of the intellect. Here he was greatly affected by the late classical interpretations, particularly that of Alexander of Aphrodisias. Al Kindi accepted the idea of an active intellect which was an external agent as the common doctrine of Plato and Aristotle but he refused to identify it with God. His treatise On the Intellect[8] contains a general classification of the types of intellect, adapted from Alexander. In it he distinguished between the active intellect and the several wholly internal intellectual aspects of the soul: the potential intellect (a receptivity to the effect of the active intellect), what may be called the activated intellect (as having been brought from potentiality to actuality) and the 'manifest' or 'demonstrative' intellect (the activated intellect considered as functioning).[9]

With Al Farabi (d. 950), a Turk who received a part of his

philosophical training at Baghdad, the influence of the *Theology of Aristotle* becomes apparent. Al Farabi accepted the Neoplatonist vision of the universe as a necessary emanation and, again under Neoplatonist influence, ignored the Islamic doctrine of the resurrection of the body, which Al Kindi had accepted on the authority of revelation. The fact is symptomatic of a general difference of outlook between the two thinkers as to the relationship between reason and faith. Al Farabi attempted to explain revelation in terms of philosophical concepts, considering it to be an inferior vehicle of truth in a symbolic form, designed for the untrained. However, unlike his near contemporary, Al Razi (d. 925/32), he did not disparage revelation altogether but accepted it as sufficient to enlighten non-philosophers on the principles of living well and thus to qualify them for happiness in the after-life, should they act accordingly. He held that the souls of those who never attained enlightenment, either through philosophy or through symbols, would perish with their bodies.

Al Farabi too composed a treatise on the psychology of knowing, called in the west *De intellectu et intellecto* ('On the intellect and what is understood').[10] At its most basic level, intellect is the 'practical reason' of Aristotle's *Ethics*. At its highest level, it is the divine intellect of the *Metaphysics*. Of special interest, though, is his treatment of the intellect described in Aristotle's *De Anima*. Like Al Kindi, Al Farabi understood the active intellect as a separate substance, activating the potential intellect in man. The active intellect itself he located within the Neoplatonist system of emanations from the One and within Aristotle's astronomical framework. It is the last of the immaterial, spiritual substances and the mediator between the heavenly and the sublunar world. As such, it is eternally the same; its function, the shedding of intellectual light, is unconscious; the diversity of its effects – the fact that men's understanding varies – stems from variety in the potential intellects upon which it acts. The location of the active intellect within a cosmological model is the most significant feature of this analysis for subsequent development. However, it is interesting to note that elsewhere Al Farabi found a place for it too within the 'symbolic truth' of Islamic revelation. There it is represented by the angel who communicated the Koran to Mohammed.[11]

Al Farabi was arguably the most original philosopher of the eastern Islamic world but the leading figure from the European viewpoint is undoubtedly the Persian, Ibn Sina (980–1037), known to the Latins as Avicenna. Although some of his works are in Persian, he chiefly wrote in Arabic, which is the language of his great philosophical encyclopaedia, the *Kitab al-Shifa* ('Book of Healing'), and of its abridgement, the *Kitab al-Najat* ('Book of Salvation'). It is not clear whether the *Najat* was known in the west, but the *Shifa*, called in Latin the *Liber Sufficientiae* ('Book of Sufficiency'), exercised an important influence through independent circulation of its sections on metaphysics and psychology.

One of the fundamental aspects of Avicenna's cosmology was his distinction between necessary and possible being. This he also expressed as a distinction between essence and existence, between the concept of the nature of a specific being and its instantiation. The perception was not perhaps his own. He may have found the germ of it in a logical distinction made by Aristotle, and similar ideas occur in Plotinus and in Al Farabi.[12] Moreover, the distinction between necessary and possible being, that is between uncaused and caused, may well have followed from philosophical reflection on the Islamic doctrine of creation from nothing,[13] although Avicenna developed the point in quite a different fashion. Whatever its source, the analysis underlay much of his own thought and was a major influence on western treatment of the matter. The dependence of possible being on a cause of its existence, combined with rejection of an infinite chain of causation, is Avicenna's main proof for the existence of God, though he also accepted the Aristotelian argument to a prime mover.[14] The relationship between God and the sensible world is traced through a chain of intelligences which as in Neoplatonist doctrine are the product of a succession of emanations. The first intelligence is produced by the self-contemplation of the One. Although a necessary emanation, it is not the cause of its own existence. The notional possibility which is a part of its essence gives rise in its self-contemplation to the matter of the first sphere, while its inherent necessity gives rise to the soul by which the first sphere is informed. From the first intelligence there also emanates, through its contemplation of the One, a lower intelligence. It too has its proper sphere, produced as before. So there emanate in all ten intelligences. The last of these is the agent intelligence, the 'giver of forms' to the sublunar world. Although the caused universe is contingent in the sense that all its beings depend for their existence on a cause – unlike the first cause, God, in whom essence and existence are synonymous – Avicenna regarded the process of causation itself as necessary. This mechanical, determinist view of creation was at best remote from Islamic teaching and was perhaps irreconcilable with it but it need not be assumed that Avicenna took this view. Because he allowed no distinction between God's knowledge and his will, emanation as a result of divine self-knowledge could equally be seen as a product of the will.[15]

In his account of knowing, Avicenna followed the now established view that the agent intellect was an external principle, which he identified with the tenth intelligence. The latter was therefore the source of forms epistemologically as well as ontologically. If the soul, considered as mind, is to apprehend the forms, according to Avicenna's theory it is necessary for it to acquire the disposition to unite itself to the agent intelligence. During the soul's union with a body, the stimulus for this is experience, generating images in the mind. After separation from the body, the soul can accomplish the union without the mediation of images. Clearly, Avicenna has taken the Aristotelian terminology in a Platonist sense, not least in conceiving of the soul as a substance in its own right, spiritual, immortal and capable of independent existence. For him as for Aristotle the soul is the actuality or perfection of the human being, conferring specific determination (constituting the being as one which can grow, reproduce, move and reason). However, in Avicenna's theory the principle which the soul informs is not prime matter considered absolutely but prime matter which already possesses a degree of unspecific organisation, the aptitude or 'form' of a body.[16] The dissolution of body therefore carries no insinuation that soul too passes out of existence.[17] But while holding firmly to the continued existence of the human soul, Avicenna rejected the Platonic notion that it exists before its union with a body. His reason is that pre-existing souls of the same species would be indistinguishable.[18] It is through union with a body that the soul acquires individuality, which it retains after separation upon bodily death.

With Avicenna, Islamic philosophy reached a peak of systematisation. As a fully elaborated explanation of the universe his thought could easily seem to pose a challenge to the theological account. The emergence of a strain of fundamentalism in Islamic theology as represented by the Asharite school has already been noted, in particular its concern with the absolute power of God. Later thinkers of the type developed the implications of absolute power in new directions, which militated against the perceptions of a system such as

Avicenna's. While they admitted the argument for God's existence from the contingency of the world, they were shy of the Aristotelian–Neoplatonist structure of necessary causation and as a philosophical counterblast fell back instead on versions of the atomic theory. The association or indeed the duration of atoms, of which creation was seen to be composed according to this, was left wholly subject to the divine will. The relationship between cause and effect in the universe was illusory: what appeared to be an effect of a natural cause was really, like the existence of the cause itself, an effect of divine action.[19]

The fullest development of this anti-rationalist critique was a treatise by the Persian philosopher and mystic, Al Ghazali (Algazel) (1058–1111), a product of the Asharite movement. His *Incoherence of the Philosophers* (*Tahāfut al-Falāsifah*) was radically intransigent on the main issues. Among other propositions, Al Ghazali asserted the creation of the world in time against the theory of eternal emanation. He defended God's knowledge of particulars, a central doctrine of the Koran, against the view that the prime mover or One was unconscious of the effects which it generated. He disallowed a refinement by Avicenna who had given God a knowledge of the universe through its operating causes, as disclosed in his self-knowledge, but not of particulars as such which Avicenna had held to be the subject of finite knowledge. And he maintained the 'occasionalist' thesis, that the relationship of what appears as cause and effect is not a necessary one but a result of the two events being joined in that sequence by God. This divine conjunction of 'cause' and 'effect' is distinct from the miracle, which is God's production of the 'effect' without his first producing the 'cause'.[20] Al Ghazali's aim was to cast doubt on the theses of the philosophers in order to emphasise the indispensability of Scripture. However, when his thought first became known to the west in the twelfth century, it was through an earlier treatise, the *Intentions of the Philosophers* (*Maqasid al-Falāsifah*), in which he patiently and scrupulously summarised the views which he intended to demolish. Ironically, therefore, he was taken as a representative of the very perspective which he opposed and served as a source for understanding the systems of Al Farabi and Avicenna, where their own treatises were unavailable.[21]

After Al Ghazali, the interest in Arabic philosophy from the Latin viewpoint switches from the eastern to the western part of the Islamic world. The beginnings of the philosophical and scientific movement in Islamic Spain probably date from the ninth century. However, it was in the second half of the tenth century that a determined effort was made under the Ommayad caliph, Al Hakam II, to establish Cordova as a centre of learning in competition with Baghdad and to equip it with the necessary texts. A theological reaction set in after Al Hakam's death but it proved to be merely a temporary check. The high point of the western Islamic philosophical movement was the twelfth century, at a time when Almohad rulers, with a power base in Morocco, were making strenuous attempts to hold off the Christian reconquest of southern Spain. The two earliest Islamic figures of note, Ibn Bajja (Avempace) and Ibn Tufayl (Abubacer), were hardly more than names to the Latin world. They continued the strand of Arabic Neoplatonism and asserted the harmony of faith and reason. Ibn Bajja used the techniques both of synthetic exposition and of commentary on the Aristotelian texts.

Close textual study, inherited from the classical scholastic tradition, had been the principal activity of Arabic thinkers until Avicenna. He too is known to have commented on the Aristotelian corpus[22] but his influence was chiefly exercised through his synthetic expositions. With the next and greatest thinker of the western group, Ibn Rushd (Averroes), there was a deliberate return to textual exposition as a means of restoring what was meant to be a more faithful Aristotelianism than that of Avicenna. Averroes was born in Cordova about 1126 and spent his life partly in Spain and partly at the court of the Almohad caliphate in Morocco. It was at the suggestion of the caliph, Abū Ya'qūb Yūsuf (d. 1184), an informed patron of learning, to whom he had been introduced by Ibn Tufayl (c. 1168), that Averroes began the task of expounding Aristotle's works, thus earning his Latin title, 'the Commentator'. His commentaries were of several kinds: 'small' and 'middle' commentaries, which were really paraphrases of the texts, and 'great' commentaries, in which the text was presented separately and was accompanied by a detailed interpretation. In all, of the several types, Averroes composed thirty-eight commentaries on Aristotle, of which fifteen were translated into Latin in the thirteenth century.[23] Apart from them, he also wrote several independent treatises. The most notable of these were an analysis of the relationship between reason and faith and a defence of philosophising aimed against Al Ghazali's views and trenchantly entitled *The Incoherence of the Incoherence* (*Tahāfut al Tahāfut*, translated into Latin as *Destructio Destructionis*, 'The Destruction of the Destruction'). Of

Averroes' commentaries, the most important were the 'great' commentaries on the *Physics*, *Metaphysics* and *De Anima*, written between 1180 and 1190. The first two of these, with the *Tahāfut*, set out his cosmology. The great commentary on the *De Anima* contained his important interpretation of Aristotle's psychology.

Averroes' cosmology reveals a different perspective from that of Avicenna, whose emanation theory he criticised. Instead of viewing the universe as the result of a series of emanations, Averroes sought to explain it in terms of the doctrines expounded chiefly in Aristotle's *Physics* and *Metaphysics*, in terms of matter and form, potentiality and actuality and motion. The material world was a compound of matter and form. For Averroes the central question regarding it was not what was the source of form but what explained the process by which material substances eternally took on new forms or were drawn from states of potentiality to actuality. The answer was that there existed a 'final' cause, an unmoved prime mover whose condition the whole universe strove to resemble. Averroes accepted the astronomical evidence for a multiplicity of moving causes, the intelligences, but reconciled this with monotheism by ranking them in a hierarchy with one highest cause, that is, God. This highest cause he considered capable of affecting all the intelligences directly and not simply of producing the first intelligence, as in the emanation theory. In keeping with his adherence to Aristotle's analysis, he also dismissed Avicenna's distinction between essence and existence and especially the implication that essence was logically prior to existence and that existence was an accident of essence. For Averroes, existence was an inherent feature of all substance.

In his psychology Averroes agreed with Avicenna in taking the agent intellect to be a substance external to the soul. However, he made a significant departure from Avicenna's account. For Averroes, the potential or 'material' intellect is not a property of the individual soul but an effect of contact between the agent intelligence and what he called the 'passive' intellect of the individual. The latter was the Aristotelian 'imagination', a product of sense knowledge and as such an aspect of bodily function. Not only did an external agent cause the transition from intellectual potentiality to actuality, as in Avicenna's system, but the very potentiality which became actualised was external to the soul and only temporarily united with it. This strange analysis is a complex of philosophical perceptions. The soul informing the body was individual – being individuated by the matter which it informed – but it was wholly conterminous with the body and upon the disintegration of the latter gave way to new forms. Intellection, by contrast, was a spiritual act, transcending bodily function, and as such was immortal. But the intellect was not individualised; it did not inform matter and was the same for all members of the species. In his insistence that intellect in both its active and potential aspects was separate from the soul, Averroes can be seen to have been making several points. He preserved the principle that soul is simply form to the body's matter; he accepted that intellect was incorruptible; and he affirmed the similarity and hence the unity of the act of understanding throughout the species at the cost of reducing to a minimum or even abolishing its individual character. In so far as understanding had an individual character this derived from the images produced by sense experience in the passive intellect, which ceased on death. Whatever his own rationalisation of his position may have been as a Moslem believer,[24] his interpretation offered the least possible scope within the Aristotelian framework for a concept of personal immortality. It was the gradual appreciation of this threat which rendered his views so controversial in the thirteenth century.

The several apparent incompatibilities between Averroes' philosophical conclusions and Islamic faith have often given rise to a feeling that he was insincere as a believer or that he maintained a doctrine of 'double truth', an acceptance of the disharmony and yet of the equal validity of the teachings of faith and reason. It is now clear that such an interpretation is unfounded.[25] Averroes was continuing a long tradition among the Islamic philosophers which saw reason and revelation as teaching essentially the same truths though expressing them differently. Their spheres, though distinct, are complementary. In some respects revelation goes beyond the capacity of reason, in which case it is a necessary supplement.

Medieval Jewish Thought

In a general review, medieval Jewish thought may be treated as a branch of Arabic culture. Arabic translations were the source for Jewish thinkers' knowledge of the ancient tradition and several of the principal Jewish philosophical treatises were themselves written in Arabic. So the *Guide of the Perplexed* by the twelfth-century Jew, Moses Maimonides, was written in Arabic and translated into Hebrew, from which the influential Latin version stemmed. Like their Islamic counterparts, these Jewish treatises served the Latin Christian world in two ways. On a basic level they were a source of knowledge of the classical systems, mainly Aristotelianism and Neoplatonism. On a higher level they served as a paradigm of systematic treatment and a stimulus to further reflection, particularly as regards the relationship between philosophy and faith. Here, the problems in the Jewish and Christian contexts were similar and partly shared.

The earliest figure of note from the western viewpoint was the Egyptian, Isaac Israeli (d. *c.* 955). He is usually held to have been the first Jewish Neoplatonist thinker. He was also a medical writer and it was as such that he was regarded by Maimonides, who dismissed his claims as a philosopher.[26] Certainly he was unoriginal but his *Book of Definitions*, translated at least twice into Latin, was a secondary source for such theories as Aristotelian causation, the Neoplatonist concepts of 'Intelligence' and 'Nature' and the Platonic doctrine on the soul.[27]

The first and most original Jewish synthesiser was the Spaniard, Solomon Ibn Gabirol (*c.* 1021–58), known to the west as Avicebron. His *Fountain of Life* (*Fons Vitae*), in five books, was a concentrated argument cast in dialogue form expounding Neoplatonist doctrine. It contained no internal evidence that its author was a Jew and it did not expressly deal with religious dogma. However, Avicebron's firm ontological distinction between God and created being and his analysis of the process of creation were important modifications of Neoplatonism in favour of Jewish belief. Avicebron saw created being, considered without further specification, as constituted of 'universal matter' and 'universal form'.[28] The theory did not imply that all created being was corporeal. It served to distinguish created being from the Creator, who was perfectly simple and unitary. Corporeal being was constituted by a common, unspecific form, the form of being a body. In addition to this common form, all corporeal beings had forms proper to the various levels of activity which characterised their species.

Besides making this ontological distinction between God and creatures, Avicebron stressed the contingency of creation. In this he may be compared with Avicenna. However, where Avicenna saw the contingency as theoretical, for Avicebron it was real. The basis of this contingency is the divine will, which Avicebron treats almost as if it were a separate divine being. Will is a divine power 'constituting and moving all things'; it is that 'retaining and sustaining the essence of all things'; it is a power 'creating the intelligible substances' and 'making matter and form and binding them together'. 'Nothing exists without it, since from it is the being of all things and their constitution.'[29] Will is thus interposed between Creator and creation. Its role is to correct the Neoplatonist schema of necessary emanation in favour of divine freedom and purpose.

To the extent that the *Fountain of Life* reconciled Neoplatonist cosmology with the requirements of Jewish belief, it did so tacitly. It contained no explicit treatment of the problem of relating pagan thought to a revealed religion. This problem is the theme of the best-known work of medieval Jewish thought, the *Guide of the Perplexed* by Moses Maimonides (1135–1204). Maimonides was born at Cordova, like his contemporary, Averroes, but was forced into exile in Egypt in his early twenties by the intolerance towards non-Moslems of the new Almohad rulers of Spain. The *Guide* was written in Egypt but its philosophical perceptions seem to reflect the cultural background of Spain and Maimonides may have derived his interest in the central problem which it tackles from similar debates in western Islam. It is not formally a philosophical work, though it contains much philosophical teaching. It sets out to explain to a Jewish reader, already versed in philosophy, the true meaning of difficult terms and passages in Scripture, which might otherwise give rise to an intellectual tension between the promptings of intellect and the apparent demands of the Law. This is the perplexity to which the title alludes and the purpose of the work is to resolve it by showing the essential compatibility of Scripture and philosophy. It is an esoteric discussion avowedly cloaked in obscurity so as to be inaccessible to more than a sophisticated elite. Not only are philosophy and religion compatible but study of philosophy is seen by Maimonides as a duty imposed by the fact that knowledge is the precondition for love and that apprehension of nature is the preparation for true worship of God.[30] Furthermore, knowledge or more particularly 'acquisition of the rational virtues . . . the conception of intelligibles, which teach true opinions concerning divine things' is the individual's 'true perfection' which gives him 'permanent perdurance'.[31] The Aristotelian influence cannot be missed here but there is also perhaps a hint of the insistence on enlightenment as a precondition of immortality evinced by Al Farabi, for whom Maimonides had a high regard. Maimonides' own views on the philosophical grounds for immortality are difficult to decipher. He seems to accept that intellects, though immortal, do not have individual differences, a view for which he quotes the authority of Avempace.[32] However, he does not treat the subject as a major issue between philosophy and religion. As regards the eternity of the world, which had been a vexed question in Islam as it was later to be in the west, Maimonides held it to be a possibility and cautioned that proof of God's existence should not rest on the proposition that the world was created in time. In this respect he anticipated the views of St Thomas Aquinas who maintained a similar position, probably under Maimonides' influence.

II   Western Translations

Translation into Latin of the philosophical works of Aristotle and of the Arabic philosophers and commentators whom we have been considering took place over more than a century and was accomplished by scholars of various provenance. The process is conveniently described under two aspects: translation from Greek and translation from Arabic.

The greatest figure of the Graeco-Latin movement in the twelfth century is James of Venice. As noted already, he was responsible for completing and partially revising the Graeco-Latin corpus of Aristotle's logical treatises.[33] Besides this important contribution, he translated (c. 1125–50) the *Physics* – with an anonymous introduction to it, called *On Intelligence* (*De intelligentia*) – the *De Anima*, the *Metaphysics*, at least in part,[34] and five of the lesser scientific treatises of Aristotle, known as the *Parva Naturalia* (the 'small works on nature'). James points to the importance of the Mediterranean world, and probably of Constantinople, as a source of extended knowledge of the Greek tradition. From this world too came the only medieval translations of Plato – Henricus Aristippus' versions of the *Meno* and *Phaedo* (the latter begun in 1156), the dialogues in which Plato developed his doctrine of the soul, its immortality, pre-existence and recollection of the Forms. Henricus Aristippus appears as archdeacon of Catania in Sicily in 1156 and as a representative of the king of Sicily at Constantinople in 1158. In 1160 he became the king's chief minister. Of Aristotle, he translated only Book IV of the *Meteorology*. The identity of the other Graeco-Latin translators of the century is not known. A version of the *Physics* was made anonymously about the middle of the century but it survives only in small part and in a single manuscript.[35] Another anonymous worker rendered *On Coming to Be and Passing Away* (*De generatione et corruptione*), more or less contemporaneously with an Arabo-Latin translation of the same treatise. Another provided an almost complete translation of the *Metaphysics*, the version known as the 'middle *Metaphysics*' from its chronological place in the transmission of this text. Yet another provided Books II and III of the *Nicomachean Ethics*, the text known as the 'old Ethics'. Thus, by the end of the twelfth century a considerable amount of Aristotle's philosophical writings had been translated directly. It was little used, however, before about the second quarter of the thirteenth century. The 'middle Metaphysics', for instance, apparently remained unknown until the middle of the thirteenth century, a fact which explains the ready demand for the Arabo-Latin version of Michael the Scot. Nor was the corpus of Graeco-Latin translations of Aristotle much enlarged in the interval. Someone did render the whole of the *Nicomachean Ethics* in the early thirteenth century but only Book I circulated, being known accordingly as the 'new Ethics'. From about the middle of the century, however, there was a transformation. By now the translations of James of Venice were circulating widely. Moreover, new and improved versions were in hand or were soon to be made. Robert Grosseteste, bishop of Lincoln and formerly, as is thought, first chancellor of Oxford university, translated the *Nicomachean Ethics* (c. ?1246). His version, with some revisions, became the standard text. He also translated Aristotle's *De Caelo* ('On the heaven') – perhaps completely, though only a fragment survives – a commentary on it by the sixth-century commentator, Simplicius, two spurious Aristotelian treatises and the works of the pseudo-Denis, on which he commented himself.[36] Among his assistants were an Englishman, John of Basingstoke, who had studied in Athens, and Master Nicholas the Greek, a Sicilian who became a member of Grosseteste's household c. 1237. But the most important translator of the century was the Dominican, William of Moerbeke (c. 1215–86), a native of the Low Countries, who travelled and worked in Greece and in central Italy and died as archbishop of Corinth. Mainly in the years c. 1260–70, he made new translations or revisions of texts of Aristotle already available or partly available in Graeco-Latin versions. He also enlarged the corpus by adding the *Politics*, which was as yet quite unknown, and the *Poetics* – on literary theory – the teaching of which was already known through Hermannus Alemannus' translation of Averroes' middle commentary. His achievement was fundamental. With a few exceptions – the *Poetics*, for which Averroes' commentary continued as the most influential source, the logical works, for which the old translations remained authoritative, and Grosseteste's *Ethics*, the more influential, revised version of which may itself be by Moerbeke – the medieval Latin texts of Aristotle were henceforward virtually those established by him. In addition to Aristotle, he translated several treatises of Proclus – statements on providence and on the nature of evil, a commentary on Plato's dialogue, the *Parmenides*, and, most notably, the *Elements of Theology*. He was therefore almost certainly the first to recognise the true attribution of the doctrine contained in the pseudo-Aristotelian *Book of Causes*, derived from it.[37] He also translated a body of ancient commentary on Aristotle: Alexander on the *Meteorology* and *De Sensu*, Ammonius (fifth century AD) on the *De Interpretatione*, Simplicius on the *Categories* and *De Caelo*, and, as part of the contemporary concern with determining Aristotle's psychological teaching, Themistius on the *De Anima* and the discussion of intellect by the sixth-century Alexandrian Mono-physite Christian, John Philoponus. The two last were translated in 1267 and 1268 respectively while Moerbeke was a chaplain at the papal court of Clement IV in Viterbo. Although there is no sound evidence that in any of this activity Moerbeke was being directed by his confrère, Thomas Aquinas, the latter as we shall see made early use of most of his translations.

While the long process of translation from the Greek was in train, there was a steady absorption into Latin of Aristotelian and Neoplatonist doctrine from Arabic. This took place mainly in the Spain of the Christian reconquest but Sicily too was an important centre. Like the southern coast of the Italian peninsula, the island had been anciently settled by Greek colonists. From 902 to 1091 it had been under Arab rule and there remained a considerable Moslem element after its conquest by the Normans. Its culture was thus a unique blend of Latin, Greek and Arabic strains.

The meeting of cultures in Spain attracted scholars from many parts of Europe. Among foreign translators known to have been active in the twelfth century are Hermann of Carinthia (*c.* 1138–43) and his pupil, Rudolf of Bruges, Hermann's contemporary and occasional colleague, Robert of Chester, Plato of Tivoli (*c.* 1134–45), Daniel of Morley (*c.* 1180), Alfred of Sareshel (*c.* 1180) and, most important of all, Gerard of Cremona (d. 1187). In the early years of the century, Adelard of Bath may have worked in Spain, as he did in southern Italy and in Syria. If so, he is one of a significant English contingent there. With Robert of Chester, Daniel of Morley and Alfred of

Sareshel, he played a part in the awakening of a scientific interest in England. Besides these foreign scholars there were several native figures, including the shadowy Petrus Alfonsi (c. 1115), Hugh of Santalla (c. 1135), John of Seville (c. 1130–40) and Dominic Gundisalvi (c. 1150–90).

The earliest phase of this activity was the translation of mathematical, medical and astronomical texts. It was carried on in a number of cities – Barcelona, Tarazona, Segovia, Leon and Pamplona. The most important translations from a philosophical viewpoint were those made in the middle and later years of the century at Toledo. Historians are now cautious about attributing them to a 'school' or otherwise going beyond the meagre evidence which exists for the methods used to produce them. A famous letter attached to the translation of Avicenna's psychology dedicates that work to Archbishop John of Toledo (c. 1152–66) and names the translators as Avendauth, a Jew of whom little else is certainly known, and Archdeacon Dominic, who is generally taken to be Gundisalvi. According to it, Avendauth translated word for word from Arabic into the vernacular and Dominic translated the vernacular word for word into Latin.[38] It is unsafe however to assume that this was the standard method of translation from Arabic to Latin. It is also unsafe to identify Avendauth with the 'John' who is found elsewhere as a collaborator, apparently with the same Dominic, in the translation of Al Ghazali's *Intentions of the Philosophers*, or to identify that 'John' with John of Seville.[39]

In fact, the Spanish translation movement in the twelfth century is full of unresolved problems. Attributions are subject to revision. However, a general picture emerges clearly enough to show the main lines of the process of transmission. Avicenna's psychology, referred to above, was an extract from the *Kitab al-Shifa*, its provenance being indicated in its alternative title, *Book of the Soul (Liber de Anima)* or *Sixth on Natural Phenomena (Sextus de Naturalibus)*. His metaphysics was similarly extracted and entitled *Book of First Philosophy or Divine Knowledge (Liber de Philosophia Prima sive Scientia Divina)*.[40] It was translated at Toledo after 1150 either by Gundisalvi or Gerard of Cremona. To them is also variously attributed the translation of Al Farabi's *On the intellect*. As noted already, Gundisalvi is credited with a share in the translation of Al Ghazali's *Intentions*. This had a complicated circulation: it was sometimes known as the *Summa of the Theory of Philosophy* and sections became separated as the 'Logic' and

'Philosophy' or 'Metaphysics' of Algazel.[41] Gundisalvi is credited too with a share in the translation of Ibn Gabirol's *Fountains of Life*. He may also be the author of several independent treatises, on cosmology and psychology, derived in part from the works of Al Farabi and Ibn Gabirol.[42] These were influential in the thirteenth century, especially for their arguments in favour of immortality. Gerard of Cremona by contrast appears only as a translator. Apart from the doubtful attributions referred to, he is credited with one of the two Latin translations of Al Kindi's *On the intellect*.[43] He has also the distinction of being the only known twelfth-century translator of Aristotle from the Arabic. His interests here seem to have been strictly in the scientific books: the *Meteorology* (Books i–iii); the *Physics*; *On the heaven* (*De caelo*); *On Coming to Be and Passing Away* (*De generatione et corruptione*); and the *Posterior Analytics*, which though a logical work was valued as an explanation of scientific theory.[44] Besides these genuine works he also translated the pseudo-Aristotelian *Book of Causes*.

Activity at Toledo continued into the thirteenth century. Hermannus Alemannus completed his translations of Averroes' middle commentaries on the *Nicomachean Ethics* and *Poetics* there in 1240 and 1256, respectively. The Latin translation of Maimonides' *Guide of the Perplexed*, from the Hebrew rather than the Arabic, was made there *c.* 1240. But the main extensions to the Latin world's knowledge of the Arabic tradition in the thirteenth century were carried out elsewhere. Michael the Scot is the principal figure. His earliest known connection indeed was with Toledo, where he translated an Arabic astronomical treatise, in 1217, and, shortly after, part of Aristotle's zoology (*De Animalibus*). In 1220 he appears in Italy and he seems to have done his main work there, dying in 1236 after several years as astrologer at the court of Frederick II in Sicily. Michael translated Averroes' great commentaries on the *Physics*, *De Caelo*, *De Anima* and *Metaphysics*. His translation of this last provided Latin readers with a valued text of Aristotle's work. The passages of the *Metaphysics*, preserved as lemmata in the commentary, were extracted and circulated as a continuous text (the 'new *Metaphysics*'). Though not complete, it was still the best available while the Graeco-Latin 'middle *Metaphysics*' remained unknown. The number of surviving manuscripts indicates a lively demand for it.[45] Michael is perhaps also the translator of several of Averroes' short and middle commentaries – the short commentaries on the *De Caelo*, the *Parva Naturalia* and the *De Animalibus* and the middle commentaries on *On Coming to Be and Passing Away* and on the *Meteorology* (Book IV). Of other translations of Averroes during the century may be noted William of Luna's rendering of the middle commentaries on most of the *Organon* and on Porphyry's *Isagoge*. William seems to have been a Spaniard but he worked in Naples; his precise dates are not known. Averroes' main independent work was not made available until the translation of the *Incoherence of the Incoherence* by Calo Calonymus at Arles in 1328, long after the reception of the commentaries had established him as both a corner-stone and a stumbling block of Latin Aristotelianism.[46]

III   New Institutions – the Rise of the Universities

Forms of Organisation

Over the same period that new sources were becoming available to western scholars, the structures of teaching and learning were being transformed by the rise of the universities.[47] From now until the Italian Renaissance and the advent of the Christian humanist movement in northern Europe in the fifteenth century they are the dominant feature of the intellectual scene. The earliest universities were spontaneous developments from the educational trends of the twelfth century. In its original, customary use, the term *studium generale* ('general centre of study'), eventually the most common medieval designation of a university, probably indicated the capacity of certain centres to attract students from beyond their immediate area. The first to emerge were the law schools of Bologna, the arts and theology schools at Paris and Oxford and, with a more doubtful claim, the medical school at Salerno. Of these, Salerno gave way to Montpellier as the leading medical centre but the others continued to be premier institutions within their principal disciplines. Later, universities were established by enactment: as with the creation of notaries public, the function attached peculiarly to the two universalist authorities, the empire and the papacy. By the end of the middle ages, it has been estimated,[48] Europe had some seventy universities, all but a handful of which were deliberate creations. Several of the already existing *studia generalia* had their status ratified under this procedure. However, their original status was a simple recognition of acquired prestige and the emergence of formal structures for the organisation and protection of the *studium* was equally a spontaneous response to circumstances. The response varied according to local conditions. This is clearly seen in the case of the two prototype universities – the students' university, or rather universities, of Bologna, and the masters' university of Paris. The history of their development illustrates the essential nature of the medieval university.

The history of the Bologna *studium* in particular reveals clearly the nature of the 'university' as at once a monopolistic professional association and an organisation for the protection of its members. In Bologna, the tension between the predominant element of the academic body, the foreign or non-citizen students, and the civic context resulted in the development of a startling constitution. The students gained the controlling power, which they exercised through their elected representatives – rectors and councillors – and through their mass meetings or congregations. Though this constitution was imitated elsewhere – notably at Padua, where it lasted longer, and in several of the fifteenth-century French provincial and Spanish foundations – it was uniquely indigenous to Bologna.

A principal expression of the twelfth-century renaissance in central Italy was the vigorous concentration on Roman civil law. Its most famous early exponent was Irnerius, who taught at Bologna between 1116 and 1140 and whose reputation was possibly the crucial factor in determining the location of the main Italian law *studium* there.[49] The special governmental features of an Italian city state themselves fostered a concentration on civil law. At the same time, they posed problems for an emergent *studium generale*, drawing the bulk of its student population from outside the commune, for such students had no rights of citizenship. Moreover, since civil law was particularly attractive to laymen, for whom it opened up a lucrative career, there was a community in Bologna unprotected either by citizenship or by clerical privilege. The special vulnerability of foreign lay students as well as the Hohenstaufen political interest in cultivating Roman law study is reflected in the Authentic *Habita* of Emperor Frederick Barbarossa, issued in 1158. Besides according the student a general protection, this decree gave him the right of trial at his choice by either his doctor or the bishop, as an alternative to the podestà of the commune. One feature of the Authentic is that its natural tendency would be to convert the original contractual bond between masters and students into a stronger, jurisdictional one and make the masters the natural defenders of academic freedom. However, this was counterbalanced by the fact that the commune began to require an oath from the masters to restrict their teaching to Bologna, a manoeuvre aimed at depriving the *studium* of mobility. This development, dating from about 1189, is seen as crucial and it was followed within a few years by the emergence of the student guilds or 'universities'. At an early stage, there were four of these – Lombards, Tuscans, Romans and Ultramontanes – but by the middle of the thirteenth century they had resolved into two: the university of citramontanes, for 'foreign' law students of the Italian peninsula, and the university of ultramontanes, for law students from beyond the Alps. These acted as communal bargaining groups both with the masters, over fees and the general regulation of the academic life, and with the commune. The latter by 1252 had accorded them full recognition as the competent authority within the *studium*.

Whereas Bologna is the archetype of the student university and of the law *studium*, Paris represents the masters' university and the arts and theological *studium*. Theology was taught at Bologna, mainly by the friars, but it was not incorporated into the university system. The germ of the Paris *studium* was the cathedral school of Notre Dame. It was the chancellor of Notre Dame who licensed teachers, though his claim to a licensing monopoly was challenged by the abbot of St Geneviève. The precise aspect of tension between town and gown which promoted the formation of the guilds at Bologna was absent here for both masters and students had clerical status, as confirmed by Pope Celestine III in 1194 and King Philip Augustus in 1200. In Paris, the threat to academic independence came from the same source which had fostered the development of the *studium* in the first place – the chancellor of the cathedral. Moreover, the problem affected masters rather than students. Hence the emergence of a masters' guild or 'university', known from the last quarter of the twelfth century. This guild succeeded, with the aid of a decree of the Third Lateran Council (1179), in carrying its point that the chancellor should license all qualified candidates without charge. At this stage, the chancellor still determined the qualification of a candidate for licensing and the corporate identity of the masters who by the subsequent ceremony of inception controlled entry into their guild was a check on the use of his prerogative. The statutes granted to them by the papal legate, Robert de Courcon, in 1215, recognised their right generally to control the *studium*, short of dissolving it. For his part, the chancellor was required to license any candidate in the higher faculties of theology, canon law and medicine who was presented by a majority of the masters and any candidate in arts who had the support of six masters. A dispersal by the masters in 1229 over a dispute between town and gown ended in a broader settlement which confirmed and augmented their privileges against chancellor and bishop. This settlement was enshrined in the papal bull *Parens scientiarum* ('Parent of sciences') of 1231, which is taken as the symbol of the university's effective independence.

During this early and critical stage of its development, the university enjoyed the advantage of continuous papal support. In the problem which it confronted immediately after the settlement with the chancellor, this support was lacking and the university initially failed in its object. The fresh crisis arose over the emergence of an important new element in the teaching system – the mendicant friars, particularly the Franciscans and Dominicans, founded in 1209 and 1215 respectively. The friars' schools at Paris served as centres of study in theology for the ablest members of the orders throughout the provinces. Accordingly they insisted that their members who had already taken an arts training elsewhere be exempt from the general requirement at Paris that entrants to the higher faculties should first be masters of arts and thereby members of the masters' guild. There were other grounds of friction. The mendicants had remained at Paris during the dispersal of 1229–31 and by opening their schools to seculars had strengthened their position in the theology faculty, which they were for a time to dominate. In 1253 matters came to a head when the university stipulated that masters in all faculties swear obedience to its statutes, including the important obligation of taking strike action by ceasing to teach if called upon. When the mendicant masters again refused to cooperate they were expelled from the university. Pope Alexander IV, elected in December 1254, took their part and when they were readmitted in 1261 it was with a diminished position in the theology faculty but otherwise on the same terms as before.

The university of Paris consisted of four faculties – arts, theology, canon law and medicine – each with its own internal organisation. The arts faculty was by far the most populous and it succeeded in establishing itself as the predominant voice in the university. It alone, because of its size, was divided into nations – French, Norman, Picard and English–German. The rector of these nations from the second half of the thirteenth century was recognised as head, under the chancellor, of the university, though he had no authority to interfere in the affairs of the superior faculties. In the general congregation of the university, each nation of the arts faculty and each of the superior faculties had one vote and a simple majority was decisive. Since the congregation at Paris, being a much smaller institution than its counterpart at Bologna, played a principal role in the direction of the *studium*, the arts faculty had an effective controlling interest.

The Structure of Studies

The structure of studies in the universities varied from one institution to another and within the same institution at different stages of its development. It is impossible therefore to do more than present a composite picture, reflecting the basic features of the system in its maturity. The central feature of the programme was the 'lecture', or expository reading, based on the prescribed books of the syllabus. In the law universities these were the texts of Roman or canon law. In the theology faculties they were the Bible and the *Sentences* of Peter Lombard. In the arts faculties they were the trivium, with its expanded logical content, parts of the quadrivium, though this was sometimes totally neglected, and the philosophical works of Aristotle, as these came to be approved. The staple lectures were those given 'ordinarily', by the regent masters – masters who had completed the full course, had incepted and now remained to teach, or 'rule the schools', either in accordance with their statutory obligation, discharging their 'necessary regency', or by choice. The ordinary lectures were supplemented by 'cursory' lectures, given by bachelors at times when the masters were not lecturing. The bachelor's cursory lectures served a double function: they inculcated the text on students and they provided the future master with a forum in which to develop his own expertise. Conferral of the 'degree' of bachelor was in the masters' universities the prerogative of the regents. In the Bolognese system it was controlled by the students. In both cases the masters controlled admission to their own ranks. In the masters' universities the procedure was as follows: after completing all the statutory exercises, including participation in disputations as well as lecturing, the bachelor was given leave to incept. There followed an interval of six months or a year, varying from one university to another, until the inceptor proceeded to the public acts which marked the commencement of his magistracy. These were in two stages: a disputation in the evening (the *vesperiae*) and another the next day. After incepting, the new master was bound to a period of regency lasting one or two years, the time varying between different universities and faculties. The process was a lengthy one for those students who completed the full programme or who followed a degree in arts with a degree in a higher faculty. Though again there were variations, the magistracy in arts might take six years, followed by a necessary regency. The magistracy in theology, for instance, might take a further ten to fourteen years. At Paris, the bachelor in this faculty, who must be at least twenty-five years old and have studied theology for seven or eight years, was admitted to lecture first on the Bible for two years. He then became a bachelor of the *Sentences*, lecturing on the Lombard's text for two years or later for one. At Oxford, lecturing on the *Sentences* preceded lecturing on the Bible.

One function of the master was to lecture. Another was to hold formal disputations. These were of two kinds: 'ordinary' disputations on a specific theme ('disputed questions') and the free questions or 'quodlibets'. The first type may have had its origin in the less formalised analysis of problems arising from the texts. It was a major part of the teaching programme and was conducted at frequent intervals – 'disputable days' – throughout the year. The 'quodlibet' (literally, 'whatever you will') was an opportunity to explore matters of current topicality and its incidence was restricted to two seasons – specific weeks in Advent and Lent. In the disputation, a problem was posed, a 'respondent' bachelor or advanced student, at least, tried to resolve it and to deal with criticisms of his solution and finally the master gave his views or 'determination'. In time, the determination tended to become separate from the process of disputation.

In essence, lecturing and disputing were oral exercises but their respective methods of textual exposition and dialectical presentation of issues became the basis of a substantial body of theological and philosophical writing. The disputation is well represented in the surviving literature, both in the form of texts approved by the master himself – 'authorised texts' or *ordinationes* – and in the form of unrevised notes of the proceedings – 'reported texts' or *reportationes*. In either case these may be of ordinary or of quodlibetal disputations. The influence of the disputation is clear also in works which were not themselves the direct products of university teaching, as in St Thomas Aquinas' *Summa Theologiae* ('*Summa* of Theology'), whose method is the posing of a question, the presentation of difficulties and their resolution. The most important literature of speculative theology generated by university lecturing is the *Commentary on the Sentences*, extant usually in an edited form for many late medieval theologians. The disputations of the arts faculty are sometimes referred to as 'sophismata' (literally 'sophisms') because the discussion and resolution of logical problems was a major feature of them. The lecturing technique of the arts faculty both directly and by imitation has left a very large literature of philosophical commentary.

5. Aristotelian Philosophy in the University – the First Phase of Assimilation

ARISTOTLE's thought, both in its own right and as interpreted in the Neoplatonist and Arabic traditions, contained several areas of special interest and sensitivity for Christians. Among the problems posed by his *Physics* and *Metaphysics* were the nature of causation, in particular the compatibility of his analysis with the idea of a free creation and of a contingent universe, whether he had taught that the world was eternal and whether, if he had, this error could be refuted philosophically.

The questions posed by his psychological theory were especially important and difficult. They revolved round the nature of soul and of intellect. The relation of soul and body raised a complex of problems, of which three were central. Could the soul of man be considered at once as a substantial form in the true Aristotelian sense and as an entity capable of surviving the death of the body? In the composition of soul and body what was the principle from which man's individuality derived? Should the various operations of the higher species of life – possessed of sensation and, in the case of man, rationality, as well as the capacity to grow and reproduce – be attributed to a plurality of souls coexisting within the organism or should they be regarded as faculties of one soul?[1] A related question concerned the origin of soul. From a theological perspective all were agreed that the rational soul – whether as a single substantial form with sensitive and vegetative powers or as the final perfection supervening upon separate, lower forms – was directly created. Within this agreement, there was a wide range of views as to the stage at which the rational soul was infused into the organism, most opinion favouring a late entry. However, there was disagreement as to whether lesser souls were also directly created or were produced in the natural process of generation.

There was also a complex of problems bearing on intellection. Was abstraction from sense experience a sufficient explanation of all our concepts? How did abstraction work? Were concepts derived by the agency of the soul itself or must they be referred to an external source? In other words, was the active intellect of which Aristotle had spoken a power of the soul or was it something influencing the soul from outside? Al Farabi and Avicenna had taken the latter view and were clearly understood to have done so. Averroes had gone a stage further and had made both the active and passive aspects of intellection external to the soul, with devastating consequences for the philosophical basis of individual immortality. However, his theory was at first misunderstood by his Latin readers. His description of the operation of the agent intellect led some to think that he made it part of the soul.[2] Paradoxically, therefore, the effect of Averroism in its first phase, from 1230 to *c.* 1250, was to promote the doctrine of the agent intellect as a power of the soul. It did not engender that doctrine, which can be seen some ten years before the reception of Averroes' works at Paris in the treatise *On the powers of the soul* (*De potentiis animae et obiectis*), written by an English master *c.* 1220. This presented Augustinian 'illumination' and Aristotelian 'abstraction' as two operations, higher and lower respectively, of the human intellect and seems to have been an important influence in the direction of maintaining the intellectual integrity of the soul.[3] The mistaken interpretation of Averroes to the same effect was therefore congenial to and in all probability largely prompted by a theory already current.[4]

Finally, there were problems stemming from Aristotle's *Ethics*, such as the nature of happiness, man's capacity to attain it and whether the will was determined by knowledge – that is, whether the maxim that all human action was directed towards the achievement of a good which was perceived entailed an intellectual determinism incompatible with freedom of will. The relationship between intellect and will also raised theological problems, particularly regarding divine freedom in creation. These topics were often to be debated, especially in the later middle ages, under the abstruse and at first sight highly remote question whether the intellect or the will was supreme.

The attempt to reconcile the claims of Christian teaching and of Aristotelian philosophy in these areas is one of the most prominent and most interesting preoccupations of the great systematic thinkers of the thirteenth century, St Bonaventure and St Thomas Aquinas. But the same themes and problems recur, with varying degrees of emphasis and often tackled piecemeal, in the work of lesser figures both in the arts and theology faculties throughout the period. Inevitably, the reconciliation between the Aristotelian and Christian dimensions was on some points an uneasy one, involving transformations of perspective which disturbed conservative minds and invited censure from authority. However, there was an intellectual penalty to be paid for failure to maintain a synthetic approach. This was the sundering of unity between the philosophical and theological planes with a resulting agnosticism in the face of theological issues, an agnosticism founded not upon unbelief but upon the assertion that faith and revelation alone afforded the basis for understanding the relationship between God and man. The threat will become real only after the close of our period but already it is evident in the tensions which begin to be felt in the first three-quarters of the thirteenth century.

The Influence of Aristotle in the West to c. *1250*

Little is known about the earliest phase of the reception of Aristotle's philosophical works at Paris. The first substantial evidence of their impact is indirect. In 1210 the provincial synod of Sens, of which the bishop of Paris was a member, issued a condemnation of two minor thinkers, Amaury of Bène and David of Dinant, and a number of named clerics who are otherwise unknown. The tenet with which Amaury and David are associated is pantheism, failure to distinguish between the universe and God. It was not an Aristotelian position, though it could perhaps be loosely derived from the Neoplatonist emanation theory of the *Book of Causes*, still at this time part of the Aristotelian corpus, or from a Neoplatonist elaboration of Aristotle's authentic works. In fact, Amaury's principal authority was the *Periphyseon* of John Scotus Eriugena, which was condemned with Amaury's own doctrine at the Fourth Lateran Council in 1215. David of Dinant, whose thought has been reconstructed in part from the strictures of Albert the Great against him and from fragments of his writings, did use the *Physics* and *Metaphysics* of Aristotle.[5] At all events, the condemnation at Sens was extended to include the stipulation that 'neither the books of Aristotle on natural philosophy nor the commentaries shall be read (*legantur*) at Paris publicly or secretly and this we forbid under penalty of excommunication'.[6] The effect of this decree was incorporated in the statutes promulgated for the university by the papal legate, Robert de Courcon, in 1215. Regulating the syllabus of the arts faculty, he repeated the ban on Aristotle's 'books of metaphysics and of natural philosophy' the '*Summae* upon them' and the 'doctrine of Master David of Dinant and of Amaury, the heretic' and added the name of 'Maurice of Spain' (*Mauricii hispani*).[7]

The identity of this last figure has been much discussed but remains unknown. One suggested explanation of the name is that it is a corruption of 'Spanish Moor' (*Maurus hispanus*), in which case the reference would be to Averroes. If so, the measure was perhaps preventive since it was another decade before the works of Averroes are known to have been received at Paris. The *Summae* or commentaries referred to are generally taken to be the works of Avicenna.

Several points must be noted about these early prohibitions. First, they were local to Paris. Other universities were not affected. Indeed, the university of Toulouse in 1229 was advertising as one of its advantages the fact that 'those who wish to scrutinise nature's bosom to the marrow may there hear the books [of] natural [philosophy] which were prohibited at Paris'.[8] Study of the philosophical works continued unimpeded at Oxford throughout the period to 1277 and there will be occasion later to notice their free study in the arts faculty at Naples. Secondly, the prohibition on 'reading' is best understood to refer to reading in the sense of lecturing rather than to personal use. Thirdly, the prohibition seems to have been felt in the arts faculty rather than in the theology faculty at Paris. It may well be that its origin lies in an incipient tension between the two faculties such as was to come to a head in the years 1270–7.[9] Certainly, one of its effects was to retard the penetration of Aristotelian scientific doctrine among the arts masters, as is shown by the evidence in so far as it exists of their activity in the period up to *c*. 1240.

One of the most valuable documents for assessing the state of teaching in the Paris arts faculty at this time is a 'crib' to aid students preparing for examination, composed by a master of arts around 1230–40.[10] From this, it is clear that the staple fare then was logic and grammar. Of Aristotle's philosophy, the *Ethics* alone (both the 'new' and 'old' *Ethics*) was examined in detail, though a general knowledge of the subject of the *Physics* and *Metaphysics* was expected, of such a kind as to confirm that these books were not taught.

The impression gained from this source is corroborated by what is known of the teaching directly. The most important writing in the area of grammar and logic comes in fact from just after 1240. This is the *Logical Textbooks* (*Summulae Logicales*) of Peter of Spain, which is assigned with probability to his period as a master of arts at Paris a little before 1246. A pupil of the English master, William of Shireswood, who also wrote on the subject, Peter went on after a further period teaching at Siena to become archbishop of Braga in

Portugal and, briefly, pope as John XXI (1276-May, 1277). His *Summulae*, one among several works of its kind by himself and others, established itself as a standard textbook for the rest of the middle ages.[11] It combined the techniques derived from Aristotle's *Organon* with a close attention to language as a vehicle of meaning. The properties of terms and the modes of signification became the focus of attention for logicians who were thoroughly accomplished in all that Aristotle's *Organon* could teach them. Although the emphasis was new and to that extent merited the description 'logic of the moderns' (*logica modernorum*) by which the development came to be known, the interest itself was not new. It has already been noted as a feature of the earlier period. Nor was the terminist logic at first overtly speculative. However, when the great task of absorbing Aristotle and his commentators was complete the development served as a fresh stimulus and to an extent provided a new vocabulary and new rules for philosophical discourse.

Besides logic, the surviving literature of the arts faculty at this time reflects study of Aristotle's *Ethics*.[12] This work was not affected by the prohibition. However, the interpretation given to Aristotle's doctrine was heavily conditioned by a theological perspective. This at least is the evidence of a surviving fragment of a course given by an arts master, *c*. 1235–40, on the 'new' *Ethics* – that is, on Book I of the *Nicomachean Ethics*.[13] In accordance with a doctrine otherwise known to have been current in the faculty, the master took the wholly unAristotelian position that happiness is something to which man unites himself rather than holding that it consists in an activity of man. In other words, happiness is identified with God. Aristotle's criticism of the Platonic doctrine of a 'subsistent Good' the master explained as being directed against an implication that man was capable by his own efforts of uniting himself with the good. The doctrine, that is, which Aristotle had rejected was the denial that grace was necessary for happiness![14] This and some other aspects of the master's interpretation is a warning against identifying too readily the reading of Aristotle with the absorption of his teaching. As already noted in the case of Averroes, the first reaction to an unfamiliar position might be a confused attempt to accommodate it within the existing outlook.

Allowing for occasional breaches of the prohibition, which are known of only indirectly,[15] the evidence such as it is agrees in suggesting that until about 1240 Aristotle's natural philosophy was not taught in Paris. When the change came it seems not to have been as a result of a revocation of the ban. Gregory IX had repeated it in 1231 to the effect that the forbidden works should not be 'used' until they had been examined and purged of all suspicion of error and had established a commission, of which nothing more is heard, for the purpose.[16] Indeed in 1245, just when it was falling into disuse in Paris, the ban as reformulated by Gregory was extended by Innocent IV, as part of the Paris statutes, to the university of Toulouse which had so far rejoiced in its liberty.[17] Moreover, as late as 1263 it reappeared for Paris, probably as a diplomatic fossil, in a bull of Urban IV.[18] However, by the time at least of Roger Bacon's magistracy in arts at Paris, which fell within the period 1240 to 1247, the constraint was no longer felt. Bacon was probably not the first to lecture on the scientific works there after the prohibition. He may, for instance, have been preceded in this by Robert Kilwardby, the later archbishop of Canterbury, who had been regent in arts at Paris in the late 1230s and early 1240s.[19] The matter is not certain but Bacon was without doubt one of the first in the field, leaving extant commentaries from this time on the *Metaphysics*, *Physics*, *On coming to be and passing away*, the zoology, the *De Anima*, *On the heaven and earth*, the pseudo-Aristotelian work *On Plants* (*De Plantis*) and the *Book of Causes*.[20]

The breadth of Bacon's teaching is a valuable if puzzling witness to the progress of Aristotelianism in Paris at this time. A few years later, the *de facto* recognition of the prohibited Aristotle to which his regency attests finds a limited formal confirmation. In 1252, new statutes promulgated for the English–German nation – one of the four groupings within the arts faculty – made Aristotle's *De Anima* required reading, along with the traditional texts of logic and grammar. Then, unambiguously and definitively, in 1255, an act of the entire faculty listed as part of the programme all the available philosophical works – the important item still missing from the corpus being the *Politics* – together with several pseudo-Aristotelian treatises, including the *Book of Causes*. Probably the intention of the act was not to innovate but to regulate existing practice and to ensure uniformity in the syllabus.[21]

It is unsafe to attribute the fact of Bacon's commenting on the scientific works at Paris or the content of his commentaries to the influence of a scientific tradition at Oxford, reaching back to the twelfth century and now reinforced by the unfettered study of Aristotelian philosophy. For one thing, the details of Bacon's early

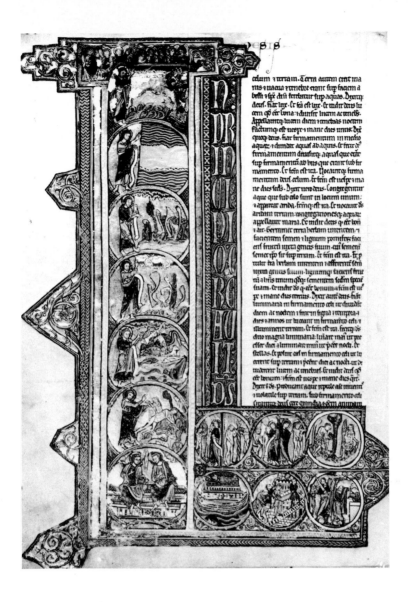

1. Genesis initial, showing the creation. (Thirteenth century)

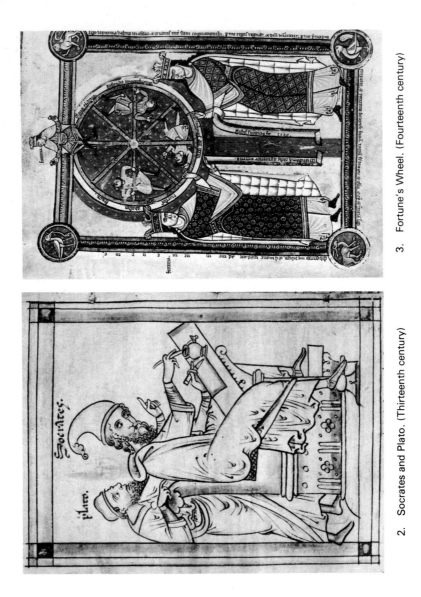

3. Fortune's Wheel. (Fourteenth century)

2. Socrates and Plato. (Thirteenth century)

studies are very imperfectly known.[22] For another, it has not been shown that the English scholars who had contact with Spain in the twelfth century were associated with an Oxford school. As regards the first decades of the thirteenth century, there is some evidence, though by no means abundant, for the progress of Aristotelianism at Oxford. One name of importance is that of John Blund, who was born probably c. 1175. It is not known whether he studied arts at Paris or at Oxford; perhaps the former is more likely. After a brief regency at Oxford before the strike of 1209 there, he taught at Paris where he began to study theology, becoming a master in that faculty c. 1220. As a result of the strike in Paris in 1229 he returned to Oxford to teach theology. His treatise *On the Soul* (*De Anima*) is the work of a master of arts rather than of a theologian.[23] It is overtly based on Aristotle, from whom there are many quotations, but it is Aristotle as interpreted by Avicenna, whom John follows in emphasising the substantiality of the soul and its capacity for independent existence. A later figure, almost exactly contemporary with Bacon himself, is Adam Buckfield, whose commentaries on several of Aristotle's scientific works survive.[24] In addition, Adam Marsh, who is otherwise known only as a theologian, was respected by Bacon as an expert in the natural sciences and in languages.[25]

The greatest representative of Aristotelianism at Oxford, however, was Robert Grosseteste (1170/75–1253), whose activity as a translator has been noticed earlier.[26] Grosseteste began to study Aristotle's philosophical works after c. 1220, when he was already a theologian of standing.[27] In common with other thinkers of the period, his view of Aristotle was heavily influenced by the Neoplatonism of the commentators. This is very clear as regards his understanding of Aristotle's theory of the soul, where Grosseteste accepted broadly the interpretation of Avicenna in taking the soul to be a substance in its own right.[28] In epistemology, he accepted the theory of abstraction but combined it with the Augustinian theory of illumination, at least in so far as it made God the ultimate source of intelligibility.[29] As regards Aristotle's *Physics*, he recognised clearly the doctrine of the eternity of the world and wrote against it in a treatise *On Finitude* (*De Finitate*).[30] In view of the preoccupations of contemporaries these are important points on which to note his reactions to Aristotelianism. But the most interesting meeting between Aristotelianism and Grosseteste's general outlook was in a more technical area of cosmology as explored by his famous metaphysics of light.

The theory was expounded principally in the treatise *On Light* (*De Luce*), written *c.* 1225–8. Its sources are partly biblical – Genesis, as interpreted notably by St Augustine and by St Basil, the fourth-century Greek Father, whose *Hexaemeron* (*Work on the Six Days of Creation*) Grosseteste read; partly philosophical – the Neoplatonist emanation theory, absorbed probably through the *Book of Causes* and Avicebron, and the notion of a form of corporeality which Grosseteste identifies with light; and partly scientific, with influences from Arabian astronomy, from alchemy and, characteristically, from mathematics.[31] All these strands are combined with principles derived from Aristotle to produce a cosmology whose distinctiveness rests on two main features, the concept of light and the appeal to mathematics. The production of the spheres is attributed to the radiation of light. The spheres themselves, thirteen in number, are a hierarchy; the outermost sphere is most rarefied, the innermost – that of the earth – is most dense. The assertion of a common principle binding the heavens and the earth was at odds with Aristotle's system in which the heavens are composed of a fifth element, ether, qualitatively different from the four elements of the sublunar world. However, although Grosseteste was evidently ill at ease with Aristotle's account and seems to have been conscious of his own originality,[32] he did not find it necessary to break with Aristotle completely. His cosmology in fact blends the two ideas. So, despite the fact that light is common to the spheres, the qualitative gap which separates the superlunary and sublunary world of Aristotle's system is maintained. The four lowest spheres are the elemental regions of fire, air, water and earth, in descending order of rarefaction, and, as in Aristotle, are alone subject to generation and corruption. The second distinctive feature of Grosseteste's cosmology is his appreciation of mathematics as the key to understanding the universe. His universe is, of course, unAristotelian in that it is the product of a free act of divine creation. But the real novelty is his conceiving God as a mathematician, an idea reminiscent of Plato's portrayal of the Craftsman in the *Timaeus*. Like Plato, Grosseteste saw the universe as constructed on numerical and geometrical principles. It is not useful to compare his outlook with that of a modern scientist. Nor is it necessary to do so in order to appreciate that his emphasis on the quantitative aspect is notable of its time.[33]

This is a convenient point at which to notice another attempt to reorientate scientific method, since although it falls outside the period under discussion it may have been prompted in part by Grosseteste's example. Perhaps partly under the influence of Grosseteste, whom he greatly respected, Roger Bacon abandoned the method of his Paris commentaries in favour of an approach which centred on the study of languages and the use of mathematics, optics, alchemy, astrology and analysis of experience – mystical as well as sensory. His views were to be expounded in a series of treatises – the *Opus Maius* (*Greater Work*), the *Opus Minus* (*Lesser Work*) and the *Opus Tertium* (*Third Work*) – written in 1266–7 in an unsuccessful attempt to secure papal patronage for a reorganisation of the programme of learning. Bacon's was an eccentric and at times incoherent genius but his intellectual acumen was shrewd; though himself a pioneer in the introduction of the Aristotelian treatises to the university curriculum and a great admirer of Aristotle, he was quick to see the danger of confining the curriculum to a narrow exposition of authority.

While the arts faculty at Paris had been moving slowly towards a study of Aristotle's philosophical works, members of the theology faculty had been absorbing the new material and applying it in their teaching. The *Summa Aurea* (*Golden Summa*) of William of Auxerre, written about 1220, is an early example of the process. It is of considerable interest for its transitional quality, combining as it does a knowledge – necessarily partial – of Aristotelian philosophy and a recognition of some of the problems which the latter posed, with preoccupations which will soon appear anachronistic. The *Summa* follows the order of material in the *Sentences* of Peter Lombard. Books I and II provide the main topics for assessing William's philosophical outlook. In Book I he deals with the relations between reason and faith, the knowability of God and proofs of his existence. As regards the last, he uses the argument from causality and the impossibility of an infinite series of causes.[34] He also adopts St Anselm's proof, both in its own right and in a developed way: the idea of the highest or best, he suggests, must include the possession of all perfections, including 'being'.[35] Later, in a manner which recalls so much twelfth-century theology, he tries to demonstrate rationally the doctrine of the Trinity. He then deals with God as creator and the relationship between the world and the divine ideas. In his explanation of creation he is evidently much influenced by the Neoplatonist perspective. Thus, he uses the term 'outflowing' (*fluere*) to describe the production.[36] But he is at pains to confute a principal aspect of the Neoplatonist account, according to which the One was separated from the world by a series of intermediate effects.[37] He also rejects the opinion, which he knows to be Aristotle's, that the world is eternal. He rejects too Plato's teaching that the world was made out of pre-existing material. Plato's error, he says, lay in his conceiving God as a human craftsman.[38] However, while William does thus address himself to problems posed by the cosmology of the ancient philosophers, it is significant of the contemporary climate and of his own perceptions of the intellectual threat faced by Christian theology that he pursues in much greater detail the Manichean analysis, the basis of the Cathar heresy in southern France. As may be expected, he relies heavily for his criticism of it on the arguments of St Augustine.[39]

William has absorbed something of the Aristotelian theory of knowledge from the *De Anima*[40] and is familiar with the theory of abstraction, current in the schools from the mid-twelfth century, but his own account of cognition is principally influenced by St Augustine. He seems to be uninterested in or only barely aware of the distinction between the several types of intellect. Similarly, he shows no sign of interest in the problems posed by the relationship between form and matter in the composition of man.

William of Auxerre was active in theological circles at Paris from at least 1219 until 1231 – the year of his death – when he was named by Gregory IX as one of the commission to examine Aristotle's works. He was, therefore, professionally a close contemporary of Philip the Chancellor. Philip had taught theology probably from before 1210 and in 1218 had become chancellor of the university. His *Summa de Bono* (*Summa on the Good*) was probably completed *c.* 1228.[41] William's *Summa Aurea* is one of the sources used but whether due to the interval between the two works or to Philip's special interests, the greater attention which he gives to Aristotle's metaphysical doctrine, at least in its psychological aspect, is striking. As its title suggests, Philip's treatise is an analysis of goodness in general. He explores the relation between goodness and being, unity and truth. Beginning with the supreme Good he moves to created natural good, discussing in turn the angels, corporeal beings, man and moral good and evil. Then he turns to supernatural good – that is grace – first as regards angels, then as regards man. He discusses the relationship between grace and human action, with subsequent treatment of the virtues.

The section on man considers especially his metaphysical composition. Philip's main problem is how man should be described in the Aristotelian terminology, an investigation which he conducts under the question 'whether in man the rational and sensible soul is one or whether they are different souls'.[42] His own preference is difficult to determine. He quotes Aristotle's concept of soul as being 'the perfection of a natural organic body' and seems clear that such a view is incompatible with a plurality of souls in man – one which he would have in common with vegetable life, a second which he would have in common with brutes and a third which would be his specifically human soul. However, he quotes the opinion of 'some' that man is composed of three 'substances' of this sort, which combine in one soul to give him life. According to this theory, there would be not three souls but three component parts:

> But although [according to this theory] there are three incorporeal substances, yet there are not three souls, in that 'soul' is the designation of a perfecting principle (*anima nomen est perfectionis*). Therefore there is no vegetable soul except in plants and such like because it is their complete perfection. And there is no sensitive soul except in brutes, because there again it is the perfection. In man, though, these are as it were the matter for the rational; the rational is the completion and it alone is the soul in man. And these three are united so that there is one soul; and that they are a soul they owe to the completing principle (*habent a completivo*); and so there are three incorporeal substances and one soul. . . .[43]

This attempted compromise between the propositions that there are three souls in man and that there is one soul only seems to invite several objections in terms of contemporary preoccupations. Thus, it might well be asked whether the human soul remains a 'soul' after vegetation and sensation cease, since whatever an 'incorporeal substance' is it is something less than a soul according to the distinction suggested. Similarly it would appear that what is created by God – in accordance with the theological doctrine on the human soul – would not in this analysis be a soul but something which by virtue of the naturally generated 'substances' becomes a soul. Philip, however, seems to find the view tolerable. It is by no means clear, though, that he subscribes to it, for later he goes on to say that he has been able to find nothing in Scripture contrary to the thesis that there is one substance with rational and sensitive – including therefore vegetative – powers and that Augustine is hesitant on the point.[44] The great interest of his treatment is not for his resolution of the dilemma but for the evidence which he provides of contemporary discussion and the extent to which it was stimulated by the penetration of Aristotelian ideas.

Problems of the soul have an important part also in the thought of William of Auvergne. He taught theology from 1222 to 1228, after which he was bishop of Paris until his death in 1249. His most important works are sections of an encyclopaedic review of theology and philosophy entitled *Magisterium divinale sive sapientiale* ('Magisterial survey of theology or philosophy'). It was planned in seven parts of which the first three had as their subjects respectively the Trinity, the created universe and the soul, while the remainder were on the incarnation, ecclesiastical institutions and morality. Several of these parts circulated as independent treatises. Despite its theological title, the first part, *De Trinitate* ('On the Trinity'), has a good deal of more general interest. Its first thirteen chapters cover the topics of existence and essence and the divine attributes and operations.[45] However, the most explicitly philosophical parts are those on the created universe (*De universo creaturarum*), which was probably written mainly *c*. 1231–6, and on the soul (*De anima*), which is judged to be later.[46] In these treatises he made a determined effort to assimilate the new material where possible and to correct it where necessary. William seems to have been well acquainted with the theories of Avicenna and Avicebron. The latter he took to be a Christian because of the resemblance between the divine will as expounded in the *Fountain of Life* and the Christian doctrine of the Logos or Word.[47] He refers to Averroes as a 'most noble philosopher' and regards him as one of the fundamental sources but he gives no indication which of his writings he had read.[48] It will be remembered that this was well before the true import of Averroes' interpretation of Aristotle's psychology was recognised. William knew a broad range of Aristotle's own works including the *Metaphysics*, the *De Anima*, the *Physics*, *On Coming to Be and Passing Away*, the meteorology, the minerology, the zoology and part at least of the *Nicomachean Ethics*. He also used the *Book of Causes*.[49]

William's discussion of the soul amply reveals the dilemma which faced Christian thinkers of the period in trying to combine the concepts of the human soul as capable both of independent existence and of being related to the body in such a way that the unity of the resulting organism was not imperilled. His treatment is much influenced by Avicenna and amounts to a Platonic concept of the soul expressed in Aristotelian terminology. Thus it is the soul rather than the man that thinks,[50] a position required not least, according to William, to guarantee knowledge to the separated soul – the soul after bodily death. He denies that soul and body constitute a single substance[51] or that matter is the principle of individuation.[52] He appears to hold that in all bodies there is a form of corporeality so that in living beings there is a medium between soul and unorganised matter.[52] This idea will be met again as it recurs in various forms throughout the century. However, he rejects the proposition that there is a plurality of souls in man – rational, animal and vegetative.[53] He is at pains to stress the unity of soul.[54] Moreover, despite his general Platonist bias, he is anxious to adhere to the language of Aristotelian hylomorphism. He uses it to confute the Platonist doctrine of the pre-existence of the soul and rejects any insinuation that the union of soul with body is a degradation or the result of a fall.[55]

Besides his general discussion of soul, William tackles the problems of intellection as bequeathed by Arabic elaborations of Aristotle. The separate active intellect of Avicenna is replaced by God, who is the ultimate source of intellectual concepts in the sense that he is the foundation of all intelligibility.[56] The soul as 'placed on the horizon of two worlds' – the sensible and the spiritual – has by the nature with which it is created an apprehension of absolute principles.[57] The problem which caused Plato to posit the world of ideas and which William believes caused Aristotle to posit a separated active intellect is thereby explained, through what is in effect a variant of the Augustinian theory of illumination.

In his cosmology, William takes trouble to deny that the world is eternal.[58] He follows Avicebron in seeing the divine will as the cause of the universe, being careful to make clear that although the divine will operates from eternity its effect is not necessarily eternal.[59] In this respect his argument foreshadows that adopted later by Thomas Aquinas. However, William goes beyond this to insist that the world must necessarily have had a beginning,[60] a tenet which was also to have currency later.

All the theologians considered so far in this context were seculars. However, the new philosophical material was also finding its way into the theology being taught within the recently established mendicant orders whose members were so soon to emerge as the dominant figures on the scene. It was bound to do so since the orders were around this time attracting established secular teachers into their ranks. The first mendicant master of theology at Paris was the Dominican, Roland of Cremona. He had lectured on the *Sentences* under John of St Giles, a secular master teaching in the order's convent of Saint-Jacques, in 1228–9. Although he continued to lecture on the *Sentences* after his inception, his *Summa on the Sentences* must be from close to this date as it seems to have been completed before the reception of Averroes.[61] He shows some familiarity with Aristotle's philosophical works. About a year after Roland's inception, his master, John of St Giles, entered the order, thus giving the Dominicans at an early stage two chairs within the faculty. The Franciscans were not far behind. The Englishman, Alexander of Hales, who had been a regent master for some ten years, entered the Franciscan order in 1236. He continued teaching apparently until his death in 1245. He is thought to have been the first to use the *Sentences* of Peter Lombard as an 'ordinary' textbook in theology. His commentary on it, which survives, was completed before 1230. It reveals a knowledge of Aristotle's philosophical works as also of the *Book of Causes* and Avicenna, though the exact degree of acquaintance is difficult to judge. The *Summa Theologica* (*Summa of Theology*) attributed to him is, rather, representative of the first generation of Franciscan theological work at Paris. It was compiled over the period *c.* 1240–56 and includes, among other contributions, work by Alexander's pupil, the Franciscan John of la Rochelle.[62]

John of la Rochelle is an interesting figure in his own right. His *Tractatus de Anima* (*Treatise on the Soul*) and the later *Summa de Anima* provide welcome evidence from which to assess the impact of Averroes in the first phase. In his analysis of the powers of the soul, John identifies a lowest sense of the term 'reason' (*ratio*), as the point at which the soul is mingled with the body and is dependent on it. This he finds to correspond to the corruptible element of intelligence which Averroes opposes to the incorruptible intellect. The function of this 'reason' is to act as an intermediary between sensation, which does not have the intelligible as its object, and intellection which does not have the sensible as its object. Moreover, it is the specific feature of man, distinguishing him from the angels, with whom he has intelligence in common, and the brute animals, with whom he has sensation in common. It exists in the rational soul only by virtue of soul's union with body. It therefore perishes with the body, whereas the intellective faculty, which for John is also part of the soul, survives.[63] It has been pointed out that despite the superficial similarities between John's doctrine on the matter and that of Averroes, their perspectives are in fact very different.[64] The 'reason' of which John speaks here is a power of the spiritual soul, by which the lowest spiritual substance – the human soul – is joined to a body. What he conceives to be the counterpart in Averroes is a power of a soul indissolubly linked to a body but temporarily joined through this power to the separated and immortal intellect. John's 'reason' is perishable because the soul, which is capable of independent existence, is only temporarily joined to a body. The dissolution of the counterpart in Averroes is the dissolution of the individual personality. If it is clear that John was in contact with the new access of authority it is equally clear that on this point he misunderstood its import. Given the complexity and unfamiliarity of the issues involved, it is hardly to be wondered at that their treatment by the first generation of Latin thinkers to encounter them should in some respects be naïve. Even so, these initial attempts to read and absorb were a necessary preparation for what was to follow.

6.   Aristotelian Philosophy and Christian Theology – System Building and Controversy

Bonaventure: Life and Works

St Bonaventure was born Giovanni Fidanza in Bagnoregio near Viterbo probably in 1217. He studied arts at Paris (*c.* 1236–42) before joining the Franciscan order there in 1243. He then studied theology under the regency of Alexander of Hales and, after the latter's death in 1245, under lesser known Franciscan masters. He received the licence in theology in 1253 and taught until 1257, though because of the dispute between secular and mendicant masters he was not recognised as a master of the faculty until the autumn of 1257. Earlier in the same year he had become minister general of the Franciscan order and from this time he ceased to teach. However, in several series of university sermons he exercised an important influence at Paris in the period around 1270, when the first condemnation of the tenets of 'radical Aristotelianism', as current in the arts faculty, was issued. In 1273 he was appointed cardinal bishop of Albano. He died at Lyons, where he had been attending the general council, on 15 July 1274.

Bonaventure's earliest and most substantial work is the *Commentary on the Sentences*, composed while he was a 'bachelor of the Sentences' in 1250–2. Also academic in origin and form are several 'Disputed Questions': 'On the knowledge of Christ', 'On the mystery of the Trinity' and 'On evangelical perfection'. The last set are only of marginal interest in a philosophical context; they relate to the dispute (1254–6) between the mendicant orders, Dominican and Franciscan, and William of St Amour, a secular master in the theology faculty, over the question whether the life of poverty was sanctioned by the Gospel. In addition to the academic works, several non-academic treatises are valuable as sources of Bonaventure's thought. These include *On the Retracing of the Arts to Theology* (*De reductione artium ad theologiam*), which is possibly contemporaneous with the *Commentary on the Sentences*, the *Breviloquium* (literally 'a short treatise'), composed *c.* 1257, and a mystical work, the *Itinerary of the Mind to God* (*Itinerarium Mentis in Deum*), written in 1259 while Bonaventure was staying at the Franciscan convent of La Verna where St Francis had received the

161

stigmata in 1224. In addition to the treatises, several hundred of Bonaventure's sermons survive, either in an authorial or in a 'reported' version. The sermons are an additional source from which to illustrate themes developed in his teaching works and non-academic treatises. Many, especially of the more than one hundred delivered in Paris, reflect contemporary issues of debate and developments within the university.

The *Commentary on the Sentences* is the chief source of Bonaventure's thought, containing a systematic exposition of all its main features. As usual with the genre, Book II, especially the sections on creation (distinctions 1–16) and man (distinctions 17–23), and to a lesser extent Book I, on the divine trinity and unity, are the most important for a treatment of philosophical topics. Among the many theological points discussed in the 'Disputed Questions' there are some of particular philosophical concern. Question 2 'on the knowledge of Christ' discusses how God knows creation, thereby raising the issue of exemplarism. Question 4 examines the knowledge of the human intellect. The questions 'on the mystery of the Trinity' are mainly devoted to arguing that doctrine, but article I of Question 1 contains a treatment of the existence of God as a matter beyond doubt.

On the Retracing of the Arts to Theology considers briefly how the various disciplines and levels of knowledge, the mechanical arts, sense experience, philosophy, study of scripture, contribute to and are part of a theological knowledge. The work is influenced by the *Didascalicon* of Hugh of St Victor but is much less detailed in its survey of the arts than Hugh's work, familiarity with which is clearly supposed. The *Breviloquium* is a digest of theology. Part II contains an account of creation and of metaphysical constitution, though presented in a dogmatic rather than an argued fashion. The short *Itinerary of the Mind to God* is a powerful statement of Bonaventure's conviction that created reality is a world of signs pointing to the creator, that the creator is present in it and that reflection upon it at its various levels leads to knowledge of God. The treatise is full of Platonist perceptions derived from St Augustine and the pseudo-Denis who, with St Anselm, are the chief influences upon it, but the influence of Aristotle is also evident, in the treatment of sense experience. Chapter 1 outlines the theme of ascent. Chapter 2 considers how the visible world 'that enters our mind through the bodily senses' leads to contemplation of God. It is an account of the process of sensation and 'imagination' and of the exercise of judgement on sensation. Our judgement is exercised on the basis of 'laws by which we judge with certainty about all sense objects that come to our knowledge'.[1] These laws are immutable, absolute, eternal and simple 'since they are intellectual and incorporeal, not made but uncreated, existing eternally in the Eternal Art, by which, through which, and according to which all beautiful things are formed'.[2] Chapter 3 considers how the working of the intellect leads to God, again by way of the Platonic argument:

> Our intellect does not make a full and ultimate analysis of any single created being unless it is aided by a knowledge of the most pure, most actual, most complete and absolute Being, which is Being unqualified and eternal, and in whom are the essences of all things in their purity. For how could the intellect know that a specific being is defective and incomplete if it had not knowledge of the Being that is free from all defect?[3]

A similar point emerges from the perception of necessary inferences:

> Necessity of inference does not follow from the existence of the thing in matter, since it is contingent; nor from its existence in the mind, because that would be a fiction if the thing did not exist in reality. Hence it must come from the exemplarity in the Eternal Art, in reference to which things have an aptitude for each other and a relation, because they are represented in the Eternal Art.[4]

Similarly, a consideration of the various sciences leads to God, in accordance with the argument of *On the Retracing*: 'All these branches of knowledge have certain and infallible laws and beacons shining down into our mind from the eternal law. And this our mind, enlightened and overflooded by so much brightness, unless it is blind, can be guided through itself to contemplate that eternal Light.'[5] Above the evidence of the human intellect is the evidence of the human soul, considered as the image of God, reformed through grace (Chapter 4). Having thus considered God as outside, through his vestiges in the visible world, and as within, in the soul, the next step is to consider him as above the soul, as 'Being Itself', 'so absolutely certain that it cannot be thought not to be' (Chapter 5).[6] Here is a clear echo of the Anselmian argument, already adopted by Bonaventure in the *Commentary on the Sentences* and invoked by him again in his

Collations on the Six Days.[7] Chapter 6 is a consideration of God as goodness which is self-diffusive in the highest degree. The treatise ends (Chapter 7) with the transition to mystical contemplation.

Of Bonaventure's sermons, three series are of particular relevance in the present context. They are the *Collations on the Ten Commandments* (*Collationes de decem praeceptis*), the *Collations on the Seven Gifts* (sc. of the Spirit) (*Collationes de septem donis*) and the *Collations on the Six Days* (sc. of creation) (*Collationes in Hexaemeron*). The term 'collation' or 'conference' has various meanings but in this case denotes university sermons delivered in the Franciscan convent at Paris. A note to one, the shorter and probably unofficial, version of the *Collations on the Six Days* records that they were given in the presence of 'various masters and bachelors of theology and other friars to the number of about one hundred and sixty'.[8] The *Collations on the Ten Commandments* were preached in the Lent of 1267. For the most part they are a straightforward exposition of the decalogue, but the sermon on the first commandment attacks in passing the eternity of the world and the unity of the intellect.[9] The *Collations on the Seven Gifts* date from February to May of the following year. The seventh collation in this series, on the gift of 'counsel', contains an attack on secular masters critical of the friars' vocation.[10] The eighth, on the gift of 'understanding', contains an attack on three principal errors associated with radical Aristotelianism: the eternity of the world, determinism and the unity of the intellect,[11] though Bonaventure does not say that he has university masters in mind. The *Collations on the Six Days* were preached between Easter and Pentecost 1273. They are specially interesting in that they were given at a time when the threat from radical Aristotelianism had been clearly perceived and in that their subject demanded close attention to cosmological theory. Collation I contains criticism of those 'who believe the world to have been created in eternity'.[12] Collation IV, on natural understanding, includes discussion of fundamental metaphysical divisons – substance and accident, universality and particularity, potentiality and actuality, unity and multiplicity, simplicity and composition, causation – with criticism of rival philosophical theories. Collation VI contains a trenchant defence of exemplarism and of Platonic ideas and divine foreknowledge and providence against Aristotle. The same theme and the questions of the eternity of the world, the unity of the intellect and the afterlife are taken up in Collation VII. Aristotle is identified with the first and third of these errors – the eternity of the world and the failure to envisage an afterlife. It is noted that Averroes (the 'Commentator') interprets him as having taught the unity of the intellect. However, Aristotle is excused on the eternity of the world 'for he understands it as a philosopher, speaking in the order of nature, i.e. saying that it could not have a beginning by nature'.[13] Moreover, Bonaventure allows that Aristotle 'may have had an opinion concerning eternal happiness, but did not mention it because it may not have seemed relevant'.[14] He also suggests an acceptable interpretation of Aristotle's supposed view on the intellect, 'that he understood intelligence to be one in relation to the influencing light' – a theory which would be in harmony with divine illumination – 'and not in itself, for it is numbered according to the subject',[15] that is, according to the individuals who possess intellect. Thus, although the collation is at pains to show the shortcomings of the philosophers and how their conclusions are surpassed by the certainty of revelation, it cannot be said to be hostile to Aristotle. This remains the impression even after allowing for the fact that there may have been an incentive when countering the radical views of rival interpreters to show that Aristotle could be read in an acceptable sense. Collation XIX is more reactionary. It cautions against descending from Scripture and patristic writings to the 'summas of the masters because error is sometimes found in them'.[16] This applies even to the masters of theology, who are the class referred to here. However, philosophy is regarded as 'the greatest danger'. 'Let the masters beware, then, not to commend or appreciate too highly the sayings of the philosophers, lest the people take it as a pretext to return to Egypt [a symbol of defection from godliness], or dismiss because of their example the *waters of Siloe* [cf. Isa. 8.6.7] in which is supreme perfection, and go to the waters of the philosophers in which there is eternal deceit.'[17] These strictures, unusually severe for Bonaventure in their apparent dismissal of philosophy, have to be read in the context of contemporary controversy. The series of collations continues with expositions of mystical theology and ends incomplete, being interrupted by Bonaventure's elevation to the cardinalate in May 1273.

The Character of St Bonaventure's Thought

The characterisation of Bonaventure's thought has been one of the most debated topics in medieval intellectual history.[18] In particular, the interplay of Augustinian and Aristotelian elements in it has proved difficult to evaluate. Certainly, there is no missing the Augustinian spirit of his outlook. It is apparent not so much from the high regard in which he holds Augustine's authority – for Augustine was regarded as a common master by all western theologians[19] – as from the way in which his thought is dominated by man's search for God. This dominating concern gives his writings the quality already noted in those of Hugh and Richard of St Victor, both heavily influenced by St Augustine. Like the Victorines, Bonaventure integrates the several levels of human knowledge into a singleminded quest and, as in their case, the spiritual dimension is always overt in his treatment of philosophical and theological problems. However, if there is no missing the Augustinian and mystical aspects of his thought there is no missing either the fact that he writes in an intellectual context revolutionised by the reception of Aristotle's 'scientific' works. It is the question of his reaction to the new material that has divided scholars – whether he should be regarded as generally hostile to it or, in so far as he was favourable to it, the degree to which he assimilated it and whether in his assimilation he is best regarded as an eclectic. Therefore he has been described alternately as an Augustinian–Neoplatonist who opposed the invasion of Aristotelian 'scientific' doctrine and as a representative of a less completely developed Aristotelianism than that espoused by St Thomas Aquinas. More recently, his thought has been convincingly presented as a genuine and original synthesis, a systematic rather than an eclectic blend of Augustinian–Neoplatonist and Aristotelian perceptions.[20] The nature of this system as well as its relevance to the issues of contemporary controversy can be illustrated by examining three central themes: Bonaventure's theories on sense perception and knowledge, on creation and causality and on the relationship between soul and body in man.

Bonaventure: Sense Perception and Knowledge

Bonaventure's account of sense perception is fundamentally that of Aristotle, whose definition of the subject he prefers to those offered by Augustine and Boethius.[21] Sensation is attributed to the soul and body as a composite rather than being referred, as in Augustine, to the soul. The Aristotelian terminology of the 'common sense' and the 'imagination' is accepted and nothing in the Aristotelian account is contradicted.[22] However, while sensation is the only route to

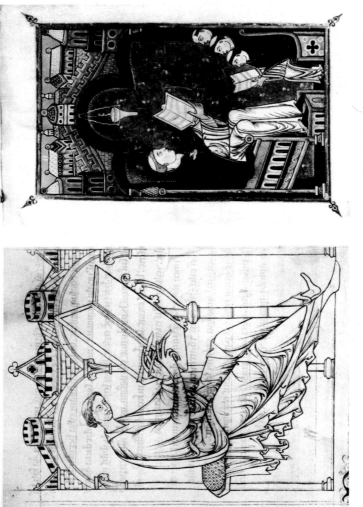

4. Monk writing. (Twelfth century)

5. Monastic school, probably representing that of St Victor (Thirteenth century)

6. A scholar's hand of the thirteenth century—considered to be that of Thomas Aquinas.

knowledge of the sensible world and is taken to be the starting point of all knowledge, when it comes to our judgements on the nature of experience and in particular to our value judgements, Bonaventure follows Augustine in requiring access by the mind to unchanging standards against which the data of sense experience can be measured.[23] As in Augustine's analysis, this awareness of an immutable, absolute and perfect order is regarded as being beyond what can be attained by sense experience of a contingent and changing world and is attributed to a divine illumination of the mind. The theory of divine illumination is the epistemological complement of the theory of exemplarism in creation, which Bonaventure also holds. Denial of exemplarism he regards as the major weakness of Aristotle's system, containing within it the seeds of other errors, including the absence of divine providence and the assertion that the world is eternal.[24] This double function of the theory of exemplars in Bonaventure's thought is quite in keeping with Augustine's perceptions, though the cosmological aspect – the role of exemplarism in creation – has acquired a particular point in the thirteenth-century context. More generally, divine illumination for Bonaventure has similar implications to what it had for Augustine. It at once emphasises man's dependence on God in the progress to understanding and guarantees him an internal, reflective route to certainty of God's existence, though it does not convey a knowledge of God's essence. The religious, even mystical, dimension to the epistemological theory explains the fervour with which its defenders adhered to it in the face of challenge from those who insisted on the sufficiency of the Aristotelian account of the way in which the mind knows.[25]

Bonaventure: Creation and Causality

For Bonaventure, as for other Christian theologians, the origin and explanation of the universe is a God who creates deliberately and freely from nothing – that is, without any pre-existing substratum, like chaos or matter, as in classical theories – and who knows the effects of his activity. As in the Augustinian system, God knows the universe by knowing the exemplar ideas upon which it is modelled. These ideas are coeternal with God and are part of him – in Trinitarian doctrine they are the Word, the second person of the Trinity – not separate and independent as in the original Platonic version of the Craftsman's activity. In this perspective, the universe is clearly posterior to God, in the sense of being related to him as effect to cause. Bonaventure also holds that it is posterior in the sense of being created in time. He is flatly opposed to the thesis, which he diffidently recognises as being Aristotle's, that the universe is eternal. Not only is such a theory repugnant to revelation, it is also in Bonaventure's view absurd. This position, clearly taken up in Bonaventure's *Commentary on the Sentences*,[26] was a subject of controversy. It was challenged implicitly by St Thomas' analysis, which treated the eternity of the world as an open question philosophically while being resolved theologically through revelation. It also seemed to be challenged by the radical Aristotelians of the arts faculty at Paris in so far as they were prepared to defend Aristotle's account.

In his investigation of the structure and production of the universe, Bonaventure uses Aristotle's terminology of causation[27] but with certain modifications and extensions which alter the import of Aristotle's theory in significant respects. In the first place, he has absorbed Avicebron's doctrine that there is matter and form in all created beings.[28] As with Avicebron, this doctrine of 'universal hylomorphism' is meant to contrast the complexity of creatures with the simplicity and unity of the Creator. It does not imply for Bonaventure that all creation is corporeal. In accordance with biblical revelation and supported by an argument from hierarchical symmetry in creation,[29] he accepts the existence of angels, who are spirits without bodies but who are nonetheless, on this metaphysical analysis, compounded of form and matter. In their case, the matter is a pure spiritual matter, which expresses the element of contingency and potentiality in their nature – the fact that they have been brought into being and are mutable, for instance in their will – but which does not carry the implications of capacity for spatial extension or for substantial change which attach to matter in the physical world. For Bonaventure, hylomorphic composition is the corollary of complexity and contingency and the counterpart of any distinction between potentiality and actuality.

The concept of a matter which is the created substratum of the universe, spiritual and corporeal, combined with reflection on the description of creation in the Book of Genesis, prompted Bonaventure to further refinements on the Aristotelian analysis. With Aristotle, 'form' and 'matter' were principles deduced from the actual state of the physical world. When these principles were introduced into an account of how the world came to be, there was a subtle shift of perspective. It was tempting to think of matter not as a notional abstraction simply but in the sense of an actual principle from which things could be and were produced. Both concepts are present in Bonaventure's thought. Certainly, he takes matter in its ultimate degree of abstraction to be characterless and so incapable of being distinguished as the matter of spiritual and corporeal beings.[30] However, a distinction at some point between the matter of spiritual and corporeal beings is necessary. While the matter of spiritual beings has the function in his thought simply of expressing their complexity and contingency in contrast to God, the matter of corporeal beings serves, in addition, to explain their capacity for being bodies and for undergoing substantial change. Bonaventure therefore treats the matter of the physical world as having several layers of actuality. Like Avicenna, he attributes the common features of corporeal beings – their spatial extension and other properties – to a preliminary, non-specific organisation of matter, a 'form' of corporeality.[31] Moreover, he regards corporeal matter as having inbuilt dispositions for acquiring forms. These inherent dispositions were created in matter by God along with matter itself. Following Augustine, from whom he borrows the theory, Bonaventure refers to them as the 'seminal reasons'. Like Augustine, he employs them in order more clearly to subordinate secondary causality to the overall creative activity of God. The secondary, natural causation is real in that its agency is necessary for the actualisation of the potential form but the secondary cause is not the originator of the form, which is already latent in the seminal reason. Besides its role as a safeguard for the unique creativity of God, the doctrine of seminal reasons had other uses. It helped to emphasise the sense of continuity underlying substantial change, for the form which gives way to new form does not wholly go out of existence any more than it wholly came into existence under the influence of the secondary agent; it returns to a potential state in matter from which it can again be actualised given the right conditions. Bonaventure found this particularly apt when considering the theological doctrine that man's body would be resurrected.[32] 'Seminal reasons' also served to mitigate the bluntness of Aristotelian theory on the composition of living beings. According to this, form was united with matter directly, a doctrine which Bonaventure in the height of the controversies described as 'insane',[33] though he does not seem to have thought that Aristotle taught it.[34] By contrast, Bonaventure insisted that the union of substantial form with matter was accomplished by virtue of a preliminary level of organisation in the matter itself, which had a form of corporeality and contained within it in a latent fashion all the principles of higher organisation, except, as will be seen, for the human soul. It was this last aspect – the union between the human soul, the highest form of the corporeal world, and the body – which lent the whole question a special edge.

Bonaventure: Soul and Body in Man

For Bonaventure, the human soul is a compound of matter and form. Several considerations prompted him to adopt this view. In the first place, as with the angels, this composition expressed the complexity and contingency which characterised all created beings. As in the case of angels, the matter of which the soul is compounded is spiritual matter. Secondly, hylomorphic composition in the soul was part of Bonaventure's contention that it was a substance in its own right, not dependent for its substantiality on its informing a body. Thirdly, hylomorphic composition provided the soul with a principle other than corporeal matter by which its individuality could be explained. Bonaventure considered that individuation must be attributed to the union of matter and form, not to form or to matter alone.

Since Bonaventure accepted the Aristotelian principle that soul is the actuality of a living body, his theory of soul must show how a substance, already composed of matter and form, could enter into a true unity of composition such as that posited in the Aristotelian analysis between soul and body. So he emphasised that it was an inherent aspect of the form of soul that it should inform a body as well as its spiritual matter. Its union with a body is not therefore considered to be a demeaning of its true condition, as in the Platonist view, but is a completion of its natural condition and a satisfaction of its appetite. It is tempting to compare this appetite to the desire for imposing order which is the motivation for the embodiment of soul in matter according to the optimistic strand of Neoplatonist thought on the subject, though with Bonaventure there is no question of the soul's pre-existing its union with a body.[35] In the completeness of its union with a body and in its life-giving and organising function, the human soul is the counterpart of the animal soul in brutes and the vegetable soul in plants. It differs from them however in its origin and in its destiny. The souls of lower beings are activated from the seminal reasons of matter. The human soul is directly created by God when the matter exists for its informing activity. It does not pre-exist the body but is created when the appropriate matter is engendered in the natural process of reproduction. As for its destiny, the human soul is unique in surviving bodily death.

This soul is the single substantial form of the body. It is the principle of man's intellective and voluntary functions. Bonaventure rejected the position adopted by Avicenna that the active aspect of intellection was to be attributed to an external principle – the agent intellect. A fortiori, he rejected the externalisation of the potential intellect, as attributed to Aristotle by Averroes. The soul is also the principle of the sensitive and vegetative functions of the human organism. A theory of the plurality of forms has sometimes been ascribed to Bonaventure whereby the human soul would be regarded as the final, rational, perfection of a being whose vegetative and sensitive functions are due to separate and lower informing principles. Although some passages of his thought can be taken to suggest such a theory, careful analysis of his views as a whole has shown that he held the unity of substantial form in all organisms.[36] However, as explained above, in discussing Bonaventure's views on causality, the substantial form supervenes upon a matter which according to him already possesses a degree of organisation – matter disposed in a non-specific way to be a body and disposed through the combination of the four elements so as to be capable of being informed by a soul.[37]

Albert the Great

Just about the time that Bonaventure joined the Franciscans and began his studies in theology, his older contemporary, Albert of Lauingen, arrived in Paris. Albert was by then in middle age, though the work for which he is remembered lay in front of him. Born in Swabia of knightly family, around 1200, he had been sent as a young man by his uncle to the nascent university of Padua.[38] There he joined the Dominicans in 1223 under the influence of Jordan of Saxony, St Dominic's successor as master general. He probably went immediately to Cologne for his novitiate and theological study. For approximately the next twenty years there are only slight indications of his intellectual interests. He wrote on Scripture, is said to have lectured on the *Sentences* at Cologne and to have been 'lector' in various Dominican convents of the German province. He also acquired some knowledge of Aristotelian philosophy and conducted investigations into natural phenomena, especially the metals mined in eastern Germany.

In 1243–4 or perhaps earlier, Albert was sent by the then master general of the Dominican order, John of Wildeshausen, to study theology at Paris. After a period lecturing on the *Sentences* under Gueric of St Quentin, the longstanding occupant of the Dominican chair for foreigners,[39] he became a master of theology in the spring of 1245 and succeeded to the chair. His extant *Commentary on the Sentences* is an edited version on which he was engaged up to March 1249, that is four years after his inception as master, by which time he had already returned to Cologne (1248) as founding regent master of the Dominican *studium generale* there. Before the completion of his *Commentary*, or perhaps before he had even begun it, he had written a large theological work known as the *Summa Parisiensis* ('Paris *Summa*'),[40] based in part at least on disputations which he held during his regency.[41]

Although the date of Albert's Aristotelian commentaries is not generally agreed, some historians assigning them early in his career, more recent scholarship takes them to have been written between 1250 and 1270.[42] Already in his theological works he had given proof of his interest and erudition in the Aristotelian philosophical texts but now he moved from writing on theology to writing on those texts themselves. This was a startling enough transition for a medieval theologian but it was doubly so for a Dominican. The 1228 statutes of the order directed that the brethren 'shall not study in the books of the Gentiles and the philosophers, although they may inspect them briefly'; they forbade them to learn secular sciences, even the liberal arts, without special dispensation, and required that they read only theological works.[43] It is hardly surprising then that Albert should have encountered some hostility and criticism.[44] However, rather like St Anselm of Bec in his day, he also seems to have met an inquisitive demand among the brethren, for in his *Physics* he claims that it was they who had over a number of years been asking him for such a book so that they could attain the whole of natural knowledge and understand Aristotle.[45]

Albert's commentaries more resembled the type composed by Avicenna than those by Averroes. They were paraphrases, with amplifications, digressions and explorations of areas which it seemed had either not been dealt with by Aristotle or where Aristotle's treatment if it existed had not come down. He declared his intention in this fashion of making Aristotle intelligible to the Latins. Many of his additions and elaborations were truly Aristotelian in spirit, being based on his own observations of natural phenomena, from which he was quite prepared to correct the ancient authorities where necessary. In other respects, his understanding of Aristotle was much affected by Neoplatonist influences. Chief among these must be counted the pseudo-Denis, in whom he was deeply read and on whom he commented, the pseudo-Aristotelian *Book of Causes*, on which he also commented, and Avicenna. In particular, he borrowed heavily from the latter's psychological doctrine. He differed from him indeed in his account of intellection, making the active intellect a power of the soul whereas Avicenna had made it an external principle. But in his explanation of the soul's relation to the body the influence of Avicenna is very clear.[46] Albert tries to fuse the Platonist and Aristotelian perspectives, with the emphasis being laid on the soul's substantiality as the basis of its immortality. He thinks of the soul therefore in two ways. The first way is as it is in itself, a spiritual substance, with a disposition towards being the perfection of a body; he considers 'perfection' – Avicenna's usage – more in keeping with the notion of substantiality than 'form'. The second way is as it is related to the body, to which it is the principle of operation as a sailor to a ship:[47]

This is more evident if the intellective or rational soul be said to move the body and to be its actuality (*actus*), as a sailor is the activity and mover of a ship. For the sailor moves the ship by intellectual design, which is the science of navigation, and yet the sailor exercises no function in the ship which is not accomplished by a physical movement and instrument, such as the top-sail or tiller or rudder or oar; and yet the navigator is wholly separated from the ship. And similarly, if the soul thus moves the whole body under the command of intellect, the whole soul is essentially separated from the body, although it has many powers and operations of sensation and vegetation, which are not accomplished without physical instruments.[48]

As a sailor has a status independently of a ship so has the soul independently of a body; but there is also a certain dependence between them. The interdependence between soul and body is such in Albert's view that a substantial union results – an idea certainly not conveyed by the analogy of the sailor and the ship, as Thomas Aquinas pointed out.[49] Despite his efforts to combine the two, Albert is clearly closer to the Platonist than to the Aristotelian perspective. His analysis is markedly cruder than that of Bonaventure. However, while insisting on the soul's substantiality, Albert does not make it derive from composition of matter and form within the soul. Indeed he wholly rejects the concept of spiritual matter.[50] The soul, like all created beings, is complex – and thus stands in contrast to God, who is simple – but the complexity stems from distinction within it of a principle of existence, not from hylomorphic composition, as in Bonaventure's account.[51]

Albert's teaching responsibilities at Cologne came to an end in 1254 on his election as prior of the German province of the order, a position which he held for three years. The commentary on the *De Anima* is known to have been written during his period as provincial. It has proved a useful reference point for the dating of many of his other commentaries.[52] It was preceded by a batch of commentaries on aspects of inanimate nature, including the *Physics*, the *De Caelo* ('On the heaven'), *De Generatione et Corruptione* ('On Coming to Be and Passing Away'), meteorology and minerology, though these need not perhaps be supposed all to have existed in a finished state.[53] It was followed by commentaries on other works of Aristotelian natural science – on the *Parva Naturalia* (the 'small treatises on nature', dealing with a range of biological and psychological topics: sensation, memory, breathing, sleep, dreams and divination, length of life, youth and age, life and death), on plants and on zoology. This last, the commentary on Aristotle's *De Animalibus*, he is known to have been engaged on *c.* 1261, during his time as bishop of Regensburg, the see to which he was appointed by Pope Alexander IV in 1260 but which he resigned in 1262. His commentaries on the *Ethics*, *Politics* and *Posterior Analytics* may come from the period *c.* 1262–3. His commentary on the *Metaphysics* seems to be later, *c.* 1264–7. Around 1263 or a little after, he wrote a short treatise *On the Unity of the Intellect* (*De unitate intellectus*), which may have been based at least in part on a disputation which he had held while at the papal curia in Anagni in 1256–7.[54] It defends individual immortality but does so in an abstract fashion, against the view of Averroes rather than against any contemporary proponents of it. The atmosphere had quite changed when, some six or seven years afterwards, in reply to a query sent to him by an observer in Paris, perhaps just before the condemnation of

1270, Albert dealt with the same matter – and with twelve other doctrines included in that condemnation – as proceeding from ignorance of philosophy, 'since many at Paris have followed not philosophy but sophisms'.[55] From 1269 until his death in 1280, Albert lived in semi-retirement at Cologne. He continued to write at least until c. 1275. His unfinished Summa Theologiae (Summa of Theology), in two books, dates from this period.

Albert's immense output has yet to be evaluated fully. The difficulties in doing so are increased by the explanatory form of his philosophical writings and by his own warnings that what he says in the course of exposition should not necessarily be taken as his own view.[56] As compared with the great synthetic undertakings of St Thomas, his pupil from the Cologne studium, his approach is inevitably seen as a transitional phase in the reception of Aristotle. However, in one respect at least its significance is apparent. Albert realised very clearly that Christian thinkers could not ignore the huge access of new learning, that they would have to examine it closely and while preserving their own principles work out the terms of an intellectual relationship. This involved for the first time in the Latin tradition a definition of the scope of philosophy and theology. Albert addressed the problem at the beginning both of his Commentary on the Sentences and of his Summa Theologiae.[57] The clearest delineation is in the later work:

> There are two manners of revelation. One manner is through the light connatural with us, and this is the manner of revelation to the philosophers. This light indeed cannot be except from the first light, of God, as Augustine says in the book, The Teacher, and this is very well proved in the Book of Causes. The other light is for the perception of entities above the world and this is raised above us. And in this latter light this science [sc. theology] is revealed. The first light shines forth in things known through themselves, but the second in the articles of faith.[58]

The Augustinian–Neoplatonist character of the statement is explicit. Philosophy and theology are distinct disciplines with different starting points but underlying them is a common foundation. They are unified in their origin. Both considerations are important for an understanding of Albert's purpose.

St Thomas Aquinas: Life and Works

St Thomas was born *c.* 1224–5, probably at Roccasecca, one of the family castles, in the north-west of the kingdom of Sicily.[59] The name Aquinas is from the family lordship around Aquino. At the age of five or six, Thomas was brought as an oblate to the Benedictine abbey of Monte Cassino, perhaps with the intention that he should become abbot in due course. This event probably took place after the treaty of San Germano (1230) the immediate prelude to which had seen strife at Monte Cassino between forces of Emperor Frederick II and the papacy. During his lifetime, Thomas' family was associated with both the imperial and papal causes, the connection being closer at first with the interests of Frederick II. However, after the latter's formal deposition by the council of Lyons in 1245, Thomas' brother Reginald was involved in an assassination plot on the emperor and was executed. The period of peace initiated by the treaty of San Germano was terminated by the excommunication of Frederick in March 1239 and in April of that year Monte Cassino was occupied and fortified by imperial troops. There is no evidence that Thomas had made his profession as a monk and he probably returned home at this time. In the autumn of 1239 he entered on the arts course at Naples university and here first began to study Aristotle – probably the *Metaphysics* as well as the works on nature and the logic. The fact that Thomas was thus introduced to Aristotle's philosophy at Naples when it was forbidden to arts students at Paris is a reminder of the diversity of reaction to the new material and of the importance of the region as a centre for translations.

Thomas did not incept in arts at Naples but instead joined the Dominican order, possibly in April 1244. While on his way to a general chapter at Bologna in May, in company with the master general, he was seized and detained by his family for over a year in an attempt to make him follow a more established regular life. A little treatise, *On Fallacies for certain Nobles in Arts* (*De fallaciis ad quosdam nobiles artistas*), and another on a logical subject may be products of this period of confinement.[60] After his release, he was sent by the order to Paris where it is likely that he spent the years 1245–8, as a member of the convent of Saint-Jacques. When, in the middle of 1248, Albert the Great went to establish a Dominican *studium generale* at Cologne, Thomas may have accompanied him. Certainly, he studied under him there from 1248 to 1252, during which time Albert is known to have lectured on the Bible, the pseudo-Denis and the *Nicomachean Ethics*.

In the autumn of 1252 Thomas went to Paris, on Albert's recommendation, to study theology. In view of the biblical training which he had already had he began immediately as a 'bachelor of the Sentences', on which he lectured for four years. He received the chancellor's licence to incept in theology probably a little before March 1256, during the dispute between secular and mendicant masters, and incepted in April or May. He began teaching as a regent master in September 1256 but it was not until about a year later that, with Bonaventure, he was accepted by the university.

In this first academic period, Thomas produced a number of works. They include, besides his *Commentary on the Sentences*, treatises *On Being and Essence* (*De ente et essentia*) and *On the Principles of Nature* (*De principiis naturae*), written before his inception, and a number of questions disputed during his regency, quodlibets and a series of questions *On Truth* (*De veritate*). As a regent he would also have been engaged on biblical exegesis. The corpus of his works includes a substantial body of scriptural commentaries, which scholars assign with varying degrees of certainty to the several phases of his teaching career. The *Summa contra Gentiles* (*Summa against the Pagans*) too is generally thought to have been begun before Thomas returned to Italy at the end of the academic year 1258–9. According to an early fourteenth-century source, the work was undertaken at the request of St Raymund of Pennaforte, a former master general of the Dominican order, as a tool for missionaries among the Moors in Spain. Despite the 'against' of its title, the work is not polemical but is rather a serious and meticulous attempt to build on philosophical foundations which were now in large part shared by both Christian and Moslem cultures. Of its four books, the first three aim to set out theological positions which can be established by philosophical reasoning alone, while the fourth book complements them by an exposition of scripturally revealed doctrine. Book I treats of God, the manner of discussing him, whether his existence can be proved, his nature and attributes; Book II considers God as creator and the nature of creation, with special attention to the nature of man; Book III considers God as the good and the end of purposive action and his providential government, particularly as regards rational creatures; Book IV expounds Christian teaching on the Trinity and Incarnation (Chapters 2–55), the sacraments (Chapters 56–78) and the resurrection of the dead and their final states

(Chapters 79–97). The earliest date for the writing of Book II is 1261, established by the fact that Thomas there uses William of Moerbeke's translation of Aristotle's *On the Generation of Animals*, completed in December of the previous year. Book IV was completed in 1264, while he was at the court of Urban IV in Orvieto.[61]

In September 1265 Thomas was assigned by the chapter of the Roman province of the order to establish a centre of study in the convent of Santa Sabina on the Aventine hill in Rome.[62] He remained based at Santa Sabina until his departure for Paris late in 1268.[63] His teaching there has left a substantial legacy. The ten disputed questions *On the Power of God* (*De potentia*) probably belong to his first year at Santa Sabina and most of the series of sixteen questions *On Evil* (*De malo*), to his second and third years there. Among the topics treated in *On the Power of God* which are of central relevance to his thought are the nature of creation and of created matter and the simplicity of the divine essence. The questions *On Evil* discuss the nature of evil and examine the seven deadly sins. A question *On Spiritual Creatures* (*De spiritualibus creaturis*) was possibly disputed in the period *c.* 1267–8 and edited later. It considers the union of the human soul and body, the Averroist doctrine of the unicity of the potential intellect and the nature of 'separated substances', that is, angels.

During his teaching at Santa Sabina, Thomas seems also to have lectured again on the first book of Peter Lombard's *Sentences* – the book which dealt with the divine trinity and unity and the divine attributes – perhaps as part of a deliberate programme to set the more usual Dominican theological training, with its emphasis on moral and sacramental theology, in a more general, dogmatic framework.[64] This interpretation would help to explain too the character of Thomas' greatest work, the *Summa Theologiae* (*Summa of Theology*).[65] Begun at Santa Sabina, avowedly 'for the instruction of beginners', it was intended as a complete and systematic guide to the subject. The *Summa* is divided into three principal parts, the second part being subdivided into a first and second part. The sections are known accordingly as *Prima Pars* ('First Part'), *Prima* (*Pars*) *Secundae* (*Partis*) ('First Part of the Second Part'), *Secunda* (*Pars*) *Secundae* (*Partis*) ('Second Part of the Second Part') and *Tertia Pars* ('Third Part').[66] The *Prima Pars* deals, after preliminary discussion of the nature of theology, mainly with God and creation but includes treatment of human nature and the intellectual life. The *Secunda Pars* deals with the moral life of man, the first subpart dealing with general aspects, the second with particular vices and virtues. The unfinished *Tertia Pars* deals with the Incarnation, the life of Christ and the church's sacraments. The *Prima Pars* was completed in Italy before Thomas' return to Paris. The *Secunda Pars* was probably begun in Italy but was mainly written in Paris, the first subpart being completed late in 1270 and the second early in 1272. The *Tertia Pars* was begun in Paris and was continued in Naples – where Thomas went after leaving Paris – from September 1272 to December 1273, at the point when he gave up writing altogether.[67]

It is probable that Thomas' recall from Rome to Paris in 1268 by the Dominican master general was intended primarily to strengthen the order there against the renewed anti-mendicant attacks of certain secular masters, most notably the theologian Gerard of Abbeville, rather than to combat radical Aristotelianism within the arts faculty.[68] He was however to be heavily engaged on both fronts during his second Paris regency. In reading the final questions of the *Secunda Secundae*, on action and contemplation and the pastoral and regular life, it is well to remember that they were written not as an abstract essay but at a time when religious vows as a means to perfection and in particular the place of the mendicant orders within the church were being hotly debated in the university. The controversy over radical Aristotelianism was the occasion of two polemical treatises by Thomas, *On the Unity of the Intellect* (*De unitate intellectus*) and *On the Eternity of the World* (*De aeternitate mundi*), both written in 1270. The subtitle, 'against the Averroists', given to the treatise *On the Unity of the Intellect* in some manuscripts, correctly denotes its purpose. It was written to refute the views of certain Paris upholders of the doctrine of Averroes on the unity of the intellect and was directed perhaps in particular at Siger of Brabant. About a year before, probably, in the theological faculty, Thomas had examined the same and related matters in a set of *Disputed Questions on the Soul* (*Quaestiones Disputatae de Anima*), which are a very full source for his views on this subject.[69] The topic of *On the Eternity of the World* was also relevant to the views of the radical Aristotelians. However, contrary to what was long the view of historians, it was not in fact aimed at them. Its target was rather the approach of conservative members of the theology faculty, apparently as represented by the Franciscan, John Pecham, in two questions disputed shortly after his inception which took place, probably, late in 1269.[70] *On the Eternity of the World* maintained the position which Thomas had already taken up in his *Commentary on the Sentences*

(2.1.1.5), in the *Summa contra Gentiles* (2.38) and most recently in the *Summa Theologiae* (1. 46. 1–2), that the eternity of the world was an open question which could not be determined philosophically.[71]

During his second Paris regency Thomas had first-hand experience of the ease with which Aristotle could, to his mind, be misinterpreted. This may well have been a consideration behind the effort which he devoted, at a time when he was otherwise already overburdened, to producing commentaries on the Aristotelian texts.[72] In the case of two texts at least there may, however, have been a more particular motive. It has been shown that the commentary on the *De Anima*, the completion of which is certainly after late November 1267, need not be considered to post-date *On the Unity of the Intellect*, as is sometimes thought, and that on the evidence of the manuscript tradition there are grounds for supposing that it was in fact completed before Thomas left Italy. In that case, the suggestion that it was part of the 'research' for his work on the corresponding section of the *Prima Pars* (questions 75–89) is a very attractive one.[73] The commentary on the *Nicomachean Ethics* can be regarded as having an analogous role in relation to the writing of the *Secunda Secundae*,[74] which is in turn broadly contemporaneous with the exploration of related topics in the disputed questions *On the Virtues* (*De Virtutibus*), held during the second regency.[75] But Thomas' commenting activity at this time went beyond what would seem necessary on the score of research alone and the needs of the arts faculty may indeed have been the stimulus. Less well known than the controversy between Thomas and the radical Aristotelians is the fact that he had a considerable following among the masters of arts. In a letter written after his death to the Dominican chapter, the rector and procurators of the arts faculty recalled how they had earlier petitioned for his return to Paris and now specifically asked that they be sent philosophical writings on which he was thought to have been engaged since his departure, including works on logic which they had asked him to write.[76] It is very likely therefore that Thomas would have been conscious of a demand for explanatory aids. In this period he commented on the *Physics*, the *Posterior Analytics*, the *De Interpretatione*, which he left unfinished, the *Politics*, the *Ethics* and two of the *Parva Naturalia* (*On Sense and Sensation* and *On Memory*). He also began work on the *Metaphysics* and *Meteorology*. These he continued at Naples, where he also took up the *De caelo* (*On Heaven*) and *On Coming to Be and Passing Away*, both of which, and the *Meteorology*, he was to leave unfinished. While at Paris he commented too on the *Liber de Causis*, now recognised as by Proclus rather than by Aristotle.

Late in April 1272, Thomas left Paris for Italy. In June of the same year he was assigned by the chapter of the Roman province of his order to found a new provincial *studium*, which it was intended would eventually become a general *studium* of the order, at a place of his choice. He chose Naples and from the autumn of 1272 until December 1273 lectured in theology at the Dominican priory there, apparently as a master both in the Dominican *studium* and in the university of Naples.[77] During this period, he worked on the *Tertia Pars* of the *Summa Theologiae* and the commentaries on Aristotle, already noted, as well as on works of biblical exegesis. To it may belong also the unfinished treatises, *Compendium Theologiae* (*Compendium of Theology*), the date of which is very uncertain, and *De substantiis separatis* (*On Separate Substances*, sc. angels), which may however belong rather to the second Paris regency.

From December 1273 Thomas ceased to write. In February 1274, his health already severely impaired, he died north of Naples while on his way to attend the general council due to meet at Lyons later in that year.

Aquinas: Existence and Nature of God

A principal characteristic of Aquinas' thought is the way in which he combines a clear and scrupulous distinction between two sources of knowledge – reason and revelation – with a confidence that truth itself is one and common to them both. The point is not that the conclusions of the two sources are always rigidly separated – though this is the strategy of the *Summa contra Gentiles* – or that Aquinas' philosophising is not influenced by his belief. It is that his writing exhibits a general critical awareness, arising from the distinction between reason and faith, of the method of procedure and the foundation of an argument. This is explicit and especially pertinent in his consideration of what can be known of God.

Regarding proof of God's existence in the *Summa contra Gentiles*, Aquinas addresses two preliminary objections from quite different perspectives. There are those who consider the undertaking superfluous since they hold the existence of God to be self-evident and there are those on the other hand who hold that the attempt is vain, that the matter cannot be rationally established but must be accepted on faith.[78] In the first case he has principally in mind those who rely on the 'ontological argument' as advanced by St Anselm, the force of which he denies on the grounds that it involves an illicit transition from the conceptual to the real order.[79] The main part of his answer to the second position is to offer a series of proofs for God's existence. He is well aware however of the limitations and difficulties of the exercise. The human intellect cannot 'through its natural power' comprehend the substance of God – what God is: 'For according to its manner of knowing in the present life, the intellect depends on sense for the origin of its knowledge; and so those things that do not fall under the senses cannot be grasped by the human intellect except in so far as the knowledge of them is gathered from sensible things.'[80] The principle here is that while the recognition that something is an effect implies recognition – and in that sense knowledge – of the cause, it does not imply knowledge of all the characteristics of the cause. Aristotle acknowledged this when he said that our intellect was as deficient in relation to the prime beings (sc. the unmoved movers) as the eye of a bat in relation to the sun.[81] Evidently, there is need for revelation if men are to know the truth about God in so far as it is unattainable by reason. However, even the truth attainable by reason is so profound that it cannot be reached except after much study or without risk of error. It is not effectively within the grasp of most men. Aquinas argues therefore that it is fitting that that body of truth too should be revealed and proposed as a subject of belief. He thus explains how Scripture and Christian credal formulae to an extent duplicate what can in his view be established by philosophical inquiry.[82]

Aquinas' proofs for God's existence proceed from the nature of external reality. In the *Summa Theologiae* he sets out five proofs. The first is Aristotle's argument from the fact of motion in the universe to a cause of motion which is itself unmoved.[83] The proof did not rest on a contention that there was a beginning to motion. Aquinas was prepared to accept as philosophically tenable the proposition, held by Aristotle himself, that motion was eternal. It rested rather on the contention that an infinite series of dependent causes is absurd. In the *Summa contra Gentiles*, this presupposition is examined and defended in detail.[84] The contention that an infinite series is impossible underlies too the second and third proofs. The second – also from Aristotle – asserts that there cannot be an infinite series of efficient causes.[85] The third is based on the distinction between essence and existence, drawn by Avicenna, and is an argument from contingent to necessary being. In the *Summa contra Gentiles*, Aquinas explains it as follows:

> We find in the world . . . certain beings, those namely that are subject to generation and corruption, which can be and not-be. But what can be has a cause because . . . it must be owing to some cause that being accrues to it. . . . We must therefore posit something that is a necessary being. Every necessary being, however, either has the cause of its necessity in an outside source or, if it does not, it is necessary through itself. But one cannot proceed to infinity among necessary beings the cause of whose necessity lies in an outside source. We must therefore posit a first necessary being which is necessary through itself.[86]

The fourth proof is the Platonist perception, already familiar from the thought of St Augustine and Anselm, that relative states of being and relative values require the postulation of an absolute. The absolute in each case is identified with God, who as the supreme being is also the supreme truth and the supreme good.[87] This argument should not be regarded as a Platonist stray marshalled into the service of proving God's existence. It is in fact one of the central concepts of Aquinas' thought as will be seen from the role it plays in his ethical theory where it caps the teleological structure taken over from Aristotle. The fifth proof is itself teleological and derives from the apparently intelligent design of the world, especially the observation that unconscious things betray a purpose in their mutually beneficial ordering, which cannot derive from themselves and cannot be attributed to chance. The conclusion is that there exists an intelligent being directing all natural beings to their ends.[88]

Having in this fashion shown that 'a first being, whom we call God'[89] exists, the next step is to investigate his properties. Aquinas applies two methods to the purpose. The first is the negative theology of which the most thorough exposition known in Latin was the works of the pseudo-Denis. Granted that one cannot know what God is, 'for by its immensity, the divine substance surpasses every form that our intellect reaches',[90] the philosopher may still proceed by knowing what he is not. So, God is immutable, without beginning or end, and thus eternal,[91] lacking potentiality[92] or matter[93] or any composition,[94] including composition of essence and existence,[95] incorporeal,[96] without accidents[97] and, as absolute being, not classifiable in terms of genus or species.[98] Finally, the most general of the negative predications, God is infinite, that is, his manner of being is not limited.[99] However, Aquinas does not rely only on negative attributes to describe God's nature. In the *Summa contra Gentiles* he goes on to analyse the basis of positive predication concerning God. The gulf which separates the infinite being from finite beings forbids the application of predicates to them 'univocally' – that is, in precisely the same sense.[100] But neither are predicates applied to them 'purely equivocally' – in totally different senses.[101] There is, Aquinas maintains, a likeness between creatures and Creator: it is the likeness of relative to absolute on which the fourth of his proofs of God's existence rests. This means that attributes applied to God and creatures signify a likeness; but they also signify an unlikeness. The perfections which are attributed are like; the manner in which they are attributed is unlike. This type of predication, which is neither 'univocal' nor 'equivocal' but has something in common with both, Aquinas calls 'analogical'. Perfections in creatures are attributed to God – to whom they properly belong – but in an absolute sense of which we have no experience and which we cannot therefore fully understand. What is said of God on the basis of rational inquiry remains always a description of the cause in terms of the effect and is inevitably deficient, 'for every effect which does not equal the power of the agent cause receives the likeness of that agent not to the full measure but incompletely'.[102]

The philosopher may then, in this analogical fashion, attribute to God perfections the concept of which has been derived from creatures. So, God is said to be good – supremely good – one, intelligent, possessed of will, and so on. This may, though, give rise to a misunderstanding. The perfections in question are not synonymous: they express different concepts, derived from experience. However, the description of God's nature in this diverse and piecemeal fashion is a reflection of man's intellectual processes and limitations rather than of diversity in God. As has already been stated, God is simple, without composition of any kind. The attributes predicated of God are distinct only in man's perception of them. In God, knowledge, will, goodness, truth and so on are perceived aspects of a perfect unity and simplicity. The point is fundamental, not only to the matter immediately in hand – the inquiry into what the philosopher can know about God – but also to the solution of another, related problem. God must be shown to know and will a multitude of things without derogation from his own simplicity. Aquinas' answer to the difficulty is tacitly to borrow the Platonist theory of exemplar ideas,[103] now identified with the divine essence. God knows and wills his own essence and all actual and possible imitations of it. It is in this way that his knowledge and will is conceived to extend to individual beings.[104] God is utterly simple and his knowing and willing, which are identical with him, are also simple. The suggestion of complexity and plurality, while inescapable, is wholly anthropomorphic.

Aquinas: Creation and Causality

The basic attribute of God from the philosopher's viewpoint is that he is the cause of the universe. In common with all Judaeo-Christian thinkers Aquinas differs from the classical Greek theories in seeing God as a creator – as having made the world from nothing.[105] God creates deliberately but creation must not be taken as implying a change in him; it is an eternal act of his will. It does not follow, however, that the effect of the creative act is eternal: 'Just as the [divine] intellect determines every other condition of the thing made, so does it prescribe the time of its making. . . . Nothing, therefore, prevents our saying that God's action existed from eternity, whereas its effect was not present from eternity but existed at that time when, from all eternity, he ordained it.'[106] As has already been noted, Aquinas considered that the question whether the universe is eternal is capable of being neither proved or disproved philosophically. The arguments for either position were stated in the *Summa contra Gentiles*[107] but Aquinas was to have occasion to return to the matter, specifically in his polemical treatise, *On the Eternity of the World*, the circumstances of which have already been noted.

God's creative activity is unique but this does not involve for Aquinas, as it did for Bonaventure, the postulation of seminal reasons as incomplete forms in created matter. Nor does his view of matter accord it any level of actuality such as attached to it in Bonaventure's thought. His understanding of the structure of the physical universe adheres closely to the Aristotelian account of causation both in its terminology – when allowances are made for the idea of deliberate creation – and in its spirit.[108] Creation is not thought of as involving the production of a matter which has actuality apart from a substantial form. For Aquinas, creation involved the production of distinct substances which as far as the physical world is concerned are substances compounded of matter and form.[109] The process of generation and decay in which substances take on new forms is sufficiently explained, in the normal pattern and for non-rational beings, by the influence of created substances as agents. These secondary agents are maintained in being by God's conserving power and are therefore subordinated to his creative activity but they have a real agency of their own, for the exercise of which they were created.[110] By this line of thought, Aquinas renders seminal reasons in the Bonaventurean sense superfluous.

The only principle in relation to which matter has any actuality for Aquinas is substantial form.[111] The union between matter and substantial form is therefore direct, as in the classic Aristotelian theory, without the mediation of a form of corporeality or of substantial dispositions in matter. The pure potentiality of matter – its lack of character – and the direct union of matter and form are for him indispensable to the unity of the substance. In his developed thought, he accepts fully and literally the Aristotelian view of soul as a body's 'first actuality', in virtue of which the substance is constituted a member of a species. As with Bonaventure's analysis, the critical issue in this regard for Christian theology was the union between body and soul in man. It is in this context that the implications of the theory must now be considered.

Aquinas: Soul and Body in Man

In Aquinas' thought, as with Aristotle, composition of matter and form is restricted to substances which are either subject to substantial change – the condition of all terrestrial substances – or to local motion, as in the case of the heavenly bodies. The attribution of matter to angels and the rational soul is rejected. Both angels and the rational soul are composite but the composition is of potentiality and actuality, essence and existence, not of matter and form. Angels are created spiritual substances, wholly separate from matter – that is, neither having matter in their composition nor any affinity for matter. Since it is in relation to matter that substances are individuated in the Aristotelian theory, there is no principle whereby multiple members of an angelic species could be distinguished. Therefore each angel must be its own species.[112] The rational soul is directly created by God as the form of a human substance.[113] Although it is without matter it has a natural aptitude for informing matter, in contrast with an angel. Having no principle of individuation within itself – like all other substantial forms it is specific rather than individual in character, considered in the abstract – it is individuated by the act of informing matter. It does not pre-exist the human body, which itself only comes into existence as a result of the informing act of soul. However, although the beginning of the soul's existence is the beginning of the existence of the body of which it is the life-giving act, the soul does not pass out of existence when, at death, it is separated from the body. The principal reasons for supposing the soul's immortality are two. Firstly, although it comes into existence with a body it does not owe its existence to a body. Secondly, its characteristic feature, rational functioning, by which it is distinguished from lower forms, is conceived to be immaterial. Hence it is taken in the last analysis to be independent of body, although while soul and body are united the soul is dependent on the body for the sense experience upon which, again in accordance with the Aristotelian theory, intellection is based.[114]

In his account of the process of knowing, Aquinas adopted the Aristotelian epistemology fully and dispensed with the theory of divine illumination as it was understood in the Augustinian tradition. What the mind knows it knows by abstraction from sense experience in virtue of its natural intellectual powers. In accordance with Aristotle's account in the *De Anima*, Aquinas conceives these powers as active and potential (or passive). The distinction accords with the general principle already noticed that there is potentiality in all created things. The human intellect as created and finite must have an element of potentiality, for only the divine intellect is wholly actual; a created intellect 'is not actual in relation to all that can be understood'.[115] Since the human intellect has no innate ideas it is clear that 'initially we are solely *able* to understand and afterwards we come actually to understand'.[116] There must also be an active intellective power. The reason is that Aristotelian 'forms' are not actually intelligible, existing as they do united with matter, so that 'nothing in the physical world is actually ready for understanding'.[117] The process of intellection is not therefore considered to be adequately explained by the mind's receptivity to the intelligible forms latent in the images produced, as in the Aristotelian account, by sensation. These provide the material of but do not themselves constitute criticised mental concepts. The extraction of the universal element from the particular images produced by sense experience is attributed to an activity on the part of mind itself. This is Aquinas' understanding of the Aristotelian active intellect and he insists that it is a power which belongs to the soul.[118] The first argument advanced in support of this in the *Summa Theologiae* is that even if there were a separate active intellect it would still have its counterpart in the soul. This is an argument based on the very Neoplatonist perspective from which the concept of a separate agent intellect itself derives, that lower realities reflect higher realities. The second argument is rather an assertion: experience of our intellectual functioning confirms that we possess this active power.[119] From this follows the resolution of the next question posed, 'whether there is one abstractive intellect for all men': 'For if the abstractive intellect were some disembodied substance not belonging to the soul, there would be one abstractive intellect for all men. Those who speak of the unity of the abstractive intellect think just that. But if the abstractive intellect is a power belonging to the soul then there must be as many of them as there are souls, and there are as many souls as there are men. . . . It is impossible for a single identical power to inhere in distinct substances.'[120]

Through his treatment of intellection Aquinas makes the union of soul and body to be the most intimate possible. Intellective function is seen as integral to the soul, while the dependence of soul on body for the exercise of this function through abstraction from sense experience shows that its union with body is to its advantage, not a mark of its degradation as frequently implied in the Platonic theory. Here are the two supporting pillars of Aquinas' structure, which collapses if either is weakened. If the unity of the human substance requires that soul and body be seen to form a real composition and not as in the Platonic theory an accidental union of two substances in which one, the soul, enters another, the body, and moves or uses it to the latter's advantage only, the immortality of the soul in such a composition requires that an immaterial intellective function should be assigned to it. This latter requirement is clearly opposed to the theory of Averroes who had wholly separated the principles of intellection and that by which the body was informed. Aquinas regarded the opinion of Avicenna, who had made only the active aspect of intellection external, as more tolerable.[121] However, as will be clear from what has been said, he was opposed to this also, insisting that both the active and potential principles of which Aristotle had spoken were integral to the soul. Through the translation of Themistius' commentary on Aristotle's *De Anima*, completed by William of Moerbeke in

November 1267, he found himself equipped to challenge the Arabic psychological tradition on its own grounds – the interpretation of Aristotle's theory. Insistence that separation of the intellect from the soul is a corruption of Aristotle is the main line of attack in the polemical treatise *On the Unity of the Intellect* (*De Unitate Intellectus*) written in Paris in 1270.

The natural bond between soul and body and the dependence of the soul on the imaginative power as its source of and point of reference for abstracted concepts has a further implication. That is, that the soul in its disembodied condition between death and the final judgement when, according to Christian belief, the body is resurrected, is in a state contrary to its nature.[122] One consequence of this, which Aquinas himself seems to have developed only over a period,[123] is that its natural power of knowing is impaired – though Aquinas held that the souls of the beatified would enjoy a supernatural degree of knowledge. Another consequence is that the separated soul is an imperfect substance, an incomplete personality: it is something less than the man, who is a composite of soul and body.[124] For this and related reasons, Aquinas argues that the doctrine of the resurrection of the body is supported and apparently demanded by philosophical considerations.[125] The point was a bold one, expressing at once the reality of the hylomorphic composition of man and the harmony and convergence of reason and revelation.

Aquinas: Moral and Social Theory

Aquinas' epistemology, cosmology and psychology are recognisably Aristotelian, when allowance is made for significant differences such as the concept of a providential creator, the elaboration of the distinction between essence and existence to which his perception of the gulf between creator and creation led him and his precision concerning personal immortality. In his moral and social theory, however, his belief in man's supernatural end prompted him to transcend Aristotle's account. Therefore, although the influence of Aristotle on this part of his system is considerable, it rather provides the starting point and affects the method of the analysis than constitutes its principal import and direction. Thus the Aristotelian teleological norm, that man's actions – those of the will, *actus humani* ('human actions'), rather than the involuntary *actus hominis* ('actions of a man'), as Aquinas distinguished them – are directed towards the achievement of the good, underlies his moral theory. But this has a different significance for him from that it had for Aristotle. Given the doctrine that man has a supernatural final state of happiness, it was impossible for a Christian thinker to adhere to the spirit of Aristotle's ethics without proposing two ends, one attainable on the natural level and another on the supernatural level. As will be seen, Aquinas does indeed recognise such a distinction – in view of Aristotle's treatment he could hardly do otherwise – but he does not allow himself to be forced by it into compartmentalising his moral theory. For him, no good can satisfy man short of the ultimate, knowledge and possession of the Good. It is towards this that man's desires are seen as being directed. So, although a large part of Aquinas' discussion of morality is modelled on the *Nicomachean Ethics*, eventually Aristotle's account is superseded. Since man has a supernatural end, there are also supernatural virtues which he can acquire only through supernatural grace:

> A man is perfected by virtue towards those actions by which he is directed towards happiness. . . . Yet man's happiness is twofold. . . . One is proportionate to human nature, and this he can reach through his own resources. The other, a happiness surpassing his nature, he can attain only by the power of God, by a kind of participation in the Godhead. . . . Because such happiness goes beyond the reach of human nature, man's natural resources by which man is able to act well according to his capacity are not adequate to direct him to it. And so to be directed towards this supernatural happiness, he needs to be divinely endowed with some additional sources of activity; their role is like that of his natural capacities, which direct him, not, of course, without God's help, to his connatural end.[126]

These additional sources of activity are the theological virtues of faith, hope and charity.[127]

Among the most important insights which Aquinas did derive from Aristotle were his perception of man as a continuous agent in his moral choices and of virtue as a general disposition.[128] The latter in particular is the inspiration for the very fine and full treatment of the intellectual and moral virtues, and by extension, for the similar treatment of the theological virtues, in the *Secunda Pars* of the *Summa of Theology*. The treatment is in two parts: a general consideration of virtue, in the First Part of the *Secunda Pars*, and a detailed investigation of individual virtues in the Second Part of the same. But Aristotle may not have been the only model. It has been argued very plausibly that this whole latter part (*Secunda Secundae*) may have been intended as a substitute for the less organic type of *Summa of Virtues and Vices* (*Summa de Virtutibus et Vitiis*) which was one of the principal sources of contemporary moral theology at a pastoral level, both within the Dominican order – which Thomas probably had chiefly in mind – and outside.[129] The suggestion of a clear practical purpose of this kind seems to be confirmed by the distinction of approach outlined in the prologue to the *Secunda Secundae*. According to this, individual treatment of the moral topics is to be followed by an examination of 'people in their respective callings', with the promise firstly of 'themes related to all stations in life' and secondly 'details related to particular callings'.[130] Analysis of the relationship between moral obligation and social or vocational standing was one of the most prominent subjects of medieval moralising. It was the foundation of a thriving genre of 'estates' literature – Latin and vernacular – in the later middle ages and in the hands of the canon lawyers and writers on penance was an important vehicle for the application of precept to social organisation. Measured against that tradition, Aquinas' consideration of the 'particular callings' is in fact sketchy and on a very general level. Perhaps he felt that the area had been or was being sufficiently explored by the canonists – such as his confrère, Raymund of Pennaforte – whose speciality it had become.[131] But there does seem in what he says, by way of outlining his subject, to be a hint of this particular dimension. However that may be, what he did achieve was a magisterial analysis of the virtues and vices – with special emphasis on justice and injustice. It found a ready demand. It was adopted in large part by another Dominican, John of Freiburg (*c.* 1297–8), into what became perhaps the most important *Summa for Confessors* of the middle ages and was used, directly and indirectly, by other treatises of the type.[132] Thus vicariously and through the wide circulation achieved by the *Secunda Secundae* in its own right[133] Aquinas' treatment of the subject must be reckoned one of the most influential theoretical essays ever written.

The determinant of morality throughout Aquinas' system is reason. Reason proposes the object for the will's exercise of choice, 'for will . . . is directed by reason and understanding, not only in us but in God'.[134] Its role is central to the discussion of virtue in the

Secunda Pars where, as in Aristotle's *Ethics*, the link between the intellectual and moral virtues is forged by prudence, which is 'right reason about things to be done',[135] 'a virtue of the utmost necessity for human life'.[136] Reason, indeed, is at the very basis of the moral law. Law at its most fundamental level, as stated by Aquinas, is the 'eternal' law, which is the divine will for the ordering of the created universe in accordance with the divine reason. That part of the divine law which stems from the nature of man and is discernible by him through rational reflection is the 'natural' law.[137] It incorporates such principles, at their broadest, as the rational pursuit of good, the preservation of one's life and the perpetuation of the species. Since man is a political animal – and, as Aquinas tends to express it also, a social animal – the precepts of natural law will also be precepts which are conducive to good social organisation. However, these precepts will also be expressed in 'human', positive law, which is morally binding in so far as it is true to its purpose – that is, in so far as it is just. In case of conflict with divine law, human law must always be disobeyed.[138]

Compared with St Augustine's view of the state, Aquinas' most important departure was his acceptance of Aristotle's principle, set out in the *Politics*, that man was by nature political and that the state was a natural society.[139] He knew the *Politics* from about 1260 and commented on part of it about 1270. However, the greatest influence on his theory of society was exercised by the *Nicomachean Ethics*. He had been introduced to this by St Albert at Cologne, in Grosseteste's translation, with particular direction towards its social and political implications.[140] Aquinas drew on the treatment of association developed under the topic of friendship in Book VIII of the *Ethics* to support his defence of the regular life against William of Saint-Amour in the treatise *Against the attackers of divine service and the regular life* (*Contra impugnantes Dei cultum et religionem*), written in October 1256.[141] Friendship itself, between governed and governing, is recommended as one of the sources of political stability in the unfinished treatise *On Princely Government* (*De regno* or *De regimine principum*) which Aquinas wrote for a king of Cyprus – probably the young Hugh II, who died in December 1267.[142] With the rule of the well-loved king is contrasted that of the tyrant, which 'being hated by the community, cannot long endure; for that cannot last for long which is against the desire of many'.[143] As was no doubt inevitable in the context, Aquinas endorses monarchy as the best form of government and that which is to be preferred, despite the risk that it may degenerate into tyranny.[144] It will be remembered that Aristotle, though he considered monarchy of the virtuous man to be a theoretical ideal, recommended polity in practice. This latter was the constitutional theory on which Marsiglio of Padua, writing some sixty years later than Aquinas and with a quite different political context in mind, was to base his *Defender of the Peace*, the most thorough-going medieval application of Aristotelianism to political organisation.

Aquinas' political thinking is as much a transformed Aristotelianism as is his general morality. The occasion of the transformation was the same in each case – regard for a higher dimension than that developed by Aristotle. The difference between the Christian and the classical perspectives is apparent in the treatment of the ruler's motivation in *On Princely Government*. Aristotle had proposed honour and glory as the proper and sufficient reward of a ruler, meaning by that to restrain his self-interest. Aquinas thinks it fragile and inferior: 'Human glory is an insufficient reward for the kingly office'.[145]

> Rather, we consider them happy who rule wisely, who prefer the suppression of evil to the oppression of peoples, and who carry out their duties, not from a desire of empty glory but for love of eternal blessedness. We say of such christian rulers that they are happy in this life by reason of their hope and will be so hereafter, when all our hope shall be fulfilled. Nor is there any other reward which could make a man happy or which could be considered a fitting recompense for kingship . . . God alone is fitting reward for a king.[146]

In this respect the ruler is merely the man writ large. His reward will be greater in that his responsibilities are greater.[147] His fundamental responsibility derives indeed from the Aristotelian nature of society, the object of which is the virtuous life.[148] But here again what is in question is the virtuous life with a supernatural dimension.[149] Kings cannot guide to this end; it is the duty of priests.[150] Temporal affairs and spiritual are distinct but there is a hierarchy of ends. Therefore, 'Those who are concerned with the subordinate ends of life must be subject to him who is concerned with the supreme end and be directed by his command';[151] and 'because the aim of a good life on this earth is blessedness in heaven, it is the king's duty to promote the welfare of the community in such a way that it leads fittingly to the happiness of heaven; insisting upon the performance of all that leads thereto, and forbidding, as far as possible, whatever is inconsistent with this end'.[152] Aquinas is far from envisaging a hierocracy. The state has a natural justification and an autonomy within its peculiar sphere. But while not dependent on the church for its *raison d'être*, it is notionally subordinate to it and in matters affecting the supernatural end must be actually so. In view of the point of departure from Augustine the destination at which Aquinas has arrived comes as a surprise, though the position is entirely consistent with his principles. While according the state a natural legitimacy, in contrast with Augustine, he requires from it a positive role bearing on the supernatural end, a thesis from which Augustine, in the abstract at least, had stopped short.

Radical Aristotelianism and the Condemnations

The inclusion of the new philosophical material on the syllabus of the Paris arts faculty had important repercussions. It meant that in the foremost arts-theology studium of Christendom, *pari-passu* with the great developments in theology, Aristotle and his pagan and Islamic commentators were being studied by masters who had no formal responsibility to relate his teaching to that of Christianity. Given their statutory obligation from 1255 to teach Aristotle, it was not difficult for regents in arts to conceive their function as that of expounding the sense of the text. This is what the most outstanding and controversial figures among them, Siger of Brabant and Boethius of Dacia, claimed to do. It was not part of the programme of the arts faculty to make a theological synthesis nor would its members have been considered competent to do so. There is no reason to suppose that either Siger or Boethius saw their method as innovatory. It is more likely that they conceived their function to be that of exegetes, in accordance with what was a well established scholastic practice of 'lecturing' upon an authority. Nor are there any grounds for attributing to them a theory of 'double truth', such as was denounced by the prologue to the 1277 condemnation: 'For they [sc. the unnamed teachers of the errors condemned] say that these things are true according to philosophy but not according to the catholic faith, as if there were two contrary truths and as if the truth of sacred Scripture were contradicted by the truth in the sayings of the accursed pagans of whom it is written, *I will destroy the wisdom of the wise* [1 Corinthians 1. 19] inasmuch as true wisdom destroys false wisdom.'[153] So far as the direct written evidence of teaching goes, the idea of a 'double truth' was a gloss on the position of those who held the offending articles rather than a theory maintained by them.[154] When forced to confront a divergence between Aristotle and faith, Siger identified truth with the latter. In the early phase of his teaching it does not appear that he gave any attention to the problem of such divergence. In the later phase he made it clear that he considered Aristotle capable of error and that philosophical conclusions might be wrong even when the reasoning behind them could not be faulted. This is not a doctrine of 'double truth' and it is something less too than a claim that philosophy is autonomous. Taken at face value, it is not so very far removed in substance from the attitude of Augustine and Bonaventure. The perspective however is different. In Siger there is lacking the sense of spiritual vision that supports Augustine and Bonaventure in their conviction that reason is a fallacious guide to truth.

There has been much debate over how the views of Siger and his associates in the arts faculty may best be characterised. For long they were identified as 'Latin Averroists'. While the term serves to describe a position on the nature of intellect, it has been rightly criticised as being too narrow and in some other respects inaccurate as a description of the body of controversial teachings. The term 'integral Aristotelianism' has some merit except that it ignores the fact that the masters concerned, like the rest of their generation, expounded Aristotle in the light of Avicenna and Averroes, among other commentators, and with a large contribution from Neoplatonism. More recently, Professor van Steenberghen, whose own researches have transformed our understanding of Siger and his context, has given currency to the term 'radical Aristotelianism' as a description of the movement. This does capture very neatly the effect upon contemporaries, though it has to be remembered that Aristotelianism itself was radical in a Christian context and required little teasing from its expositors to render it so. It is clear from the writings or recorded lectures of Siger and Boethius that they had arrived at a compelling insight into the nature of the universe based on Aristotelian principles. There is no doubt that they were fascinated by it. No doubt also they communicated their fascination to their youthful audiences. Judging by the written evidence, neither was a lacklustre teacher. Their flair and the sensitive character of the material which they handled combined powerfully to disturb a balance which was already precarious.

The works of Siger of Brabant and Boethius of Dacia are the principal literary witnesses to radical Aristotelianism. Siger was born around 1240 and became master of arts at Paris in about 1265 or a little before. From shortly after that time until his flight from Paris in 1276 he was a prominent figure in the arts faculty.[155] The substantial written corpus of his teaching consists partly of unrevised *reportationes* – that is, notes taken by a member of the audience – and partly of 'official' versions, apparently edited by the master himself. They fall into several periods, reflecting important developments in Siger's outlook. The first period which has been distinguished is that preceding the condemnation issued by the bishop of Paris, Stephen Tempier, on 10 December 1270. To it belong two works of interest as sources for Siger's controverted views, a logical question exploring the relationship between concept and reality and entitled 'Whether it would be true to say "Man is an animal", if no man existed' (*Quaestio utrum haec sit vera "homo est animal" nullo homine existente*), and the important set of *Questions on the Third Book of the De Anima* (*Quaestiones in Tertium De Anima*), which are held to date from the beginning of the academic year 1269–70. In the logical question, Siger resolves the problem posed by dismissing it as an unreal one since the human species is eternal. He does so without any reference to the discrepancy between the Aristotelian and Christian perspectives.[156] The work on Book III of the *De Anima* consists of eighteen questions, divided into four chapters. The first chapter is devoted to differentiating between the intellect and the sensitive and vegetative parts of the soul; the second discusses the nature of intellect, considered in itself; the third discusses intellect considered in relation to bodies; the fourth deals with the possible, that is the 'potential', and agent intellect. In his treatment, Siger subscribes with minor differences of expression and emphasis to Averroes' theory that intellect is external to the individual. He gives no sign that he is aware of or concerned by a conflict between this outlook and Christian teaching on immortality.[157]

This direct evidence of radical teaching in the arts faculty in the period before the 1270 condemnation is complemented by several other literary sources. The Augustinian friar, Giles of Rome, was at Paris as student, master and bachelor from probably the early 1260s to 1278, when his attack on the doctrine of the plurality of forms resulted in his expulsion for a time from the university. He was the author of, among other works, a treatise *On the errors of the philosophers*

(*De erroribus philosophorum*), written between 1268 and 1274, but perhaps around 1270,[158] in which he catalogued what he considered to be the errors of Aristotle himself and of his Arabic disciples. The work is a valuable judgement on the controversial aspects of Aristotelianism but it is not linked specifically to contemporary expositions. However, Giles knew some at least of what was being taught by the radical masters. In a passage of his *Commentary on the Sentences*, the redaction of which dates from after 1295, he recalled how as a bachelor he had seen a great master, 'a major figure in philosophy, who was then at Paris, resolved on holding the opinion of the Commentator [sc. Averroes] that man does not understand [sc. as an individual]'.[159] If this refers to Giles' period as a bachelor of arts – as suggested by the context in which he saw the 'major figure' concerned – rather than as a bachelor in theology, it is a scene from *c*. 1265.[160] There is no means of identifying the teacher in question.

The *Collations* of Bonaventure ('On the Ten Commandments' and 'On the Seven Gifts') are important as the first known stirrings of disquiet at current views in the years 1267 and 1268. As already noted, the 1267 set attacked though in general terms and without attribution the doctrines of the eternity of the world and the unity of the intellect – two tenets which appear in the works of Siger discussed above. Criticism of the eternity of the world and the unity of the intellect was renewed in the 1268 set, which also attacked necessitarian determinism.[161]

The next piece of evidence is of outstanding interest. This is Thomas Aquinas' tract *On the unity of the intellect*, written in 1270. In it he attacked two contentions: first, that the possible (or potential) intellect was a separate substance and not the form of the body, and secondly that it was one for all men. The approach to the first is in large part an exploration of Aristotle's own meaning and the views of his interpreters, Greek and Arabic. As far as the Greek tradition went, Aquinas took full advantage of the recently available text of Themistius' commentary on the *De Anima*. The weight of authority, he found, was heavily against Averroes who emerged therefore as 'not so much a Peripatetic [sc. an Aristotelian] as a perverter of Peripatetic philosophy'.[162] He then proceeded to consolidate his own interpretation by a series of arguments in favour of the doctrine that the intellect was a power of the human soul. A principal consideration advanced is the difficulty otherwise of explaining how it is that the individual understands. Nothing in what Aquinas says suggests that he was aware of any challenge to the view that it is the individual who understands. As regards the second contention against which he wrote, his task was easy, since the position became untenable if it were accepted that the intellect was a part of the soul which informed a body. Having made his point and having raised a number of absurd consequences of the doctrine that the intellect is one, he proceeded to criticise the arguments put up against the doctrine that it is multiplied by the number of individual men. A notable feature of the tract is that it is aimed both at a particular figure – not named, but taken to be Siger, a view which has some manuscript authority – and at a group who teach Averroes' doctrine on the intellect. However, although it tackles the same general teaching as that contained in Siger's *Questions on the Third Book of the De Anima*, there is no certainty that Thomas had this text to hand and he must at least have had some other source for the views which he combated. Such a source might have been notes taken at Siger's lectures.[163] The challenge offered in the final paragraph of Thomas' tract ('If there be anyone . . . who wishes to say something against what we have written here, let him not speak in corners, nor in the presence of boys who do not know how to judge about such difficult matters; but let him write against this teaching if he dares')[164] suggests that he was thinking to some extent of oral teaching. This is confirmed by the impression gained from the tract that he was in doubt on certain points about the exact nature of the opposed views.

Another piece of supplementary evidence for radical Aristotelianism in its early phase is by its nature somewhat hazardous but it agrees well enough in its main features with what is known otherwise. This is the syllabus condemned in 1270. To a considerable extent it reflects the preoccupations evident in Bonaventure's collations and in some other of his sermons. It may be that Bonaventure exercised a significant influence in the framing of the condemnation, though it is not known by what procedure Bishop Tempier drew up his list – whether or not, that is, he was assisted by a commission, as in 1277.[165] The text is brief enough and of sufficient interest to quote in full:[166]

These are the errors condemned and excommunicated together with all who shall have taught them knowingly or have asserted them, by the Lord Stephen, bishop of Paris, in the year of Our Lord 1270, on the Wednesday after the feast of the blessed Nicholas in winter:

The first article is: that the intellect of all men is one and the same in number.

2. That this is false or inappropriate: man understands.
3. That the will of man wills or chooses out of necessity.
4. That everything that is done here below is subject to the necessary causation of the heavenly bodies.
5. That the world is eternal.
6. That there never was a first man.
7. That the soul which is man's form in that he is man is corrupted on the corruption of the body.
8. That the soul separated [sc. from the body] after death does not suffer from corporeal fire.
9. That free will is a passive not an active power; and that it is moved necessarily by the object of desire.
10. That God does not know individual things.
11. That God does not know things other than himself.
12. That human acts are not ruled by the providence of God.
13. That God cannot give immortality or incorruption to a corruptible or mortal being.

How far do these articles respond to what is known of radical teaching in the period up to 1270? For some of them no contemporary source has as yet been found to which they might refer. This is the case with articles 4 (astrological determinism) and 13 (divine power regarding immortality). The remote pedigree in Aristotelian and Neoplatonist thought of the articles which bear on free will, divine knowledge and divine providence is clear enough, and an exposition of the texts could easily give rise to them. Neither providence nor divine knowledge of the world had any place in the Aristotelian or Neoplatonist systems. The knowledge of Aristotle's unmoved Mover is self-centred. There are traces in Siger of this outlook as regards the way in which subsistent intelligences have knowledge but his point was not a denial that God knows individuals and such a contention is not compatible with his general views.[167] As regards free will, Thomas Aquinas had already pointed out in *On the unity of the intellect* how it was subverted by the doctrine of a unique intellect, for it 'follows that there would be no difference among men in respect to the free choice of the will, but it [the choice] would be the same for all, if the intellect in which alone would reside pre-eminence and dominion over the use of all other powers is one and undivided in all. This is clearly false and

impossible. For it is opposed to what is evident and destroys the whole
of moral science and everything which relates to the civil intercourse
which is natural to man.'[168] Moreover, apart from this aspect and the
more general cosmic determinism condemned in the syllabus, the
framers of it were concerned by the Aristotelian account of human
motivation, as reflected in the second part of article 9. This subject
would receive more detailed attention in the condemnation of 1277.
Siger does not seem to have consciously denied freedom of will but the
psychology of motivation was a delicate topic and it is noteworthy
that his treatment of moral responsibility in a treatise on *Impossibles*
(*Impossibilia*), which probably comes from the period 1271–4, does
have a determinist flavour.[169]

Four articles of the syllabus reflect Siger's teaching directly. These
are articles 1 (the unicity of the intellect), articles 5 and 6 (the eternity
of the world and of the human species) and article 8 (that the
separated soul does not suffer corporeal fire). The last point Siger had
maintained in the *Questions on the Third Book of the De Anima*.[170] Some
others, for instance article 2 (that the individual does not understand)
and article 7 (that the soul which is the human form disintegrates with
the body) might have been thought to follow from his known views on
the intellect, but they are not found in the writings. Article 2, if
directed at him, seems to be a distortion of his actual position.[171] Siger
held that the union between the principle by which man understood
and his body was not the union of substantial form and matter, in
Aristotelian terms. But his view of the interaction between the
principle of intellection and man's sense experience left room, in his
own opinion at least, for an individual character to thought. It
appears however that some of the arts masters were more extreme in
this respect. Giles of Rome's recollection, already quoted, is one
testimony to the extreme position. Moreover, in a treatise written in
1275, *On the plurality of the possible intellect (De pluralitate intellectus
possibilis)*, he records that there were divergent reactions among the
radical masters to the criticisms of Thomas' *On the unity of the intellect*.
Some defended their position while conceding Thomas' point that the
individual does understand. Others denied the point.[172] As already
noted, Thomas himself showed no sign in his tract that he was aware
of a contention that the individual does not understand. However,
that is the view maintained a little later in an anonymous commentary on the *De Anima* emanating from the arts faculty at some time
after Thomas' tract and before 1275. Here the presupposition that the

individual understands is rejected flatly. 'They accept', says the anonymous author, 'that man properly understands; but they do not prove it. On this basis, they have an argument. But if the basis is untrue they have no argument. Well then, I do not concede that man understands, in a proper use of language. If the point is once conceded I do not know how to reply; but I deny the point, and rightly so; therefore my reply will be easy.'[173] This is an example of precisely the extreme reaction of which Giles speaks. If, as is possible, the anonymous commentary intervened between the publication of Thomas' tract in 1270 and the condemnation of the same year, it may be the source of the view stigmatised in article 2.

Several of Siger's writings or reported lectures are judged to come probably from the period 1271 to 1274. Those which contain insights on the controversial questions include a *Treatise on the eternity of the world* (*Tractatus de eternitate mundi*), the treatise on *Impossibles* (*Impossibilia*), already noted, a lecture *On necessity and contingency of causes* (*De necessitate et contingentia causarum*), a commentary on Aristotle's *Metaphysics* and a treatise *On the intellective soul* (*De anima intellectiva*). In several, the author is at pains to emphasise that his approach to the subject is expository rather than dogmatic. In discussing the eternity of the world, Siger sets out the Aristotelian position on species, carefully noting that the doctrine is that of Aristotle, and denies that the contrary can be proved. The treatise on *Impossibles* is devoted to a series of sophisms including, besides the matter already noted, the proposition 'God does not exist'. In his analysis of it Siger expounds the Neoplatonist theory of necessary causation, but makes it clear that he does so 'according to the statement of the philosophers'. Similarly, in discussing necessity and contingency, he sets out the Neoplatonist theory, again stressing that this is the viewpoint of the philosophers. In commenting on the *Metaphysics*, however, he departs from this apparent professional detachment. He does again purport to set out the opinions of the philosophers. But he also faces the question how there can be a contradiction between their conclusions and the doctrines of faith. His explanation is that any philosopher, however great, can be mistaken. The truths of faith, on the other hand, are founded on the prophets and catholic truth is not to be denied on grounds of philosophical argument, even where the argument cannot be refuted. It would seem that there has been a development either in Siger's views or in his sensitivity to their effect.[174] The same sensitivity is evident in *On the intellective soul*. This is his next extant treatise on the highly charged psychological problem after the *Questions on the Third Book of the De Anima*. There is late authority from an Italian source that Siger composed a reply to Aquinas' criticisms. The reply, referred to by the title, *On the Intellect* (*De intellectu*), maintained the earlier teaching, at least in its main lines. It was a different work from *On the intellective soul* and is now lost. The latter itself is incomplete, though the final chapter was probably never written.[175] It is a confused treatise. Siger argues that on the very Aristotelian principles accepted by Aquinas the intellect must be one. He then concedes that several philosophers, Avicenna, Algazel and Themistius, have held otherwise. Because of this difficulty and others he has for long been uncertain what the solution is and what Aristotle's own position was. Accordingly, it is necessary to adhere to faith which surpasses all human reason. However, he then proceeds to analyse man as a composite – his intellect coming from outside – in a modified version of the Averroist position.[176] The equivocal attitude here proved to be merely a stage in the development of Siger's thoughts on the subject. These are revealed again by his *Questions on the Book of Causes* (*Quaestiones super librum de causis*) which probably date from *c*. 1275–6. Now Siger recognises that the doctrine of the unique intellect is 'in our faith heretical and it seems also to be irrational'. After setting out the arguments on either side he takes a stand remarkably similar to that of his former opponent in the matter, Thomas Aquinas.[177] Thus in his last known lectures Siger did a volte-face on his original teaching about the intellect.

Of the life and career of Boethius of Dacia little is known. A native of what is modern Denmark, he taught in the arts faculty at Paris up to *c*. 1277. After the condemnation of that year he seems to have entered the Dominican order.[178] There is manuscript evidence that teachings by him were included in the condemnation of 1277 and this is confirmed by recent investigation.[179] About a dozen writings by him survive. Most important among them are two treatises: *On the highest good or on the life of the philosopher* (*De summo bono sive de vita philosophi*) and *On the eternity of the world* (*De eternitate mundi*).[180]

In *On the eternity of the world* Boethius takes a position similar to that of Thomas Aquinas: he holds that the philosopher as such cannot show the world to have begun – that is, not to be eternal – but he affirms vigorously that it must be held as an article of faith that the world did begin and he regards the contrary as false. His treatment includes an explicit analysis of the division between reason and faith which is of considerable interest as an example of thinking in the arts faculty on this point:

> There are many things in faith which cannot be demonstrated by reason, for instance that a dead body returns to life as the same individual and that a thing which is generated returns without generation [references to the Christian doctrine that the body is resurrected at the end of the world]. On the one hand, he who does not believe this is a heretic; on the other, he who seeks to know it by reason is a fool. Therefore, because effects and works are from power and power is from substance, who dares to say that he knows perfectly by reason the divine substance and all its power? That would be to say that he knows perfectly all the immediate effects of God: how they are from him, whether in time or from eternity, and how they are conserved by him in being and how they are in him. . . . And who is there who can sufficiently investigate this? And since there are many points in these matters which faith posits and which cannot be investigated by human reason, therefore where reason falls short, faith supplies the defect. . . .[181]

The most notable feature of his thinking here is how far it is removed from the notion of a 'double truth'.[182]

Boethius' treatise *On the highest good* is a very fine and concise essay on the Aristotelian doctrine that the intellectual life is the highest good for man. The author declares at the outset that his investigation is being conducted 'by reason', with the implication that he is eschewing theological insights. There is no doubt that this formal method explains the almost complete lack of Christian content, the only hint of such being a suggestion that 'he who is more advanced in the happiness which we know by reason to be possible for a man in this life, is closer to the happiness to which we look forward by faith in a future life'.[183] To suppose that the author intended to exclude a theological dimension from human happiness would be wrong. However, as it stood, the work was an unnervingly powerful statement of how far the *Nicomachean Ethics* could carry towards a purely naturalistic account of human orientation and activity. The threat was felt, as appears from the inclusion in Tempier's 1277 syllabus of the proposition 'that there is no more excellent state than to devote oneself to philosophy'.[184]

The period between the condemnation of 1270 and that of 1277 was

one of great turbulence in the Paris arts faculty.[185] The disarray
manifested itself in the contest over the election of a rector in
December 1271. A majority – representing conservative views, as
appears – supported one candidate, Alberic of Reims. A minority
supported an unnamed figure who was in all probability Siger
himself. In March 1272 the split was aggravated when the dissident
minority elected a rector and other officers of its own. This situation
lasted until a settlement was effected by the papal legate, Cardinal
Simon de Brion, in 1275. In April 1272 the conservatives enacted
statutes forbidding any arts master to determine in theological
matters or to teach against faith in philosophical matters. This
indicates the nature of the underlying issue. The episode is a salutary
caution against identifying the whole of the faculty with the views of
its most famous and most outspoken masters.

The settlement of 1275 had a large measure of success but it did not
solve all the faculty's problems. The issue behind the enactment of
April 1272 was still alive.[186] In September 1276 a decree of the whole
university forbade masters or bachelors of any faculty from lecturing
in private except on books of logic or grammar. Lecturing was to be in
publicly accessible places where faithful record could be taken of what
was said. In November, the inquisitor of France, the Dominican,
Simon du Val, cited Siger of Brabant and two others, Gosvin of la
Chapelle and Bernier de Nivelles, of whom little else is known, to
appear before him. Probably Siger and Gosvin had already fled to
Italy, where Siger was to die at the hands of a demented secretary
several years later.

Two weeks after the inquisitor's action, Cardinal Simon moved to
punish those guilty of a range of offences against clerical discipline.
Whether it was the case, as suggested by Professor van Steenberghen,
that the philosophical crisis had its counterpart in a moral decline,[187]
it seems likely that the ecclesiastical authorities thought so and were
determined to bring the university to order on both counts. On 18
January 1277, the day on which Siger and his colleagues were due to
appear before the inquisitor, Pope John XXI – the former Master
Peter of Spain – took the initiative. He wrote instructing Bishop
Tempier to inquire into the errors current in the university and to
report on them. The bishop immediately appointed a commission of
sixteen theologians, including the prominent secular master, Henry
of Ghent, to conduct the investigation. The commission proceeded
with great urgency. With equal urgency, the bishop, by his own

authority, on 7 March published a list of 219 propositions said to emanate from the arts faculty. The propositions were 'strictly forbidden' and 'totally condemned' and those who taught or held them excommunicated, unless they approached the bishop within seven days. In a further hint of a perceived connection between moral and intellectual decadence, there was also banned, in the prologue to the syllabus of propositions, a late twelfth-century work on courtly love, a work on divination and several unnamed works on the same subject and on magic and astrology.

Tempier's 1277 condemnation does not lend itself readily to summary but a general outline is necessary. The list of propositions is usually studied in the ordering given it by the pioneering researcher in the subject, P. Mandonnet.[188] Mandonnet grouped them in two broad sections: errors in philosophy (179 propositions) and errors in theology (40 propositions). He also subdivided them thematically. The errors in philosophy fall under the following subject headings:[189] the nature of philosophy (seven propositions, including 'that there is no more excellent state than to devote oneself to philosophy' (1;40)); the knowability of God (three propositions); the nature of God (two propositions); divine knowledge (three propositions, including that 'God does not know things other than himself' (13;3) and that 'the first cause has no knowledge of future contingents' (15;42)); divine will and power (eleven propositions, including that 'in making whatever is caused directly by him God does so necessarily' (20;53)); the causation of the world (six propositions); the nature of the intelligences (twenty-three propositions); the function of the intelligences (eight propositions); the heaven and the generation of lower beings (nineteen propositions); the eternity of the world (ten propositions); necessity and contingency (fifteen propositions); the principles of material beings – that is, matter, form and the elements – (five propositions); man and the agent intellect (twenty-seven propositions); the operation of the human intellect (ten propositions); human will (twenty propositions, including several asserting the determination of the will by the good); ethics and morality (ten propositions, including several concerning immortality and the nature of happiness).

The important questions of the sources of the propositions and the immediate targets of the condemnation have been greatly illuminated by recent scholarship.[190] In the case of those for which an exact or close parallel exists in contemporary writings it seems that one need look no further than the arts faculty, the explicit object of the proceeding as announced in Tempier's prologue. Of the propositions which can be attributed with either certainty or probability, some forty-four come from Siger, sixteen from Boethius and fourteen from the works of anonymous arts masters. In a large number of other cases it is possible that the views of Siger or Boethius were implicated. Commentators both in the middle ages and in modern times have noted that a number of propositions reflect doctrines of Thomas Aquinas. In fact, only one can be said with certainty to be directly drawn from him and this is not a doctrine but rather an explanatory comment of no importance.[191] However, several other propositions do correspond to Aquinas' views even though it is likely that the source was similar statements by arts masters. The most generally interesting examples of this category are a series of propositions expressing the theory of individuation by matter and founding all knowledge on sense experience.[192] Several also dealt with the relationship between knowing and willing in a manner which would have been hostile to Aquinas' outlook.[193] No reference was made however to the sensitive doctrine of the unicity of substantial form. This now became the object of attention elsewhere.

Eleven days after the Paris condemnation, Archbishop Robert Kilwardby, a Dominican and former master at Paris, in a visitation of the university of Oxford, forbade the teaching there of a series of thirty propositions, of which sixteen were philosophical.[194] The most important feature of the list was the determined attack which it mounted on the unicity of substantial form. Included in it was not only the unicity of substantial form (propositions 7 and 12) but various related theories. Thus, it was forbidden to teach that there was no form of corporeality (proposition 13), that the intellective soul was united directly to matter – the position, it will be remembered, which Bonaventure had attacked so fiercely – (proposition 16), that matter had no active potentiality, that is, no inchoate form or seminal reason (proposition 3), that privation (lack of form) was pure nothingness (proposition 4) and that form corrupted into pure nothingness (rather than into a pristine state of 'active potentiality') (proposition 2). In all this, Kilwardby had made a significant departure. It might very well have been imitated in its turn. On 28 April the pope ordered Bishop Tempier to proceed to a new investigation, this time to include the theology as well as the arts faculty. However, three weeks later John XXI was dead and no further condemnation ensued at Paris.

7. The Condemnations in Context

IT is convenient to end an account of the medieval recovery of ancient thought and its penetration of western consciousness with the 1270s. The Aristotelian corpus was now complete and, except for the recently discovered *Politics*, its implications had been recognised and its doctrine had made a massive impact on the intellectual system. The impact of the *Politics* is part of the wider political and ecclesiastical as well as intellectual history of the fourteenth century. However, to end in the 1270s carries one serious risk, that of attributing too much importance to the local condemnations and censures[1] which mark the decade so heavily. Unquestionably the condemnations are significant but it needs to be distinguished in what their significance lies and in what it does not.

To take the former aspect first: apart from their immediate implications for the two universities concerned, the chief significance of the condemnations is that they were symptomatic. They are the high-water point of a tide of unease which had ebbed and flowed over Aristotle's doctrines and the comments of his interpreters since these began to be understood. In their apprehension of the dangers of naturalism and determinism associated with the new philosophical material they expressed a real mood of anxiety. They did not discover the problems. Still less did they resolve them. What they did was to publicise them and for a time to focus attention sharply on them. The intellectual content of the condemnations was slight. The 1277 Paris list in particular was hastily drawn up, uncoordinated and misconceived in many of its assumptions. The effect of Tempier's interventions even on the 'radical Aristotelianism' which occasioned them is difficult to gauge. It is clear that in the case of Siger of Brabant, the principal representative of that outlook, there had been a marked development towards moderation before his flight from Paris. How far this development was due to the constraints imposed by the condemnation of 1270 and the fear of further disciplinary action and how far to the force of Thomas Aquinas' critique is difficult to judge. *A fortiori*, it is impossible to estimate the respective effects of argument and repression on that part of radical Aristotelianism which is largely hidden from historical view.

One can more confidently state two respects in which the

condemnations were not significant. They did not end, nor did they aim to, the study of Aristotle's philosophy either at Paris or at Oxford, either in the arts or the theology faculty. This is true moreover even of the study of Aristotle with the aid of Averroes' commentaries. In this respect the later condemnations are different to that of 1210. Aristotle was firmly established as the core of the university arts course and continued as such for the rest of the middle ages and long beyond. Neither did the condemnations, in effect, seriously threaten the Thomist system as a contribution to medieval theology. The glancing blow struck by the 1277 Paris list at certain positions defended by Aquinas, notably individuation by matter, and the more directly aimed shots of the Oxford condemnations were more than counterbalanced in their potentially damaging consequences by the speed with which the authorities and individual members of the Dominican order rallied to the support of its greatest teacher.

The speed of the Dominican reaction is indeed impressive. The general chapter of the order meeting at Milan in 1278 despatched two visitors to England in the aftermath of Kilwardby's censures to punish, exile and deprive from office Dominicans critical of Thomas' teaching.[2] The following year, meeting at Paris, it provided for the punishment of all in the order who spoke or wrote irreverently or unbecomingly of him or his works, whatever their private opinions might be.[3] This official reaction, however, interesting as it is, reveals nothing about the issues judged important. The contributions of individual apologists are more informative. In 1277, Peter of Conflans, William of Moerbeke's predecessor in the title of archbishop of Corinth, wrote to Kilwardby disapproving of the content of the Oxford syllabus. Although the text of his letter is not known its substance can be deduced from Kilwardby's reply to it, written in the same year.[4] The principal points of debate between them were the interrelated questions whether prime matter should be considered as pure potentiality, whether it contained seminal reasons and whether substance was constituted by a single, simple form.

In March 1278 Kilwardby was appointed a cardinal and resigned the see of Canterbury. He was succeeded the following year by the Franciscan, John Pecham, who had established himself at Paris and later at Oxford and the Roman curia as a theologian of stature, with decided views against unicity of form. In October 1284 Pecham confirmed his predecessor's prohibitions. Then, in June 1286, he

proceeded against the Oxford master, Richard Knapwell, a Dominican, who had in a disputed question held in favour of unicity of form.
Knapwell's statement of the theory was assessed for its theological
import, in particular as regards the nature of Christ's body between
death and resurrection and the effect of transubstantiation in the
Eucharist.[5] On these grounds the theory was deemed heretical by a
synod at London and those who held it were excommunicated.

Knapwell was not an isolated figure. He must have been encouraged in his stance by the attitude of the English provincial of his order,
William Hothum, whose pupil he seems to have been. Both before
Pecham's renewal of the Oxford censures, in a meeting with him, and
soon after the renewal, in an address to the university, Hothum had
urged moderation, pointing out that there was diversity of view over
the question of substantial form. After Knapwell's condemnation,
Hothum appealed on his behalf to the pope – unsuccessfully as it
turned out, for Nicholas IV, a former Franciscan, resolved the case by
imposing perpetual silence on Knapwell. Other Oxford supporters of
the Thomist position at this time were the Dominicans, Robert
Orford, Thomas Sutton and William Macclesfield.[6] Knapwell,
Orford and Macclesfield all wrote replies to the *Correctorium Fratris
Thomae* (*Correction of Brother Thomas*) of the Franciscan, William de la
Mare, Pecham's successor to the Franciscan chair at Paris. This
treatise, compiled in 1279, consisted of propositions culled from
Aquinas' principal works and accompanied by criticisms of their
divergence, real or apparent, from the teaching of Augustine and
Bonaventure. Especially criticised were Aquinas' treatment of matter
as pure potentiality, devoid of seminal reasons, his ascribing individuation to matter, his denial of universal hylomorphism and his
maintenance of the unicity of substantial form.[7] The *Correction* became
influential in the Franciscan order through an act of the general
chapter in 1282 which directed that it be used as clarification when
the works of Thomas were read.[8]

The early Oxford upholders of Aquinas' views had their counterparts at Paris in, among others, the Dominicans Bernard of Trillia,[9]
Giles of Lessines and John of Paris. Giles of Lessines wrote a treatise,
On the Unity of Form (*De unitate formae*), in 1278, aimed at Kilwardby's
reply to Peter of Conflans.[10] John of Paris, a notable political thinker
along the lines suggested by Aquinas, wrote a criticism of William de
la Mare which circulated under the title *Correction of the Corruption of
Thomas* (*Correctorium corruptorii Thomae*).[11]

In view of the evidently denominational character which the controversy early assumed it is worth observing that there was at first dissension within the Dominican order itself over Aquinas' disputed theories. Kilwardby was a Dominican and by his forthright action he doubtless hoped to stem the progress of Thomism among his confrères as well as in the university generally.[12] That there was other opposition in the order to Aquinas' doctrine is shown by the repeated injunctions of chapters against criticism of it. However, Aquinas' doctrine was within a remarkably short time given an official status for Dominicans. The general chapter at Saragossa in 1309 required that teaching throughout the order be in accordance with it. That at Metz in 1313 was even more explicit on the point and in addition made study in Aquinas a prerequisite for those, the most able members of the order, who were to be sent to Paris university.[13] Aquinas' 'rehabilitation' was complete with his canonisation in 1323 and the subsequent declaration by the then bishop of Paris that the 1277 condemnation was void in so far as it affected him.[14] Thus, through the steady patronage of the Dominican authorities, Aquinas' system was accorded a guaranteed place among the schools of medieval theology.

With this much said by way of perspective on the condemnations, the 1270s can properly be taken as the end of an era in the intellectual tradition. Greek philosophy held no more shocks. The next major access of texts, the recovery of Plato, found a place already prepared both by the long centuries of acquaintance with his outlook and the special cultural spirit of the Italian renaissance. The character of late medieval thought does not derive from new discoveries of ancient authorities but from grappling with problems recognised in the course of reflecting on material which was already established as part of the intellectual vision and from a redefinition of the respective scope of faith and reason. Appreciation of the subtle and rigorous analyses offered by the major late medieval thinkers, Duns Scotus and William of Ockham, and their disciples, has been steadily growing in recent decades so that the fourteenth and fifteenth centuries can no longer be treated as an addendum to or even a decline from the achievements of the thirteenth. This makes it more than ever difficult to view the thirteenth century, despite its magnificent accomplishments of intellectual endeavour, as the apex of medieval thought. Such a judgement is in any case more philosophical than historical. But new regard for the later period does nothing to diminish the importance of the thirteenth century as a pivotal point in western cultural history. It represents the culmination of a lengthy process by which Latin intellectuals received increasingly more complex and challenging lessons from the ancient masters. The content of those lessons, the manner of their delivery, the challenges which they posed and the extent to which the challenges were met have been the interlocking themes of the present study.

Epilogue: Aspects of Recent Research

THE Supplementary Bibliography with this edition is an eloquent witness to the continuing vigour of scholarship on medieval thought, the more so in that the works noted are a selection along the principal themes of the book rather than an attempt at complete listing of output in the field. In thus updating the original bibliography by the addition of titles which were either published after the book was written or which came to my attention late, I hope that the text and its apparatuses will continue to discharge what I see as one of the most important functions of a survey, that of equipping the reader with a clear overview of the state of the question both as regards primary and secondary source material. In a subject so complex and with so many organs of productivity, this is not an easy task and its execution is fallible: but the highest level of bibliographical information which may be afforded is an indispensable requirement of academic study, whether at undergraduate or advanced levels. At undergraduate level especially, nothing so soon develops self-confidence as penetrating beyond the banalities of a general treatment to master directly the specialist literature and, wherever possible, the texts also on which it rests. In highlighting here some of the important directions that recent research has been taking, I focus particularly on those aspects which arise most immediately from the text of the book, which relate to judgements made in it or which represent points that I should wish to expand were I now writing it.

An area of the original bibliography which I have not generally sought to update is that relating to the classical systems and the early patristic period, since this section of the book was intended as a background introduction – a function with which I am still satisfied – rather than as an integral part of the survey. I mention, however, two points where my original account seems in retrospect to fall short. One concerns the works of Cicero, specific uses of which were instanced but regarding whom my comment in passing that 'his philosophical influence was small compared to his immense literary stature',[1] while a relative judgement, might well appear unduly dismissive.[2] Cicero was not an original thinker, though he might, paradoxically perhaps, be called an original philosophical writer

212

since he both adapted Greek thought to a Roman context and, largely, created a style and even terminology for that adaptation. Moreover, he was a thoroughly informed and acute critic.[3] Certainly, his philosophical corpus offered to the Latin culture of the middle ages a large potential source for exploitation and development and an accomplished model of philosophical discourse. With such a notable exception as the *Republic*, which suffered, *c.* 700, the indignity of being palimpsested but which was transmitted to the succeeding middle ages partially, through St Augustine and Lactantius and in Macrobius' *Commentary on the Dream of Scipio*, the bulk of Cicero's philosophical writing as it remains to us, including *On the Laws* (*De Legibus*), was known directly. It served, especially in the twelfth century, as a source of Stoic cosmological doctrine and of ethical teaching.[4] Recent literature includes argument for its having exercised a distinctive influence on political and social thought both before the reception of Aristotle's *Ethics* and *Politics* and after.[5] Political and social theory was an area in which Cicero was at his most authoritative and explicit, though even in this he was liable to misinterpretation and distortion.[6] Assessment of the general impact of his works must, in part, depend on the fullest possible study of the manuscript tradition,[7] but judged within the contours of the evolution of medieval speculative thought it does seem that Cicero's profile was less than might have been expected of such an important writer.

One explanation may appear from the qualitative differences between what Cicero provided and what was provided by Aristotle, whose impact, for good and ill, on the medieval schools must be an indication of susceptibility at least. Cicero offered rich seams of ancient theorising on a wide range of issues to the learned who wished to mine. Aristotle's ore-load, by comparison, was at the surface. More: that of the scientific and social treatises, once the implications began to be perceived, threatened a landslide. The contrast between Cicero and Aristotle was that Aristotle was trenchantly dogmatic. He could not be long ignored. He compelled address. Rather, he compelled systematic address, for which the programme of the medieval universities offered an ideal framework, though since he partly shaped that programme the argument may be illicit. His political thought, for example, depended on his ethical, and his ethical on a complex of psychology, physics and natural theology. He required argued rejection, commitment or accommodation. For all its sophistication and despite its reputation, medieval scholastic culture, taken as a body, had the weakness that given a choice it preferred conclusions – even better, applied conclusions – to abstract theorising, the security of arrival to intellectual voyaging. In this it was not unique. Even Petrarch, who was a new kind of scholar and an enthusiast, deemed 'a work more subtle than necessary or useful'[8] that of which a modern scholar and enthusiast can say that 'if one had to choose a single work upon which to rest Cicero's reputation as a respectable philosopher, it would be the *Academics*'.[9] Then again – the analogy is rough but not impertinent – in the sixteenth century, Melancthon, influentially for Protestant education, preferred Aristotle to Plato in ethics because of Plato's irony and ambiguities.[10] The preferences exercised by the medieval schools were not always advantageous for intellectual development, but they were made within and prompted by the level of expertise obtaining and for what seemed sufficient reason. The expertise was rather in dialectical analysis and the reconciliation of authorities than in historical reconstruction.[11] The demand from philosophising was more for firm and teachable positions than for mental diversion.

The second point on which my treatment of the classical background is open to criticism is in my not including a separate section on Stoicism. Here, I felt that I could conveniently explain, as they arose, those aspects to which I would refer in my later treatment. Happily for this important strand of the medieval composition, there is now very full and authoritative guidance in M. L. Colish, *The Stoic Tradition from Antiquity to the Early Middle Ages* (Leiden, 1985) on the background and early period, and in G. Verbeke, *The Presence of Stoicism in Medieval Thought* (Washington, DC, 1983), lucidly charting the course of Stoic ideas through to the chronological limit of my own account.

The extended bibliography begins, therefore, like the continuous subject of the book, with St Augustine, on whom it has been estimated that scholarly output is at the rate of more than one hundred titles a year. Far from heaping up further that insupportable burden, the *Augustinus-Lexikon*, edited by Cornelius Mayer (Basel/Stuttgart, 1986–   ), aims to alleviate it for specialist and non-specialist alike, both as regards past and continuing production. Combining the best of traditional scholarship with new technology, it has in an ancillary project assembled two computerised databanks. The first is a complete concordance of Augustine's works, which not only facilitated the compilation of the *Lexikon* itself but is designed as a supplement to it. The second is a bibliography of some 50,000 items. This, it is intended, will be maintained and improved. The *Lexikon* surveys Augustine's writings and context, through articles in German, English or French. Though the aim is to provide factual information, the *Lexikon* is no mere accumulation of detail. The essential factual foundation is there but it is judged so well in terms of the various likely requirements of the user as to constitute, in the case of many of the articles, an original outline essay analysing the topic in question. If maintained as planned, the several projects will thus supersede all other methods of keeping abreast with developments in Augustinian studies.

Among studies relating to themes of my book, three topics of distinct interest may for varying reasons be particularly noted. P. F. Beatrice's '"Quosdam Platonicorum Libros"; the Platonic Readings of Augustine in Milan', *Vigiliae Christianae*, xliii (1989), 248–81, reconsiders a much-discussed problem, to which further reference will be made below. Beatrice reviews the historiography of the issue (cf. Chapter 2 above, pp. 46–7) and argues in favour of exclusively identifying the readings in question with Marius Victorinus' Latin translation of Porphyry's *Philosophy from Oracles* (cf. Chapter 2 above, p. 44). Two stimulating studies of Augustine as controversialist throw much light on the crucial transition between the convert captivated by the classical philosophical vision of order and moral freedom and the theologian of grace: P. Fredriksen, 'Beyond the Body/Soul Dichotomy. Augustine on Paul against the Manichees and Pelagians', *Recherches Augustiniennes*, xxii (1988), 87–114, and R. A. Markus, 'Augustine's *Confessions* and the Controversy with Julian of Eclanum: Manicheism Revisited', *Agustiniana*, xli (1991), 913–25. Both agree on the central importance of Augustine's interpretation of St Paul for an understanding of his intellectual development at this time. In a felicitous summary of the influence of Paul as 'both the agent of upheaval in Augustine's thought and the thread that gave continuity to it' (Markus, p. 916), Professor Markus suggests a fertile potential for future research. Professor Fredriksen, explaining the disintegration in Augustine's outlook of 'the essentially classical model of self-improvement and moral freedom even in the extremely attenuated form in which it survived into Augustine's early Pauline commentaries' (Fredriksen, p. 103), highlights how the sudden discontinuity and externality manifested in Paul's conversion broke the mould of the classical concept of virtue. It is evident that, as with his reading of St Paul in the garden in Milan, Augustine here found that towards which he had been moving. An important point on which the two articles are particularly successful is in facing the insinuation of a continuing Manichean dualism in Augustine's thought, a charge levied against him in his own time and recurring in subsequent interpretation. Fredriksen indeed turns the tables, arguing that for Augustine the Pelagian view represented an instance of a dualism 'common to Manichees and pagan philosophers both' (Fredriksen, p. 112), in which it was the soul that was truly human. Markus subtly shows how the rejection of Manicheism led to a deepening of that interest in psychology – and as we think of it, the subconscious – which is perhaps the most original of Augustine's many contributions to the intellectual tradition. 'The self had to embrace the vast areas of darkness for which the Manichean conception had no room.' (Markus, p. 915). 'Augustine transposed into terms of conflict within the self the conflict which Manichean teaching projected onto two separate natures in permanent conflict.' (Markus, p. 923). Both studies see inner tension acutely manifested in sexuality. For this, in the contemporary context, P. Brown, *The Body and Society* (New York, 1988) is indispensable.

By contrast with these large issues of interpretation, the third topic which I isolate for mention is limited. For the intellectual historian however, whose interest is not only in ideas themselves but in the accessibility, as in the reception and understanding, of ideas, the brief study by E. Dekkers, 'Sur la diffusion au moyen âge des oeuvres moins connues de saint Augustin', in *Homo Spiritalis*, ed. C. Mayer (Würzburg, 1987), pp. 446–59, fills a gap and provides interesting notes on early medieval library holdings.

There have been important publications on Boethius both in context of his own century and of longer-term influence. S. Lerer, *Boethius and Dialogue Literary Method in the Consolation of Philosophy* (Princeton, 1985), examines Boethius' use of the dialogue in the context of earlier Latin examples, especially those of Cicero and Augustine. It also pays close attention to the more general literary artifice of the work, particularly the role of imagery in advancing its themes. F. Troncarelli, in two magisterial works, has set out the hypothesis that

Cassiodorus was the author of an edition of the *Consolation of Philosophy*, which he has proceeded to reconstruct from the manuscript tradition, identifying, among other aspects, a life of Boethius, a series of rhetorical Graeco-Latin annotations, annotations to the metres and a particular iconography. Professor Troncarelli's first book on the subject, *Tradizioni Perdute. La 'Consolatio Philosophiae' nell'alto medioevo* (Padua, 1981), was questioned in some of its assumptions[12] but Troncarelli replied to the objections, extending his thesis,[13] which he further developed in *Boethiana Aetas. Modelli Grafici e Fortuna Manoscritta della 'Consolatio Philosophiae' tra IX e XII° Secolo* (Alessandria, 1987). Apart from the high interest of the principal argument, Troncarelli's interdisciplinary pursuit of his case has resulted in the most widely ranging examination of the tradition of the *Consolation* and of its interpretation since Courcelle. On a specific theme, J. C. Frakes, *The Fate of Fortune in the Early Middle Ages, the Boethian Tradition* (Leiden, etc., 1988), examines the Roman tradition of *fortuna*, the patristic reinterpretations, Boethius' interpretation and the commentary tradition up to the Carolingian period, with a final chapter on the 'metaphysics' of Fortune – its relationship to a wider philosophical outlook. G. d'Onofrio, 'Dialectic and Theology. Boethius' *Opuscula Sacra* and their Early Medieval Readers', *Studi Medievali*, 3rd ser., xxvii (1986), 45–67, considers principally Remigius d'Auxerre against a context of school reading of these texts by Gottschalk of Orbais, Hincmar of Reims and Ratramnus of Corbie.

Troncarelli's Cassiodorus would agree well with the interesting picture of this figure to emerge independently from S. J. B. Barnish, 'The Work of Cassiodorus after his Conversion', *Latomus*, xlviii (1989), 157–89. Barnish's Cassiodorus has a distinct eye to the propagandist value of literary activity and maintains a continuing political interest, not only after his retirement from public office but after his conversion to the monastic life. 'Squillace', Dr Barnish observes (p. 166), 'was not the world's end'. He considers closely the educational work of Cassiodorus, asking of his projected foundation at Rome whether it was intended to educate laymen, still active in the world, as well as clergy and *conversi*, of Vivarium and the *Institutiones* whether they were 'a substitute for the failed school' (p. 175), and of the *Institutiones* in particular whether they were addressed to the wider public who might have been its scholars. These points are extended into a consideration of the degree to which the *Institutiones* value secular learning in its own right. While careful not to exaggerate the contemporary impact of Cassiodorus' project, Barnish sets it persuasively within its contemporary context.

The bibliography to the first edition noted that H. Bett, *Johannes Scotus Erigena* was the only full study in English of this figure. The statement is now doubly outdated since the appearance of J. J. O'Meara, *Eriugena* (Oxford, 1988) and D. Moran, *The Philosophy of John Scottus Eriugena: a Study of Idealism in the Middle Ages* (Cambridge, 1989). In the preceding decade there have been over 30 relevant published studies in the major languages, and both works contain bibliographies and judicious reviews of the state of scholarship. Professor O'Meara adds to the corpus of translated sources a fine rendering of the *Homily on the Prologue to St John's Gospel* and, among lesser poetry, of the *Aulae sidereae*, which has attracted notice for its biographical implications. The main difference between the two books is that where O'Meara's is an exposition of Eriugena's thought – especially in respect of the *Periphyseon* – Moran's is an interpretation. The scholarly understanding of Eriugena has undergone radical revision since the late David Knowles' influential survey described him as 'a voice in the wilderness',[14] a judgement which did not so much emphasise the thinker's originality as justify ignoring him. In the interval, attention has been devoted to Eriugena's rapport with the intellectual context of his time, particularly with the liberal arts programme of the Carolingian renaissance, from which he would be distinguished principally by the access which his knowledge of Greek gave him to unfamiliar source material. Professor Moran shares much of this outlook. He recognises that Eriugena the liberal arts master and Eriugena the follower of Greek Platonism should not be too strongly contrasted. The theology (most crucially the theology of pseudo-Denis) to which he was exposed in the 860s fitted well with a bias already acquired. Moran joins most scholars in seeing the *Periphyseon* as having been reworked in a coterie headed by the author. Beyond, Moran's book cries halt to assimilation. His focus is sharply on Eriugena's power and originality as a systematic thinker and his main argument is towards revision in philosophical understanding of Eriugena, presented as a radical idealist for whom mind is higher than the being of which it is productive. There are interesting views on the genesis of the *Periphyseon*, the plan of which is seen as conforming to a Neoplatonic cycle of unity–diversity–reunification. The historian benefits incidentally from what is principally an analysis for philosophers. The themes of the *Periphyseon* are examined to show that Eriugena's readers were not 'novices but ... skilled theologians and philosophers' (Moran, p. 70). The Alumnus (or disciple) is not simply a foil to Nutritor (the master): he represents in effect the Latin theologian and takes advantage artfully of the dialogue form of the treatise to articulate the Latin theologian's difficulties in the face of 'new' Greek ideas, of which the negative theology is presented as the most important. It is the commitment to this negative theology, to the exploration of non-being rather than of being and – to anticipate Nicholas of Cusa's formulation – to 'learned ignorance' that, for Moran, distinguishes Eriugena from the intellectualist tradition not only of the Carolingian renaissance, especially in its encyclopaedism, but as stemming from Augustine himself.

Of the subjects dealt with in Chapter 3 above, 'The Central Middle Ages – Logic, Theology and Cosmology', Gerbert of Aurillac now has a long-required general treatment in P. Riché, *Gerbert d'Aurillac, Le Pape de L'An Mil* (Paris, 1987). This does not so much revise perspectives as integrate the several phases of a varied career which, like that of Cicero and Boethius, combined action and contemplation. For Gerbert the influence of Boethius is fundamental but Cicero too was a conscious model, the master rhetor and the purveyor of the consolation of philosophy in time of crisis (as revealed in his letter 167; cf. Riché, p. 118). R. W. Southern has extended and deepened his earlier classic study of St Anselm of Bec in *Saint Anselm, A Portrait in a Landscape* (Cambridge, 1991), paying especially close attention to the letter collection as a source, a subject on which the author contributed in *Anselmo d'Aosta Figura Europea* (Atti del Convegno di Studi, Aosta 1° e 2° marzo 1988), ed. I. Biffi and C. Mirabelli (Milan, 1989).

Two particular studies take divergent views of Anselm's influence on Abelard; D. E. Luscombe, 'St Anselm and Abelard', *Anselm Studies*, i (1983), 207–29, and M. T. Clanchy, 'Abelard's Mockery of St Anselm', *Journal of Ecclesiastical History*, xli (1990), 1–23. Their discussion leaves little room for doubt as to the fact of Anselm's importance for Abelard, whatever the difference about its nature. As regards method, the judgement that 'Anselm's use of analogies does

seem to have been a factor in prompting Abelard to develop
discussion of the value of analysis' (Luscombe, p. 213) would appear
firmly established. Moreover, the case for Abelard's having read the
Cur Deus Homo is much strengthened by Mews' argument, referred to
below, that the 'Sentences of Hermann' represent Abelard's own
teaching. The effect may even be one of 'extensive and pervasive
submission to some of Anselm's deepest thoughts' (Luscombe,
p. 218), particularly as regards argument by analogy and the
Anselmian (and Victorine) pursuit of 'necessary reasons'. This does
not require – from Abelard least – that the intellectual debt should
betoken a more general deference. While contesting with Roscelin
there was a polemical advantage in Abelard's adducing the authority of Anselm (cf. Clanchy, p. 2). But one of his later references to
the genesis of the treatise *On the Divine Unity and Trinity* (the *Theologia
'Summi Boni'*), that 'words were useless if the intelligence could not
follow them, that nothing could be believed unless it was first
understood' (cf. Chapter 3 above, p. 111), strongly suggests criticism of Anselm's formulation (cf. Clanchy, p. 17; Luscombe,
pp. 219–20, n. 7), a criticism that, far from being incompatible with
Abelard's seriousness in the pursuit of reasoned theology, is on one
level a measure of his commitment to it and on another of the
difference of context between the monastic teacher and the master in
a secular school.[15] Even the eager pupils, to whom the sentiment
that nothing could be believed unless first understood is attributed,
may be a riposte to the brethren who drove Anselm on. They need
not perhaps be taken quite literally[16] but their stimulus, possibly
telescoped backwards so far as concerns the inferred criticism of
Anselm, is a not implausible justification of fresh thinking.[17] Certainly, if Anselm was conscious of his pupils' demands, how much
more should Abelard have been, both as regards on this point their
intellectual questioning and, less soberly, the simple need to keep
them amused. In this latter respect, an overt opportunity to
eavesdrop on the astonishing indiscretion of his teaching banter was
provided by the unlikely medium of De Rijk's edition of the
Dialectica. Here, fossilised from the period of his seduction of Héloise,
the examples 'Peter's girl loves him' and 'Peter loves his girl',
capped – no doubt as the class dissolved in merriment – by the
logical tag 'Laughter is of the nature of man', illustrate the relations
signified by pronominal adjectives, in an exposition of Aristotle's *On
Interpretation*, while 'Let my girl friend kiss me' and 'Let my girl

friend hurry' illustrate optative and jussive constructions, arising from the *Topics*.[18] There is a displeasing parade here, quite of a part with the tone of the *Historia Calamitatum* (how suggestive too that 'Peter's girl loves him' should precede 'Peter loves his girl'), but the histrionic trait revealed is probably common in some measure to most successful teachers of arid matter in a competitive context, performing before mobile audiences. It makes entirely credible Dr Clanchy's clever punctuation of the quotations from contemporary masters and from Anselm in the *Theologia Christiana* to offer us another chance of joining the flies on the wall. What he presents as a mockery is ingeniously explained by his identifying Anselm as the source of the technicality underlying Abelard's condemnation at Soissons.[19] Professor Luscombe disagrees, pointing out correctly that the terms *fistula* and *infistulatus*, glossed by Clanchy to pejorative effect, 'do not necessarily have a foul meaning',[20] a fact which would, however, have suited Abelard's purpose well since the reader might miss or be uncertain of a *double entendre* that in the classroom would be made explicit.[21] The differences, aside from detail, between the interpretations do not seem irreconcilable: they point to a general intellectual debt which was real, lasting and highly significant – even where Anselm and Abelard diverged[22] – and, in the aftermath of Soissons, a bitterness and self-justification typically vented by playing to the gallery.

There have been notable advances in the understanding of Abelardian texts. C. J. Mews' 'Peter Abelard's *Theologia Christiana* and *Theologia* 'Scholarium' Re-examined', *R[echerches de] T[héologie] A[ncienne] et M[édiévale]*, lii (1985), 109–58, considers closely the manuscript tradition of these treatises and the relationship between them, with reflections on Abelard's practice of adding to, correcting and annotating his works. The study was designed partly as the foundation of an edition of the remaining versions of the *Theologia*, brought to fruition in *Petri Abaelardi Opera Theologica*, iii, *Theologia 'Summi Boni' Theologia 'Scholarium'*, eds E. M. Buytaert and C. J. Mews (Turnhout, 1987), referred to above. In C. J. Mews, 'The Sententiae of Peter Abelard', *RTAM*, liii (1986), 130–84, it is argued, again through re-examination of the manuscript tradition and the comparison of revisions, that the so-called 'Sentences of Hermann' report the teaching of Abelard himself and not that of a disciple, on faith, sacraments (baptism, confirmation, the eucharist, extreme unction and matrimony) and charity. The extant fragments of the related *Liber Sententiarum Magistri Petri* are edited in an appendix. Dr Mews has also convincingly identified Thomas of Morigny as the compiler of the *Capitula Haeresum XIV* which were part of the campaign mounted against Abelard at Sens (C. Mews, 'The List of Heresies Imputed to Peter Abelard', *Revue Bénédictine*, xcv (1985), 73–110).

As to doctrine, E. Bertola, 'La dottrina morale di Pietro Abelardo', *RTAM*, lv (1988), 53–71, is a close examination of Abelard's ethical views which, in particular, draws attention to the principle of Augustinian psychology, 'Sensation is not of the body but of the soul through the body' – as used by Abelard with moral import – ascribing to it a fundamental significance for the interior quality of Abelard's ethics. Dr Mews' argument for the 'Sentences of Hermann' would have repercussions for Abelard's teaching on grace in so far as the latter work may be understood to attenuate the role of grace. Dr Mews, however, takes the view that the 'Sentences' do not deny the role of grace but emphasise that grace can do nothing if man does not respond, the position essentially of the 'Commentary on the Epistle to the Romans' (Mews, 'The *Sententiae*', 154; cf. Chapter 3 above, p. 110). In a thoroughly documented study, L. Moonan, 'Abelard's Use of the *Timaeus*', *AHDLMA*, lvi (1989), 7–90, shows how Abelard's regard for Plato's great dialogue reflects that of his contemporaries and absolves him of the charge of trying to christianise Plato or preferring Plato to patristic authorities.

Study of the *Timaeus* was once associated particularly with the 'school of Chartres'. The debate over this continues. A chapter of the *Metalogicon* of John of Salisbury where John, with tantalising ambiguities, reviews the sequence of his studies, has had an important bearing on the issues. The chapter is given a careful reading from different perspectives by O. Weijers, 'The Chronology of John of Salisbury's Studies in France (Metalogicon, II. 10)', in *The World of John of Salisbury*, ed. M. Wilks (Oxford, 1984), pp. 109–16, and by K. S. B. Keats-Rohan, 'John of Salisbury and Education in Twelfth-Century Paris from the Account of his *Metalogicon*', *History of Universities*, vi (1986–7), 1–45 (also in condensed form in Keats-Rohan, 'The Chronology of John of Salisbury's Studies in France. A reading of *Metalogicon* II. 10', *Studi Medievali*, 3rd ser., xxviii (1987), 193–203). Dr Keats-Rohan's interpretation of the crucial transition, 'Reversus itaque in fine triennii repperi magistrum Gilebertum', to signify scholarly redirection rather than relocation (Keats-Rohan,

'John of Salisbury and Education', 17–18) is intrinsically plausible, and 'repperi' can quite properly be taken to mean 'sought out', as suggested (ibid., 9). While uncertainties remain, it is difficult to envisage the argument's being taken further through exegesis of this chapter of the *Metalogicon*. Besides its contribution to interpreting the sequence of John of Salisbury's studies in France, Dr Keats-Rohan's article also constitutes a judicious review of the critique of contemporary education in the work. Several related aspects are considered by C. J. Nederman, 'Knowledge, Virtue and the Path to Wisdom: the Unexamined Aristotelianism of John of Salisbury's *Metalogicon*', *Mediaeval Studies*, li (1989), 268–86, who emphasises the extent of John's absorption of Aristotelian epistemological and ethical teaching both directly, through the logical works, and indirectly, through Boethius and Cicero, the latter being an important source of John's firm understanding that virtue is a mean.

Of the impact of Aristotelianism on Arabic thought, no topic has bulked so large from the western perspective as the theory of the intellect, especially that elaborated by Averroes. H. A. Davidson, 'Averroes on the material intellect', *Viator*, xvii (1986), 91–137, and 'Averroes on the active intellect as a cause of existence', *Viator*, xviii (1987), 191–225, has advanced understanding both of Averroes' actual teaching on these two aspects of Aristotelian psychology and of his method. As regards the potential or material intellect, Averroes had little guidance from his Islamic predecessors, who did not show themselves much interested in it. Behind the Great Commentary on the *De Anima* lies a succession of positions which Averroes adopted while he wrestled with the problems, though it was the Great Commentary itself that was so crucial for the West. Professor Davidson's account of its teaching is nuanced: while it made clear that the material or potential intellect was a 'separate [sc. incorporeal] substance' or more particularly 'not a body or form in a body', 'the proposition that the potential intellect is not joined to the body as its form is nowhere expressed' there (*Viator*, xvii (1986), 130), and is in Davidson's view 'at best an implication to be drawn from Averroes' (ibid., 133). On the active intellect, Professor Davidson again stresses the development of Averroes' views and cautions of Averroes' method that, although his object was to recover genuine Aristotelian doctrine and although his reading was on the whole more naturalistic, he was not always successful. O. N.

Mohammed, *Averroes' Doctrine of Immortality A Matter of Controversy* (Waterloo, Ontario, 1984), examines the relationship between Averroes' understanding of intellect and soul and his position as an Islamic believer. The two are reconciled, it is argued, because Averroes rests immortality on the resurrection and not on the nature of the soul.

Medieval Jewish thought has been the subject of a learned introductory survey by C. Sirat, *La Philosophie Juive au Moyen Age selon les Textes Manuscrits et Imprimés* (Paris, 1983), especially valuable for the less explored later phase, defined as commencing with the thirteenth century and extending to the Renaissance. The two French titles of 1988 (for details of which, see the Supplementary Bibliography) have additional bibliography. The English reader will be well served by the English title, *A History of Jewish Philosophy in the Middle Ages* (Cambridge, 1985).

Major studies have appeared of the origins and early development of the universities of Paris, Oxford and Cambridge, as noted more fully in the Supplementary Bibliography. S. C. Ferruolo, *The Origins of the University, The Schools of Paris and their Critics 1100–1215* (Stanford, 1985), is a wide-ranging investigation of twelfth-century attitudes to learning, which concludes with an attractive argument that the formation of a common guild of masters in the several disciplines at Paris is due to their consciousness of professionalism as teachers and to their shared educational ideals. J. I. Catto, ed., *The Early Oxford Schools* (Oxford, 1984), includes what are, for my themes, particularly relevant chapters on the late twelfth century and on thirteenth-century thought. For Alexander Nequam, whose theological teaching at Oxford in the 1190s is attested firmly, if at a remove, there is now a valuable study in the late Dr R. W. Hunt's thesis, as edited and revised by M. Gibson, *The Schools and the Cloister, The Life and Writings of Alexander Nequam 1157–1217* (Oxford, 1984). Among the many points of interest generated by Alexander's varied writings is the fact that although of Aristotle he had mastered fully only the logic,[23] he displays a fair smattering of at least superficial knowledge of the scientific works. He was especially well informed for his time in his treatment of the soul, in which he had absorbed the influence of Avicenna, probably through his younger contemporary, John Blund.[24] It would seem, however, that he had earlier knowledge of Aristotelian doctrine on the soul, since he refers to it in passing in a work from his first period, the *Commentary on Martianus Capella*.[25] He could recommend reading of the *De Anima* of Aristotle and also of the *Metaphysics* and of *On Generation and Corruption*, though Dr Hunt found no trace of his own use of them. Alexander has quotations from the 'old Ethics' (see Chapter 4 above, p. 133), from the *Book of the Twenty-four Philosophers (Liber XXIV Philosophorum)*, discussed below, and from the *Book of Causes*.[26] It is reasonable to think that in some of this he witnesses to the early reception of Aristotle at Paris, where he had studied before *c*. 1182. A very opaque series of remarks can be interpreted to mean that there is something furtive about lectures on the sciences,[27] though it has to be said that this is not the only possible sense of a passage which could perhaps rather be a comment on the difficulty of scientific inquiry and a criticism of reluctance to make one's knowledge public. If, however, the former reading is correct, then the reference would almost certainly be to the Parisian scene, the more valuable for the fact that the period in question is obscure. It would, moreover, give a particular sense to the famous condemnation of 1210, whose precision as to public and private readings might distinguish a practice that, in response to a perceived constraint, had grown up over several decades.

The *Book of the Twenty-four Philosophers*, referred to above, is a Latin treatise containing 24 definitions of God, each accompanied by commentary and representing, according to the prologue, the product of the discussion of that number of philosophers meeting in debate. F. Hudry, *Le Livre des XXIV Philosophes* (Grenoble, 1989), edits and translates into French a version – distinguished from that commonly transmitted – preserved in Laon, Bibliothèque Municipale Ms. 412, a thirteenth-century collection of recent advances in philosophical and scientific source-material, where the text of the *Book* is written in a hand dated here *c*. 1230–40. The editor posits a Greek original underlying her text, which, she argues, represents the doctrine of Aristotle's lost work *On Philosophy*. Extending the case inferentially, she both identifies this lost work of Aristotle with the much discussed 'Platonic books', instrumental in the conversion of St Augustine, and places it at the centre of the condemnation of Aristotelianism at Paris in 1210. The existence of two versions of the *Book of the Twenty-Four Philosophers* she sees as a product of the expurgation following this condemnation and more precisely of the prohibition issued by Gregory IX in 1231. Mlle Hudry has signalled an edition of the common version of the *Book*, previously published by C. Baeumker in 1928, and a description of the complete manuscript tradition.

Although the earliest phases of Aristotelianism at Paris continue to be murky, a great deal more precision is being given to the period *c.* 1220–50. The most exciting developments are the authoritative way in which the date 1230, adopted for the reception of Averroes since the pioneering work of R. de Vaux, is being pushed back and the new understandings of activity in the arts faculty. R. A. Gauthier, 'Le traité *De anima et de potenciis eius* d'un maître ès arts (vers 1225)', *R[evue] des S[ciences] P[hilosophiques] et T[héologiques]*, lxvi (1982), 3–56, edits an exposition of Aristotelian doctrine on the soul and intellect by a philosopher who, though he mistakenly understands Averroes to teach that the agent intellect was joined to the soul as one of its powers (cf. Chapter 5 above, p. 146) and uses him to mount an offensive against what he considers to be Avicenna's error in making it separate, is evidently well acquainted with both authors. The text, which is after 1224, can be dated plausibly to before *c.* 1228. Moreover, Dr Gauthier shows that it was drawn on by the theological text, *De potenciis anime et obiectis*, published by Fr Daniel Callus (D. A. Callus, 'The Powers of the Soul: An Early Unpublished Text', *R[echerches] de T[héologie] A[ncienne] et M[édiévale]*, xix (1952), 131–70). Accordingly, this latter text can no longer be cited as evidence for a pre-existing interpretation conditioning the reception of Averroes in this sense (see Chapter 5 above, p. 146). It is clear that such an interpretation was current in the period but its genesis, and in particular the relationship between the arts and theology faculties in its genesis, remains to be determined. Since the *Summa on the Good* of Philip the Chancellor refers to Averroes, Gauthier's case regarding the date at which Averroes was known at Paris is powerfully reinforced by the new dating of *c.* 1225–8 for that work (cf. Chapter 5 above, p. 154), independently argued in *Philippi Cancellarii Parisiensis Summa de Bono*, ed. N. Wicki (Berne, 1985).

R. A. Gauthier, *Anonymi Magistri Artium (c. 1245–1250) Lectura in Librum de Anima a quodam discipulo reportata Ms. Roma Naz. V. E. 828* (Grottaferrata, 1985), sheds light on teaching in the arts faculty at a slightly later date. Here the master does not follow either the Avicennan or pseudo-Averroist position (that is, Averroes as understood to make the agent intellect part of the soul). The agent and possible intellects are distinguished but neither is a 'part' of the soul; they both correspond to the soul as a whole, seen under different aspects – a higher and lower aspect of knowing. In general, the text shows that Aristotle was being interpreted in a fashion acceptable to Christian theology, a point already evidenced in relation to Averroes. Gauthier is accordingly led to observe that far from its having been the task of Thomas Aquinas to 'christianise' Aristotle – since that was the state in which he found him in mid-thirteenth-century Paris – it was his task to expound him in a more authentic fashion and to work out a relationship between that understanding and a Christian perspective. The continued study of the work of the arts faculty during Thomas' early period at Paris is one of the most important contributions which can be made to understanding that development.

C. Lafleur, *Quatre Introductions à la Philosophie au XIIIe Siècle Textes Critiques et Etude Historique* (Montreal/Paris, 1988) is a valuable first instalment of what is promised as a major project, focussing on the decisive process by which Aristotle's philosophical works were introduced on to the syllabus and by which philosophical perspectives were transformed. Dr Lafleur's subject is not simply the propaedeutic role of the philosophical studies of the arts faculty but their intrinsic value. He edits four new specimens of the genre of *Introductions to Philosophy*: (1) the anonymous *Accessus Philosophorum VII Artium Liberalium*, dated *c.* 1245 as a *terminus ante quem*, though judged unlikely to have been composed much after the early 1230s; (2) the anonymous *Philosophica Disciplina*, dated *c.* 1245; (3) the *Divisio Scientiarum* of Arnoul de Provence, dated probably to the early 1250s and certainly pre-1260; and (4) the anonymous *Compendium circa Quadrivium*, whose provenance and dating is least certain, though it is judged with probability to be by a Paris arts master of the early 1240s.

Close links between Paris and Oxford were evidenced in the careers of Alexander Nequam and John Blund and they continued into the early fourteenth century. Even the manuscript tradition of the works edited by Lafleur testifies to them. What more obvious than that Robert Grosseteste should fit into a well-established pattern whereby his teaching theology in Oxford, evidenced from about 1225 but on one argument inferred as early as 1214, should have been preceded by a magistracy in the arts faculty and a formation among the leading circles at Paris? A major piece of historical revision, R. W. Southern, *Robert Grosseteste, The Growth of an English Mind in Medieval Europe* (Oxford, 1986), in challenging previous assumptions has presented another Grosseteste, not the finished product of the major centres (the scholar portrayed by D. A. Callus and his collaborators in 1955) but a struggling provincial, who made his way up through local English schools and minor position until, late in the day, a fortunate combination of circumstances afforded him initial security and subsequent advancement. The interest of the thesis goes beyond the mere detail of early study, important as that is. Sir Richard Southern links Grosseteste's independence as a thinker, sensitively and humanely explored, with the eccentricity of his scholastic career thus viewed. In charting Grosseteste's intellectual development he has also proposed revision of the chronology of his works. Whether independence on the part of a brilliantly original mind is compatible with a conventional training must be moot. Would a local education itself have been innocent of the methods taught in the leading circles? Does contact with the premier English *studium*, of which Grosseteste was afterwards to be a distinguished member and in which the unsupported assertion of Thomas Gascoigne locates him as a master of arts, seem more likely than not, even for the struggling scholar? If he were early a member of that *studium*, to what extent – granted that Oxford was less developed, or even differently developed, than contemporary Paris – is the force of the intrinsically powerful argument from independence of mind reduced? The questions are impatient of answers. Professor Southern has shown how the evidence, such as it is, can be read in a new, fundamentally attractive way. Time and again the reader is brought to feel that if what is said is not absolutely necessary it is able to appear necessary for the time being. Professor Southern's thesis, moreover, accounts for a problem inadequately addressed before – the apparently retarded course of Grosseteste's career. It does so, however, from a premiss which cannot be regarded as established. The question of the date of Grosseteste's becoming head of the Oxford masters is acknowledged to be pivotal: 'if he was *not* elected chancellor in 1214, but perhaps ten or fifteen years later, then his career began to assume a different shape' (Southern, *Grosseteste*, p. vi). Professor Southern takes the view that Grosseteste came to the office at the end of the period mentioned and his book is the product of the changes consequent on that dating.

The argument here, from both perspectives, leads back quickly to the only firm source for Grosseteste's having occupied that eminence at all, without which he would assuredly be supposed never to have done so. The source is an apologetic reminiscence of Bishop Oliver Sutton of Lincoln in 1295, voiced when the proctor of the Oxford masters, Mr Peter of Medbourne, approached him for formal confirmation of the chancellor whom they had elected. It was a scene in a pantomine played out on these occasions, though this time with a script which included the tendentious word 'elected'. The crucial passage, which is from the bishop's register, reads:

> Deinde dictum fuit eidem procuratori quod cancellarii pro tempore existentes non fuerunt electi sed tantummodo nominati. Et episcopus adjecit quod beatus Robertus quondam Lincoln' episcopus qui hujusmodi officium gessit dum in universitate predicta regebat in principio creationis sue in episcopum dixit proximum predecessorem suum episcopum Lincoln' non permisisse quod idem Robertus vocaretur cancellarius sed magister scolarum. At ipse Magister Petrus ad hoc non respondit, set petiit hujusmodi negotium more solito expediri.[28]

This may for the moment be roughly paraphrased as follows: The bishop told the proctor that chancellors were nominated [sc. by him], not elected, and he added that Robert Grosseteste, who held the office at a time when he was regent at Oxford, said that he had not been allowed by his predecessor as bishop of Lincoln to be called chancellor but rather master of the schools. The proctor made no reply but sought that the business be expedited in the usual way.

The earliest mention of the office of chancellor at Oxford, which differed from Paris in not being a cathedral town, is in the settlement effected by the papal legate in 1214. This ended a five-year disruption of the *studium* when the great majority of masters dispersed following violence by the townsmen. Part of the legatine award was that the townsmen would make various reparations and one of the officials mentioned in this context was the chancellor whom the bishop was envisaged as appointing. In 1201 there is clear reference to the title 'master of the schools of Oxford'.[29] So far as is known, the title 'chancellor' was an innovation of the legatine award, possibly on the simple analogy of the Paris model or possibly in response to the insistence of the returning masters.[30]

Although misgivings are occasionally expressed about it, I see no problem in accepting the accuracy of Bishop Sutton's statement. He was a punctilious prelate, probably on the whole sympathetic to the masters, of whose number he had long been one, and his resistance to them on this and other issues was part of that 'zeal for legal rights'[31] which is a characteristic of medieval civilisation.[32] Although the declaration by Grosseteste to which Sutton refers – if it is to be dated, as it generally is, to the beginning or the early phase of Grosseteste's pontificate ('in principio creationis sue in episcopum') – had been made some 60 years before Sutton adverted to it, this is not a strong reason for doubting its authenticity. Sutton's date of birth is calculated as c. 1219. He is unlikely himself to have heard a statement made at the beginning of Grosseteste's pontificate. However, Henry of Lexington, almost certainly Sutton's uncle, had succeeded Grosseteste as bishop; Bishop Henry or his household is one possible link in an oral tradition dating perhaps from c. 1235. That it was an oral tradition is worth noting. It may be that Grosseteste, when he became bishop, took an early opportunity to make a pronouncement or was drawn to do so early, but the matter was not apparently of sufficiently high moment for him to have the pronouncement committed to writing. As vicariously recorded, Grosseteste's testimony is important but limited. All that it guarantees is that he was head of the *studium* and that there was a problem over the title of his office. It does not explain the problem, which is a matter of inference. Professor Southern understands the problem to have been a dispute over the method of appointment, a foreshadowing of the dispute which evoked the reminiscence. Such a dispute over the method of appointment is out of the question in 1214.[33] It is, marginally, less inconceivable in 1225 and Professor Southern has interpreted Grosseteste's testimony to refer to that date or thereabout. If, on the other hand, the dispute was over title solely and not method of appointment, then it is inconceivable after 1221, by which date it has been established clearly that the title chancellor was in use and the chancellor had his seal.[34] Indeed, in those terms, a dispute would be most tidily placed some time between 1214, the date of the legate's award – or from slightly before the award itself, if the masters had already taken the initiative and if the mention of chancellorship in the award was a result of their pressure – and 1216, in June of which year Mr Geoffrey de Lucy is considered to have acceded to the chancellorship.[35] The dating 1214 × 1221 for Grosseteste's headship of the schools was adopted by Fr Callus. The reader of the two views of Grosseteste's intellectual development in its broad lines must decide, insofar as he does not wish simply to enjoy both versions, which of these resolutions of the problem of 'chancellorship' is more plausible. A decision in favour of the Callus view on the 'chancellorship' would do nothing to supply the defect of evidence for Grosseteste's early academic career but it would, by emphasising Grosseteste's status at the earlier date, shift the balance of probability in hypothesising, and it would provide a different framework within which to fit the only scraps of evidence so far available which might tentatively be pleaded in support of the hypothesis that he had been a member of the Paris *studium*. These are his apparent familiarity with some of the great figures of the Parisian scene,[36] a death-bed reminiscence concerning a campaign which he had witnessed, probably after 1210, to expel Cahorsin usurers 'from the parts of France',[37] and an attempt by him in the middle of the 1240s to dissuade the Oxford theologians from an innovation in the course prompted by a relatively recent development at Paris.[38] In this, he may be seen as defending not only the Oxford custom but the old custom at Paris that he would have known had he taught or studied there.[39] The reference to France is of more than geographical interest, in that, taken at face value, it constitutes evidence – uncertain but not to be dismissed lightly – that, of the four people named in the context, more than one had been his teacher.[40] Indeed, if the order of names in the list were deliberate and the last two named were taken to have been his teachers, then not only would he be held to have studied in Paris, but the commencement of his theological study there would be set before early 1206, the term of Stephen Langton's regency. He would thus, neatly, and even by the strictest criteria of the statutes shortly afterwards enacted by Robert de Courson, be accorded an interval to have incepted at Paris before the resolution of the Oxford dispute.

If the problem recalled in Grosseteste's statement did relate to title solely rather than method of appointment and is to be dated accordingly 1214 × 1221, or more narrowly 1214 × 1216, in what may it be supposed to have consisted? Although it is a reasonable assumption, which I share, that Grosseteste, if he were head of the

schools in 1214 would in effect have been elected by his peers, it is
not a datum. If he were, rather, appointed by the bishop and
especially if he were appointed on an interim basis until the
reconstitution of the *studium* was complete, other considerations than
academic seniority might have influenced the choice. (Grosseteste
might, for instance, have been used as an intermediary in negotiat-
ing the return of the dispersed masters.)[41] Nor is it a datum, though
again it is the reasonable inference, that Grosseteste's regency as
referred to in Sutton's reminiscence was in theology. This line of
speculation would be to import the hypothesis of the provincial
outsider into the earlier dating of his headship of the schools. The
bishop's denial of what, by the legate's award, was the correct title
would in these terms be an implicit concession to the fact that
Grosseteste was under-qualified. However, this is a notional possibility only, to be raised in order to be discountenanced. That a man
so judged to be unqualified should have been an acceptable head of
the schools, whatever his title, must be dismissed as implausible in
the extreme. Moreover, neither is it a circumstance that Grosseteste
is likely to have wished to recall nor, if that had been the context and
unless all memory of the context had been forgotten, would the
example have served Sutton's purpose, since it would have been
open to an immediate retort. Sutton may be construed, rather, in
this sense: not only has the bishop absolute discretion as to whom he
appoints to the chancellorship but – for good measure ('episcopus
adjecit') – he need not, in strictest theory, bestow the title at all;
there was an occasion when he withheld it and that when there was
a most worthy candidate. Master Peter, perhaps genuinely impressed by the recondite lore, more probably recognising as well as
Sutton that the history lesson had no practical relevance to the
everyday world in which the head of the university was a chancellor,
made no reply fit for an episcopal register. The curtain then opened
on the next scene – the bishop's ritual inquiry why the (well-
qualified) candidate had not appeared in person.

On the assumption still that what was at issue was title, the
problem would most plausibly have been the age-old antipathy of an
administration to novelty, compounded by the fact that 'chancellor'
was in context rather awkward.[42] There is some slight evidence that
no later than August 1214 the term was causing difficulty of
interpretation to the episcopal side and perhaps even misgiving. It
comes from a draft of the charter to be issued, in accordance with the

legate's award, by the commune of Oxford. On palaeographical grounds the draft has been assigned to the bishop's chancery[43] and this agrees well with aspects of its content. At one reference to the chancellor, the words 'constituted by the bishop' were interlineated. At another reference, the legate's chancellor ('whom the bishop shall appoint over the scholars there') has become 'the chancellor of the schools of Oxford'.[44] In view of its provenance, this draft has been taken to suggest that the bishop, Hugh of Wells, had by now committed himself to the new title. But in applying the settlement vis-à-vis the town, the question how to style the head of the university would have been peripheral. The essential point would have been to ensure that there should be no room for doubt that the town was implementing the award. It would have been quite the wrong context in which to introduce confusion of terminology as against the award or to reveal dissension in the clerical camp. The more so since the legate was intended to have letters patent showing what had been done.[45] The variation noted may have seemed the most that could be managed. The problem would be more safely raised, as it would be more acute, when the time came, a month or two after – no doubt postponed, in the way of administrations, as late as possible – formally to appoint a clerk with a novel title, at once cathedral and extra-cathedral. The disappearance of the 'chancellor' now would not affect the town's obligations as expressed either by the award or by the draft charter. Nor need Hugh of Wells' putative demurral be thought of as disrespectful. Medieval bishops in dealing with outside authority were past masters of deferential prevarication. There may have been genuine doubt whether the title 'chancellor' was fundamental to the award and whether the earlier, unproblematical title 'master of the schools' would not adequately serve the essential purpose. Comfort may have been taken in this context too from the fact that the legate, at the second mention of the chancellor in his award (referring to poor scholars 'whom the bishop of Lincoln or the archdeacon of the place or his official or the said chancellor – *ipse cancellarius* – or another deputed to this by the bishop of Lincoln shall provide') had allowed for an alternative agent ('vel alius ad hoc ab episcopo Lincolniensi deputatus') in this specific instance. Also, he had included a similar formulation allowing variety as regards the persons competent to demand and receive the return of clerks from lay custody: 'by the bishop of Lincoln or the archdeacon of the place or his official or the chancellor or him whom the bishop shall have deputed to this office'[46] [sc. of receiving the return, but the bishop would have been poorly served by advisers who missed the room for wider legal argument from an ambiguity]. The moratorium on the first office-holder's use of the title would have lasted until the bishop quietly satisfied himself that resistance was unlikely to be successful in the longer term, that it might result rather in the conversion of the legate's future tenses into imperatives and that the prudent course was to accept the award with the rights of nomination which it purported to confer. Since the relations between Grosseteste and Hugh of Wells were warm, the transition may have been the easier.[47]

None of this is capable of proof nor is, perhaps, likely ever to be. If however some firm evidence were to establish that Grosseteste was indeed the first head of the schools after the return of the dispersed masters, then the certainty on that score might invite – it would not compel – an interpretation of Sutton's reminiscence different from that usually adopted. There is some difficulty in reconciling the supposition that Grosseteste deemed it of sufficient urgency to clarify the details of his tenure of the 'chancellorship' so soon in his pontificate that that circumstance – but no other of his declaration – would be specially remembered and signalled sixty years later, with his having made only an oral pronouncement. Sutton, who was well enough informed on the substance, appears to have had no stronger evidence than hearsay. The mystery is greater if one takes the statement quite literally to have been 'at the inception of his creation as bishop'. But perhaps the point was not that Grosseteste had made the statement early in his pontificate, let alone right at the beginning. The question arises whether the adverbial phrase 'in principio creacionis sue in episcopum' modifies 'dixit' or whether it does not rather modify 'permisisse'. 'Suus' for 'eius' is a not uncommon laxity of medieval Latin[48] and, in the present context, if the 'sue' refers to Grosseteste the following 'suum' is redundant. With 'sue' read to mean 'eius', the effect of the Latin is, without loss of syntactical coherence, to throw into a position of emphasis that which establishes a fundamental parameter: 'In the beginning it was not so.' The 'dixit' is quite unstressed, the verb of importance to Sutton's point being 'permisisse'. The nearest English translation, on this suggestion, would be: 'And the bishop added that blessed Robert, late bishop of Lincoln, who held this office at a time when he was regent in the university, said that at the inception of his creation as bishop [? at the beginning or in the early phase of his pontificate], the bishop of Lincoln, his immediate predecessor, had not permitted that the said Robert [sc., for Sutton's purpose, the head of the university] be called chancellor but master of the schools.' (The ambiguity, as I perceive it, of the Latin can be recovered in English by omitting 'that' after 'said'.) The statement itself Grosseteste might have made at any time, perhaps perfectly casually, perhaps in reaction to a particular issue. If the latter, then it may have been a reflection on the contrast between a stage of the university's history when the very title of chancellor was in doubt and the development marked by the university's self-confident adoption of a common seal, the subject of a dispute c. 1251–3. For what the consideration is worth, the longevity of the oral tradition would be reduced by a quarter. Apart from formulation, there is the difficulty that Hugh of Wells' pontificate, formally calculated from his consecration, was almost five years old by the Michaelmas term of 1214. But, because of the papal interdict, he did not have restoration of the temporalities of his see until July 1213. In the casual context of a verbal statement, verbally recalled, as opposed to the dating of an episcopal act, 'the inception of his creation as bishop' – if those were Grosseteste's actual words – might be thought of as running from his effectively entering on his diocese. However, as Fr Callus soberly observed of the passage, possibilities and guesses do not ever amount to valid evidence.[49] The evidence as it is cannot resolve the vexed issue on which the informed reader will have to reach his own judgement before returning to ponder an inspired account of the intellectual development of one of medieval England's and Europe's most dazzling thinkers.

The presence of Grosseteste as an *éminence grise* – on some points influential, on some constricting, on some forcing departures – is evident in the teaching of the first Franciscan theologian at Oxford whose works have survived, convincingly identified and lucidly analysed by P. Raedts, *Richard Rufus of Cornwall and the Tradition of Oxford Theology* (Oxford, 1987). Though a theologian of second rank, Rufus is of first-rank interest to the historian. His wrestling with Aristotelian epistemology, with the definition of theology and with its method – especially the distinction between dialectical and allegorical exposition – and with the relationship between intellect and will, his debt to the Aristotelian model of nature and his naive appreciation of Aristotelian psychology illustrate vividly the process of absorption of the new ideas, while his theory, so far as it can be glimpsed, of individuation is an interesting anticipation of a later development. Among other points of interest, Rufus is plausibly revealed as a discriminating pioneer in the introduction of Bonaventure's work to Oxford. Conversely, Dr Raedts' patient unravelling of the transmission of Rufus' works casts the notable sidelight on the relations between the Paris and Oxford scenes that intellectual contact was not wholly one way and that Bonaventure or his immediate circle made shift to keep abreast of English currents of thought.

A topic on which Richard Rufus preferred Grosseteste's analysis of Aristotle to that of Bonaventure was the eternity of the world, one of the great concerns of the century. L. Bianchi, *L' Errore di Aristotele La Polemica contro l'Eternità del Mondo nel XIII Secolo* (Florence, 1984) scrutinises thoroughly the general course of the debate and the issues underlying it, showing how it raised and concentrated attention on large problems of logic, mathematics, physics, cosmology, metaphysics and theology and on such specific points as ontological relations and the nature of time. His conclusions are a powerful complement to the contribution of Professor van Steenberghen in pioneering the concept of a 'radical Aristotelianism' to replace the earlier 'Latin Averroism' and of Fr Callus and others in mitigating the exaggerated dualism between Augustinianism and Aristotelianism. The impression of fluidity and of 'non-denominationalism' which emerges on this topic from Professor Bianchi's work is confirmed by the findings of R. C. Dales, summarised in his *Medieval Discussions of the Eternity of the World* (Leiden etc., 1990). Professor Dales, too, while adverting to the rancour which the dispute engendered, has noted the general absence of, for example, a Franciscan or Dominican position on the problems arising. The results of the separate studies emphasise the more general fluidity which is evident in the immediate aftermath of the 1277 condemnation (see above, Chapter 7).

The studies of Bianchi and Dales continue the 'rehabilitation' of the radical arts masters at the expense of their critics. The process is advanced separately by R. C. Dales, 'The Origin of the Doctrine of the Double Truth', *Viator*, xv (1984), 169–79, which traces the underlying distinction between the physical and theological orders to theologians, such as Philip the Chancellor and, most influentially,

Alexander of Hales, in their anxiety to defend the created origin of
the world. Its invocation by members of the arts faculty at Paris in
the 1260s and 1270s was, in this illuminating argument, 'apparently
on the assumption that the distinction was by now traditional and
would be understood by the whole academic community' (p. 176).
The process is advanced, in relation to another issue, by C. J. Ryan,
'Man's Free Will in the Works of Siger of Brabant', *Mediaeval Studies*,
xlv (1983), 155–99, where this aspect of Siger's thought is re-
examined in the light of the Vienna and Peterhouse reportations of his
Questions on the *Metaphysics* and on the *Book of Causes*, and where
Siger is shown to be committed to the defence of free will even if his
metaphysics of the subject is relatively undeveloped. On yet another
issue, A. Maurer, 'Siger of Brabant and Theology', *Mediaeval Studies*,
l (1988), 257–78, argues that Siger's brief comments on sacred
theology reveal his acceptance that its teachings have greater
certainty than those of metaphysics. Professor Dales summarises his
conclusions on the confrontation between Tempier and the radical
masters as follows: 'The picture which emerges . . . is one of able
and devout Christian philosophers and theologians being attacked
for largely non-doctrinal reasons, and condemned by a dishonest
and vengeful committee of theologians . . . who had the ear of a
fairly unintelligent, though fearful and conservative bishop' (Dales,
Medieval Discussions, p. 176). The judgement is the measure of how
far historical revision has gone on what was once known as 'Latin
Averroism'. It may well be that as the debris of past misunderstanding of the issues in question is removed, the next phase of research
on the subject will take the direction of re-examining in the light of
new clarities why the crisis was perceived as it was, with that
intensity which prompts men of principle to act ignobly.[50]

Notes

1. MASTERS OF THOSE WHO KNOW – PLATO, ARISTOTLE AND THE NEOPLATONISTS

1. Dante, *Inferno*, Canto IV, l. 131.
2. *Ibid.*, l. 134.
3. It is also known as the theory of 'Ideas'. 'Forms' is preferable, however, since 'Ideas' in so far as it implies subjectivity conveys the wrong impression of Plato's doctrine.
4. See D. Ross, *Plato's Theory of Ideas* (Oxford, 1951), p. 172.
5. Plato, *Meno*, 81a.
6. From his birthplace, Stageira in Chalcidice, Aristotle is sometimes, usually in older works, referred to as 'the Stagirite'.
7. The Lyceum, so-called from an area of the city, sacred to Apollo, had an adjoining promenade or 'Peripatos'. From this the school acquired the soubriquet 'Peripatetic' which is sometimes used to refer to it.
8. The great contribution in this direction was made by W. Jaeger, *Aristotle. Fundamentals of the History of his Development* first published in German in 1923. (2nd edn, Oxford, 1948.)
9. Aristotle, *De Generatione et Corruptione*, I.2; 317^a 25. Elsewhere, Aristotle distinguishes 'change of size' and 'local motion' from 'alteration' but the most important point is the isolation of the special character of substantial change.
10. Aristotle, *Topics*, I.5; 102^a–102^b.
11. Aristotle, *De Generatione et Corruptione*, I.2; 317^a 25.
12. This is the characteristic application of the doctrine. 'Being which undergoes substantial change' is almost synonymous with 'material being'. The exceptions are the heavenly bodies which, however, as explained below, are also thought of as composites of matter and form.
13. A similar difficulty existed in Greek.
14. The term derives from the Greek for 'matter' and 'form' or 'shape'. The following account of the tension between Aristotle's theory of knowledge and of being derives from the analysis of E. Zeller, for which see his *Aristotle and the Earlier Peripatetics* (translated from his *Die Philosophie der Griechen in ihrer geschichtlichen Entwicklung* by B. F. C. Costelloe and J. H. Muirhead), I (London, 1897), 328–80. Not all scholars follow Zeller's interpretation. For a recent review of the problem, see W. K. C. Guthrie, *Aristotle an Encounter* (A History of Greek Philosophy, vol. VI; Cambridge, 1981), pp. 209–22.
15. The four causes are reviewed in *Physics*, II.3; 194^b 16–34.
16. The elements are not to be confused with the notional 'first matter', being themselves substances compounded of matter and form.
17. Aristotle, *Physics*, 242^a 19.
18. *Ibid.*, 258^b 10 *et seq.*
19. Aristotle, *Metaphysics*, Λ, especially Ch. 7; 1072^a–1072^b.
20. *Ibid.*, Book Λ.8; 1074^a 30–5.
21. Aristotle, *De Anima*, II, 1; 412^a 27.
22. *Ibid.*, III, 11; 434^a 5–10. Sometimes he tends to the view that animals do not have imagination. The conflict is probably a matter of definition.
23. *Ibid.*, 10; 433^b 21 *et seq.*
24. *De Anima*, III, 5; 430^a 15–25. Translated by J. A. Smith, in *The Works of Aristotle translated into English*, ed. W. D. Ross, vol. III (Oxford, 1931). For another translation,

with minor differences, see *Aristotle's De Anima Books II and III*, translated with Introduction and Notes by D. W. Hamlyn (Clarendon Aristotle Series, Oxford, 1968), p. 60. The thirteenth-century Latin translation by William of Moerbeke rendered the last part of the passage as follows: 'Only separated, however, is it what it really is. And this alone is immortal and perpetual. It does not remember, because it is impassible; the passive intellect is corruptible, and the soul understands nothing apart from this latter.' See *Aristotle's De Anima in the Version of William of Moerbeke and the Commentary of St Thomas Aquinas*, translated by K. Foster and S. Humphries with an introduction by I. Thomas (London, 1951), pp. 425–6.

25. In an early dialogue, the *Eudemus*, of which only fragments survive.

26. References to the *Ethics* below are all to the *Nicomachean Ethics*.

27. Aristotle, *Nicomachean Ethics*, v, 2; tr. J. A. K. Thomson (Harmondsworth, repr. 1971), p. 144. Aristotle, *Politics*, iii, 4, tr. T. A. Sinclair (Harmondsworth, repr. 1970), p. 107.

28. *Nichomachean Ethics*, iii, 7; tr., p. 95.

29. *Ibid.*, iii, 11; p. 105.

30. *Ibid.*., vi, 7; p. 180.

31. *Ibid.*, i, 1; p. 25.

32. *Ibid.*, 5; p. 31.

33. *Ibid.*, 7; pp. 36–7.

34. *Ibid.*, 13; pp. 53–4.

35. *Ibid.*, vii, 2; p. 195.

36. *Ibid.*, 3; p. 202.

37. *Ibid.*, ii, 6; p. 66.

38. *Ibid.*, v, 6–7; pp. 156–68.

39. *Ibid.*, 10; pp. 166–8.

40. *Ibid.*, ix, 9; p. 277. For an earlier statement of the dictum, cf. *ibid.*, i, 7; p. 37.

41. *Ibid.*, ix, 9; p. 279.

42. Aristotle, *Politics*, i, 2; tr. p. 28.

43. *Ibid.*, p. 29.

44. See below, pp. 42–3.

45. See R. T. Wallis, *Neo-Platonism* (London, 1972), p. 166; J. Dillon, *The Middle Platonists* (London, 1977), pp. 401–8.

46. *Enneads*, iv. 7. 13; cf. Plotinus, *The Enneads*, tr. S. McKenna (3rd edn, London, 1962), p. 356.

47. Porphyry, *Life of Plotinus*, in McKenna, cited above, p. 2.

2. FROM ANCIENT WORLD TO MIDDLE AGES: ADAPTATION AND TRANSMISSION

1. On this subject see R. W. Southern, *Western Society and the Church in the Middle Ages* (Harmondsworth, 1970), pp. 53–67.

2. The classic account is that of G. Boissier, *La Fin du Paganisme* (Paris, 1909), pp. 231–91.

3. St Augustine, *Epistula* 228, ed. A. Goldbacher, *CSEL*, vol. lvii, part 4 (Leipzig, 1911; repr. New York and London, 1961), 484–96.

4. For a detailed account, see P. Brown, *Augustine of Hippo* (London, 1967), and J. J. O'Meara, *The Young Augustine* (London, 1954).

5. St Augustine, *Confessions*, ix. 6, 14; tr. R. S. Pine-Coffin (Harmondsworth, 1961), p. 190.

6. See e.g. *Confessions*, ii. 5; tr. Pine-Coffin, p. 48; cf. *Soliloquies*, xii: tr. J. H. S. Burleigh, *Augustine: Earlier Writings* (London, 1953), pp. 35–6. For a review of this aspect see Brown, *Augustine of Hippo*, pp. 200–2.

7. This is not to accept the absolute historicity of these dialogues. Cf. J. J. O'Meara,

tr., *St. Augustine Against the Academics* (Ancient Christian Writers, no. 12, Westminster, Maryland, 1950), pp. 23–32, and his 'The Historicity of the Early Dialogues of St Augustine', *Vigiliae Christianae*, 5 (1951), 150–78.

8. See *Confessions*, III. 4; tr. Pine-Coffin, pp. 58–9; *Soliloquies*, x, Burleigh, *Augustine*, p. 33.

9. *Confessions*, III. 5; tr. Pine-Coffin, p. 60.

10. The mood of enthusiastic doubt, giving way to a quest for new certainty, is captured with remarkable intensity in *Confessions*, VI. 11: 'What great men the Academics are! Can there be nothing known for certain about the rule of living?'

11. *Confessions*, VII. 9; tr. Pine-Coffin, p. 144. *Ibid.*, VIII. 2; p. 159.

12. For an examination of Augustine's progress in Greek, see P. Courcelle, *Late Latin Writers and their Greek Sources* (Cambridge, Mass., 1969), pp. 149–65.

13. For a convenient summary of the bibliography and arguments, see R. J. O'Connell, *St. Augustine's Early Theory of Man, A.D. 386–391* (Cambridge, Mass., 1968), pp. 1–28.

14. The view that Augustine was converted to Platonism and adapted Christianity to that outlook rather than vice versa is an extreme statement of the case and does not accord with his later treatment of the differences between them. He resolved these by a highly eclectic approach to Platonist doctrines. For a judicious review of this question, see O'Meara, *St. Augustine Against the Academics*, pp. 19–22 and his *Charter of Christendom: The Significance of the City of God* (New York, 1961), pp. 62–87. Augustine's thought in the period immediately after conversion is analysed in detail, from the point of view of Plotinian indebtedness, by O'Connell, *St. Augustine's Early Theory of Man*.

15. For a list of St Augustine's works, see H. Marrou, *Saint Augustine and his Influence through the Ages* (New York, London, 1957), pp. 182–6.

16. St Augustine, *City of God*, XIX, 1, 2. Varro's lost compendium, *On Philosophy*, was probably an important source of St Augustine's knowledge of ancient schools.

17. E.g. *ibid.*, XVI. 18–40 *passim*; XVII. 17–22 *passim*.

18. See O'Meara, *Charter of Christendom*, pp. 74 ff., and his *Porphyry's Philosophy from Oracles in Augustine* (Etudes Augustiniennes, Paris 1959). On this aspect of Neoplatonism, see R. T. Wallis, *Neoplatonism* (London, 1972), pp. 105 ff.

19. See H. Chadwick, 'Philo and the Beginnings of Christian Thought', in *CHLGEMP*, pp. 150–2.

20. 'When Augustine speaks of understanding he always has in mind the product of a rational activity for which faith prepares the way.' E. Gilson, *The Christian Philosophy of St. Augustine* (London, 1961), p. 36.

21. It may even be that Porphyry himself can be considered an example of the type. He may have been a Christian for a time or, perhaps, disposed to become one. Cf. F. Copleston, *A History of Philosophy*, I, part 2 (New York, 1962), 218.

22. Tertullian, *Prescription against Heretics*, 7, in A. Roberts and J. Donaldson tr., *The Ante-Nicene Fathers*, III (repr. Grand Rapids, Michigan, 1973), 246.

23. St Augustine, *On Christian Doctrine*, II. 40; tr. D. W. Robertson, Jr (The Library of Liberal Arts Press, 1958), p. 75.

24. Cf. *ibid.*, p. x.

25. See e.g. *Confessions*, VII and *City of God*, VIII. See also J. J. O'Meara, 'Neo-platonism in the Conversion of St Augustine', *Dominican Studies*, III (1950), 331–43 and his 'Augustine and Neoplatonism' in *Recherches Augustiniennes* (Paris, 1958), I, 91–111.

26. See O'Meara, *St. Augustine Against the Academics*, III, 7–9; pp. 113–21.

27. For detailed references to these, see Gilson, *Christian Philosophy*, pp. 41–2.

28. *De Quantitate Animae*, XIII. 22; ed. Migne, *PL*, XXXII, 1048.

29. St Augustine, *De Trinitate*, XV. 7. 11; ed. W. J. Mountain and F. Glorie (Corpus Christianorum, Series Latina, La, 1968), p. 474. Cf. Gilson, *Christian Philosophy*, p. 47.

30. 'He felt from the beginning that the body and soul together make the man, but he continued throughout his life to reason as though the soul were one substance which uses that other substance, the body.' Gilson, *Christian Philosophy*, p. 48.

31. For a full discussion of this subject, see *ibid.*, pp. 59–65.

32. In the *Soliloquies*, Augustine had been prepared to suppose that this reminiscence might indeed be the route by which the mind attained to higher knowledge. (*Soliloquies*, xx. 35; tr. Burleigh, *Augustine Earlier Writings*). Later, he rejected the theory. Cf. Gilson, *Christian Philosophy*, pp. 71–2. For Augustine's discussion of whether knowledge is learned, see *The Teacher (De Magistro)*, tr. Burleigh, *Augustine Earlier Writings*.

33. 'Plato . . . saw that God alone could be the author of nature, the bestower of intelligence and the kindler of love by which life becomes good and blessed.' St Augustine, *City of God*, xi. 25; tr. P. Schaff, in *A Select Library of the Nicene and Post-Nicene Fathers*, series 1, vol. ii (repr. Grand Rapids, Michigan, 1973), p. 219. For Augustine's acquaintance with the doctrine, through Neoplatonism, see Gilson, *Christian Philosophy*, p. 77.

34. For a discussion of the difficulties, see Gilson, *Christian Philosophy*, pp. 80–96.

35. St Augustine, *On Free Will*, i. xiii–xiv; tr. Burleigh, *Augustine Earlier Writings*, pp. 129–30.

36. *Ibid.*, xv, p. 131.

37. St Augustine, *To Simplician, On Various Questions*, tr. *ibid.*, pp. 376–406.

38. *On Free Will*, iii. xxv. 74; *ibid.*, p. 215.

39. See *De Genesi ad Litteram*, v. 7. 20. ed. I. Zycha (*CSEL*, xxviii), p. 150. Cf. *CHLGEMP*, pp. 397–400.

40. St Augustine, *On the Nature of the Good*, iii; Burleigh, *Augustine Earlier Writings*, p. 327.

41. *Ibid.*, viii; p. 328.

42. For the whole schema, see *ibid.*, i–xxiii; pp. 326–33.

43. Augustine attempted to show, against Porphyry, that even the resurrection was in keeping with Platonist principles. *City of God*, xiii,. 16–18.

44. *Ibid.*, viii. 11; xi. 21.

45. See *City of God*, xxii. 30; in *ibid.*, xx. 8, Augustine says that it is called 'a thousand years'. See further, R. A. Markus, *Saeculum: History and Society in the Theology of St Augustine* (Cambridge, 1970), pp. 17–21, and G. Folliet, 'La typologie du sabbat chez Saint Augustin: son interprétation millénariste entre 388 et 400', *Revue des Etudes Augustiniennes*, ii (1956), 371–90.

46. On the history of medieval millennial speculation and activity, see N. Cohn, *The Pursuit of the Millennium* (London, 1957) and M. Reeves, *The Influence of Prophecy in the Later Middle Ages* (Oxford, 1969).

47. *City of God*, xiv, 28.

48. For fine insights into this, see A. H. Armstrong and R. A. Markus, *Christian Faith and Greek Philosophy* (London, 1960), especially pp. 91–2.

49. Cf. Gilson, *Christian Philosophy*, pp. 134–5.

50. *Confessions*, xiii. 9. 10.

51. *City of God*, xx. 7; tr. Schaff, *Select Library*, p. 427.

52. See, e.g., *City of God*, i. 35. On the problem of ambiguity in Augustine's use of his terms, see Gilson, *Christian Philosophy*, p. 181.

53. Augustine probably owed the idea of two mystical cities to the African theologian, Tyconius, who had abandoned the Donatist view that the church was a pure society. See further, Markus, *Saeculum*, pp. 115–22.

54. See *ibid.*, pp. 95, 204–5, 210.

55. See P. Brown, 'St Augustine', in B. Smalley (ed.), *Trends in Medieval Political Thought* (Oxford, 1965), pp. 1–21 (reprinted in P. Brown, *Religion and Society in the Age of St Augustine* (London, 1972)); see also M. J. Wilks, 'St Augustine and the general will',

Studia patristica IX (Texte und Untersuchungen 94, Berlin, 1966), 487–522 and H. A. Deane, *The Political and Social Ideas of St Augustine* (New York, 1963), pp. 144, 235–6.

56. E.g. *Epistle* CLXXXV, ii. 8–9: *CSEL*, LVII, 7–8; *Contra Litteras Petiliani*, II, 20, 45: *CSEL*, LII, 45. This is not to deny that obedience is part of his general doctrine nor to imply that it was assumed for the purpose of coercing opponents. Cf. Deane, *Political and Social Ideas*, p. 190.

57. Cf. Deane, *Political and Social Ideas*, pp. 151–2.

58. *City of God*, II. 21; XIX. 21.

59. *Ibid.*, XIX. 24.

60. *Ibid.*, 27.

61. St Augustine, *Epistola* 153; tr. W. Parsons, *St Augustine's Letters*, III (The Fathers of the Church; Washington, 1953), 302.

62. Cf. Gilson, *Christian Philosophy*, p. 177: 'To transfer the rules obtaining on one level to the other is to confuse and upset everything.'

63. St Augustine, *Enarrationes in Psalmos*, LI. 6 (Corpus Christianorum, Series Latina, XXXIX, 627); cf. Deane, *Political and Social Ideas*, p. 130.

64. St Augustine, Epistola 138. 13; tr. P. Schaff in *A Select Library of the Nicene and Post-Nicene Fathers*, series 1, vol. I (repr. Grand Rapids, Michigan; 1973), 481–8.

65. On the doctrine of the just war, see F. H. Russell, *The Just War in the Middle Ages* (Cambridge, 1975).

66. For important treatment of the subject, see P. Brown, 'St Augustine's Attitude to Religious Coercion', *Journal of Roman Studies*, LIV (1964), 107–16 and also his 'Religious Coercion, in the later Roman Empire: the case of North Africa', *History*, XLVIII (1963), 283–305 (both reprinted in *Religion and Society in the Age of St Augustine*).

67. Cassiodorus, *Variae*, II. 27; quoted H. M. Barrett, *Boethius, Some Aspects of his Times and Work* (New York, 1965), p. 31.

68. Boethius' father-in-law was a great-grandson of Symmachus, the champion of paganism against St Ambrose.

69. The fullest statement of his intention is contained in *In librum de Interpretatione* (*editio secunda*), I. 2; ed. Migne, *PL*, LXIV, 433.

70. Boethius' authorial intentions and his achievements of them have been examined by A. Kappelmacher, 'Der schriftstellerische Plan des Boethius', *Wiener Studien, Zeitschrift fur Klassische Philologie*, XLVI (1929), 215–25 and L. M. De Rijk, 'On the Chronology of Boethius' Works on Logic', *Vivarium*, II (1964), 1–49, 125–62.

71. See J. Shiel, 'Boethius' Commentaries on Aristotle', *Mediaeval and Renaissance Studies*, IV (1958), 217–44.

72. The evidence is summarised in W. H. Stahl, R. Johnson and E. L. Burge, *Martianus Capella and The Seven Liberal Arts*, vol. I (New York, 1971),p. 115.

73. See H. Chadwick, 'The Authenticity of Boethius' Fourth Tractate De Fide Catholica', *Journal of Theological Studies*, n.s. XXXI (1980), 551–6 and *Boethius, the Consolations of Music, Logic, Theology and Philosophy* (Oxford, 1981), pp. 175–80.

74. See *CHLGEMP*, pp. 331–40.

75. See Barrett, *Boethius*, p. 143.

76. See W. C. Bark, 'Theodoric vs. Boethius: Vindication and Apology', *American Historical Review*, XLIX (1944), 410–26. See also V. Schurr, *Die Trinitätslehre des Boethius im Lichte der Skythischen Kontroversen* (Paderborn, 1935) and Chadwick, *Boethius, the Consolations*, pp. 180–90, for the background.

77. See especially, P. Courcelle, *Late Latin Writers and their Greek Sources*, tr. H. E. Wedeck (Cambridge, Mass. 1969), pp. 295–322. Professor Courcelle's account of Boethius' dependence on Alexandrian writers for his logical doctrine must be read in the light of Shiel, 'Boethius' Commentaries on Aristotle'.

78. See the argument of A. Momigliano, 'Cassiodorus and Italian Culture of his Time', *Proceedings of the British Academy*, XLI (1955), 207–45. The question has been

reviewed by Chadwick, *Boethius, the Consolations*, who suggests that the *Consolation* 'is a work written by a Platonist who is also a Christian but is not a Christian work', p. 249.

79. For example, by E. K. Rand, *Founders of the Middle Ages* (Cambridge, Mass., 1928), Ch. 5.

80. See W. Schmid, 'Boethius and the Claims of Philosophy', in *Studia Patristica, Papers Presented to the Second International Conference on Patristic Studies held at Christ Church, Oxford*, 1955, part II, eds K. Aland and F. L. Cross (Berlin, 1957), pp. 368–75. On other aspects of literary design in the work, see A. Crabbe, 'Literary Design in the *De Consolatione Philosophiae*' in M. Gibson, ed., *Boethius, his Life, Thought and Influence* (Oxford, 1981), pp. 237–74.

81. *Boethius, The Consolation of Philosophy*, eds H. F. Stewart and E. K. Rand (Loeb edition; London; Cambridge, Mass., repr. 1953), p. 157.

82. *Ibid.*, p. 181 (slightly revised).

83. The references to God here and elsewhere in the *Consolation* are not evidence of the author's Christianity. Nor is his use of the Platonic doctrine of recollection proof against it (for example, Book v, metric 3).

84. It occurs also in *De Trinitate*, IV.

85. For details of these, see H. R. Patch, *The Tradition of Boethius* (New York, 1935); P. Courcelle, *La Consolation de Philosophie dans la Tradition Littéraire* (Paris, 1967) and 'Étude critique des commentaires sur la *Consolatio Philosophiae* de Boèce du IXe au XVe siècle', *Archives d'histoire doctrinale et littéraire du Moyen Age*, XIV (1939), 5–140, J. Beaumont, 'The Latin Tradition of the *De Consolatione Philosophiae*' in Gibson, ed., *Boethius*, pp. 278–305.

86. The term 'quadrivium' or more authentically 'quadruvium' derived from Boethius himself. Its complement, 'trivium', seems to have been a coinage of the Carolingian period. See M. L. W. Laistner, *Thought and Letters in Western Europe AD 500 to 900* (2nd edn London, 1957), p. 41.

87. He did not actually found intellectual monasticism. On earlier and independent contemporary examples of the type, see P. Riché, *Education and culture in the Barbarian West Sixth through Eighth Centuries*, tr. J. J. Contreni (Columbia, S.C., 1976), pp. 158–61. The importance of the library at Vivarium for the transmission of classical texts is not now considered to have been so great as was once thought. For a recent statement, see L. D. Reynolds and N. G. Wilson, *Scribes and Scholars* (Oxford, 1974), pp. 72–4.

88. See R. W. Southern, *The Making of the Middle Ages* (repr. London, 1967), p. 166.

89. Among other works of Isidore which served to transmit a knowledge specifically of ancient philosophical schools may be noted the *De natura rerum* (on the physical world), the *De differentiis rerum* (on biblical and theological terms) and the *Liber numerorum* (on the symbolism of numbers).

90. I acknowledge my debt for what follows to the two fundamental studies by P. Riché, *Education and Culture* and *Les Ecoles et l'Enseignement dans l'Occident Chrétien de la Fin du Ve Siècle au Milieu du XIe Siècle* (Paris, 1979).

91. See J. Marenbon, *From the Circle of Alcuin to the School of Auxerre: Logic, Theology and Philosophy in the Early Middle Ages* (Cambridge, 1981), pp. 44–55, 151–66.

92. See *ibid.*, pp. 57–62.

93. *Ibid.*, pp. 39–40.

94. *Ibid.*, pp. 64–5.

95. See *ibid.*, pp. 67–70 and *CHLGEMP*, pp. 573–5.

96. See Marenbon, *From the Circle of Alcuin*, pp. 105–11; cf. J. J. Contreni, 'The Irish Colony at Laon during the time of John Scottus' in *Jean Scot Erigène et l'Histoire de la Philosophie* (Actes du Colloque no. 561 du CNRS à Laon, du 7 au 12 juillet 1976, organisé par R. Rogues; Paris, 1977), pp. 59–67.

97. See L. Bieler, *Ireland, Harbinger of the Middle Ages* (Corrected reprint, Oxford, 1966), p. 166.

98. M. Cappuyns, *Jean Scot Erigène: sa vie, son oeuvre, sa pensée* (Paris, 1933); J. J. O'Meara, *Eriugena* (Cork, 1969).

99. I. P. Sheldon-Williams, 'Eriugena's Greek Sources' in J. J. O'Meara (ed.), *The Mind of Eriugena* (Dublin, 1973), pp. 2–5.

100. See *CHLGEMP*, pp. 577–8 and O'Meara, *Eriugena*, p. 19.

101. See *CHLGEMP*, p. 523, n. 5.

102. Eriugena already knew Origen's *De principiis* by this time, see *ibid.*, pp. 583–4.

103. Cf. M. L. Uhlfelder and J. A. Potter, *John the Scot, Periphyseon, On the Division of Nature* (Indianapolis, 1976), pp. xxvii–xxviii.

104. *Annotationes in Marcianum*, ed. C. Lutz (Cambridge, Mass., 1939), 57.15, p. 64. This might be thought, from the context, to apply to the classical heaven only but as the editor shows, pp. xvi–xvii, it is part of a general emphasis in the work on the power of reason.

105. *Periphyseon*, I. 69. I. P. Sheldon-Williams, ed. and tr. *John Scotus Eriugena, Periphyseon*, I (Dublin, 1968), pp. 197–9.

106. *Periphyseon*, IV. 4; tr. Uhlfelder and Potter, *John the Scot*, p. 215.

107. *Periphyseon* ('Concerning Nature') is the more general title; cf. *CHLGEMP*, p. 520, n. 2.

108. *Periphyseon*, I. (Prologue); Sheldon-Williams, p. 37.

109. Sheldon-Williams, 'Eriugena's Greek Sources', p. 5.

110. *Periphyseon*, V. 38; tr. Uhlfelder and Potter, *John the Scot*, p. 351.

111. See, for example, *Periphyseon*, V. 8; Uhlfelder and Potter, *John the Scot*, pp. 288–9.

112. On Origen's doctrine, see, e.g. *CHLGEMP*, pp. 190–2.

113. Marenbon, *From the Circle of Alcuin*, pp. 88–109.

114. See *ibid.*, pp. 111–12.

115. See *ibid.*, pp. 109–11.

116. See *CHLGEMP*, pp. 532–3. Cf. *Periphyseon*, ed. Sheldon-Williams, I (Dublin, 1968), 24.

117. See M. Gibson, 'The Continuity of Learning circa 850–circa 1050', *Viator*, VI (1975), [1–13], 12.

3. THE CENTRAL MIDDLE AGES – LOGIC, THEOLOGY AND COSMOLOGY

1. St Anselm's defence of Trinitarian doctrine and his report of Roscelin's views is contained in his *Epistola de Incarnatione Verbi*, of which there are two recensions, edited in F. S. Schmitt, *Sancti Anselmi Cantuariensis Archiepiscopi, Opera Omnia*, vols I and II (Edinburgh, 1946).

2. See the account in R. W. Southern, *The Making of the Middle Ages* (repr. London, 1967), Ch. 2.

3. See J. J. Contreni, *The Cathedral School of Laon from 850 to 930, its Manuscripts and Masters* (Münchener Beiträge zur Mediävistik und Renaissance-Forschung, 29; Munich, 1978).

4. Gerbert may have taught less intensively during his second period at Reims. Cf. P. Riché, *Les Ecoles et l'Enseignement dans l'Occident Chrétien de la Fin du Ve Siècle au Milieu du XIe Siècle* (Paris, 1979), p. 180.

5. See Peter Abelard, *Historia Calamitatum*, ed. in J. T. Muckle, 'Abelard's Letter of Consolation to a Friend (*Historia Calamitatum*)', *Mediaeval Studies*, XII (1950), [163–213], 175–6; tr. B. Radice, *The Letters of Abelard and Héloise* (Harmondsworth, 1974), p. 58.

6. See B. Smalley, *The Study of the Bible in the Middle Ages* (2nd edn., Notre Dame, 1964), pp. 83–4.

7. See E. A. Moody, *Truth and Consequence in Medieval Logic* (Amsterdam, 1952),

pp. 1–3. On the difficulties experienced by early twelfth-century scholars in disentangling logic and grammar, see R. W. Hunt, 'Studies in Priscian in the Eleventh and Twelfth Centuries', *Mediaeval and Renaissance Studies*, I (1941–3), 214–23.

8. See J. Marenbon, *From the Circle of Alcuin to the School of Auxerre: Logic, Theology and Philosophy in the Early Middle Ages* (Cambridge, 1981), p. 16; cf. L. Minio-Paluello, 'Nuovi impulsi allo studio della logica: la seconda fase della riscoperta di Aristotele e di Boezio', in *La Scuola nell' Occidente Latino dell' Alto Medioevo*, II (Settimane di studio del Centro Italiano di Studi sull' Alto Medioevo, XIX, Spoleto, 1972), pp. [743–66] 747–8. In what follows, I rely heavily on this lucid article which supplements the earlier standard account by A. van de Vyver, 'Les Etapes du Développement Philosophique du Haut Moyen-Age', *Revue Belge de Philologie et d'Histoire*, VII (1929), 425–52.

9. See Minio-Paluello, 'Nuovi impulsi', pp. 753–4. The vulgate text of the literal translation of the Categories was a composite of a polished version by Boethius and what was probably an earlier version by him, see Minio-Paluello, *Aristoteles Latinus, I 1–5, Categoriae vel Praedicamenta*, pp. x–xi, xxi.

10. See H. Chadwick, *Boethius, the Consolations of Music, Logic, Theology and Philosophy* (Oxford, 1981), pp. 167, 173.

11. See Minio-Paluello, 'Nuovi impulsi', p. 751; Chadwick, *Boethius, the Consolations*, pp. 255–6. Cf. O. Lowry, 'Boethian Logic in the Medieval West', in M. Gibson, ed., *Boethius, his Life, Thought and Influence* (Oxford, 1981), pp. 95–6.

12. See Minio-Paluello, 'Nuovi impulsi', pp. 751–4.

13. *Ibid.*, p. 760 and see A. van de Vyver, *Abbonis Floriacensis Opera Inedita: Syllogismorum Categoricorum et Hypotheticorum Enodatio* (Bruges, 1966).

14. See Minio-Paluello, 'Nuovi impulsi', p. 765.

15. See the analysis of sources of Abelard's independent textbook of logic, the *Dialectica*, in *Petrus Abaelardus, Dialectica*, ed. L. M. de Rijk (2nd edn, Assen, 1970). pp. xiv–xviii. These include all the Boethian commentaries and independent treatises, besides the texts of the *Isagoge*, the *Categories* (in the composite literal version) and the *De Interpretatione*.

16. The intense interest in the new or less familiar texts of the *Organon* at this time resulted in new versions even of those translated by Boethius; see Minio-Paluello, 'Nuovi impulsi', pp. 749–50.

17. See de Rijk, *Petrus Abaelardus*, pp. xvii–xviii, on Abelard. For the text of Adam of Balsham's *Ars Disserendi* see L. Minio-Paluello, *Twelfth Century Logic*, I (Rome, 1956). Cf. L. Minio-Paluello 'The *Ars Disserendi* of Adam of Balsham "Parvipontanus" ', *Mediaeval and Renaissance Studies*, III (1954), 116–69; Lowry, 'Boethian Logic', in Gibson, ed., *Boethius*, pp. 111–12.

18. For an outline of the *Heptateuchon*, which now survives only on microfilm, see Gibson, ed., *Boethius*, pp. 108–9. Cf. A Clerval, *Les Ecoles de Chartres* (Paris, 1895), pp. 220–48. For John of Salisbury's understanding, see *Metalogicon*, II. 3; tr. D. D. McGarry, *The Metalogicon of John of Salisbury. A Twelfth Century Defense of the Verbal and Logical Arts of the Trivium* (Berkeley; Los Angeles, 1962), p. 78. John of Salisbury was *avant-garde* in this respect. The absorption of the new logic into the educational syllabus was gradual. The *Posterior Analytics* in particular caused difficulty. See L. Minio-Paluello, 'Iacobus Veneticus Grecus, Canonist and Translator of Aristotle', *Traditio*, VIII (1952), [265–304] 267, 270 n. 13.

19. See A. C. Lloyd, 'Neo-platonic Logic and Aristotelian Logic', *Phronesis*, I (1955–6), 58–72, especially pp. 155–7.

20. Porphyry, *Isagoge*, I 10–14, in *Aristoteles Latinus, I 6–7, Categoriarum Supplementa*, eds L. Minio-Paluello and B. G. Dods (Bruges; Paris, 1966), p. 5.

21. Boethius, *In Isagogen Porphyrii Commenta, editio secunda*, at I 10–11, ed. S. Brandt (*CSEL*, XLVIII; 1906), pp. 159–67.

22. *Metalogicon*, II. 17; McGarry, *The Metalogicon*, p. 112.

23. *Historia Calamitatum*, edition cited in n. 5 above, 178; Radice, *Letters of Abelard and Héloise*, p. 60.

24. The *Logica* 'Ingredientibus' is edited in B. Geyer, *Peter Abelards Philosophische Schriften (BGPMA*, vol. xxi, Parts 1–4; Münster, 1919–33), to which there is an addendum in Minio-Paluello, *Twelfth Century Logic*, ii (Rome, 1958), pp. 1–108. The commentary on *De Differentiis Topicis* edited in M. dal Pra, *Pietro Abelardo Scritti Filosofici* (Rome; Milan, 1954), is probably also to be grouped with the *Logica* 'Ingredientibus' which may have been intended also to include commentaries on the other Boethian independent treatises. The *Logica* 'Nostrorum Petitioni Sociorum' is edited in Geyer, *Abelards Philosophische Schriften*, 505–80. Several lesser works, called *Introductiones Parvulorum*, are edited in dal Pra, *Pietro Abelardo*.

25. M. M. Tweedale, *Abailard on Universals* (Amsterdam; New York; Oxford, 1976), is a convenient source of reference to his texts on this problem.

26. On Abelard's varying terminology see B. Stock, *The Implications of Literacy. Written Language and Models of Interpretation in the Eleventh and Twelfth Centuries* (Princeton, 1983), p. 394, n. 340.

27. Cf. Tweedale, *Abailard on Universals*, p. 185.

28. *Metalogicon*, iv. 35; McGarry, *The Metalogicon*, p. 259.

29. See *ibid.*, p. 260; cf. *ibid.*, ii. 17, pp. 113–14.

30. See N. Häring, *The Commentaries on Boethius by Gilbert of Poitiers* (Toronto, 1966), pp. 80–90, 100. Gilbert, who became bishop of Poitiers in 1142, was tried before the council of Reims (1148) over theological implications of his theory but managed to clear himself.

31. *Metalogicon*, ii. 17; McGarry, *The Metalogicon*, p. 115.

32. On Peter Damian's attitude to secular learning, see Riché, *Les Ecoles*, pp. 339–43.

33. R. W. Southern, 'Lanfranc of Bec and Berengar of Tours' in *Studies in Medieval History presented to Frederick Maurice Powicke*, eds R. W. Hunt, W. A. Pantin, R. W. Southern, (Oxford, 1948), pp. 27–48, describes the methods of the participants. M. Gibson, *Lanfranc of Bec* (Oxford, 1978), describes the dispute against its historical and theological background. See also, J. de Montclos, *Lanfranc et Bérenger, la Controverse Eucharistique du XIe Siècle* (Spicilegium Sacrum Lovaniense, Etudes et Documents, 37; Louvain, 1971).

34. The philosophical terminology was still uncertain, see Southern, 'Lanfranc of Bec', pp. 40–1; cf., Gibson, *Lanfranc of Bec*, pp. 89–91.

35. See Smalley, *Study of the Bible*, pp. 47–8.

36. The details of Anselm's biography are known from the *Vita Anselmi* written by his friend Eadmer, a monk of Canterbury. The standard secondary account is R. W. Southern, *St. Anselm and his Biographer* (Cambridge, 1960).

37. See *ibid.*, p. 51.

38. *Monologion*, i; translated in *Anselm of Canterbury, Monologion, Proslogion, Debate with Guanilo and Meditation on Human Redemption*, tr. and ed. J. Hopkins and H. Richardson (London, 1974), p. 5.

39. *Ibid.*; Hopkins and Richardson edn, p. 6.

40. *Ibid.*, iii; Hopkins and Richardson edn, p. 6.

41. St Anselm dealt with the topic again in connection with the status of evil in his *De Casu Diaboli* ('On the Devil's Fall'), written about a decade later.

42. *Monologion*, xv; Hopkins and Richardson edn, p. 24.

43. *Ibid.*, xxvii; Hopkins and Richardson edn, p. 42.

44. *Ibid.*, xxvi; Hopkins and Richardson edn, p. 41. For Boethius' use of 'supersubstance' see *De Trinitate*, iv, in *Boethius, The Consolation of Philosophy*, eds H. F. Stewart and E. K. Rand (Loeb edn; London; Cambridge, Mass., repr 1953), pp. 16–17. However, he also used the term 'substance' as peculiarly appropriate to God, *ibid.*, pp. 16–17. On

the terminological contradiction see Marenbon, *From the Circle of Alcuin*, pp. 28–9.

45. St Anselm, *Monologion*, xxvi; Hopkins and Richardson edn, p. 41.

46. Boethius, *Contra Eutychen*, iii; Stewart and Rand, *Boethius*, pp. 84–5.

47. St Anselm, *Monologion*, lxxix; Hopkins and Richardson edn, p. 85.

48. *Ibid.*, lxxx; Hopkins and Richardson edn, p. 85. 'Therefore it seems – or rather it is unhesitatingly affirmed – that this Being which we call God is not nothing.'

49. *Ibid.*, Preface; Hopkins and Richardson edn, p. 3.

50. *Ibid.*, Hopkins and Richardson edn, p. 5.

51. 'The demonstrations of reason are in varying degrees provisional.' Southern, *St Anselm*, p. 56.

52. *Proslogion*, i; translated in E. R. Fairweather, *A Scholastic Miscellany: Anselm to Ockham* (The Library of Christian Classics, x; Philadelphia, 1956), p. 73. St Anselm's quotation follows St Augustine's preferred reading of Isaiah, vii. 9, from a pre-Vulgate translation of the Bible.

53. See K. Barth, *Anselm: Fides Quaerens Intellectum* (London, 1960).

54. See Southern, *St. Anselm*, pp. 23–5, 58, and also his 'Lanfranc of Bec and Berengar of Tours', 46.

55. This aspect of St Augustine's thought, with its implications for St Anselm's argument, is examined in J. F. Callahan, *Augustine and the Greek Philosophers* (Villanova, 1967), pp. 1–47.

56. Cf. above, pp. 47–8.

57. See Hopkins and Richardson, *Anselm of Canterbury*, pp. 115–20, 123–34.

58. For suggestions as to St Anselm's intention here, see G. R. Evans, *Anselm and Talking about God* (Oxford, 1978), p. 67.

59. The treatise is translated in R. McKeon, *Selections from Medieval Philosophers*, i (New York; Chicago; Atlanta; San Francisco; Dallas, 1929), pp. 150–84.

60. Cf. Evans, *Anselm and Talking about God*, p. 7.

61. See Southern, *St Anselm and his Biographer*, pp. 82–3.

62. See *ibid.*, pp. 85–91.

63. See *ibid.*, pp. 203–26. St Anselm's influence and the change from the monastic to the cathedral scene are the subject of G. R. Evans, *Anselm and a New Generation* (Oxford, 1980).

64. The collected edition of Abelard's works is *Opera Petri Abaelardi*, ed. V. Cousin (2 vols; Paris, 1849–50). The texts mentioned are available in individual editions, as follows: *Peter Abaelards Theologia 'Summi Boni'*, ed. H. Ostlender (*BGPMA*, xxxv, 2–3; Münster, 1939); *Petri Abaelardi Opera Theologica*, ed. F. M. Buytaert (Corpus Christianorum, Continuatio Mediaevalis, xi–xii; Turnhout, 1969) contains the 'Commentary on Romans' (CCCM, xi) and the *Theologia Christiana* and the shorter versions of the *Theologia 'Scholarium'* (CCCM, xii); *Peter Abailard, Sic et Non, A Critical Edition*, ed. B. B. Boyer and R. McKeon (Chicago; London, 1976–7); *The Ethics of Peter Abelard*, ed. and tr. D. E. Luscombe (Oxford, 1971); *Petrus Abaelardus, Dialogus inter Philosophum, Judaeum et Christianum*, ed. R. Thomas (Stuttgart; Bad Cannstatt, 1970) and *Peter Abelard. A Dialogue of a Philosopher with a Jew, and a Christian* tr. P. J. Payer (Toronto, 1979).

65. See D. E. Luscombe, *The School of Peter Abelard* (Cambridge, 1969), pp. 103–42. E. M. Buytaert, 'The Anonymous Capitula Haeresum Petri Abelardi and the Synod of Sens, 1140', *Antonianum*, xliii (1968), 419–60, reviews some of the textual problems.

66. *Epistola*, xvii, 375c; Radice, *Letters of Abelard and Héloise*, p. 270.

67. *Dialectica* iv. 1 (prologue); ed. de Rijk, pp. 469–70.

68. See R. E. Weingart, *The Logic of Divine Love. A Critical Analysis of the Soteriology of Peter Abailard* (Oxford, 1970), pp. 13, 16.

69. St Augustine, *De Civitate Dei*, viii. 9–12.

70. See Weingart, *Logic of Divine Love*, p. 14.

71. See *ibid.*, pp. 38–9.

72. On the medieval use of the maxim, see P. Courcelle, ' "Nosce teipsum" du Bas-Empire au Haut Moyen-Age. L'héritage profane et les développements chrétiens', *Il Passaggio dall' Antichità al Medioevo in Occidente* (Settimana di studio del Centro Italiano di Studi sull' Alto Medioevo, IX, Spoleto, 1962), 265–95, and also Courcelle's *Connais Toi-Même de Socrate a saint Bernard* (Etudes Augustiniennes, 3 vols, Paris, 1974–5). See also *The Ethics*, ed. Luscombe, p. xxxi, n. 2.

73. See Luscombe, *The School*, pp. 130–2, 139.

74. Abelard however did not advocate the abolition of the canonical penances themselves, which he saw as a safeguard against arbitrary decisions on the part of the confessor. See D. E. Luscombe, 'The Ethics of Abelard: Some Further Considerations' in E. M. Buytaert (ed.), *Peter Abelard. Proceedings of the International Conference Louvain May 10–12, 1971* (Louvain, the Hague, 1974), pp. [65–84], 83–4.

75. This has been studied by O. Lottin, *Psychologie et Morale aux XIIe et XIIIe Siècles*, II (Louvain; Gembloux, 1948), especially pp. 421–89.

76. Abelard, *Sic et Non*, eds Boyer and McKeon, p. 103.

77. *Ibid.*, p. 96.

78. The argument is developed at length in *Theologia Christiana*, V, ed. Buytaert (see n. 64 above), xii, 347–72. For the critical reaction, see Luscombe, *The School*, pp. 134–6.

79. See Weingart, *Logic of Divine Love*, pp. 83–4.

80. See *ibid.*, p. 88.

81. See *ibid.*, pp. 71, 93, 202.

82. On the critical reaction to Abelard's soteriology, see Luscombe, *The School*, pp. 137–9.

83. See Weingart, *Logic of Divine Love*, pp. 74–8, 202.

84. Abelard, *Commentarium in Epistolam Pauli ad Romanos*, IV (IX. 21); ed. Buytaert (see n. 64 above), XI, 240.

85. Such is the view of the 'Sentences of Hermann', see Luscombe, *The School*, pp. 162–3. The anonymous *Sententie Parisienses I* are more faithful to Abelard's written position but show some wavering, see *The School*, p. 167. For other echoes of the dilemma, see *The School*, p. 171. Cf. now Mews, *RTAM*, LIII (1986), 130–84.

86. Abelard, *Historia Calamitatum*, edition cited in n. 5 above, 192; Radice, *Letters of Abelard and Héloise*, p. 78.

87. See Weingart, *Logic of Divine Love*, p. 3.

88. A careful discussion of the affinities of the *Didascalicon* and original features of the work is found in *The Didascalicon of Hugh of St Victor*, tr. J. Taylor (New York; London, 1961), pp. 28–36.

89. The modification is the distinction of logic as a fourth branch. For the sources of Hugh's schema, see *ibid.*, pp. 161–2 (note 21).

90. See *ibid.*, p. 8.

91. The work is edited in Migne, *PL*, CLXXVI, cols 173–618.

92. *Ibid.*, cols 214–15 (*De Sacramentis* I. 2. 22). Cf. Luscombe, *The School*, pp. 190–1. For a general comparison of the thought of Abelard and Hugh, see *The School*, pp. 183–97.

93. *De Sacramentis*, I. 3. 21, 26–9; Migne, *PL*, CLXXVI, cols 225, 227–31.

94. See M. Th. d'Alverny, 'Achard de Saint-Victor, De Trinitate, de Unitate et Pluralitate Creaturarum', *Recherches de Théologie Ancienne et Medievale*, XXI (1954), 299–306 and J. Ribaillier, *Richard de Saint Victor, De Trinitate. Texte critique avec introduction, notes et tables* (Textes philosophiques du moyen age, VI; Paris, 1958), pp. 27–33.

95. *De Trinitate*, Prologue (890 D). For a Latin text with French translation, see G. Salet, *Richard de Saint-Victor, La Trinité* (Sources Chrétiennes, 63; Paris, 1959). The passage quoted is on, p. 58.

96. *De Trinitate*, I. 1; Salet, *La Trinité*, pp. 64–5.

97. *Ibid.*, 3; pp. 68–9.

98. *Ibid.*, 4; pp. 70–1.

99. *Ibid.*, 8; pp. 78–9.

100. *Ibid.*, iv. 21–2; pp. 278–83. On the significance of the definition, see Salet, *La Trinité*, pp. 487–9.

101. Walter of St Victor, *Contra Quatuor Labyrinthos Franciae*, ed. P. Glorieux, *AHDLMA*, xix (1952), 187–335.

102. Cf. Smalley, *Study of the Bible*, p. 105.

103. Chalcidius translated the Greek word for matter (*hyle* – meaning also 'wood') as silva ('wood'). Thus, in the twelfth century, matter – the principle organised by form – was variously referred to as *hyle*, the transliteration of the Greek also found in Chalcidius, *silva* and *materia*.

104. See *Guillaume de Conches, Glosae super Platonem*, ed. E. Jeauneau (Textes Philosophiques du Moyen Age, 13; Paris, 1965), p. 211.

105. The treatise known in the middle ages as *De Hebdomadibus*, edited by Stewart and Rand, *Boethius*, pp. 38–51.

106. The glosses of Thierry and Clarembald have been edited by N. M. Häring, for which see the Bibliography. For William of Conches' glosses on the *Timaeus*, see Jeauneau, *Guillaume de Conches*; for his glosses on Boethius' *Consolation*, see J. M. Parent, *La Doctrine de la Création dans l'Ecole de Chartres* (Publications de l'Institut d'Etudes Médiévales; Paris and Ottawa, 1938). William's *Philosophy of the World (De Philosophia Mundi)* is printed in Migne, *PL*, clxxii, 39–102, as a work of Honorius Augustodunensis; also *ibid.*, xc, as a work of Bede. There is a modern edition of the first book, ed. G. Maurach (Leiden, 1974). On Bernard Silvestris, see *Bernard Silvestris, Cosmographia*, ed. P. Dronke (Leiden, 1978) *The Cosmographia of Bernardus Silvestris*, trans. W. Wetherbee (New York; London, 1973), B. Stock, *Myth and Science in the Twelfth Century, a Study of Bernard Silvester* (Princeton, 1972), and for the wider literary context, W. Wetherbee, *Platonism and Poetry in the Twelfth Century, the Literary Influence of the School of Chartres* (Princeton, 1972).

107. Migne, *PL*, clxxii, 43.

108. *Ibid.*, 46. On William's difficulties with the 'World Soul' and his changing views about it, see R. W. Southern, *Platonism, Scholastic Method and the School of Chartres* (The Stenton Lecture, 1978; University of Reading, 1979) pp. 21–4.

109. See R. McKeon, 'Medicine and Philosophy in the Eleventh and Twelfth Centuries', *The Thomist*, xxiv (1961), 211–56. Cf. T. Silverstein, 'Guillaume de Conches and Nemesius of Emesa', *H. A. Wolfson Jubilee Volume* (Jerusalem, 1965), ii, 719–34.

110. See R. W. Southern, *Medieval Humanism and Other Studies* (Oxford, 1970), pp. 61–86.

111. See *ibid.*, p. 78.

4. NEW SOURCES AND NEW INSTITUTIONS

1. On the isolation of philosophy in Islamic culture, see F. E. Peters, *Aristotle and the Arabs: the Aristotelian Tradition in Islam* (New York; London, 1968), pp. 71–5.

2. For the issues involved, see above, p. 63.

3. In what follows, I am much indebted to Peters, *Aristotle and the Arabs*, as also to his *Aristoteles Arabus* (Leiden, 1968), M. Fakhry, *A History of Islamic Philosophy* (New York; London, 1970) and R. Walzer, *Greek into Arabic, Essays on Islamic Philosophy* (London, 1962).

4. On this aspect, see especially, G. C. Anawati, 'Le néoplatonisme dans la pensée musulmane: état actuel des recherches', in *Plotino e il Neoplatonismo in Oriente e in Occidente* (Accademia Nazionale dei Lincei; Rome, 1974), pp. 339–405.

5. According to the different views, the work may have been compiled at Baghdad in

the ninth or tenth century or not until the twelfth century in Moslem Spain. The former view is now more generally favoured. Cf. *ibid.*, pp. 352–60.

6. *De Generatione Animalium* II. 3; 736ᵇ 27 ff.

7. See A. Nagy, 'Die philosophischen Abhandlungen des Ja'qub ben Ishaq Al-Kindi', *BGPMA*, II, Part v (Münster, 1897).

8. There were two medieval Latin translations, of which one was by Gerard of Cremona. Both are printed in *ibid.*, pp. 1–11.

9. Al Kindi's treatment is discussed by E. Gilson, 'Les sources gréco-arabes de l'augustinisme avicennisant', *AHDLMA*, IV (1929–30), [5–149], 22–6.

10. The Latin text of Al Farabi's treatise is edited with a French translation in *ibid.*, 108–41 and discussed in pp. 27–38.

11. Cf. R. Walzer, 'Early Islamic Philosophy', *CHLGEMP*, pp. 643–69, at p. 663.

12. Cf. S. M. Afnan, *Avicenna, his Life and Works* (London, 1958), p. 118; A.-M. Goichon, *La Philosophie d'Avicenne et son Influence en Europe Médiévale* (2nd edn; Paris, 1979), pp. 22–7.

13. Cf. Afnan, *Avicenna*, pp. 121–2.

14. Cf. *ibid.*, pp. 130–2; Coichon, *La Philosophie d'Avicenne*, p. 22–6.

15. Cf. Afnan, *Avicenna*, pp. 172–3.

16. Cf. Goichon, *La Philosophie d'Avicenne*, pp. 47–8; G. Verbeke, 'Introduction sur la Doctrine Psychologique d'Avicenne' in S. van Riet (ed.), *Avicenna Latinus, Liber de Anima seu Sextus de Naturalibus*, IV–V (Louvain; Leiden, 1968), pp. [1*–73*], 40*–1*.

17. For the central discussion of this see *Avicenna Latinus, Liber de Anima*, part v, Ch. 4; *ibid.*, pp. 113–26.

18. Cf. Verbeke, 'Introduction'; *ibid.*, p. 31*.

19. Cf. Fakhry, *History of Islamic Philosophy*, pp. 238–9.

20. Cf. *ibid.*, pp. 244–61.

21. Cf. below, pp. 135–6.

22. See Peters, *Aristotle and the Arabs*, pp. 166–7.

23. On the history of Averroes' commentaries, see H. A. Wolfson, 'Revised Plan for Publication of a *Corpus Commentariorum Averrois in Aristotelem*', *Speculum*, XXXVIII (1963), 88–104.

24. For an interesting discussion of this, see F. C. Copleston, *A History of Medieval Philosophy* (London, 1972), p. 124.

25. See M. Fakhry, 'Philosophy and Scripture in the Theology of Averroes', *Mediaeval Studies*, (1968), 78–89.

26. See S. Pines, tr., *Moses Maimonides, The Guide of the Perplexed* (Chicago; London, 1963), p. lx.

27. Two Latin versions – one by Gerard of Cremona, the other an abridgement probably of an independent translation – are edited in J. T. Muckle, 'Isaac Israeli, *Liber de Definicionibus*', *AHDLMA*, XI (1937–8), 299–340.

28. A detailed analysis of this doctrine and of the confusions implicit in it is found in J. Schlanger, *La Philosophie de Salomon ibn Gabirol, Etude d'un Néoplatonisme* (Leiden, 1968), Ch. viii.

29. See C. Baeumker, ed., '*Avencebrolis (Ibn Gabirol), Fons Vitae ex Arabico in Latinum translatus ab Iohanne Hispano et Dominico Gundissalino*', *BGPMA*, vol. I, Part 2 (Münster, 1892) (containing Books I–III of the *Fountain of Life*) and Parts 3–4 (Münster, 1895) (containing Books IV–V of the same). The passages quoted are respectively from *Fons Vitae* I. 2, Baeumker edn, p. 4, ll. 14–15; I. 5, p. 7, ll. 14–15; III. 57, p. 205, l. 23; v. 37–8, p. 326, ll. 1–7; v. 39, p. 327, ll. 14–17.

30. See *Guide*, III. 51; Pines, *Moses Maimonides*, pp. 618–22 and cf. also pp. cxvi–cxvii.

31. *Ibid.*, III. 54; p. 635.

32. *Ibid.*, ll. 74; p. 221. Cf. Pines, *Moses Maimonides*, p. ciii.

33. Cf. above, p. 90. The fundamental account of James' activity is L. Minio-

Paluello, 'Iacobus Veneticus Grecus, Canonist and Translator of Aristotle', *Traditio*, VIII (1952), 265–304.

34. Only Books I–III and part of Book IV survive.

35. See Minio-Paluello, 'Iacobus Veneticus Grecus', p. 265, n. 2. Cf. also his 'Note sull' Aristotele latino medievale', *Rivista di Filosofia Neo-Scolastica*, XLII (1950), 222–31.

36. For a survey of Grosseteste's career, translations and writings, see J. McEvoy, *The Philosophy of Robert Grosseteste* (Oxford, 1982), especially, as regards the present, pp. 8–11, 21–4, 69–123.

37. See L. Minio-Paluello, 'Aristotele dal Mondo Arabo a quello Latino' in *L'Occidente e l'Islam nell'Alto Medioevo* (Settimane di Studio del Centro Italiano di Studi sull' Alto Medioevo, XII, 2–8 aprile 1964; Spoleto, 1965), pp. [603–37], 632–3.

38. The Latin text of this dedicatory letter is printed in S. van Riet, ed., *Avicenna Latinus, Liber de Anima seu Sextus de Naturalibus* I–II–III (Louvain; Leiden, 1972), pp. 103*–4*.

39. Cf. *ibid.*, pp. 98*–100*; L. Thorndike, 'John of Seville', *Speculum*, XXXIV (1959), 20–38. For argument that Avendauth should be identified with the contemporary savant and author Abraham ibn Daud, see M. T. d'Alverny, 'Avendauth?', *Homenaje a Millas-Vallicrosa*, I (Barcelona, 1954), 19–43, 35–8.

40. See S. van Riet (ed.), *Avicenna Latinus, Liber de Philosophia Prima sive Scientia Divina I–IV* (Louvain; Leiden, 1977).

41. On this, see D. Salman, 'Algazel et les Latins', *AHDLMA*, x (1935–6), 103–27; J. T. Muckle (ed.), *Algazel's Metaphysics, A Mediaeval Translation* (Toronto, 1933); C. H. Lohr, 'Logica Algazelis. Introduction and Critical Text', *Traditio*, XXI (1965), 223–90.

42. See Gilson, 'Les sources gréco-arabes', 80, and his 'Avicenne en Occident au Moyen Age', *AHDLMA*, XXXVI (1969), [89–121], 99–100. One psychological treatise, entitled *De Anima*, is edited by J. T. Muckle, *Mediaeval Studies*, II (1940), 23–103. Another, *De Immortalitate Animae*, is edited by G. Bülow (*BGPMA*, vol II, Part 3; Münster, 1897).

43. Cf. Nagy, 'Die philosophischen Abhandlungen'. On the techniques of Gundissalvi and Gerard see M. A. Alonso, 'Traducciones del Arcediano Gundisalvo', *Al-Andalus*, XII (1947), [295–338], 308–15.

44. See Minio-Paluello, 'Aristotele dal Mondo Arabo', pp. 612–13.

45. The numbers of surviving manuscripts for the several translations of the *Metaphysics* are as follows: James of Venice (original), 5; James of Venice (revised, c. 1220–30), 41; 'middle Metaphysics', 24; Michael the Scot, 126; William of Moerbeke, 217. These figures are taken from the calculations by B. G. Dod, tabulated in *The Cambridge History of Later Medieval Philosophy*, eds N. Kretzmann, A. Kenny and J. Pinborg (Cambridge, 1982), p. 77, and see pp. 74–9 for the circulation of other texts. Surviving manuscripts are surveyed in *Aristoteles Latinus, Codices, Pars Prior & Pars Posterior*, eds G. Lacombe *et al.* (Rome, 1939–Cambridge, 1955), and in the editions of individual texts within the series.

46. A minor treatise of Averroes, *De substantia orbis* (On the substance of the globe), being an analysis of Aristotelian physics, was available from about 1230–1.

47. The following account draws on A. B. Cobban, *The Medieval Universities, their Development and Organization* (London, 1975), and on the classic study, H. Rashdall, *The Universities of Europe in the Middle Ages*, eds F. M. Powicke and A. B. Emden, 3 vols (Oxford, 1936).

48. See Cobban, *The Medieval Universities*, p. 116.

49. Irnerius' role as a teacher of civil law at Bologna may have been paralleled by Gratian in canon law. But the evidence for Gratian's career is slight and it is not certain that he taught. See J. T. Noonan, 'Gratian Slept Here: the Changing Identity of the Father of the Systematic Study of Canon Law', *Traditio*, XXXV (1979) 145–72.

5. ARISTOTELIAN PHILOSOPHY IN THE UNIVERSITY – THE FIRST PHASE OF
ASSIMILATION

1. On the history of this question, see the important study by D. A. Callus, 'The origins of the problem of the unity of form', *The Thomist*, XXIV (1961), 120–49. Cf. O. Lottin, 'La pluralité des formes substantielles avant saint Thomas d'Aquin. Quelques documents nouveaux', *Revue néo-scolastique de philosophie*, XXXIV (1932), 449–67.

2. See D. H. Salman, 'Note sur la première influence d'Averroes', *Revue néo-scolastique de philosophie*, XL (1937), 203–12, and his, 'Jean de la Rochelle et les débuts de l'Averroisme latin', *AHDLMA*, XVI (1948), [133–44], 133–4; R. Miller, 'An aspect of Averroes' influence on St Albert', *Mediaeval Studies*, XVI (1954), 57–71, 61–2.

3. See D. A. Callus, 'The powers of the soul, an early unpublished text', *Recherches de Théologie Ancienne et Medievale*, XIX (1952), 131–70 and R. Gauthier, 'Le cours sur l'Ethica nova d'un maître ès arts de Paris (1235–1240)', *AHDLMA*, XLII (1975), [71–141], 80–5. See now, however, below p. 226.

4. In this regard, Salman, 'Jean de la Rochelle', 144, seems to me very just: 'Les esprits de ce temps et de ce milieu sont rigoureusement imperméables aux erreurs d'Averroès, que leur mentalité irrémédiablement latine et chrétienne ne leur permettrait même pas de concevoir. Ils ne peuvent toucher une thèse ou un texte sans aussitôt les transposer selon des catégories augustino-chrétiennes. . . . Et c'est en fonction de cette puissante mais aveugle faculté d'assimilation qu'il faut comprendre la première influence d'Averroès dans le moyen âge latin.'

5. For further details see F. van Steenberghen, *La Philosophie au XIIIe Siècle* (Louvain; Paris, 1966), pp. 88–91 and citations there.

6. The full text is printed in H. Denifle and A. Chatelain, *Chart. Univ. Par.*, I (Paris, 1889), 70, no. 11. For a translation, see L. Thorndike, *University Records and Life in the Middle Ages* (New York, 1944; repr. 1971), pp. 26–7.

7. *Chart. Univ. Par.*, I, 78–9, no. 20. Cf. Thorndike, *University Records*, pp. 27–30.

8. *Chart. Univ. Par.*, I, 129–31, no. 72. Cf. Thorndike, *University Records*, pp. 32–5.

9. Cf. van Steenberghen, *La Philosophie au XIIIe Siècle*, pp. 94–6.

10. The document, preserved in a Barcelona manuscript, was first studied by M. Grabmann, 'Eine für Examinazwecke abgefasste Quaestionensammlung der Pariser Artistenfakultät aus der ersten Hälfte des 13 Jahrhunderts', *Revue néo-scolastique de philosophie*, XXXVI (1934), 211–29. For a recent review with notices of subsequent publications, see van Steenberghen, *La Philosophie au XIIIe Siècle*, pp. 119–31

11. See *Petri Hispani Summulae Logicales*, ed. I. M. Bochenski (Turin, 1947); *Peter of Spain, Tractatus Syncategorematum and Selected Anonymous Treatises*, tr. J. P. Mullally, with an introduction by J. P. Mullally and R. Houde (Milwaukee, Wisc., 1964).

12. See O. Lottin, 'Psychologie et Morale à la Faculté des Arts de Paris aux approches de 1250' in his *Psychologie et Morale au XIIe et XIIIe Siècles*, I (Louvain; Gembloux, 1942), 505–34.

13. See Gauthier, 'Le cours sur l'Ethica'.

14. *Ibid.*, 77–8.

15. In 1231 Gregory IX commissioned the abbot of St Victor and the prior of Saint-Jacques to absolve those who had incurred excommunication on this account. *Chart. Univ. Par.*, I, 143, no. 86.

16. *Ibid.*, 136–9, no. 79, and 143–4, no. 87; Thorndike, *University Records*, pp. 38–40. For discussion, see van Steenberghen, *La Philosophie au XIIIe Siècle*, pp. 106–9.

17. *Chart. Univ. Par.*, I, 185–6, no. 149.

18. *Ibid.*, 427, no. 384. See van Steenberghen, *La Philosophie au XIIIe Siècle*, p. 146.

19. For this suggestion, see van Steenberghen, p. 137.

20. See T. Crowley, *Roger Bacon. The Problem of the Soul in his Philosophical Commentaries* (Louvain; Dublin, 1950), pp. 73–4; D. E. Sharp, *Franciscan Philosophy at Oxford in the Thirteenth Century* (Oxford, 1930), pp. 151–71.

21. *Chart. Univ. Par.*, I, 227–30, no. 201, for the 1252 statute, 277–9, no. 246, for that of 1255. Cf. Thorndike, *University Records*, pp. 52–6 and 64–6, respectively. For discussion, see van Steenberghen, *La Philosophie au XIIIe Siècle*, pp. 357–60.

22. See Crowley, *Roger Bacon*, pp. 19–25.

23. See D. A. Callus, 'The Treatise of John Blund on the Soul' in *Autour d'Aristote. Recueil d'Etudes de Philosophie Ancienne et Médiévale offert à Monseigneur A. Mansion* (Louvain, 1955), pp. [471–95], 481. The treatise is edited by D. A. Callus and R. W. Hunt, *Iohannes Blund Tractatus de Anima* (Auctores Britannici Medii Aevi, 2; London, 1970).

24. See D. A. Callus, 'Introduction of Aristotelian learning to Oxford', *Proceedings of the British Academy*, XXIX (1943) [229–81], 258–9; cf. van Steenberghen, *La Philosophie au XIIIe Siècle*, pp. 176–7.

25. See Callus, 'Introduction', 262–3; cf. Crowley, *Roger Bacon*, pp. 27–8; J. M. G. Hackett, 'The Attitude of Roger Bacon to the *Scientia* of Albertus Magnus', in *Albertus Magnus and the Sciences. Commemorative Essays 1980*, ed. J. A. Weisheipl (Toronto, 1980), pp. [53–72], 70–1.

26. See above, p. 133.

27. See J. McEvoy, *The Philosophy of Robert Grosseteste* (Oxford, 1982), pp. 8–9.

28. See *ibid.*, pp. 268 ff.

29. See *ibid.*, pp. 346–50.

30. See *ibid.*, pp. 230–1.

31. See *ibid.*, pp. 152–5, 158–62, 165, 181.

32. See *ibid.*, pp. 180–2, 186–7.

33. On Grosseteste's concept of God as a mathematician, see *ibid.*, pp. 168–80.

34. See C. Ottaviano, *Guglielmo d'Auxerre (†1231) la Vita, le Opere, il Pensiero* (Rome [1929]), pp. 58–9.

35. See *ibid.*, p. 61.

36. See *ibid.*, p. 78.

37. The discussion of this point is found in a section which links the subject of Book I with that of Book II: fos 36v–37v in the sixteenth-century edition of F. Regnault, *Guilelmi Antissiodorensis Aurea in quattuor Sententiarum Libros perlucida Explanatio* (Paris, n.d.).

38. *Ibid.*, Book II, tractate VII, cap. i, fo. 56^r.

39. *Ibid.*, and cap. ii, fos 56v–58^r.

40. 'Aristotle says that the soul is in a certain respect all things since the images of all things come to be impressed on the soul.' *Ibid.*, tractate V, cap. i, fo. 51v(a).

41. See L. W. Keeler, *Ex Summa Philippi Cancellarii Quaestiones de Anima* (Münster, 1937), p. 8. Cf. now *Summa de Bono*, ed. N. Wicki (Berne, 1985).

42. *Ibid.*, pp. 28–39.

43. *Ibid.*, pp. 32–3.

44. *Ibid.*, p. 39. The editor notes that in fact Augustine is not hesitant but takes the view that there is one soul with several powers.

45. A. Masnovo, *Da Guglielmo d'Auvergne a San Tomaso d'Aquino* (3 vols; Milan, 1930–45) draws heavily on these sections and contains an illuminating account of William's outlook.

46. See E. A. Moody, 'William of Auvergne and his Treatise *De Anima*', in his *Studies in Medieval Philosophy, Science and Logic. Collected Papers 1933–1969* (Berkeley; Los Angeles; London, 1975), pp. [1–109], 9.

47. See *ibid.*, p. 12.

48. See R. de Vaux, 'La Première Entrée d'Averroës chez les Latins', *Revue des Sciences Philosophiques et Theologiques*, XXII (1933), pp. [193–245], 235.

49. See Moody, 'William of Auvergne', p. 12.
50. See *ibid.*, p. 27.
51. See *ibid.*, pp. 37–8.
52. See *ibid.*, pp. 55, 78.
53. See *ibid.*, p. 28.
54. See *ibid.*, pp. 28–31.
55. See *ibid.*, pp. 32, 34.
56. See *ibid.*, pp. 68–9.
57. See *ibid.*, p. 70.
58. See Masnovo, *Da Guglielmo d'Auvergne a San Tomaso d'Aquino*, pp. 133–52.
59. See *ibid.*, pp. 136–7.
60. See *ibid.*, p. 139.
61. See de Vaux, 'La Première Entrée', 234–5.
62. See van Steenberghen, *La Philosophie au XIIIe Siècle*, pp. 165–6.
63. See Salman, 'Jean de la Rochelle', 135–7.
64. *Ibid.*, 143–4.

6. ARISTOTELIAN PHILOSOPHY AND CHRISTIAN THEOLOGY – SYSTEM BUILDING AND
CONTROVERSY

1. 2. 9; *Itinerarium Mentis in Deum, with an Introduction, Translation and Commentary*, ed.
P. Boehner (*Works of St Bonaventure*, vol. 2; New York, 1956), p. 57.
2. *Ibid.*, pp. 57–9.
3. *Ibid.*, 3. 3; p. 65.
4. *Ibid.*, p. 67.
5. *Ibid.*, 7; p. 71.
6. *Ibid.*, 5. 3; p. 81.
7. *Commentary on the Sentences* I. 8. 1. 1. 2; *Opera Omnia* (Quaracchi, 1882), 154; 4.
Collations on the Six Days, v. 31; tr. J. de Vinck (*The Works of Bonaventure*, vol. 5; Paterson,
New Jersey, 1970), p. 91.
8. *S. Bonaventurae, Collationes in Hexaemeron et Bonaventuriana Quaedam Selecta*, ed. F.
Delormé (Quaracchi, 1934), p. 275.
9. *Collation II*. 25; *Opera Omnia, V* (Quaracchi, 1891) 514(b).
10. *Collation VII*. 17–18; *ibid.*, 492–3.
11. *Collation VIII*. 16–20; *ibid.*, 497–8.
12. I. 16; tr. de Vinck, p. 9.
13. VII 2; p. 110.
14. *Ibid.*.
15. *Ibid.*
16. XIX. 11; p. 289.
17. *Ibid.*, 12; p. 290.
18. For a comprehensive review, see J. F. Quinn, *The Historical Constitution of St
Bonaventure's Philosophy* (Toronto, 1973), pp. 17–99.
19. A point well made in D. A. Callus, *The Condemnation of St Thomas at Oxford* (The
Aquinas Society of London, Aquinas Paper No. 5; Blackfriars, Oxford, 1955), where it
is cautioned that Augustinians and Aristotelians ought not be be regarded as rigid
classifications.
20. By Quinn, *Historical Constitution*.
21. See *ibid.*, p. 370.
22. Cf. above, pp. 22–3.
23. Cf. above, p. 48.
24. See Quinn, *Historical Constitutions*, pp. 620–6.
25. 'The theory of illumination and of knowledge in the eternal principles appeared

to the followers of the Augustinian tradition, such as John Peckham and Matthew of Acquasparta, as a sacred repository which religious sentiment was passionately concerned to protect.' E. Gilson, *The Philosophy of St Bonaventure* (Paterson, New Jersey, 1965), p. 351.

26. II, 1. 1. 2, *Opera omnia* (Quaracchi, 1885), ii, 19–24.

27. Cf., above, p. 19.

28. Bonaventure probably absorbed this doctrine through his master, Alexander of Hales. Bonaventure seems not to refer directly to Avicebron or to the *Fountain of Life*. See Quinn, *Historical Constitution*, p. 159, n.50.

29. For the details of this, see Gilson, *Philosophy*, pp. 215–16.

30. *Commentary on the Sentences*, II. 3. 1. 1. 2. Conclusion; (edition cited in n. 7 above), II, 96–8. Cf. Gilson, *Philosophy*, pp. 225–6.

31. Cf. above, p. 125. Although some interpreters of Bonaventure consider light to be the form of corporeality, this does not seem to be correct, although light is common to bodies in Bonaventure's system. See Quinn, *Historical Constitution*, pp. 103–4, 113n.

32. See Quinn, *Historical Constitution*, pp. 305–6.

33. *Collationes in Hexaemeron* 4. 10. Cf. *The Works of Bonaventure*, tr. J. de Vinck, v. 64: 'Hence it is unsound to propose that the final form is added to prime matter without something that is a disposition or potency towards it, or without any other intermediate form.' 'Unsound' is too weak a translation for the word used (*insanum*).

34. Bonaventure interpreted Aristotle as having held a position similar to his own on 'seminal reasons'. See *Commentary on the Sentences*, II. 7. 2. 2. 1. Conclusion, 2. 18. 1. 3, edition cited in n. 7 above, II, 198(a), 440(b).

35. Cf. above, p. 33.

36. The question is exhaustively considered by Quinn, *Historical Constitution*, pp. 219–319.

37. Cf. *ibid.*, pp. 294–308.

38. I follow here the dating suggested by J. A. Weisheipl, 'The Life and Works of St Albert the Great', in his *Albertus Magnus and the Sciences, Commemorative Essays 1980* (Toronto, 1980), pp. 11–51.

39. That is, for members of other than the French province of the order. See *ibid.*, p. 23 and J. A. Weisheipl, *Friar Thomas D'Aquino, his Life, Thought and Work* (New York, 1974), pp. 58–67, for the Dominican chairs at Paris.

40. An extract from this had an independent circulation under the title, *Summa de Creaturis*. See Weisheipl, 'The Life and Works', p. 22.

41. There is a separate record of these disputations in his surviving *Quaestiones disputatae*.

42. The view of Fr Weisheipl and broadly of Franz Pelster; see *ibid.*, p. 27.

43. H. Denifle and E. Chatelain, *Chart. Univ. Par.*, I (Paris, 1889), 112 (no. 57).

44. On this, see E. A. Synan, 'Albertus Magnus and the Sciences', in Weisheipl, *Albertus Magnus*, pp. [1–12], 8–9. On differing interpretations of the passage, see F. van Steenberghen, *La Philosophie au XIIIe Siècle* (Louvain; Paris, 1966), pp. 275–7.

45. See Synan, cited in n. 44 above.

46. This aspect of Albert's thought has been well studied. See A. Schneider, *Die Psychologie Alberts des Grossen nach den Quellen dargestellt* (*BGPMA*, vol. IV; Münster, 1903–6); A. C. Pegis, *St Thomas and the Problem of the Soul in the Thirteenth Century* (Toronto, 1934), pp. 77–120; K. Park, 'Albert's Influence on Late Medieval Psychology', in Weisheipl, *Albertus Magnus*, pp. 501–35.

47. The metaphor originated with Aristotle, *De Anima*, 2. 1 (413a, 4–10), who raised the question whether the soul might not be regarded in that way but did not pronounce on it. It was taken up by Avicenna, unenthusiastically: see S. van Riet, ed., *Avicenna Latinus, Liber de Anima seu Sextus de Naturalibus I–II–III* (Louvain; Leiden, 1972), 1. 1. p. 34, ll. 19–22.

48. *De Anima*, 2. 1. 4; ed. C. Stroick (Alberti Magni *Opera Omnia*, vol. VII, Part I; Münster, 1968), p. 70(b).

49. Thomas Aquinas, *Summa contra Gentiles*, 2. 57.

50. Cf. Pegis, *St Thomas and the Problem of the Soul*, pp. 112–13.

51. Albert uses the distinction formulated by Boethius in the treatise on being and goodness known as *De Hebdomadibus* ('Quomodo substantiae in eo quod sint bonae sint cum non sint substantialia bona'), between 'being' and 'that which is', as the means to express this composition. As Albert puts it, the 'quo est', that by virtue of which something exists, is distinct from the 'quod est', that which is. Cf. *ibid.*, pp. 115–16.

52. See Weisheipl, 'The Life and Works', pp. 30–1, 39, 40–2.

53. On the dating of the minerology and discussion of cross-references between the commentaries, see *Albertus Magnus, Book of Minerals*, tr. D. Wyckoff (Oxford, 1967), pp. xxxv–xli.

54. See *De Unitate Intellectus*, ed. A. Hufnagel (*Alberti Magni Opera Omnia*, vol. XVII, Part I; Münster, 1975), pp. ix–x.

55. *De Quindecim Problematibus*, 1; ed. B. Geyer (*Alberti Magni Opera Omnia*, vol. XVII, Part I; Münster, 1975), p. 34(b). For argument in favour of dating this consultation to 1274–5, see F. van Steenberghen, *Maître Siger de Brabant* (Louvain; Paris, 1977; Philosophes Médiévaux, XXI), pp. 122–8.

56. See van Steenberghen, *La Philosophie au XIIIe Siècle*, pp. 292–300, for a review of this question.

57. See R. McInerney, 'Albert and Thomas on Theology', in A. Zimmermann, ed., *Albert der Grosse, seine Zeit, sein Werk, seine Wirkung* (Berlin; New York, 1981), pp. [50–60], 50–1.

58. *Summa Theologiae*, 1. 1. 4; ed. D. Siedler (*Alberti Magni Opera Omnia*, vol. XXXIV, Part I; Münster, 1978), p. 15(b).

59. The following account of Aquinas' career is principally and generally indebted to Weisheipl, *Friar Thomas D'Aquino*. Not all Aquinas' works are detailed but mainly those which are necessary to convey an impression of his intellectual interests and teaching activities or to provide a basis for the discussion below of the central features of his thought. Some treatises on special subjects which are sources for particular aspects are introduced at the appropriate juncture in the discussion of his thought. Weisheipl includes a full catalogue of authentic works with argument concerning their dating and details of editions.

60. See Weisheipl, *Friar Thomas D'Aquino*, pp. 34, 386.

61. See *ibid.*, pp. 144–5.

62. On the nature of this *studium*, see Leonard E. Boyle, *The Setting of the Summa theologiae of Saint Thomas* (Toronto, 1982; Etienne Gilson series, 5), pp. 8–10.

63. The idea that Thomas spent 1267–8 at Viterbo has no basis, see R. A. Gauthier, 'Quelques questions à propos du commentaire de S. Thomas sur le *De anima*', *Angelicum* LI (1974) [419–72], 438–42.

64. See the interesting argument in Boyle, *Setting of the Summa Theologiae*, pp. 11–20.

65. See *ibid.*, p. 15.

66. In citations, these parts are often abbreviated to Ia, Ia IIae, IIa IIae and IIIa respectively.

67. For a summary of the evidence, see Weisheipl, *Friar Thomas D'Aquino*, pp. 361–2.

68. See *ibid.*, pp. 236–8.

69. See *ibid.*, pp. 250–4. For criticism of the manuscript tradition which assigns these questions to Paris, see Gauthier, 'Quelques questions', 452–3, n. 44*bis*.

70. See I. Brady, 'John Pecham and the Background of Aquinas' *De Aeternitate Mundi*' in *St Thomas Aquinas 1274–1974 Commemorative Studies* (Toronto, 1974), II, 141–78, where Pecham's questions on the subject are edited, at 155–78.

71. See F. van Steenberghen, *Thomas Aquinas and Radical Aristotelianism* (Washington, D.C., 1980), pp. 9–12.

72. See Weisheipl, *Friar Thomas D'Aquino*, pp. 280–5, 316–17, for this suggestion and for a review and dating of the commentaries. For that on the *De Anima*, see Gauthier, 'Quelques questions', 443–54.

73. See *ibid.*, 452–4.

74. See *ibid.*, 454.

75. On these, see Weisheipl, *Friar Thomas D'Aquino*, pp. 254–5.

76. See *ibid.*, pp. 332–3, 294.

77. *Ibid.*, pp. 295–6.

78. *Summa contra Gentiles*, 1. 10–13.

79. The question is argued in *ibid.*, 10 and *Summa Theologiae*, 1a. 2. 1.

80. *Summa contra Gentiles*, 1. 3; tr. A. C. Pegis, J. F. Anderson, V. J. Bourke and C. J. O'Neil, *On the Truth of the Catholic Faith* (New York, 1955–7), i, 64.

81. *Ibid.*; tr., 65.

82. *Ibid.*, 1. 4.

83. *Summa Theologiae*, 1a. 2. 13.

84. *Summa contra Gentiles*, 1. 13.

85. *Summa Theologiae*, 1a. 2. 13.

86. *Summa contra Gentiles*, 1. 15, where the argument is to the conclusion that God is eternal; tr., i, 98–9.

87. *Summa Theologiae*, 1a. 2. 13.

88. *Ibid.*; cf. *Summa contra Gentiles*, 1. 13.

89. *Ibid.*, 1. 14; tr. i, 96.

90. *Ibid.*

91. *Ibid.*, 1. 15.

92. *Ibid.*, 1. 16.

93. *Ibid.*, 1. 17.

94. *Ibid.*, 1. 18.

95. *Ibid.*, 1. 21–2.

96. *Ibid.*, 1. 20.

97. *Ibid.*, 1. 23.

98. *Ibid.*, 1. 24–5.

99. *Ibid.*, 1. 43; cf. *Summa Theologiae*, 1a. 7. 1.

100. *Summa contra Gentiles*, 1. 32.

101. *Ibid.*, 1. 33.

102. *Summa Theologiae*, 1a, 13. 5.

103. In the *Summa contra Gentiles* the theory is not identified as such but in the *Summa Theologiae*, 1a. 15. 1, Aquinas says that Plato's error, for which he was criticised by Aristotle, was in making the ideas subsistent and independent of intellect, the implication being that the location of ideas in the divine intellect would have been acceptable to Aristotle.

104. *Summa contra Gentiles*, 1, 49–54, 69, 74–8.

105. The point is argued in *Summa contra Gentiles*, 2. 16.

106. *Ibid.*, 2. 35; tr., pp. 102–3.

107. 2. 31–8.

108. A good statement is Aquinas' short, early treatise, *On the Principles of Nature* (*De Principiis Naturae*), probably written during his period as a bachelor of the Sentences. See Weisheipl, *Friar Thomas D'Aquino*, p. 387, no. 59.

109. For a comparison of Aquinas and Bonaventure on this point see Quinn, *Historical Constitution*, pp. 109–12, and references there.

110. See *Summa Theologiae*, 1a. 105. 5.

111. See *Summa contra Gentiles*, 4. 81.

112. See, e.g. *Summa contra Gentiles*, II. 93.

113. A full account of Aquinas' understanding of the matter is found in *De potentia*, q. 3, a. 9.

114. *Summa Theologiae*, Ia. 75. 1; cf. *ibid.*, 5.

115. *Ibid.*, 79. 2; Blackfriars tr., p. 151.

116. *Ibid.*

117. *Ibid.*, 79. 3; tr. p. 157.

118. *Ibid.*, 79. 4.

119. *Ibid.* (Responsio).

120. *Ibid.*, tr. pp. 163–5.

121. *Compendium Theologiae*, 86.

122. Although Aquinas usually describes the state as *praeter naturam* ('beyond nature'), in the *Summa contra Gentiles*, 4. 79, when considering the implications for a resurrection of the body, he describes the state as *contra naturam* ('contrary to nature').

123. See the argument of Anton C. Pegis, 'The Separated Soul and its Nature in St. Thomas', in *St Thomas Aquinas 1274–1974*, I, 131–58.

124. See *Summa Theologiae*, Ia. 75. 4.

125. See *Summa contra Gentiles*, 4. 79.

126. *Summa Theologiae*, Ia IIae 62. 1; Blackfriars tr., vol. XXIII, 139 (slightly modified).

127. *Ibid.*, Ia IIae 62. 3.

128. Cf. the discussion in A. H. Armstrong and R. A. Markus, *Christian Faith and Greek Philosophy* (London, 1960), p. 112.

129. See Boyle, *Setting of the Summa theologiae*, pp. 15, 20–3.

130. *Summa Theologiae*, IIa IIae, Prologus; Blackfriars, tr., vol XXXI, xxi.

131. For a general review, see P. Michaud-Quantin, *Sommes de Casuistique et Manuels de Confession* (Louvain; Lille, 1962; Analecta Mediaevalia Namurcensia, XIII).

132. See Leonard E. Boyle, 'The Summa Confessorum of John of Freiburg and the Popularization of the Moral Teaching of St Thomas and some of his Contemporaries' in *St Thomas Aquinas 1274–1974 Commemorative Studies*, II, 245–68.

133. See Boyle, *Setting of the Summa theologiae*, p. 23.

134. *Quaestiones Disputatae de Veritate*, 23. 6.

135. *Summa Theologiae*, Ia IIae 57. 4; Blackfriars tr., vol. XXIII, p. 51.

136. *Ibid.*, 57. 5; p. 55.

137. The discussion of law occupies *Summa Theologiae* Ia IIae, 90–7.

138. *Summa Theologiae*, Ia IIae, 96. 4.

139. In the *Nicomachean Ethics*, Aristotle described man as a 'social' animal, so that a similar perception could have been derived from there. As has been noted already, Aquinas tends to describe him as 'political and social'.

140. See J. Catto, 'Ideas and Experience in the Political Thought of Aquinas', *Past and Present*, LXXI (1976), 3–21, 8–9.

141. Cf. *ibid.*, 10.

142. See Weisheipl, *Friar Thomas D'Aquino*, pp. 190, 194–5; Catto, 'Ideas and Experience', 12 *et seq.*

143. *De Regimine Principun*, 10; partially ed. and tr., A. P. D'Entrèves (tr. J. G. Dawson), *Aquinas Selected Political Writings* (Oxford, 1965), pp. 56–7.

144. *De Regimine Principum*, 6.

145. *Ibid.*, 7; D'Entrèves, *Aquinas*, p. 37.

146. *Ibid.*, 8, quoting from St Augustine; D'Entrèves, *Aquinas*, 45–7.

147. *Ibid.*, 9.

148. *Ibid.*, 14.

149. 'Thus the final aim of social life will be, not merely to live in virtue, but rather through virtue to attain to enjoyment of God.' *Ibid.*; D'Entrèves, *Aquinas*, p. 75.

150. *Ibid.*; D'Entrèves, *Aquinas*, pp. 76–7.

151. *Ibid.*; D'Entrèves, *Aquinas*, p. 77.

152. *Ibid.*, 15; D'Entrèves, *Aquinas*, p. 79.

153. From the text of the condemnation as translated in R. Lerner and M. Mahdi, eds, *Medieval Political Philosophy, A Sourcebook* (Toronto, 1963), pp. [337–54], 337.

154. See J. F. Wippel, 'The Condemnations of 1270 and 1277 at Paris', *Journal of Mediaeval and Renaissance Studies*, VII (1977) [169–210], 172, n. 8.

155. Throughout the following account of Siger and of radical Aristotelianism I am indebted to F. van Steenberghen, *Maître Siger de Brabant* (Philosophes Médiévaux, XXI; Louvain; Paris, 1977), 'Siger de Brabant et la condamnation de l'aristotélisme hétérodoxe le 7 mars 1277', *Académie Royale de Belgique Bulletin de la Classe des Lettres et des Sciences Morales et Politiques*, 5th ser., LXIV (1978), 63–74, and *Thomas Aquinas and Radical Aristotelianism* (Washington, D.C., 1980).

156. See van Steenberghen, *Maître Siger*, pp. 50–1.

157. See *ibid.*, pp. 339–47, for a fuller analysis.

158. Cf. *ibid.*, p. 71.

159. See M. Giele, F. van Steenberghen and B. Bazán, eds, *Trois Commentaires Anonymes sur le Traité de l'Ame d'Aristote* (Philosophes Médiévaux, XI; Louvain; Paris, 1971), p. 18, for text of the passage.

160. See *ibid.*, p. 20.

161. See above, p. 164.

162. See B. H. Zedler, tr., *Saint Thomas Aquinas On the Unity of the Intellect against the Averroists* (Milwaukee, 1968), p. 47; Leonine edition, vol. XLIII (Rome, 1976), 302 (cap. ii, 155).

163. See van Steenberghen, *Maître Siger*, p. 60.

164. Zedler, *Saint Thomas Aquinas*, p. 75; Leonine edition, 314 (cap. v, 435).

165. See van Steenberghen, *Maître Siger*, pp. 75–7.

166. *Chart. Univ. Par.*, I, 486–7; cf. van Steenberghen, *Maître Siger*, pp. 74–5.

167. *Quaestiones in Tertium de Anima*, q. 17; in B. Bazán (ed.), *Siger de Brabant, Quaestiones in Tertium de Anima, De Anima Intellectiva, De Aeternitate Mundi* (Philosophes Médiévaux, XIII; Louvain; Paris, 1972), pp. 63–4. Cf. R. Hissette, *Enquête sur les 219 Articles Condamnés à Paris le 7 mars 1277* (Philosophes Médiévaux, XXII; Louvain; Paris, 1977), pp. 37–8.

168. Zedler, *Saint Thomas Aquinas*, pp. 60–1; Leonine edition, 308 (cap. iv, 91–5).

169. See van Steenberghen, *Maître Siger*, p. 94.

170. q. 11; ed. Bazán, *Siger de Brabant*, pp. 31–5.

171. See van Steenberghen, *Maître Siger*, pp. 68, 77–8.

172. See Giele *et al.*, *Trois Commentaires*, pp. 17–18.

173. *Ignoti Auctoris Quaestiones in Aristotelis Libros I et II de Anima*, II. 4; *ibid.*, p. 75, ll. 42–7.

174. Because of this feature, van Steenberghen argues that the commentary on the *Metaphysics* is later than the *De Aeternitate Mundi*, the *Impossibilia* and the *De Necessitate* and close in time to the *De Anima Intellectiva*, c. 1273. *Maître Siger*, pp. 96–7.

175. See *ibid.*, p. 99.

176. *De Anima Intellectiva*, cc. 7–8; ed. Bazán, *Siger de Brabant*, pp. 101–11.

177. For an analysis, see van Steenberghen, *Maître Siger*, pp. 377–83.

178. See van Steenberghen, *La Philosophie au XIIIe Siècle*, p. 402.

179. See Hissette, *Enquête*, p. 314.

180. These are edited most recently, with a third treatise, in *Boethii Daci Opera*, vol. C VI, part II, ed. N. G. Green-Pedersen (Corpus Philosophorum Danicorum Medii Aevi; Copenhagen, 1976).

181. *Ibid.*, p. 356.

182. For a review of the conflicting interpretations of Boethius' position, see van Steenberghen, *La Philosophie au XIIIe Siècle*, pp. 404–5, 407–11.

183. Green-Pedersen, *Boethii Daci Opera*, p. 372.

184. See Hissette, *Enquête*, pp. 15–18.

185. See van Steenberghen, *Maître Siger*, pp. 80–8.

186. See *ibid.*, pp. 140 ff.

187. 'Le tableau qu'il trace des moeurs qui s'étaient introduites dans certaines couches de la population universitaire est éloquent; cette dégradation morale n'est sans doute pas sans relations avec le désarroi des idées et la crise philosophique.' *Ibid.*, p. 145.

188. P. Mandonnet, *Siger de Brabant et l'Averroisme Latin au XIIIe Siècle*, 2me partie (2nd edn; Louvain, 1908), pp. 175–91.

189. Dual numbering in the references to propositions represents the Mandonnet and the original ordering respectively.

190. Especially Hissette, *Enquête*.

191. In commenting on the *Nicomachean Ethics*, Aquinas refers to death as the greatest terror. The context makes it clear that the meaning is 'as regards this life'. The statement, as collected in a compendium, where the wording is 'that death is the end of terrors', is condemned in proposition 213; 178. See Hissette, *Enquête*, pp. 304–7.

192. See propositions 42;96, 43;81, 110;191; cf. 116;97, 147;124 (individuation) 142; 122. 146; 187 (knowledge).

193. Propositions 162;173, 163;163, 164;159, 165;158, 166;130.

194. *Chart. Univ. Par.*, I, 558–9, no. 474.

7. THE CONDEMNATIONS IN CONTEXT

1. For convenience, I occasionally use the term 'condemnations' to refer to the Oxford censures as well as those at Paris, although Kilwardby maintained that his was a prohibition against teaching rather than a formal condemnation.

2. *Chart. Univ. Par.*, I, 567, no. 481; see F. J. Roensch, *Early Thomistic School* (Dubuque, Iowa, 1964), p. 14.

3. Quoted *ibid.*, pp. 15, 25, n. 69.

4. See *ibid.*, pp. 174–8.

5. See D. A. Callus, 'The Problem of the unity of Form and Richard Knapwell', in *Mélanges offerts à Etienne Gilson* (Toronto; Paris, 1959), pp. 123–60, 157–8; cf. Roensch, *Early Thomistic School*, pp. 180–2.

6. See *ibid.*, pp. 41–57, for details of their careers and writings.

7. William de la Mare's *Correctorium* is edited with the text of Knapwell's reply, by P. Glorieux, *Le Correctorium Corruptorii 'Quare'* (Bibliothèque Thomiste, 9; Kain, 1927).

8. See Roensch, *Early Thomistic School*, p. 15.

9. His career and work are reviewed in the introductions to *Bernardi Triliae Quaestiones de Cognitione Animae Separatae a Corpore. A Critical Edition of the Latin Text with an Introduction and Notes*, ed. S. Martin (Toronto, 1965) and *Bernardi de Trillia Quaestiones Disputatae de Cognitione Animae Separatae*, ed. P. Kunzle (Corpus Philosophorum Medii Aevi Opera Philosophica Mediae Aetatis Selecta, 1; Bern, 1969). See also Roensch, *Early Thomistic School*, pp. 84–8.

10. See *ibid.*, pp. 89–92.

11. See *ibid.*, pp. 98–104. For his political thought, see W. Ullmann, *A History of Political Thought: the Middle Ages* (Harmondsworth, 1965), pp. 200–4.

12. Callus, 'The Problem', pp. 131–3, discusses the influence of Aquinas' teachings on the younger generation of seculars and even perhaps of Franciscans at this time.

13. See Roensch, *Early Thomistic School*, p. 18; cf. J. A. Weisheipl, *Friar Thomas D'Aquino, His Life, Thought and Work* (New York, 1974), pp. 342–3.

14. *Chart. Univ. Par.*, II, 280, no. 838.

1. Chapter 1 above, p. 29.

2. This was, most courteously, noted by Professor R. A. Markus, reviewing the first edition, in *Journal of Theological Studies*, xxxvii (1986), 237.

3. For a recent, spirited championship of Cicero's claims in this regard, see P. MacKendrick (with the collaboration of K. L. Singh), *The Philosophical Books of Cicero* (London, 1989), especially pp. 3–25.

4. An excellent short account, with specific bibliography, of Cicero's place in the development of medieval ethics may be found in the introduction to D. C. Luscombe, ed., *Peter Abelard's Ethics* (Oxford, 1971), where (p. xxi) it is shrewdly observed of one important treatment of the *De officiis* that 'when the *Moralium dogma philosophorum* raised again Cicero's questions on the relationship between honesty and utility, the questions had no edge or sharpness and were, for this author, only pegs from which to dangle classical quotations.'

5. See C. J. Nederman, 'Nature, Sin and the Origins of Society: the Ciceronian Tradition in Medieval Political Thought', *Journal of the History of Ideas*, xlix (1988), 3–26. I would disclaim the view attributed to me there, p. 3, on the basis of Chapter 1 above, pp. 28–9, 'that social and political naturalism was strictly an inheritance from the transmission of Aristotle to the West in the thirteenth century'. A fundamental distinction is between the social and political dimensions, specifically as regards the rationale of political authority. Augustine, on my understanding of the evolution of his positions, held the naturalism of the one but not of the other. His analysis of the state's legitimacy as a remedy for sin suffused the classical. D. X. Burt, 'Augustine on the State as a Natural Society', *Augustiniana*, xl (1990), 155–66, argues for calling the state a natural society in Augustine's thought when due allowance is made for the fact that 'the State in this world' 'is called upon to correct perversions more than to promote good'. This seems to me broadly equivalent to saying that for Augustine the state was a consequence of human nature only in the sense that human nature was debased (cf. Chapter 2 above, p. 55). My point in the context of the development of medieval views on society is not to deny that before the reception of Aristotle's *Ethics* and *Politics* there were indirect routes of the assimilation of Aristotelian doctrine or, more generally, that there were other sources of a naturalistic outlook. Ultimately the judgement to be made is one of proportion.

6. See H. Baron, 'Cicero and the Roman Civic Spirit in the Middle Ages and Early Renaissance', *Bulletin of the John Rylands Library*, xxii (1938), 72–97. The distortion, effected mainly through the modifications of Ciceronian values in St Ambrose's *De Officio Ministrorum* and the apologetics of St Jerome, prompted Baron (p. 79) to the judgement that 'up to the twelfth century the typical medieval Cicero was a teacher of misogyny and flight from active life'.

7. For demonstrations of what may be revealed from this painstaking exercise, see R. H. Rouse and M. A. Rouse, 'The medieval circulation of Cicero's "Posterior Academics" and the *De finibus bonorum et malorum*', in *Medieval Scribes, Manuscripts and Libraries, Essays presented to N. R. Ker*, ed. M. B. Parkes and A. G. Watson (London, 1978), pp. 333–67, and P. L. Schmidt, *Die Überlieferung von Ciceros Schrift 'De legibus'* (Munich, 1974). L. D. Reynolds, ed., *Texts and Transmission: A Survey of the Latin Classics* (Oxford, 1983) provides a most valuable overview of the classical tradition as a whole, mainly from the manuscripts selected by editors as the basis of texts. Editors' judgements in labelling witnesses *deteriores* were not always based on the level of collation necessary to support them and in any case the historian's interest embraces the complete circulation. For criticism of editing divorced from study of the manuscripts, see L. E. Boyle, '"Epistulae Venerunt Parum Dulces": the Place of

Codicology in the Editing of Medieval Latin Texts', in *Editing and Editors: a Retrospect* (New York, 1988), pp. 29–46.

8. 'subtile opus magis quam necessarium aut utile': G. Billanovich, 'Nella Biblioteca del Petrarca', *Italia Medioevale e Umanistica*, iii (1960), [1–58], 37, 35. Cf. Rouse and Rouse, 'The medieval circulation', p. 361.

9. MacKendrick, *The Philosophical Books*, p. 125.

10. Cf. *The Cambridge History of Renaissance Philosophy*, eds C. B. Schmitt and Q. Skinner (Cambridge, 1988), pp. 325–6.

11. Of the major schools, that of St Victor affords notable exceptions. See R. W. Southern, 'Aspects of the European Tradition of Historical Writing: 2. Hugh of St Victor and the Idea of Historical Development', *Transactions of the Royal Historical Society*, 5th ser., xxi (1971), 159–79. For other insights by way of comparison and contrast, see R. H. C. Davis and J. M. Wallace-Hadrill (with R. J. A. I. Catto and M. H. Keen), eds, *The Writing of History in the Middle Ages, Essays presented to Richard William Southern* (Oxford, 1981), especially M. Gibson, 'History at Bec in the Twelfth Century' (pp. 167–86). My former pupil, Fräulein Marianne Kaufmann, has written perceptively on this and other aspects in her thesis, 'The School of St Victor: an Intellectual Programme in its Context' (National University of Ireland, M. Phil. thesis, University College Dublin, 1988).

12. See M. Gibson, '"Tradizioni perdute" of the "De Consolatione philosophiae" Comments on a recent Book', *R[evue des] E[tudes] A[ugustiniennes]*, xxx (1984), 274–8.

13. F. Troncarelli, 'Tradizioni ritrovate? Risposta ad alcune obiezioni ad un libro recente', *REA*, xxxi (1985), 215–26.

14. D. Knowles, *The Evolution of Medieval Thought* (London, 1962), p. 77.

15. This is not to accept the explanation as true of the actual time of writing. Mews in *Petri Abaelardi Opera Theologica*, iii *Theologia* 'Summi Boni', *Theologia* 'Scholarium', eds E. M. Buytaert and C. J. Mews (Turnhout, 1987), pp. 41–3, argues that 'Abaelard's original intention in writing the work was to offer his students a more convincing exposition of trinitarian doctrine than anything which Roscelin could offer.'

16. Mews (as in the preceding note), p. 42, comments on the topos. For Anselm's pupils, see now the remarks of R. W. Southern, *Saint Anselm, A Portrait in a Landscape* (Cambridge, 1990), p. 119.

17. Thus John of Salisbury explains his need to recall what he had learned and his consequent attachment to Adam of the Petit Pont by his pupils' demands on him. *Metalogicon*, ed. C. C. J. Webb (Oxford, 1929), ii. 10; p. 81, 11. 3 ff. A more original teacher might well be similarly prompted to work out his own answers.

18. Petrus Abaelardus, *Dialectica*, ed. L. M. de Rijk (2nd edn; Assen, 1970), pp. 151, 152, 319: 'Osculetur me amica'; 'Festinet amica'; '"Petrum diligit sua puella" vel "eius amica"'; 'Petrus diligit suam puellam'; 'Si aliquis est homo, ipse est risibilis'. Cf. P. Bourgain, 'Héloïse', in *Abélard en son Temps* (Paris, 1981), [pp. 211–37] p. 227; Clanchy, 'Abelard's Mockery', 22. The grammatical point of the examples is largely lost in translation. The last example, expressing what was held to be a defining property of man, is formulated so as to extend Abelard's consideration here of pronominal reference. I agree with Bourgain in taking it as a comment on the class's reaction to the preceding examples rather than as self-deprecation, to which Abelard does not seem to have been much prone.

19. Clanchy, 'Abelard's Mockery', 11–17.

20. Luscombe, 'St Anselm and Abelard', 224–5 (n. 42).

21. Cf. Clanchy, 'Abelard's Mockery', 22–3, where Bernard's diagnosis of Abelard as 'totally ambiguous' is well adduced in this context.

22. I see Abelard's reference to the genesis of *On the Divine Unity and Trinity (Theologia* 'Summi Boni') as indeed a challenge to Anselm's formulation but as a serious rather than contemptuous challenge.

23. See Hunt, *The Schools and the Cloister*, p. 68.

24. See ibid., pp. 116–17. The main evidence is presented in *Iohannes Blund, Tractatus de Anima*, eds D. A. Callus and R. W. Hunt (London, 1970), pp. viii–xi. For the passage concerning the estimative faculty, cited in Hunt, *The Schools and the Cloister*, p. 117, cf. *Iohannes Blund, Tractatus de Anima*, eds Callus and Hunt, pp. 68–71 (nos 254–61).

25. See Hunt, *The Schools and the Cloister*, p. 69.

26. Ibid., pp. 68–71.

27. Ibid., p. 68 and note 10.

28. *The Rolls and Register of Bishop Oliver Sutton 1280–1299*, ed. R. M. T. Hill, v (Lincoln Record Society, lx; 1965), 60.

29. *The Letters of Pope Innocent III (1198–1216) concerning England and Wales*, eds C. R. Cheney and M. G. Cheney (Oxford, 1967), no. 279.

30. A suggestion made by G. Pollard, 'The Legatine Award to Oxford in 1214 and Robert Grosseteste', *Oxoniensia*, xxxix (1974), [62–71] 70.

31. Cf. W. A. Pantin, *The English Church in the Fourteenth Century* (Cambridge, 1955), p. 93.

32. On Sutton's relations with the university, see *Rolls and Register*, iii, ed. Hill (Lincoln Record Society, xlviii; 1954), lxix–lxxvii.

33. See R. W. Southern, 'From Schools to University', in *The History of the University of Oxford*, i, *The Early Oxford Schools*, ed. J. I. Catto (Oxford, 1984), 35.

34. Ibid., 33n.

35. See M. G. Cheney, 'Master Geoffrey de Lucy, an Early Chancellor of the University of Oxford', *English Historical Review*, lxxxii (1967), 750–63; C. H. Lawrence, 'The Origins of the Chancellorship at Oxford', *Oxoniensia*, xli (1976), 316–23.

36. See D. A. Callus, 'The Oxford Career of Robert Grosseteste', *Oxoniensia, x* (1945), [42–72], 49–51. Cf. J. McEvoy, *The Philosophy of Robert Grosseteste* (Oxford, 1982), pp. 7–8.

37. *Matthaei Parisiensis Monachi S. Albani Chronica Majora*, ed. H. R. Luard (Rolls Series; 7 vols, 1872–83), v, 404. The passage is discussed in Southern, *Robert Grosseteste*, p. 66, n. 7. J. W. Baldwin, *Masters, Princes and Merchants, The Social Views of Peter the Chanter and his Circle* (Princeton, 1970), i, 20–1, ii, 12–13, links the episode with the otherwise attested campaign against usurers in Artois and Flanders and to the strictures against usurers of the Council of Paris 1213, which it may have preceded.

38. *Roberti Grosseteste Epistolae*, ed. H. R. Luard (Rolls Series, 1861), Epistola 123, pp. 346–7. The context is reviewed by J. I. Catto, 'Theology and Theologians 1220–1320', in *Early Oxford Schools*, ed. Catto, 472–7, and by P. Raedts, *Richard Rufus of Cornwall and the Tradition of Oxford Theology* (Oxford, 1987), pp. 122–7, 142–3. For Grosseteste's own commenting on the *Sentences*, see D. A. Callus, 'The *Summa Theologiae* of Robert Grosseteste', in R. W. Hunt, W. A. Pantin and R. W. Southern, eds, *Studies in Medieval History presented to F. M. Powicke* (Oxford, 1948), pp. 180–208. This may probably be thought of as 'not more than a supplement to the study of the Bible': Catto, 'Theology and Theologians', p. 484.

39. As pointed out by C. H. Lawrence, in *English Historical Review*, ciii (1988), 977.

40. The reference is to 'sancti patres et doctores nostri quos vidimus et audivimus', followed by the personages in question: Eustace of Fly, Master James of Vitry, Stephen Langton and Master Robert de Courson. Langton's style is given as archbishop of Canterbury in exile, which was his status at the time of the preaching campaign referred to, but that does not of course exclude him from consideration as one of 'doctores nostri'.

41. As suggested, with due circumspection, by Pollard, 'The Legatine Award', 70.

42. The point is best made by Lawrence, 'The Origins of the Chancellorship' and 'The University in State and Church', in *The Early Oxford Schools*, ed. Catto, p. 100, and by M. G. Hackett, 'The University as a Corporate Body', ibid., 44.

43. See *Mediaeval Archives of the University of Oxford*, ed. H. E. Salter, i (Oxford Historical Society, lxx; 1920), 7–8.

44. Ibid., 8–9.

45. Ibid., 10.

46. Ibid., 9.

47. Cf. Hackett, 'The University as a Corporate Body', 45 and n. 4.

48. For a classical example – by a stylist – of the reflexive used equivocally, see Caesar, *De Bello Gallico*, I, 36, 4–5

49. D. A. Callus, ed., *Robert Grosseteste Scholar and Bishop* (Oxford, 1955), p. 7.

50. At date of writing, I have not yet seen L. Bianchi, *Il Vescovo e i Filosofi. La Condanna Parigina e l'Evoluzione dell' Aristotelismo Scolastico* (Bergamo, 1990). R. Hissette, 'Note sur le Syllabus "Antirationaliste" du 7 mars 1277', *Revue Philosophique de Louvain*, lxxxviii (1990), 404–16, comments on related implications of K. Flasch, *Aufklärung im Mittelalter? Die Verurteilung von 1277. Das Dokument des Bischofs von Paris übersetzt und erklärt* (Mainz, 1989).

Bibliographies (First Edition)

There are two bibliographies, the first of works in English, the second of works in other languages. Neither is comprehensive but between them they are intended to provide an orientation in the subject, to supply immediate needs for further reading on the main themes of the book beyond what could be included in endnotes, and to indicate sources of more detailed bibliography. Each bibliography is divided as follows:

1. GENERAL REVIEWS AND BIBLIOGRAPHICAL AIDS
2. SOURCES
3. SECONDARY WORKS (by chapter divisions)

A. BIBLIOGRAPHY OF WORKS IN ENGLISH

1. GENERAL REVIEWS AND BIBLIOGRAPHICAL AIDS

E. Gilson, *History of Christian Philosophy in the Middle Ages* (London, 1955) is excellent not only for its text but for the detailed discussions and references in its extensive notes. Other good surveys are A. Maurer, *Medieval Philosophy* (New York, 1962) and F. C. Copleston, *A History of Medieval Philosophy* (London, 1972) and *A History of Philosophy*, vol. II (London, 1950); see also J. R. Weinberg, *A Short History of Medieval Philosophy* (Princeton, 1964): these are clear accounts written by philosophers. D. Knowles, *The Evolution of Medieval Thought* (London, 1962) and G. Leff, *Medieval Thought St Augustine to Ockham* (Harmondsworth, 1958), are by historians. R. L. Poole, *Illustrations of the History of Medieval Thought and Learning* (2nd edn; London, 1920), was a perceptive treatment in its time and while requiring correction in the light of later work remains stimulating. R. W. Southern, *The Making of the Middle Ages* (London, 1953), has a fine discussion of the early medieval tradition of thought as part of a wider historical survey. J. Marenbon, *Early Medieval Philosophy (480–1150)* (London, 1983), tries to isolate the specifically philosophical elements in the thought of the period and pays close attention to the logical aspects. R. Klibansky, *The Continuity of the Platonic Tradition during the Middle Ages* (London, 1939), was an important corrective of an older perspective. It has been reissued with a new preface and four supplementary chapters (Kraus: New York; London; Nendeln, 1981). A. H. Armstrong, ed., *The Cambridge History of Later Greek and Early Medieval Philosophy* (Cambridge, 1970) has strong essays on late classical Greek developments, the Greek patristic tradition, with a consideration of Eriugena's relationship to it, Augustine, and the period from Boethius to Anselm. N. Kretzmann, A. Kenny and J. Pinborg, eds, *The Cambridge History of Later Medieval Philosophy from the Rediscovery of Aristotle to the Disintegration of Scholasticism* (Cambridge, 1982), is written very much with philosophical interests in mind. It has detailed treatment of logic and thematic surveys. It provides extensive biographical and bibliographical guidance. A Piltz, *The World of Medieval Learning* (Oxford, 1981), is attractive and lively. A. Murray, *Reason and Society in the Middle Ages* (Oxford, 1978), examines the relationship between aspects of intellectual development and the social context. R. R. Bolger, *The Classical Heritage and its Beneficiaries* (Cambridge, 1954), is of interest to our theme though wider than it. R. R. Bolger, ed., *Classical Influences on European Culture AD 500–1500* (Cambridge, 1971) (conference papers), has some treatment of speculative ideas. W. Ullmann, *A History of Political Thought in the Middle Ages* (Harmondsworth, 1965), is a good introduction to this subject; see also C. H. McIlwain, *The Growth of Political Thought in the West from the Greeks to the End of the Middle Ages* (New York, 1932) and A. P.

d'Entrèves, *The Mediaeval Contribution to Political Thought* (Oxford, 1939). R. W. and A. J. Carlyle, *A History of Medieval Political Theory in the West*, 6 vols (Edinburgh, 1903–36) is uneven but important. A. C. Crombie, *Augustine to Galileo: the History of Science AD 400–1650*, 2 vols (2nd edn; London, 1952), is a good introduction, providing an account of the mechanics of cosmological theories. L. Thorndike, *A History of Magic and Experimental Science*, vols 1–2 (New York, 1923), is a standard authority. For general intellectual surveys, see F. B. Artz, *The Mind of the Middle Ages AD 200–1500* (3rd edn; New York, 1965), which has an extensive bibliography, and H. O. Taylor, *The Mediaeval Mind. A History of the Development of Thought and Emotion in the Middle Ages*, 2 vols (4th edn; London, 1927). On the monastic scene, J. Leclercq, *The Love of Learning and the Desire for God* (New York, 1962), is a favourite (from French). Helen Waddell, *The Wandering Scholars* (London, 1927), is a splendid evocation of the learned world before it became over-serious.

The New Catholic Encyclopaedia, 15 vols (San Francisco; London; Toronto; Sydney, 1967), provides scholarly biographical articles on many medieval writers, with bibliographies. The relevant sections of G. C. Boyce, ed., *Literature of Medieval History 1930–1975. A Supplement to L. J. Paetow's A Guide to the Study of Medieval History*, 5 vols (Millwood, New York, 1981), are very helpful. E. A. Synan, 'Latin Philosophies of the Middle Ages', in *Medieval Studies. An Introduction*, ed. J. M. Powell (Syracuse Univ. Press, 1976), is a useful introductory and bibliographical essay. For individual authors, note: *Augustinian Bibliography 1970–1980: with Essays on the Fundamentals of Augustinian Scholarship*, compiled by T. L. Miethe, foreword by V. J. Bourke (Westport, Conn.; London, 1982); M. Brennan, 'A Bibliography of Publications in the Field of Eriugenian Studies, 1800–1975', *Studi Medievali*, 3rd ser., XVIII, 1 (1977), 401–47; *Thomistic Bibliography 1940–1978*, compiled by T. L. Miethe and V. J. Bourke (Westport, Conn.; London, 1980). On an important subject: E. J. Ashworth, *The Tradition of Medieval Logic and Speculative Grammar from Anselm to the End of the Seventeenth Century: A Bibliography from 1836 Onwards* (Toronto, 1978). C. H. Lohr, 'Medieval Latin Aristotle Commentaries', *Traditio*, XXIII (1967), 313–413; XXIV (1968), 149–245; XXVI (1970), 135–216; XXVII (1971), 251–351; XXVIII (1972), 281–396; XXIX (1973), 93–197; XXX (1974), 119–44, apart from its value as a listing, gives a good impression of the extent of activity.

Among serial publications of the English-speaking world containing material in the field may be noted especially: *Speculum* (the journal of the Mediaeval Academy of America) (1926–   ); *Mediaeval Studies* (Toronto, 1939–   ); *Mediaeval and Renaissance Studies* (London, 1941–   ); *Traditio* (New York, 1943–   ). *Vivarium* (Assen, 1963–   ) publishes mainly in English.

2. SOURCES

The subject is well served by sources in translation. Useful conspectuses are C. P. Farrar and A. P. Evans, *Bibliography of English Translations from Medieval Sources* (New York, 1946) and M. A. Ferguson, *Bibliography of English Translations from Medieval Sources 1943–1967* (New York; London, 1974). See also the listing of editions and translations in *Speculum* (1973–   ) and in the *Repertorium Fontium Historiae Medii Aevi* (Rome, 1962–   ).

The following list of selected sources reflects broadly the order of treatment in the text. Of sources used by medieval authors, the most important is Aristotle, for whom the standard translation is J. A. Smith and W. D. Ross, *The Works of Aristotle translated into English* (Oxford, 1910–52). Plato's *Timaeus, Meno* and *Phaedo* may be found, for example, in the five-volume translation by B. Jowett, *The Dialogues of Plato* (3rd edn.; Oxford, 1892). Plotinus, *Enneads*, tr. S. McKenna (3rd edn; London, 1962); also by A. H. Armstrong in the Loeb Classical Library series, 3 vols (London, 1966–7). Proclus, *Elements of Theology*, ed. and tr. E. R. Dodds (2nd edn; Oxford, 1963). Macrobius: W. H. Stahl, tr. *Macrobius, Commentary on the Dream of Scipio* (New York; London, 1952). For

Martianus Capella's *Marriage of Philology and Mercury*, see vol. II of W. H. Stahl, R. Johnson and E. L. Burge, *Martianus Capella and the Seven Liberal Arts* (New York: London, 1977).

There are many collections of translated readings from medieval authors. See especially, R. McKeon, *Selections from Medieval Philosophers*, 2 vols (New York, etc., 1929); A. Hyman and J. J. Walsh, *Philosophy in the Middle Ages: the Christian, Islamic and Jewish Traditions* (New York, 1967); J. F. Wippel and A. B. Wolter, *Medieval Philosophy from St Augustine to Nicholas of Cusa* (New York, 1969); H. Shapiro, *Medieval Philosophy* (New York, 1964). E. Grant, *A Source Book in Medieval Science* (Cambridge, Mass., 1974), is very valuable.

The principal authors are well represented in translation. Among the most useful texts thus available are, by author:

St Augustine: *A Select Library of the Nicene and Post-Nicene Fathers of the Church* (Buffalo, 1886), *The Catholic University of America Patristic Studies* (Washington, D.C., 1922–), *Ancient Christian Writers: the Works of the Fathers in Translation* (Westminster, Md; London, 1946–), *The Fathers of the Church* (New York, 1947–) and *The Library of Christian Classics* (London; Philadelphia, 1953–) have published various works of Augustine. Very useful tabular guides may be found in an addendum (adapted by J. J. O'Meara) to H. Marrou, *Saint Augustine and his Influence through the Ages* (New York; London, 1957) and interspersed through P. Brown, *St Augustine of Hippo: A Biography* (London, 1967). The following texts will be found particularly valuable: *Confessions*, tr. R. S. Pine-Coffin (Harmondsworth, 1961); *City of God*, tr. H. Bettenson (Harmondsworth, 1972); *Against the Academics*, tr. J. J. O'Meara (Ancient Christian Writers, no. 12; 1950); *On Christian Doctrine*, tr. D. W. Robertson (Indianapolis; New York, 1958). J. H. S. Burleigh, *Augustine Earlier Writings* (London, 1953), is an important collection.

Boethius: H. F. Stewart and E. K. Rand, eds and tr., *Boethius, The Theological Tractates and the Consolation of Philosophy* (London; Cambridge, Mass., 1918; rev. edn by S. J. Tester, 1973). E. Stump, tr., *Boethius's De Topicis Differentiis* (Ithaca; London, 1978) is an excellent translation and study. *The Consolation of Philosophy*, tr. V. E. Watts (Harmondsworth, 1969).

Cassiodorus: L. W. Jones, tr., *An Introduction to Divine and Human Readings by Cassiodorus Senator* (New York, 1946), for the *Institutions*.

Pseudo-Dionysius: C. E. Rolt, tr., *Dionysius the Areopagite, On the Divine Names and The Mystical Theology* (London, 1920). *The Ecclesiastical Hierarchy*, tr. T. L. Campbell (New York; London, 1981).

John Scotus Eriugena: I. P. Sheldon-Williams, ed. and tr., *Periphyseon I–III* (Dublin, 1968–81). M. L. Uhlfelder and J. A. Potter, tr., *John the Scot, Periphyseon* (Indianapolis, 1976) (an abridgement).

Fredegisus: *On Nothing and Darkness*, tr. J. F. Wippel and A. B. Wolter, *Medieval Philosophy from St Augustine to Nicholas of Cusa* (New York, 1969), pp. 103–8.

Peter Damian: *On Divine Omnipotence, ibid.*, pp. 143–52.

Anselm of Bec: S. N. Deane, tr., *St Anselm, Basic Writings* (2nd edn; La Salle, Illinois, 1962), contains *Monologion, Proslogion* and *Cur Deus Homo*, though it is not the best translation of any. J. Hopkins and G. Richardson, tr., *Anselm of Canterbury*, vol. I (London, 1974), contains *Monologion, Proslogion* and the debate with Guanilo. M. J. Charlesworth, tr., *Proslogion with a Reply on Behalf of the Fool by Guanilo and the Author's Reply to Guanilo* (Oxford, 1965). *The Cur Deus Homo* is translated with the *Proslogion* and extracts from other works in E. R. Fairweather, ed., *A Scholastic Miscellany, Anselm to Ockham* (The Library of Christian Classics, 10; Philadelphia, 1956). J. Hopkins and G. Richardson, *Truth, Freedom and Evil, Three Philosophical Dialogues* (New York, 1967). D.

P. Henry, ed. and tr., *The De Grammatico of St Anselm: the Theory of Paronymy* (Notre Dame, 1964).

Peter Abelard: D. E. Luscombe, ed. and tr., *The Ethics of Peter Abelard* (Oxford, 1971). P. J. Payer, tr., *Dialogue between a Jew, a Christian and a Philosopher* (Toronto, 1979). B. Radice, tr., *The Letters of Abelard and Héloïse* (Harmondsworth, 1974), includes the autobiography, *Historia Calamitatum*. See also J. T. Muckle, tr., *The Story of Abelard's Adversities: a Translation with Notes of the Historia Calamitatum* (Toronto, 1954). J. R. McCallum, *Abelard's Christian Theology* (Oxford, 1948), contains extracts from the *Theologia Christiana*.

John of Salisbury: D. D. McGarry, tr., *The Metalogicon of John of Salisbury* (Berkeley; Los Angeles, 1955).

Bernard Silvestris: W. Wetherbee, tr., *The Cosmographia of Bernardus Silvestris* (New York; London, 1973).

Hugh of St Victor: J. Taylor, tr., *The Didascalicon of Hugh of St Victor* (New York; London, 1961).

The Arabic and Jewish tradition: substantial extracts from this are found in A. Hyman and J. J. Walsh, *Philosophy in the Middle Ages: the Christian, Islamic and Jewish Traditions* (New York, 1967), which also gives more detailed information on translations. Al Ghazali: *Al-Ghazali's Tahafut al-Falasifah (Incoherence of the Philosophers)*, tr. (into English) S. A. Kamali (Lahore, 1958). The work can in fact be followed from reading the translation of Averroes' refutation, see below. Avicenna: *Avicenna's Psychology An English Translation of Kitab al-Najat, Book II, chapter VI*, tr. F. Rahman (London, 1952). Averroes: *The Incoherence of the Incoherence*, tr. S. van Bergh, 2 vols (Oxford, 1954). *Averroes on the Harmony of Religions and Philosophy*, tr. G. F. Hourani (London, 1961). *Averroes on Aristotle's De Generatione et Corruptione, Middle Commentary and Epitome*, tr. S. Kurland (Cambridge, Mass., 1958). Avicebron: Ibn Gabirol, *The Fountain of Life*, tr. H. E. Wedeck (New York, 1962) (an abridgement). Moses Maimonides: S. Pines, tr., *Moses Maimonides, The Guide of the Perplexed* (Chicago; London, 1963).

L. Thorndike, *University Records and Life in the Middle Ages* (New York, 1944; repr. 1971), is a splendid source of translated texts on the universities.

Robert Grosseteste: *On Light* is translated in Shapiro, *op. cit.*, pp. 254–263; also tr. C. C. Riedl (Milwaukee, 1942).

Roger Bacon: R. B. Burke, tr., *The Opus Majus of Roger Bacon* 2 vols (New York, 1928; repr. 1962). D. C. Lindberg, *Roger Bacon's Philosophy of Nature, a Critical Edition with English Translation, Introduction and Notes of De Multiplicatione Specierum and De Speculis Comburentibus* (Oxford, 1983).

Albert the Great: *On the Six Principles*, H. Shapiro, *Medieval Philosophy* (New York, 1969), pp. 266–93. *Albertus Magnus Book of Minerals*, tr. D. Wyckoff (Oxford, 1967).

On thirteenth-century logic: Peter of Spain, *Tractatus Syncategorematum and Selected Anonymous Treatises*, tr. J. P. Mullally (Milwaukee, 1964). *William of Sherwood's Introduction to Logic*, tr. N. Kretzmann (Minneapolis, 1966); William of Sherwood, *Treatise on Syncategorematic Words*, tr. N. Kretzmann (Minneapolis, 1968).

Bonaventure: *The Works of Bonaventure*, tr. J. de Vinck (Paterson, New Jersey, 1960–). *St Bonaventure's De Reductione Artium ad Theologiam*, ed. and tr. E. T. Healy (New York, 1955). *St Bonaventure's Itinerarium Mentis in Deum*, ed. and tr. P. Boehner (New York, 1956). *Breviloquium*, tr. E. E. Nemmers (St Louis: London, 1946). *Disputed Questions on the Mystery of the Trinity*, tr. Z. Hayes (New York, 1979) with an important introduction.

Thomas Aquinas: the Blackfriars edition of the *Summa Theologiae* 60 vols (London, 1964–76) has a facing English translation and is conveniently divided thematically. The *Summa Contra Gentiles* is translated by A. C. Pegis, J. F. Anderson, V. J. Bourke and C. J. O'Neil, as *On the Truth of the Catholic Faith*, 5 vols (New York, 1955–7). Among other works available in translation are (*De Regno:*) *On Kingship*, tr. G. B. Phelan and I. T. Eschmann (Toronto, 1949); see also text of Book I in A. P. d'Entrèves, *Aquinas Selected Political Writings*, tr. J. G. Dawson (Oxford, 1959). (*De Unitate Intellectus:*) *On the Unity of the Intellect against the Averroists*, tr. B. H. Zedler (Milwaukee, 1968). (*De Aeternitate Mundi:*) *On the Eternity of the World*, tr. C. Vollert (Milwaukee, 1965). (*De Ente et Essentia:*) *On Being and Essence*, tr. A. Maurer (Toronto, 1949); see also *Aquinas on Being and Essence: a Translation and Interpretation*, by J. Bobik (Notre Dame, 1965). (*Quaestio Disputata de Anima:*) *The Soul*, tr. J. P. Rowan (St Louis, 1949). (*De Libero Arbitrio:*) *On Free Choice*, tr. A. C. Pegis (New York, 1945). (*Quaestiones Disputatae de Potentia:*) *On the Power of God*, tr. L. Shapcote, 3 vols (London, 1932–4; 1 vol., Westminster, Md, 1952). (*Quaestiones Disputatae de Veritate:*) *Truth*, tr. R. W. Mulligan *et al.*, 3 vols (Chicago, 1952–4). *St Thomas Aquinas, Quodlibetal Questions 1 and 2*, tr. S. Edwards (Toronto, 1983), illustrates the method well and has a good introduction. Of the commentaries on Aristotle, see *Aristotle's De Anima with the Commentary of St Thomas Aquinas*, tr. K. Foster and S. Humphries (London; New Haven, 1951); *Commentary on the Nicomachean Ethics*, tr. C. I. Litzinger, 2 vols (Chicago, 1964); *Commentary on the Metaphysics of Aristotle*, tr. J. P. Rowan, 2 vols (Chicago, 1961). For other translations, see the catalogue of authentic works in J. A. Weisheipl, *Friar Thomas d'Aquino: his Life, Thought and Work* (New York, 1974).

Siger of Brabant: *On the Necessity and Contingency of Causes*, in H. Shapiro, *Medieval Philosophy* (New York, 1964), pp. 415–38.

Boethius of Dacia: *On the Supreme Good or On the Life of the Philosopher*, in J. F. Wippel and A. B. Wolter, *Medieval Philosophy from St Augustine to Nicholas of Cusa* (New York, 1969), pp. 369–75.

Giles of Rome, *On the Errors of the Philosophers*, in H. Shapiro, *Medieval Philosophy*, pp. 386–413.

3. SECONDARY WORKS

More information of a specialist nature may be found in the endnotes. For more detailed bibliography, consult works cited in section 1 and particular studies.

1. MASTERS OF THOSE WHO KNOW – PLATO, ARISTOTLE AND THE NEOPLATONISTS

There are several good introductions to the thinkers considered here, among them: W. K. C. Guthrie, *Socrates* (Cambridge, 1971); G. M. A. Grube, *Plato's Thought* (London, 1935) and I. M. Crombie, *Plato, the Midwife's Apprentice* (London, 1964), who offer varying interpretations. See also J. E. Raven, *Plato's Thought in the Making* (Cambridge, 1965). F. M. Cornford, *Plato's Cosmology* (London; New York, 1937) presents the *Timaeus*. J. L. Ackrill, *Aristotle the Philosopher* (Oxford, 1981) is a short review; W. D. Ross, *Aristotle* (5th edn; London, 1960) is standard; G. E. R. Lloyd, *Aristotle, the Growth and Structure of his Thought* (Cambridge, 1968) is a very stimulating presentation especially of Aristotle as a scientist. A. H. Armstrong, *An Introduction to Ancient Philosophy* (4th edn; London, 1970) is a readable general guide which covers Neoplatonism well. For more detail on late classical developments, see P. Merlan, *From Platonism to Neoplatonism* (3rd edn; The Hague, 1968), J. Dillon, *The Middle Platonists* (London, 1977), R. T. Wallis, *Neo-Platonism* (London, 1972), J. M. Rist, *Plotinus: the Road to Reality* (Cambridge, 1967) and A. H. Armstrong, ed., *The Cambridge History of Later Greek and Early Medieval Philosophy* (Cambridge, 1970).

E. Booth, *Aristotelian Aporetic Ontology in Islamic and Christian Thinkers* (Cambridge, 1983), investigates the effect on medieval thinkers of the unresolved tension in Aristotle's thought between the conception of individuals and universals. The collection of papers by H. A. Wolfson, *Studies in the History of Philosophy and Religion*, I

(Cambridge, Mass., 1973), contains important studies on several themes of central interest in the classical, patristic and later periods. D. J. O'Meara, ed., *Neoplatonism and Christian Thought* (Albany, New York, 1982), is useful generally on this subject and has treatment of Augustine, Eriugena and Aquinas. R. A. Norris, *God and World in Early Christian Theology. A Study in Justin Martyr, Irenaeus, Tertullian and Origen* (London, 1966) is a clear and readable review of this formative period. L. G. Patterson, *God and History in Early Christian Thought. A Study of Themes from Justin Martyr to Gregory the Great* (London, 1967) also provides useful background. J. N. D. Kelly, *Early Christian Doctrines* (5th edn; London, 1977), studies the development of patristic and conciliar theology. A Louth, *The Origins of the Christian Mystical Tradition – From Plato to Denys* (Oxford, 1981) is discursive but raises many points of interest to our subject. H. J. Blumenthal and R. A. Markus, eds, *Neoplatonism and Early Christian Thought: Essays in honour of A. H. Armstrong* (London, 1981) has several contributions of interest, especially regarding Augustine.

2. FROM ANCIENT WORLD TO MIDDLE AGES: ADAPTATION AND TRANSMISSION

1. St Augustine

P. Brown, *St Augustine of Hippo: a Biography* (London, 1967) is not only the best account of Augustine's life but is a classic of historiography. See also G. Bonner, *St Augustine of Hippo: Life and Controversies* (London, 1963); J. J. O'Meara, *The Young Augustine* (London, 1954).

For Augustine's thought in general, E. Gilson, *The Christian Philosophy of St Augustine* (tr. L. E. M. Lynch) (London, 1961), is a splendid guide. On his political ideas, see J. N. Figgis, *The Political Aspects of St Augustine's City of God* (London, 1921); N. H. Baynes, *The Political Ideas of St Augustine's De Civitate Dei* (Historical Association Pamphlet; London, 1936); H. A. Deane, *The Political and Social Ideas of St Augustine* (New York; London, 1963); R. A. Markus, *Saeculum: History and Society in the Theology of St Augustine* (Cambridge, 1970); J. J. O'Meara, *Charter of Christendom: the Significance of the City of God* (New York, 1961); J. H. S. Burleigh, *The City of God: a Study in St Augustine's Philosophy* (London, 1949). R. E. Meagher, *An Introduction to Augustine* (New York, 1978), has useful readings and a partial listing of Augustine's writings. R. H. Barrow, *Introduction to St Augustine, the City of God* (London, 1950) has judicious selections with summary and commentary. F. E. Cranz, 'The Development of Augustine's Ideas on Society before the Donatist Controversy', *Harvard Theological Review*, XLVII (1954), 255–316, is full of clear insights. W. H. C. Frend, 'The Roman Empire in the Eyes of Western Schismatics during the Fourth Century AD', *Miscellanea Historiae Ecclesiasticae* (Louvain, 1961), 9–22, reprinted in Frend, *Religion Popular and Unpopular in the Early Christian Centuries* (London, 1976), examines western Christian hostility to the mixture of sacred and profane, an important theme for understanding Augustine's theory. R. A. Markus, 'Two Conceptions of Political Authority: Augustine, *De Civitate Dei*, XIX 14–15, and some Thirteenth-century Interpretations', *Journal of Theological Studies*, new series, XVI (1965), 68–100, discusses Augustine's own views and the later reading.

R. A. Markus, *Christianity in the Roman World* (London, 1975), provides good background. A Momigliano, ed., *The Conflict between Paganism and Christianity in the Fourth Century* (Oxford, 1963), deals with the context and has treatment of pagan apologetic and Christian Platonism. P. Brown, *Religion and Society in the Age of St Augustine* (London, 1972), collects a number of penetrating essays by the author; his *Society and the Holy in Late Antiquity* (London, 1982), collects others written since; see especially 'Eastern and Western Christendom in late Antiquity: a parting of the Ways', which urges a new perspective on the theme with cautions against too great an emphasis on the factor of language. R. A. Markus, *From Augustine to Gregory the Great* (London, 1983), is a collection of articles by another leading interpreter. P. Courcelle, *Late Latin Writers and their Greek Sources* (English tr.; Cambridge, Mass., 1969), is an

important study of the cultural background both of Augustine and Boethius. See also C. N. Cochrane, *Christianity and Classical Culture* (London, 1939).
For rival views on the church to Augustine's, see W. H. C. Frend, *The Donatist Church* (Oxford, 1952); J. Ferguson, *Pelagius* (Cambridge, 1956); and R. F. Evans, *Pelagius Inquiries and Reappraisals* (London, 1968), which is very useful too on Augustine himself. For Augustine's contribution to doctrine, see E. Teselle, *Augustine the Theologian* (London, 1970). R. W. Battenhouse, ed., *A Companion to the Study of St Augustine* (Oxford, 1955), is helpful in general. G. R. Evans, *Augustine on Evil* (Cambridge, 1982), covers a theme of philosophical and theological interest. A. W. Matthews, *The Development of St Augustine from Neoplatonism to Christianity* (University of America Press, 1980), on a much debated aspect.

2. Boethius

H. Chadwick, *Boethius: The Consolations of Music, Logic, Theology and Philosophy* (Oxford, 1981), has replaced H. M. Barrett, *Boethius: some Aspects of his Times and Work* (Cambridge, 1940), which served English readers well for many years. M. Gibson, ed., *Boethius, his Life, Thought and Influence* (Oxford, 1981), is especially valuable on the 'influence'. See also H. R. Patch, *The Tradition of Boethius* (Oxford, 1935). E. K. Rand, *The Founders of the Middle Ages* (Cambridge, Mass., 1928), presented in Chapter 5 an influential view of Boethius.
M. W. Laistner, *Thought and Letters in Western Europe 500–900* (London, 1957), is a good general survey of this period. L. D. Reynolds and N. G. Wilson, *Scribes and Scholars. A Guide to the Transmission of Greek and Latin Literature* (2nd edn; Oxford, 1974), is a valuable introduction to the physical aspects of textual transmission. J. J. O'Donnell, *Cassiodorus* (Berkeley; London, 1979), is the most recent study of this figure. See also A. Momigliano, 'Cassiodorus and the Italian Culture of his Time', *Proceedings of the British Academy*, XLI (1955), 207–55. G. A. Kennedy, *Classical Rhetoric and its Christian and Secular Tradition from Ancient to Modern Times* (Chapel Hill, North Carolina; 1980), on this subject. P. Riché, *Education and Culture in the Barbarian West Sixth through Eighth Centuries* (translated from the 3rd French edition by J. J. Contreni; Columbia, South Carolina, 1976). M. Herren, 'On the Earliest Irish Acquaintance with Isidore of Seville', in E. James, ed., *Visigothic Spain: New Approaches* (Oxford, 1980), pp. 243–50, is interesting.

3. John Scotus Eriugena

On Eriugena's main Greek authority, see S. Gersh, *From Iamblichus to Eriugena. An Investigation of the Prehistory and Evolution of the Pseudo-Dionysian Tradition* (Leiden, 1978). J. Marenbon, *From the Circle of Alcuin to the School of Auxerre. Logic, Theology and Philosophy in the Early Middle Ages* (Cambridge, 1981), has shed new light on Eriugena's context. The most important work on Eriugena himself is in section B, but J. J. O'Meara, *Eriugena* (Cork, 1969), is a good, short introduction. P. O. Kristeller, 'The Historical Position of Johannes Scottus Eriugena', in J. J. O'Meara and B. Naumann, eds, *Latin Script and Letters AD 400–900* (Leiden, 1976), pp. 156–64, is useful as an outline. H. Bett, *Johannes Scotus Erigena* (Cambridge, 1925), is the only full study in English. J. J. O'Meara and L. Bieler, eds, *The Mind of Eriugena* (Dublin, 1973) (collected conference papers), has important contributions. The relevant chapters of Armstrong, ed., *CHLGEMP*, are very good. On Eriugena's use of his sources see the study by I. P. Sheldon-Williams in O'Meara and Bieler, *The Mind of Eriugena*, and more recently, E. Jeauneau, 'Pseudo-Dionysius, Gregory of Nyssa and Maximus the Confessor in the Works of John Scottus Eriugena', in U.-R. Blumenthal, ed., *Carolingian Essays* (Washington, D.C., 1983). D. J. O'Meara, 'The Problem of speaking about God in John Scottus Eriugena', *ibid.*, discusses the question of affirmative and negative theology. J. Marenbon, 'Wulfad, Charles the Bald and John Scottus Eriugena', in M.

Gibson and J. Nelson, eds, *Charles the Bald, Court and Kingdom* (Oxford, 1981), pp. 375–83, reviews the dispute over Eriugena's autographs.

There is also English material in the collected conference proceedings noticed in section B.

3. THE CENTRAL MIDDLE AGES – LOGIC, THEOLOGY AND COSMOLOGY

Logical revival and Schools: M. Gibson, 'The Continuity of Learning circa 850–circa 1050', *Viator*, VI (1975), 1–13, is a most useful review of school studies in a neglected period; see also her 'The Artes in the Eleventh Century', in *Arts Libéraux et Philosophie au Moyen Age* (Actes du IVème Congres International de Philosophie Médiévale; Montreal; Paris, 1969) and, a localised treatment, L. M. de Rijk, 'On the Curriculum of the Arts of the Trivium at St Gall from *c*. 850–*c*. 1000', *Vivarium*, I (1963), 35–86. R. L. Benson and G. Constable, with C. D. Lanham, eds, *Renaissance and Renewal in the Twelfth Century* (Oxford, 1982), contains a number of pertinent essays, some of which are specially noted below. On the character of medieval logic in both the central and high periods there is a substantial bibliography, for which see the bibliographical aids cited in section 1, and note T. Gilby, *Barbara Celarent. A Description of Scholastic Dialectic* (London, 1949), E. A. Moody, *Truth and Consequence in Mediaeval Logic* (Amsterdam, 1952), L. M. Rijk, *Logica Modernorum. A Contribution to the History of Early Terminist Logic*, 2 vols (Assen, 1962–7), and Ph. Boehner, *Medieval Logic. An Outline of its Development from 1250 to 1400* (Manchester, 1966). More particularly of interest to the subject of the development of logical study in the period is the very clear account by O. Lowry, 'Boethian Logic in the Medieval West', in Gibson, ed., *Boethius*, pp. 90–134. See also N. Kretzmann, 'The Culmination of the Old Logic in Peter Abelard', in Benson *et al.*, *Renaissance and Renewal*, pp. 488–511. B. Stock, *The Implications of Literacy. Written Language and Models of Interpretation in the Eleventh and Twelfth Centuries* (Princeton, 1983), ranges widely over the thinkers considered in this chapter, examining their sensitivity to the relationship between language and reality. J. W. Baldwin, *The Scholastic Culture of the Middle Ages 1000–1300* (Lexington, Mass., 1971), is a useful survey of the period.

On Gerbert of Aurillac, see O. G. Darlington, 'Gerbert, the Teacher', *American Historical Review*, LII (1946–7), 456–76.

On Berengar, A. J. MacDonald, *Berengar and the Reform of Sacramental Doctrine* (London, 1930) but see section B for more recent treatment. M. Gibson, *Lanfranc of Bec* (Oxford, 1978), is the standard work but see also the illuminating study by R. W. Southern, 'Lanfranc of Bec and Berengar of Tours', in R. W. Hunt, W. A. Pantin and R. W. Southern, eds, *Studies in Medieval History presented to Frederick Maurice Powicke* (Oxford, 1948), pp. 27–48.

Anselm of Bec: J. M. Hopkins, *A Companion to the Study of St Anselm* (Minneapolis, 1972), is very useful. R. W. Southern, *St Anselm and his Biographer* (Cambridge, 1963), is standard and a classic. On aspects of his method, see G. Evans, 'The Nature of St Anselm's Appeal to Reason in the *Cur Deus Homo*', *Studia Theologica*, XXXI (1977), 33–50; G. Evans, 'St Anselm and Sacred History', in R. H. C. Davis and J. M. Wallace-Hadrill, eds, *The Writing of History in the Middle Ages. Essays presented to R. W. Southern* (Oxford, 1981), pp. 187–209; and E. J. O'Toole, 'Anselm's Logic of Faith', *Analecta Anselmiana*, III (Frankfurt/Main, 1972), 146–54. D. P. Henry, *The Logic of St Anselm* (Oxford, 1967), is a technical treatment. R. D. Shofner, *Anselm Revisited. A Study of the Role of the Ontological Argument* (Leiden, 1974), provides a conspectus of modern interest in Anselm's method. Cf., from a philosophical viewpoint, R. R. La Croix, *Proslogion II and III. A Third Interpretation of Anselm's Argument* (Leiden, 1972). G. R. Evans, *Anselm and Talking about God* (Oxford, 1978), studies the formulation of a theological language. G. R. Evans, *Anselm and a New Generation* (Oxford, 1980), discusses Anselm's influence, and her *Old Arts and New Theology, the Beginnings of Theology as an Academic Discipline* (Oxford,

1980), is characteristically stimulating on a topic of central concern. G. R. Evans, *Alan of Lille, the Frontiers of Theology in the Later Twelfth Century* (Cambridge, 1983), provides more material for assessing the contribution of the arts to theology.

Peter Abelard: J. G. Sikes, *Peter Abailard* (Cambridge, 1932), needs to be read with more recent treatment, especially as regards the dating of some of Abelard's works. L. Grane, *Peter Abelard. Philosophy and Christianity in the Middle Ages* (English tr.; London, 1970), is very readable. M. T. Beonio-Brocchieri Fumagalli, *The Logic of Abelard* (English tr.; Dordrecht, 1969), contains an account of the relationship of his logical works and examines his method. M. M. Tweedale, *Abailard on Universals* (Amsterdam; New York; Oxford, 1976), is a convenient presentation, with analysis, of his texts on this question. R. E. Weingart, *The Logic of Divine Love. A Critical Analysis of the Soteriology of Peter Abelard* (Oxford, 1970), is an illuminating study. D. A. Luscombe, *The School of Peter Abelard* (Cambridge, 1969), is essential for Abelard's context, influence and critics. E. M. Buytaert, ed., *Peter Abelard* (Louvain; the Hague, 1974), consists of conference papers, with several of importance, in French and English. P. L. Williams, *The Moral Philosophy of Peter Abelard* (Lanham, Maryland, 1980). N. M. Häring, 'Abelard Yesterday and Today', in *Pierre Abélard, Pierre le Vénérable. Les Courants Philosophiques, Littéraires et Artistiques en Occident au Milieu du XIIe Siècle*, ed. R. Louis, J. Jolivet and J. Chatillon (Paris, 1975), pp. 341–403. R. Klibansky, 'Peter Abelard and Bernard of Clairvaux', *Mediaeval and Renaissance Studies*, v (1961), 1–27, is a good, general account of the different perspectives.

O. Brooke, 'The Speculative Development of the Trinitarian Theology of William of St Thierry in the *Aenigma Fidei*', *Recherches de Théologie Ancienne et Médiévale*, xxvii (1960), 193–211; xxviii (1961), 26–58, is an enlightening account of William's use of his sources and the point of his hostility to Abelard.

Gilbert of Poitiers: N. M. Häring, 'The Case of Gilbert de la Porrée, Bishop of Poitiers 1142–1154', *Mediaeval Studies*, xiii (1951), 1–40. L. O. Nielsen, *Theology and Philosophy in the Twelfth Century: A Study of Gilbert Porreta's Thinking and the Theological Expositions of the Doctrine of the Incarnation during the Period 1130–1180* (Leiden, 1982).

John of Salisbury: C. C. J. Webb, *John of Salisbury* (London, 1932). H. Liebeschutz, *Mediaeval Humanism in the Life and Writings of John of Salisbury* (London, 1950). R. H. and M. A. Rouse, 'John of Salisbury and the doctrine of Tyrannicide', *Speculum*, xlii (1967), 693–709, examines a crux of political theory of interest also for thirteenth-century treatment of the same problem.

R. W. Southern, 'Aspects of the European Tradition of Historical Writing: 2. Hugh of St Victor and the Idea of Historical Development', *Transactions of the Royal Historical Society*, 5th ser. xxi (1971), 159–79, discusses the theme with reference to the *De Sacramentis*.

R. Klibansky, 'Standing on the Shoulders of Giants', *Isis*, xxvi (1936), 147–9, on a famous phrase.

R. W. Southern, *Medieval Humanism and Other Studies* (Oxford, 1970), contains his important critique of the 'school of Chartres' and is otherwise of interest. For other accounts of 'Chartres' see N. Häring, 'Chartres and Paris Revisited', in J. R. O'Donnell, ed., *Essays in honour of Anton Charles Pegis* (Toronto, 1974), pp. 268–329; P. Dronke, 'New Approaches to the School of Chartres', *Anuario de Estudios Medievales*, vi (1969), 117–40; R. Giacone, 'Masters, Books and Library at Chartres according to the Cartularies of Notre-Dame and Saint-Père', *Vivarium*, xii (1974), 30–51. Cf. also R. W. Southern, *Platonism, Scholastic Method and the School of Chartres* (The Stenton Lecture, 1978; University of Reading, 1979), for an examination of the 'Platonism' of 'Chartres', and his 'The Schools of Paris and the School of Chartres', in Benson *et al.*, *Renaissance and Renewal in the Twelfth Century*, pp. 113–37. Whatever the view taken of 'Chartres', twelfth-century cosmology loses none of its interest, see: N. M. Häring, 'The Creation and Creator of the World according to Thierry of Chartres and Clarembaldus of Arras',

AHDLMA, xxii (1955), 137–216; S. Gersh, 'Platonism–Neoplatonism–Aristotelianism: a Twelfth century Metaphysical System and its Sources', in Benson *et al.*, *Renaissance and Renewal in the Twelfth Century*, pp. 512–34; J. Silverstein, 'Elementatum: its Appearance among the Twelfth Century Cosmogonists', *Mediaeval Studies*, xvi (1954), 156–62; M. Gibson, 'The Study of the "Timaeus" in the Eleventh and Twelfth Centuries', *Pensamiento*, xxv (1969), 183–94, on a principal source. P. Dronke, *Fabula. Explorations into the Uses of Myth in Medieval Platonism* (Leiden; Cologne, 1974), W. Wetherbee, *Platonism and Poetry The Literary Influence of the School of Chartres* (Princeton, 1972), and B. Stock, *Myth and Science in the Twelfth Century. A Study of Bernard Silvester* (Princeton, 1972), share interests.

M. D. Chenu, *Nature, Man and Society in the Twelfth Century* (Chicago, 1968), is selected chapters from his *La Théologie au Douzième Siècle*.

S. Kuttner, 'Gratian and Plato', in C. N. L. Brooke *et al.*, eds, *Church and Government in the Middle Ages. Essays presented to C. R. Cheney* (Cambridge, 1976), on a particular aspect of the philosophical influence and see other bibliography there for the philosophical influence on legal theory.

B. Smalley, 'Ecclesiastical Attitudes to Novelty *c.* 1100–1250', *Studies in Church History*, xii (1975), 113–33, considers the appreciation of change as development as both regards religious organisation and intellectual outlook.

R. M. Thomson, 'England and the Twelfth Century Renaissance', *Past and Present*, ci (1983), 3–21, reopens this subject with interesting reflections on the geography and regional character of learning.

4. NEW SOURCES AND NEW INSTITUTIONS

Arabic thought and its influence: N. Daniel, *The Arabs and Mediaeval Europe* (2nd edn; London; New York, 1979), provides a general survey with chapters on theological and scientific influences; see also W. Montgomery Watt, *The Influence of Islam on Medieval Europe* (Edinburgh, 1972). Montgomery Watt's *Islamic Philosophy and Theology* (Edinburgh, 1964), is very helpful as an introduction; see also *CHLGEMP*, part viii (by R. Walzer). More detailed but still offering a clear outline is M. Fakhry, *A History of Islamic Philosophy* (New York; London, 1970). I. Husik, *A History of Mediaeval Jewish Philosophy* (New York, 1916; repr. 1974), is still useful as an introduction to this strand. I. I. Efros, *Studies in Medieval Jewish Philosophy* (New York; London, 1974), is more specialised than will suit the purposes of the general reader. F. E. Peters, *Aristotle and the Arabs: the Aristotelian Tradition in Islam* (New York; London, 1968), is especially valuable and may be supplemented by consulting his *Aristoteles Arabus* (Leiden, 1968). R. Walzer, *Greek into Arabic, Essays on Islamic Philosophy* (London, 1962), is also important on the eastern translation process.

S. M. Afnan, *Avicenna, his Life and Works* (London, 1958), is less useful for the historian of the western scene than Goichon's study in section B. W. Montgomery Watt, *Muslim Intellectual: A Study of Al-Ghazali* (Edinburgh, 1963), is a valuable account not only of this figure but of the Islamic philosophical context. On the development of the theory of the intellect there is little in English but see R. Walzer, 'Aristotle's Active Intellect νους ποιητικος in Greek and Early Islamic Philosophy', in *Plotino e il Neoplatonismo in Oriente e in Occidente* (Accademia Nazionale dei Lincei; Rome, 1974), pp. 422–36. B. H. Zedler, 'Averroes on the Possible Intellect', *Proceedings of the American Catholic Philosophical Association*, xxv (1951), 164–78, is a clear analysis.

Translations: there are good general accounts by D. C. Lindberg, 'The Transmission of Greek and Arabic Learning to the West', in Lindberg, ed., *Science in the Middle Ages* (Chicago; London, 1978), pp. 52–90, and M.-T. d'Alverny, 'Translations and Translators', in Benson *et al.*, *Renaissance and Renewal in the Twelfth Century*, pp. 421–62.

C. H. Haskins, *Studies in the History of Mediaeval Science* (Cambridge, Mass., 1927), was the pioneering work and is still important. L. Thorndike, 'John of Seville', *Speculum*, xxxiv (1959), 20–38, is judicious. D. H. Salman, 'The Mediaeval Latin Translations of Alfarabi's Works', *New Scholasticism*, xiii (1939), 245–61. J. T. Muckle, 'Greek Works translated directly into Latin before 1350', *Mediaeval Studies*, iv (1942), 34–42, is useful for the early period. L. Minio-Paluello, 'Iacobus Veneticus Grecus Canonist and Translator of Aristotle', *Traditio*, viii (1952), 265–304, and see his *Opuscula, the Latin Aristotle* (Amsterdam, 1972), for the author's principal articles on this theme before 1969. C. S. F. Burnett, 'A Group of Arabic–Latin Translators Working in Northern Spain in the Mid-12th Century', *Journal of the Royal Asiatic Society*, i (1977), 62–108. L. Thorndike, *Michael Scot* (London, 1965). R. Lemay, *Abu Ma'shar and Latin Aristotelianism in the Twelfth Century: the Recovery of Aristotle's Natural Philosophy through Arabic Astrology* (Beirut, 1962). J. A. Weisheipl, *The Development of Physical Theory in the Middle Ages* (University of Michigan, 1959), is a useful short survey of some of the effects of the translations. W. F. Ryan and C. B. Schmitt, eds, *Pseudo-Aristotle. The Secret of Secrets. Sources and Influences* (London, 1982), contains specialist studies on this, the most widely diffused of the spurious works attributed to Aristotle in the middle ages.

Universities: H. Rashdall, *The Universities of Europe in the Middle Ages*, ed. F. M. Powicke and A. B. Emden, 3 vols (Oxford, 1936), is fundamental. A. B. Cobban, *The Medieval Universities, their Development and Organization* (London, 1975), is a very clear account. Of particular relevance is G. Leff, *Paris and Oxford Universities in the Thirteenth and Fourteenth Centuries. An Institutional and Intellectual History* (New York, 1968). L. J. Daly, *The Medieval University 1200–1400* (New York, 1961), is also useful. D. L. Douie, *The Conflict between the Seculars and the Mendicants at the University of Paris in the Thirteenth Century* (Aquinas Society of London, Aquinas Papers, no. 23; London, 1954), on this problem. J. W. Baldwin, 'Masters at Paris from 1179 to 1215: a Social Perspective', in Benson *et al.*, *Renaissance and Renewal in the Twelfth Century*, pp. 138–72. A. G. Little and F. Pelster, *Oxford Theology and Theologians c. AD 1282–1302* (Oxford, 1934), though a little later than our period has among other aspects a good account of academic exercises.

5. ARISTOTELIAN PHILOSOPHY IN THE UNIVERSITY – THE FIRST PHASE OF ASSIMILATION

and

6. ARISTOTELIAN PHILOSOPHY AND CHRISTIAN THEOLOGY – SYSTEM BUILDING AND CONTROVERSY

Much of the material for the period covered by Chapter 5 is of a specialist nature. For particular aspects, see the endnotes. The best survey is that by F. van Steenberghen, noted in section B. As the bibliography for the thirteenth century and especially for St Thomas Aquinas is very large, I mainly confine the present to more general works. I have also kept in mind the interests of historians rather than of philosophers. For more detailed bibliography, consult the works mentioned and the bibliographical guides listed above.

F. van Steenberghen, *Aristotle in the West. The Origins of Latin Aristotelianism* (2nd edn; Louvain, 1970), is a good introduction to the period; see also his *The Philosophical Movement in the Thirteenth Century* (Belfast; Edinburgh, 1955) (lectures). A series of studies by W. H. Principe, under the general title, *The Theology of the Hypostatic Union in the Early Thirteenth Century* (Pontifical Institute of Mediaeval Studies, Studies and Texts, vii, xii, xix, xxxii; Toronto, 1963–75), though concerned with a specific theological doctrine, contain treatment of the philosophical presuppositions and provide short biographies and extensive bibliographies for the theologians considered. These are:

William of Auxerre (vol. I; 1963); Alexander of Hales (vol. II; 1967); Hugh of Saint-Cher (vol. III; 1970); Philip the Chancellor (vol. IV; 1975). On the early period at Oxford, see D. A. Callus, 'Introduction of Aristotelian Learning to Oxford', *Proceedings of the British Academy*, XXIX (1943), 229–81; cf. Callus, 'Two Early Oxford Masters on the Problem of Plurality of Forms. Adam of Buckfield. Richard Rufus of Cornwall', *Revue Néoscolastique de Philosophie*, XLII (1939), 411–45. C. H. Lawrence, *St Edmund of Abingdon* (Oxford, 1960), is the standard study of a figure whose scholastic career is of interest. S. P. Marrone, *William of Auvergne and Robert Grosseteste. New Ideas of Truth in the Early Thirteenth Century* (Princeton, 1983), considers developments in epistemology in the period.

L. J. Bowman, 'The Development of the Doctrine of the Agent Intellect in the Franciscan School of the Thirteenth Century', *The Modern Schoolman*, L (1972–3), 251–79, sketches the doctrine through the century among teachers of this order. There are several important studies of Bonaventure: J. G. Bougerol, *Introduction to the Works of Bonaventure* (Paterson, New Jersey, 1964; translated from French), is very useful; E. Gilson, *The Philosophy of St Bonaventure* (Paterson, New Jersey, 1965; translated from French), is a valuable interpretation; J. F. Quinn, *The Historical Constitution of St Bonaventure's Philosophy* (Toronto, 1973), is exhaustive and judicious. R. McKeon, 'Philosophy and Theology, History and Science in the Thought of Bonaventura and Thomas Aquinas', in D. Tracy, ed., *Celebrating the Medieval Heritage: a Colloquy on the Thought of Aquinas and Bonaventure* (*The Journal of Religion*, LVIII, Supplement, 1978), is a useful consideration of the method of the two thinkers.

J. A. Weisheipl, ed., *Albertus Magnus and the Sciences, Commemorative Essays 1980* (Toronto, 1980), serves as a valuable review of the main features and problems. J. Dunbabin, 'The Two Commentaries of Albertus Magnus on the Nicomachean Ethics', *Recherches de Théologie Ancienne et Médiévale*, XXX (1963), 232–50, is an important study. L. A. Kennedy, 'The Nature of the Human Intellect according to St Albert the Great', *The Modern Schoolman*, XXXVII (1959–60), 121–37.

J. A. Weisheipl, *Friar Thomas d'Aquino, his Life, Thought and Work* (New York, 1974), is the standard biography, with a useful catalogue of authentic works. Among the introductions to Aquinas' thought note especially: J. Pieper, *Guide to Thomas Aquinas* (New York, 1962): M.-D. Chenu, *Towards Understanding St Thomas* (Chicago, 1964); F. C. Copleston, *Aquinas* (Harmondsworth, 1955); A. Kenny, *Aquinas* (Oxford, 1980). The two latter are readable discussions from a philosophical viewpoint. E. Gilson, *The Christian Philosophy of St Thomas Aquinas* (New York, 1956), is an excellent study. A. C. Pegis, *St Thomas and the Problem of the Soul in the Thirteenth Century* (Toronto, 1934), is also excellent on this aspect. *St Thomas Aquinas Commemorative Studies*, 2 vols (Toronto, 1974), contains important articles, some of which are signalled in the endnotes; see also, G. Verbeke and D. Verhelst, eds, *Aquinas and the Problems of his Time* (Mediaevalia Lovaniensia, series I, Studia 5; Louvain, 1976) and A. Parel, ed., *Calgary Aquinas Studies* (Toronto, 1978) (especially E. Synan, 'Aquinas and his Age'). B. Mondin, *St Thomas Aquinas' Philosophy in the Commentary to the Sentences* (The Hague, 1975), is technical but useful in examining a rather neglected work. J. Doig, *Aquinas on Metaphysics. A Historico-Doctrinal Study of the Commentary on the Metaphysics* (The Hague, 1972), is a close exposition. R. J. Henle, *Saint Thomas and Platonism. A Study of the Plato and Platonici Texts in the Writings of Saint Thomas* (The Hague, 1956), on an aspect of Aquinas' thought which has received insufficient emphasis. The evolving interpretation of Aquinas' political thought as bearing on the *De Regno* in particular may be followed in L. E. Boyle, 'The *De Regno* and the Two Powers', in O'Donnell, ed., *Essays in honour of Anton Charles Pegis*, pp. 237–47, and J. Catto, 'Ideas and Experience in the Political Thought of Aquinas', *Past and Present*, LXXI (1976), 3–21; cf. also the first study (by L. Genicot, in French) in Verbeke and Verhelst, eds, *Aquinas and the Problems of his Time*, which provides a convenient review. T. Gilby, *Principality and Polity: Aquinas and the Rise of State Theory in the West* (London, 1958). P. E. Persson, *Sacra Doctrina: Reason and Revelaton in Aquinas* (Oxford, 1970). R. McInerney, *Ethica Thomistica: the Moral Philosophy of Thomas Aquinas* (Washington, D.C., 1982).

J. McEvoy, *The Philosophy of Robert Grosseteste* (Oxford, 1982), is a splendidly clear analysis. See also J. McEvoy, 'The Chronology of Robert Grosseteste's Writings on Nature and Natural Philosophy', *Speculum*, LVIII (1983), 614–55. A. C. Crombie, *Robert Grosseteste and the Origins of Experimental Science 1100–1700* (Oxford, 1953), for an assessment of Grosseteste within this strand.

D. E. Sharp, *Franciscan Philosophy at Oxford in the Thirteenth Century* (Oxford, 1930), was pioneering and remains fundamental. T. Crowley, *Roger Bacon. The Problem of the Soul in his Philosophical Commentaries* (Louvain; Dublin, 1950). S. C. Easton, *Roger Bacon and his Search for a Universal Science* (Oxford, 1952).

E. M. F. Sommer-Seckendorff, *Studies in the Life of Robert Kilwardby* (Rome, 1937), and D. Douie, *Archbishop Pecham* (Oxford, 1952), on these figures.

J. A. Weisheipl, 'The Parisian Faculty of Arts in Mid-Thirteenth Century: 1240–1270', *American Benedictine Review*, XXV (1974), 200–17, is a general account of developments in the curriculum and of the academic exercises.

Controversy and condemnation: F. van Steenberghen, *Thomas Aquinas and Radical Aristotelianism* (Washington, D.C., 1980). E. P. Mahoney, 'Sense, Intellect and Imagination in Albert, Thomas and Siger', in Kretzmann *et al.*, eds, *Cambridge History of Later Medieval Philosophy*, pp. 602–22, is recommended as a clear survey, which gives careful attention to the nuances in Siger's position. J. F. Wippel, 'The Condemnations of 1270 and 1277 at Paris', *Journal of Medieval and Renaissance Studies*, VII (1977), 169–201. D. A. Callus, 'The Condemnation of St Thomas at Oxford' (The Aquinas Society of London, Aquinas Paper no. 5; London, 1955).

B. Bibliography of Works in Other Languages

1. GENERAL REVIEWS AND BIBLIOGRAPHICAL AIDS

M. Grabmann, *Die Geschichte der scholastischen Methode*, 2 vols (Freiburg, 1909–11; repr. Darmstadt, 1961) is by a scholar who did much to establish the study of the subject; also by him are *Die Philosophie des Mittelalters* (Berlin, 1921), and, with more specialised treatments, *Mittelalterliches Geistesleben*, 3 vols (Munich, 1926–56). Also fundamental treatments and the starting point for much subsequent work were M. de Wulf, *Histoire de la Philosophie Médiévale*, 3 vols (6th edn; Louvain, 1947) (also available in English), and B. Geyer, *Die patristische und scholastische Philosophie* (vol. II of F. Ueberweg, *Grundriss der Geschichte der Philosophie*) (Berlin, 1928). P. Vignaux, *La Pensée au Moyen Age* (Paris, 1938) is a good synthesis.

A. Siegmund, *Die Überlieferung der griechischen christlichen Literatur in der lateinischen Kirche bis zum 12. Jahrhundert* (Munich, 1949), covers an important strand. C. von Prantl, *Geschichte der Logik im Abendlande*, 4 vols (Leipzig, 1855–70; repr. 1955), is still basic for this subject. For more recent studies, consult Ashworth, *The Tradition of Medieval Logic*, cited in section A1. O. Lottin, *Psychologie et Morale aux XIIe et XIIIe Siècles*, 6 vols (Louvain, 1942–60), is a study of a specific theme which casts light on the thought of many major and minor figures. W. Beierwaltes, *Platonismus in der Philosophie des Mittelalters* (Darmstadt, 1969), is a collection of essays on a subject for which there is more bibliography below (Chapters 1–3). P. Wilpert, ed., *Die Metaphysik im Mittelalter ihr Ursprung und ihre Bedeutung* (Berlin, 1963; Miscellanea Mediaevalia, 2) (conference papers), has a number of specialist studies of central interest. P. Duhem, *Le Système du Monde: Histoire des Doctrines Cosmologiques de Platon à Copernic*, 10 vols (Paris, 1913–59), is the monumental account of this subject.

F. van Steenberghen, *Introduction à l'Étude de la Philosophie Médiévale Recueil de Travaux offert à l'Auteur par ses Collègues, ses Etudiants et ses Amis* (Louvain: Paris, 1974: Philosophes médiévaux, XVIII), is a mine of information on the history of study of the subject and some of its principal themes. Steenberghen's *La Bibliothèque du Philosophe Médiéviste* (Louvain; Paris, 1974; Philosophes médiévaux, XIX), is very useful. For St Augustine there are C. Andresen, *Bibliographia Augustiniana* (Darmstadt, 1962) and T. van Bavel, *Repertoire Bibliographique de Saint Augustin (1950–1960)* (The Hague, 1963). C. Vasoli, ed., *Il Pensiero Medievale, Orientamenti Bibliografici* (Bari, 1971), is an invaluable guide.

Of serial publications may be noted especially: *Archives d'Histoire Doctrinale et Littéraire du Moyen Age* (Paris, 1926–), *Recherches de Théologie Ancienne et Médiévale* (Louvain, 1929–) and *Revue du Moyen Age Latin* (Lyons–Strasbourg, 1945–). The various monograph volumes of *Beiträge zur Geschichte der Philosophie [und Theologie] des Mittelalters* (Münster, 1891–), have supplied a wealth of studies and texts. The series *Settimana di Studio del Centro Italiano di Studi sull' Alto Medioevo* (Spoleto, 1954–) has explored a number of central themes. *Revue d'Histoire Ecclésiastique* (Louvain, 1900–) publishes an annual bibliography of publications in this and related fields. Other indications of relevant serial publications may be got from the endnotes, within, or from the list in Vasoli, *Il Pensiero Medievale*. C. Leonardi, ed., *Medioevo Latino: Bolletino Bibliografico della Cultura Europea dal Secolo VI al XIII* (Spoleto: Centro Italiano di Studi sull' Alto Medioevo, 1980) is the first of what is intended as an annual review.

2. SOURCES

The following list of selected sources reflects broadly the order of treatment in the text.

Though more and more replaced by critical editions, J. P. Migne, ed., *Patrologia Latina*, 221 vols (Paris, 1844–55), remains an immensely valuable collection for texts up to the early thirteenth century. The series *Corpus Christianorum* (with its *Continuatio Medievalis*) (Turnhout, 1954–) and *Corpus Scriptorum Ecclesiasticorum Latinorum* (Vienna, 1866–) are also fundamental. There are series devoted to individual authors as will be noted below. It is not possible here to provide a comprehensive guide to the works of individual authors; for more detail see the works cited under sections A1 and B1 above and the bibliographies in specialised secondary studies.

St Augustine: for a full list of Augustine's works and of editions to that date see the bibliographical guide (adapted by J. J. O'Meara) in H. Marrou, *Saint Augustine and his Influence through the Ages* (New York; London, 1957). Important additions, from the *Corpus Christianorum Series Latina*, are as follows: vol. XXXII (1962) – *De Doctrina Christiana, De Vera Religione*; vols L, LA (1968) – *De Trinitate Libri XV*; vol. XXIX (1970) – *Contra Academicos, De Beata Vita, De Ordine, De Magistro, De Libero Arbitrio*; vol. XLIV (1970) – *De Diversis Quaestionibus ad Simplicianum*; vol. XXVII (1981) – *Confessionum Libri XIII*. The Bibliothèque Augustinienne edition of the *City of God*, *Oeuvres de Saint Augustin, La Cité de Dieu*, 5 vols (Desclée de Brouwer [Paris], 1959–60), is conveniently divided and has facing Latin text and French translation.

Martianus Capella: *De Nuptiis Philologiae et Mercurii*, ed. A. Dick (Leipzig, 1925; corrected repr., Stuttgart, 1970); also ed. J. C. King (Tübingen, 1979).

Macrobius: *In Somnium Scipionis*, ed. J. Willis (Leipzig, 1970).

Boethius: *De Consolatione Philosophiae*, ed. L. Bieler (Corpus Christianorum, XCIV; 1954). *Opuscula Sacra* (with *De Consolatione Philosophiae*), ed. H. F. Stewart and E. K. Rand (London; Cambridge, Mass., 1918; rev. edn by S. J. Tester, 1973). Logical Works: the Commentaries on Porphyry's *Isagoge* are edited by S. Brandt (*CSEL*, XLVIII; 1906); those on *De Interpretatione*, by C. Meiser (Leipzig, 1877–80); that on Cicero's Topics in *M. Tullii Ciceronis Opera Omnia*, ed. J. C. Orelli and J. G. Baiter, V, 1 (Zurich, 1833). *De Syllogismis Hypotheticis*, ed. L. Obertello (Brescia, 1969). Otherwise the text is that of *PL*, LXIV. Boethius' translations are edited in *Aristoteles Latinus* as follows: I (1–5) (Bruges; Paris, 1961), *Categoriae vel Praedicamenta*; I (6–7) (Bruges; Paris, 1966),

Categoriarum Supplementa (including *Porphyrii Isagoge*): II (1–2) (Leiden, 1965), *De Interpretatione vel Periermenias*; III (1–4) (Bruges; Paris, 1962), *Analytica Priora*; V (1–3) (Leiden, 1969), *Topica*; all the foregoing are edited by L. Minio-Paluello; VI (1–3), ed. B. G. Dod (Leiden; Brussels, 1975), *De Sophisticis Elenchis*. The treatises *De Arithmetica* and *De Musica* are edited by G. Friedlein (Leipzig, 1867).

Cassiodorus: *Institutiones*, ed. R. A. B. Mynors (Oxford, 1937).

Isidore of Seville: *Etymologiarum sive Originum libri XX*, ed. W. M. Lindsay, 2 vols (Oxford, 1911). *Etymologies: Livre XVII, de l'Agriculture*, ed. and tr. (into French), J. André (Auteurs Latins du Moyen Age; Paris, 1981) (the first volume of a series which will eventually cover all twenty books). *Traité de la Nature*, ed. and tr. J. Fontaine (Bordeaux, 1960).

Fredegisus: *De Substantia Nihili et de Tenebris*, ed. *Monumenta Germaniae Historica, Epistulae*, IV (Berlin, 1895), 552–5; see also, C. Gennaro, *Fridugiso di Tours e il De Substantia Nihili et Tenebrarum Edizione Critica e Studio Introduttivo con una Aggiunta Palaeografica* (Padua, 1963). Agobard's Letter to Fredegisus is edited in *Monumenta Germaniae Historica, Epistulae*, V (Berlin, 1898), 210–21.

John Scotus Eriugena: *Periphyseon, I–III*, ed. I. P. Sheldon-Williams (Dublin, 1968–81). *De Divina Praedestinatione Liber*, ed. G. Madec (*Corpus Christianorum, Continuatio Medievalis*, L: 1978). *Annotationes in Marcianum*, ed. C. Lutz (Cambridge, Mass., 1939). *Expositiones in Ierarchiam Coelestem* (*Corpus Christianorum, Continuatio Medievalis*, XXXI; 1975). *Homélie sur le Prologue de Jean*, ed. É. Jeauneau (Paris, 1969). *Commentaire sur l'Évangile de Jean*, ed. É. Jeauneau (Paris, 1972). É. Jeauneau, *Quatre Thèmes Erigéniens* (Montreal; Paris, 1978), prints in Part II, a version of Book I of a commentary on Martianus Capella, *De Nuptiis*, liber I, which differs from that edited by Lutz.

Ratramnus of Corbie: *Liber de Anima ad Odonem Bellovacensem*, ed. D. C. Lambot (Namur; Lille, 1952).

Remigius of Auxerre: *Remigii Antissiodorensis Commentum in Martianum Capellam*, ed. C. E. Lutz (Leiden, 1962–5).

For commentaries by Bovo of Corvey (late ninth or early tenth century) and Adalbold of Utrecht (early eleventh century) on Boethius' *Consolation*, see R. B. C. Huygens, 'Mittelalterliche Kommentare zum O qui perpetua', *Sacris Erudiri*, VI (1954), 373–427. See also for Adalbold, E. T. Silk, 'Pseudo-Johannes Scottus, Adalbold of Utrecht and the Early Commentaries on Boethius', *Mediaeval and Renaissance Studies*, III (1954), [1–40], 14–24.

Abbo of Fleury: *Syllogismorum Categoricorum et Hypotheticorum Enodatio*, ed. A. van de Vyver (Bruges, 1966).

Gerbert of Aurillac: Gerbert's pupil, Richer, left an important account of his master's method; see *Richeri Historiarum Libri Quatuor*, III, 46–7, ed. G. Waitz (*Monumenta Germaniae Historica, Scriptorum Rerum Germanicarum*; Hanover, 1877).

Peter Damian: *Pierre Damien Lettre sur la Toute-Puissance Divine*, ed. A. Cantin (Sources Chrétiennes, 191; Paris, 1972). Latin text with facing French translation.

Lanfranc and Berengar: Lanfranc, *Liber de Corpore et Sanguine Domini, PL,*, CL, 407–42. Berengar, *De Sacra Coena adversus Lanfrancum*, ed. A. F. and F. T. Vischer (Berlin, 1834) also W. H. Beekenkamp (The Hague, 1941).

Anselm of Bec: *Opera Omnia*, ed. F. S. Schmitt, 6 vols (Edinburgh, 1946–61).

Gilbert Crispin: C. C. J. Webb, 'Gilbert Crispin, Abbot of Westminster: Dispute of Christian with a Heathen Touching the Faith of Christ', *Mediaeval and Renaissance Studies*, III (1954), 55–77. *Giselberti Crispini Disputatio Judei et Christiani*, ed. B. Blumenkranz (Utrecht: Antwerp, 1956).

Peter Abelard: the *Historia Calamitatum* is edited by J. T. Muckle in *Mediaeval Studies*, XII (1950), 163–213 and by J. Monfrin (2nd edn; Paris, 1962). (Note that although the title *Historia Calamitatum* is universally established, it has poor manuscript authority and is probably a construction.) For logical and theological works respectively see notes 24 and 64 to Chapter 3.

A certain amount of specialised material, by anonymous or attributed authors, illustrative of the logical movement from the twelfth century, has appeared in the periodical, Université de Copenhague, *Cahiers de l'Institut du Moyen-Age Grec et Latin* (cited below as *CIMAGL*); see especially: S. Ebbesen, 'Anonymi Bodleiani in Sophisticos Elenchos Aristotelis Commentarii Fragmentum', *CIMAGL*, VIII (1972), 3–32 (a fragmentary survival, dated *c*. 1150); Ebbesen, 'Paris 4720A. A Twelfth Century Compendium of Aristotle's *Sophistici Elenchi*', *CIMAGL*, x (1973), 1–20 (edited extracts); Ebbesen, 'Anonymus Aurelianensis II, Aristotle, Alexander, Porphyry and Boethius. Ancient Scholasticism and Twelfth Century Western Europe', *CIMAGL*, XVI (1976), 1–128; N. J. Green Pedersen, 'William of Champeaux on Boethius' Topics according to Orléans Bibl. Mun. 266', *CIMAGL*, XIII (1974), 13–30 (edited fragments from a manuscript which contains many references to contemporaries of Abelard; with argument that a *Magister W.* is William of Champeaux); Green Pedersen, 'On the Interpretation of Aristotle's Topics in the Thirteenth Century', *CIMAGL*, IX (1973), 1–46 (a consideration of the terminology used by a number of thirteenth-century commentators on the work, with edited selections).

John of Salisbury: *Metalogicon*, ed. C. C. J. Webb (Oxford, 1929); *Policraticus*, ed. C. C. J. Webb (Oxford, 1909).

Gilbert of Poitiers: *The Commentaries on Boethius by Gilbert of Poitiers*, ed. N. Häring (Toronto, 1966).

Peter Lombard: *Libri IV Sententiarum*, ed. A. Heysse (Quaracchi, 1916). *Sententiae in IV Libris Distinctae* (Quaracchi, 1971–   ).

Hugh of St Victor: *Didascalicon, De Studio Legendi*, ed. C. H. Buttimer (Washington, D.C., 1939).

Richard of St Victor: *Richard de Saint Victor, De Trinitate Texte Critique avec Introduction, Notes et Tables*, ed. J. Ribaillier (Paris, 1958). *Richard de Saint-Victor, La Trinité*, ed. and tr. G. Salet (Sources Chrétiennes, LXIII; Paris, 1959) (Latin text with facing French translation).

Walter of St Victor: P. Glorieux, 'Le *Contra Quatuor Labyrinthos Franciae* de Gauthier de Saint-Victor, Edition Critique', *AHDLMA*, XIX (1952), 187–335.

Thierry of Chartres: *Commentaries on Boethius by Thierry of Chartres and his School*, ed. N. M. Häring (Toronto, 1971).

William of Conches: see notes 104 and 106 to Chapter 3. The *Dragmaticon* was printed as *Dialogus de Substantiis Physicis*, ed. G. Gratarolus (Strasbourg, 1567).

Clarembald of Arras: *Life and Works of Clarembald of Arras*, ed. N. Häring (Toronto, 1965).

Bernard Silvestris: *Cosmographia*, ed., with introduction and notes, P. Dronke (Leiden, 1978).

Al Farabi: for his treatise on the intellect, see note 10 to Chapter 4.

Avicenna: *Avicenna Latinus*, ed. S. van Riet, 3 vols (Louvain; Leiden, 1968–77).

Al Ghazali: see note 41 to Chapter 4.

Averroes: Mediaeval Academy of America, *Corpus Commentariorum Averrois in Aristotelem*, including *Compendia Librorum Aristotelis qui Parva Naturalia Vocantur*, ed. A. L. Shields (Cambridge, Mass. 1949); *Commentarium Medium in Aristotelis De Generatione et Corruptione Libros*, ed. F. H. Fobes and S. Kurland (Cambridge, Mass., 1956): *Commentarium Magnum in Aristotelis De Anima Libros*, ed. F. S. Crawford (Cambridge, Mass., 1953). Other commentaries are printed in *Aristotelis Opera cum Averrois Commentariis* (Venice, 1562–74).

Isaac Israeli: J. T. Muckle, 'Isaac Israeli, Liber de Definicionibus', *AHDLMA*, XI (1937–8), 299–340, prints two versions of a translation.

Ibn Gabirol (Avicebrol): see note 29 to Chapter 4.

Domininic Gundisalvi: see note 42 to Chapter 3.

Plato Latinus, ed. R. Klibansky (London, 1940–62): I, *Meno*; II. *Phaedo*; III. *Parmenides*; IV. *Timaeus a Calcidio translatus commentarioque instructus*, ed. J. H. Waszink.

Aristoteles Latinus, ed. G. Lacombe, L. Minio-Paluello *et al.* (variously at Bruges-Paris, Louvain-Leiden, 1939–).

The *Corpus Latinum Commentariorum in Aristotelem Graecum* under the direction of G. Verbeke has published a number of Latin texts of late antique Greek commentaries; see especially,

Themistius: *Commentaire sur le Traité de l'Ame d'Aristote Traduction de Guillaume de Moerbeke* (Louvain; Paris, 1957);

John Philoponus: *Jean Philopon Commentaire sur le De Anima d'Aristote Traduction de Guillaume de Moerbeke*, ed. G. Verbeke (Louvain; Paris, 1966);

Nemesius of Emesa: *Némésius d'Émèse De Natura Hominis Traduction de Burgundio de Pise*, ed. G. Verbeke and J. R. Moncho (Leiden, 1975) (a mid-twelfth-century translation of a treatise from the late fourth-century AD in which medical and philosophical theory blends).

H. Denifle and A. Chatelain, eds, *Chartularium Universitatis Parisiensis*, 4 vols (Paris, 1889–97), is indispensable for documentation on the history of the university and the thirteenth-century philosophical context.

P. Glorieux, *Répertoire des Maîtres en Théologie de Paris au XIIIe Siècle*, 2 vols (Paris, 1933–4), and *La Faculté des Arts et ses Maîtres au XIIIe Siècle* (Paris, 1971), A. B. Emden, *A Biographical Register of the University of Oxford to AD 1500*, 3 vols (Oxford, 1957–9), and *A Biographical Register of the University of Cambridge to 1500* (Cambridge, 1963), are standard guides to individual figures.

John Blund: *Iohannes Blund Tractatus de Anima*, ed. D. A. Callus and R. W. Hunt (London, 1970).

William of Auxerre (Guilelmus Antissiodorensis): *Aurea in Quattuor Sententiarum Libros Perlucida Explanatio* (Paris [1500]). A new edition is in progress: *Magistri Guillelmi Altissiodorensis Summa Aurea*, ed., J. Ribaillier (Spicilegium Bonaventurianum, 16– Paris; Quaracchi, 1980–).

William of Auvergne (Guilelmus Alvernus): *Opera Omnia* (Venice, 1591); also printed Paris, 1516 and Orleans, 1674–5. J. R. O'Donnell, ed., 'Tractatus Magistri Guillelmi Alvernensis De Bono et Malo', *Mediaeval Studies*, VIII (1946), 245–99, and 'Tractatus Secundus Guillelmi Alvernensis De Bono et Malo', *ibid.*, XVI (1954), 219–71. B. Switalski, ed., *William of Auvergne De Trinitate. An Edition of the Latin Text with an Introduction* (Toronto, 1976).

Alexander of Hales: *Summa Theologica*, 4 vols (Quaracchi, 1942–8). *Glossa in Quatuor Libros Sententiarum Petri Lombardi*, 4 vols (Quaracchi, 1951–7).

Philip the Chancellor: *Ex Summa Philippi Cancellarii Quaestiones de Anima*, ed. L. W. Keeler (Münster, 1937).

John of La Rochelle: *Tractatus de Divisione Multiplici Potentiarum Animae, Texte Critique avec Introduction*, ed. P. Michaud-Quantin (Paris, 1964).

Robert Grosseteste: *Die philosophischen Werke des Robert Grosseteste*, ed. L. Baur (*BGPMA*, IX; Münster, 1912). *Roberti Grosseteste Commentarius in VIII Libros Physicorum Aristotelis*, ed. R. C. Dales (Boulder, Colorado, 1963). Robert Grosseteste *Hexaemeron*, ed. R. C. Dales and S. Gieben (London, 1982).

Roger Bacon: *The Opus Maius of Roger Bacon*, ed. J. H. Bridges 3 vols (Oxford, 1897–1900). *Fratris Rogeri Baconi Opera Quaedam hactenus inedita*, ed. J. S. Brewer (Rolls Series; London, 1859), for *Opus tertium*, *Opus Minus* and *Compendium Philosophiae*. *Fratris Roger Bacon Compendium Studii Theologiae*, ed. H. Rashdall (Aberdeen, 1911). *Rogeri Baconis Moralis Philosophia*, ed. F. Delorme and E. Massa (Zurich, 1953). *Opera hactenus inedita Rogeri Baconis*, ed. R. Steele and F. Delorme, 16 fascicles (Oxford, 1905–40). K. M. Fredborg, L. Nielsen and J. Pinborg, ed., 'An Unedited Part of Roger Bacon's Opus Maius: De Signis', *Traditio*, xxxiv (1978), 75–136.

Robert Kilwardby: *De Ortu Scientiarum*, ed. A. G. Judy (London, 1976).

St Bonaventure: *S. Bonaventurae Opera Omnia*, 10 vols (Quaracchi, 1882–1902). *Collationes in Hexaemeron*, ed. F. Delorme (Quaracchi, 1934): another redaction of this work.

Albert the Great: *Opera Omnia*, ed. A. Borgnet, 38 vols (Paris, 1890–9). A new, critical edition is in progress: *Opera Omnia*, ed. B. Geyer *et al.* (Münster, 1951–   ).

St Thomas Aquinas: for the various editions see the catalogue of authentic works in J. A. Weisheipl, *Friar Thomas d'Aquino, his Life, Thought and Work* (New York, 1974). The preferred edition is generally the Leonine edition of the *Opera Omnia* (Rome, 1882–   ). Two important sets of texts have been published in this series since Weisheipl's catalogue was compiled: *Opera Omnia*, vol. xlii (Rome, 1979) (containing, *inter alia, De Regno ad Regem Cypri*); *Opera Omnia*, vol. xliii (Rome, 1976) (containing, *inter alia, De Principiis Naturae, De Aeternitate Mundi, De Unitate Intellectus*). The Blackfriars edition of the *Summa Theologiae*, 60 vols (London, 1964–76), provides a Latin text with facing English translation, in conveniently divided sections.

Siger of Brabant: *Questions sur la Métaphysique*, ed. C. A. Graiff (Louvain, 1948; Philosophes médiévaux, i). *Les Quaestiones super Librum de Causis de Siger de Brabant*, ed. A. Marlasca (Louvain; Paris, 1972; Philosophes médiévaux, xii). *Quaestiones in Tertium de Anima. De Anima Intellectiva. De Aeternitate Mundi*, ed. B. Bazán (Louvain; Paris, 1972; Philosophes médiévaux, xiii). *Siger de Brabant, Ecrits de Logique, de Morale et de Physique* (Louvain; Paris, 1974; Philosophes médiévaux, xiv). *Questions sur la Physique d'Aristote*, ed. P. Delhaye (Louvain, 1941; Les Philosophes Belges, xv).

Boethius of Dacia: *Opera* in *Corpus Philosophorum Danicorum Medii Aevi*, ed. J. Pinborg (Copenhagen, 1969–   ).

Three anonymous commentaries dating from the 1270s on the *De Anima* are edited in M. Giele, F. van Steenberghen and B. Bazán, *Trois Commentaires Anonymes sur le Traité de l'Ame d'Aristote* (Louvain; Paris, 1971; Philosophes médiévaux, xi).

3. SECONDARY WORKS

More information of a specialist nature may be found in the endnotes. For more detailed bibliography, consult works cited in section 1 and particular studies. As the bibliography is intended primarily for English readers, the list does not normally include titles for which there is a satisfactory English translation or studies the results of which are incorporated in English publications.

1. MASTERS OF THOSE WHO KNOW – PLATO, ARISTOTLE AND THE NEOPLATONISTS

J. Danielou, *Platonisme et Théologie Mystique* (2nd edn; Paris, 1953), is an important study both for general background and for the character of Christian mysticism. On particular influences, see P. Henry, *Plotin et l'Occident* (Louvain, 1934) and J. Flamant, *Macrobe et le Néoplatonisme Latin à la Fin du IVe Siècle* (Leiden, 1977). The collection, *Plotino e il Neoplatonismo in Oriente e in Occidente* (Accademia Nazionale dei Lincei; Rome, 1974), has several important articles.

2. FROM ANCIENT WORLD TO MIDDLE AGES: ADAPTATION AND TRANSMISSION

1. St Augustine

On the Platonist contribution to Patristic thought, see E. von Ivánka, *Plato Christianus Übernahme und Umgestaltung des Platonismus durch die Väter* (Einsiedeln, 1964), and as affecting Augustine in particular, C. Boyer, *Christianisme et Néo-platonisme dans la Formation de Saint Augustin* (Paris, 1920). See also Boyer's *L'Idée de Vérité dans la Philosophie de Saint Augustin* (Paris, 1920), and his *Essai sur la Doctrine de Saint Augustin* (Paris, 1932). R. Holte, *Béatitude et Sagesse: St Augustin et le Problème de la Fin de l'Homme dans la Philosophie Ancienne* (Paris, 1962), covers a theme of considerable interest. On the more general context, H. I. Marrou, *Saint Augustin et la Fin de la Culture Antique* (2nd edn, with *Retractatio*; Paris, 1949), is stimulating. For the *Confessions* see P. Courcelle, *Recherches sur les Confessions de Saint Augustin* (Paris, 1950). E. Lamirande, *L'Eglise Céleste selon Saint Augustin* (Paris, 1963), examines the development and implications of Augustine's idea of the city of God. J. Chaix-Ruy, *Saint Augustin Temps et Histoire* (Paris, 1956), examines an important aspect of Augustine's outlook. G. de Plinval, *Pélage, ses Ecrits, sa Vie et sa Réforme* (Lausanne, 1943), is a useful treatment of this figure.

2. Boethius

The best treatment is now that by Chadwick, in section A, which provides an up to date bibliography, but see also L. Obertello, *Severino Boezio*, 2 vols (Genoa, 1974). On Boethius' influence, two studies by P. Courcelle remain fundamental: *La Consolation de Philosophie dans la Tradition Littéraire Antécédents et Postérité de Boèce* (Paris, 1967), which includes iconography, and 'Etude Critique sur les Commentaires de la Consolation de Boèce, IX–XVe Siècles', *AHDLMA*, XII (1939), 5–140. See also F. Troncarelli, 'Per una Ricerca sui Commenti Alto medievali al *De Consolatione* di Boezio', in *Miscellanea in Memoria di Giorgio Cencetti* (Turin, 1973), pp. 363–80. As regards the tradition of commentary, H. Silvestre, 'Le Commentaire Inédit de Jean Scot Érigène au Mètre IX du Livre III du "De Consolatione Philosophiae" de Boèce', *Revue d'Histoire Ecclesiastique*, XLVII (1952), 44–122, is of interest although the commentary in question is not now thought to be by Eriugena. On the influence of the sacred treatises see G. Schrimpf, *Die Axiomenschrift des Boethius (De Hebdomadibus) als philosophisches Lehrbuch des Mittelalters* (Leiden, 1966) and M. Cappuyns, 'Le plus ancien Commentaire des "Opuscula sacra" et son Origine', *Recherches de Théologie Ancienne et Médiévale*, III (1931), 237–72.

On Macrobius: J. Flamant, *Macrobe et le Néo-Platonisme Latin à la Fin du IVe Siècle* (Leiden, 1977), and for influence beyond, M. Schedler, *Die Philosophie des Macrobius und ihr Einfluss auf die Wissenschaft des christlichen Mittelalters* (*BGPMA*, vol. 13, Part 1; Münster, 1916). P. Courcelle, 'La Postérité Chrétienne du Songe de Scipion', *Revue des Etudes Latines*, XXXVI (1958), 205–34, considers the early influence and the formation of the tradition.

J. Fontaine, *Isidore de Séville et la Culture Classique dans l'Espagne Wisigothique*, 2 vols (Paris, 1959), is authoritative.

3. John Scotus Eriugena

On other philosophical work contemporary with Eriugena, a subject, which has received important recent attention in English, see J.-P. Bouhot, *Ratramne de Corbie Histoire Littéraire et Controverses Doctrinales* (Paris, 1966), and P. Delhaye, *Une Controverse sur l'Ame Universelle au IXe Siècle* (Lille; Namur, 1950). M. Cristiani, *Dall' Unanimitas all' Universitas da Alcuino a Giovanni Eriugena: Lineamenti Ideologici e Terminologia Politica della Cultura del Secolo IX* (Rome, 1978), considers the intellectual history in its wider context and shows how the predestinarian controversy had political implications.

On Eriugena's major Greek authority, see R. Roques, *L'Univers Dionysien: Structure Hiérarchique du Monde selon le Pseudo-Denys* (Paris, 1954).

M. Cappuyns, *Jean Scot Érigène sa Vie, son Oeuvre, sa Pensée* (Louvain; Paris, 1933; reprinted Brussels, 1969), is fundamental; see also M. dal Pra, *Scoto Eriugena* (Milan, 1951). P. Mazzarella, *Il Pensiero di Giovanni Scoto Eriugena Saggio Interpretativo* (Padua, 1957) and G. Bonafede, *Scota Eriugena* (Palermo, 1969), are both centred on the *Periphyseon*. G. Schrimpf, *Das Werk des Johannes Scottus Eriugena im Rahmen des*

Wissenschaftsverständnisses seiner Zeit eine Hinführung zu Periphyseon (*BGPMA*, Neue Folge, XXIII; Münster, 1982), presents that work more comprehensively. On particular aspects and problems, see C. Allegro, *Giovanni Scoto Eriugena Fede e Ragione* (Rome, 1974) (on the theme of faith and reason); E. Jeauneau, *Quatre Thèmes Erigéniens* (Conférence Albert-le-Grand, 1974, Montreal; Paris, 1978), Part I of which consists of short, pleasing essays on themes in Eriugena; Jeauneau, 'Jean Scot Erigène et le Grec', *Archivum Latinitatis Medii Aevi*, XLI (1979), 5–50, on Eriugena's knowledge of Greek and motives in translating. *Jean Scot Erigène et l'Histoire de la Philosophie* (Colloques Internationaux du C.N.R.S., Laon 7–12 juillet 1975; Paris, 1977), consists of collected conference papers ranging over Eriugena's context, thought and influence. G. d'Onofrio, 'Giovanni Scoto e Boezio: tracce degli "Opuscula Sacra" e della "Consolatio" nell' Opera Eriugeniana', *Studi Medievali*, 3rd ser. XXI, 2 (1980), illuminates aspects both of Eriugena's thought and Boethius' influence. Also on sources is a collection of conference papers, W. Beierwaltes, *Eriugena Studien zu seinen Quellen* (Heidelberg, 1980). See also Beierwaltes, 'Eriugena Aspekte seiner Philosophie', in H. Löwe, ed., *Die Iren und Europa im früheren Mittelalter*, II (Stuttgart, 1982), 799–818. The latter collection also includes a study of the controversy over predestination: G. Schrimpf, 'Der Beitrag des Johannes Scottus Eriugena zum Prädestinationsstreit', *ibid.*, 819–65. P. Lucentini, *Platonismo Medievale: Contributi per la Storia dell' Eriugenismo* (Florence, 1979), on the tradition.

3. THE CENTRAL MIDDLE AGES – LOGIC, THEOLOGY AND COSMOLOGY

Schools: P. Riché, *Les Ecoles et l'Enseignement dans l'Occident Chrétien de la Fin du Ve Siècle au Milieu du XIe Siècle* (Paris, 1979). *La Scuola nell' Occidente Latino dell' Alto Medioevo* (Settimane di Studio del Centro Italiano di Studi sull' Alto Medioevo; 2 vols, Spoleto, 1972), has particularly important sections on the school from Cassiodorus to Alcuin, and the Carolingian school from Alcuin to Remigius of Auxerre. See too G. Beaujean, 'L'Enseignement du "Quadrivium" ', *ibid.*, pp. 639–67; L. Minio-Paluello, 'Nuovi impulsi allo studio della logica: la seconda fase della riscoperta di Aristotele e di Boezio', *ibid.*, pp. 743–66; J. Chatillon, 'Les Ecoles de Chartres et de Saint Victor', *ibid.*, pp. 795–839. G. Paré, A. Brunet and P. Tremblay, *La Renaissance du XIIe Siècle: les Ecoles et l'Enseignement* (Paris; Ottawa, 1933), and see also, P. Delhaye, 'L'Organisation Scolaire au XIIe Siècle', *Traditio*, V (1947), 211–68, which is a useful, brief review of the educational context before the universities. E. Lesne, *Histoire de la Propriété Ecclésiastique en France*, 6 vols in 8 (Lille, 1910–43), V (1940): *Les Ecoles de la Fin du VIIIe Siècle à la Fin du XIIe Siècle*, has a wealth of information.

Logic: A. van de Vyver, 'Les Etapes du Développement Philosophique du Haut Moyen-Age', *Revue Belge de Philologie et d'Histoire*, VII (1929), 425–52, is fundamental; see also Minio-Paluello, 'Nuovi impulsi'. Jean Isaac, *Le Peri Hermeneias en Occident de Boèce à Saint Thomas* (Paris, 1953), on this book of Aristotle's *Organon*. J. Reiners, *Der Nominalismus in der Frühscholastik* (*BGPMA*, vol. VIII, Part 5; Münster, 1910), on one aspect. On a major figure, F. Picavet, *Gerbert un Pape Philosophe d'après l'Histoire et d'après la Légende* (Paris, 1897), and U. Lindgren, *Gerbert von Aurillac und das Quadrivium: Untersuchungen zur Bildung im Zeitalter der Ottonen* (Wiesbaden, 1976).

J. Gonzette, *Pierre Damien et la Culture Profane* (Louvain; Paris, 1956), on this figure.

J. de Montclos, *Lanfranc et Bérenger, la Controverse Eucharistique du XIe Siècle* (Louvain, 1971), is the fullest study of the dispute. A. Cantin, 'Ratio et Auctoritas dans la Première Phase de la Controverse Eucharistique entre Béranger et Lanfranc', *Revue des Etudes Augustiniennes*, XX (1974), 155–86, discusses the application of logic to theology.

Anselm of Bec: the best general study is in English. More recent treatment of particular aspects includes: R. Pouchet, *La Rectitudo chez Saint Anselme Un Itinéraire Augustinien de l'Ame à Dieu* (Paris, 1964), on a concept which involves philosophical and theological insights, especially bearing on soteriology; F. S. Schmitt, 'Anselm und der (Neu-)Platonismus', *Analecta Anselmiana*, I (Frankfurt/Main, 1969), 39–71, which re-examines Anselm's Platonism on a number of specific points: K. Flasch, 'Der Philosophische Ansatz des Anselm von Canterbury im Monologion und sein Verhältnis zum Augustinischen Neuplatonismus', *ibid.*, II (Frankfurt/Main, 1970), 1–43; P. Mazzarella, 'L'Esemplarismo in Anselmo d'Aosta e in Bonaventura da Bagnoregio', *ibid.*, I, 145–64, which examines the role of creation as an image of the creator in both thinkers. See also R. Javelet, *Image et Rassemblance au Douzième Siècle de Saint Anselme à Alain de Lille*, 2 vols (Strasbourg, 1967).

M.-Th. d'Alverny, 'Achard de Saint Victor, Evêque d'Avranches – Disciple de Saint Anselme', *Analecta Anselmiana*, II (Frankfurt/Main, 1970), 217–22, briefly places this figure within the tradition.

Peter Abelard and contemporary theology: J. Jolivet, *Arts du Langage et Théologie chez Abélard* (Paris, 1969). J. Cottiaux, 'La Conception de la Théologie chez Abelard', *Revue d'Histoire Ecclésiastique*, XXVIII (1932), 247–95, 535–51, 787–828 (defending Abelard's orthodoxy, with close textual analysis). R. Thomas, ed., *Petrus Abaelardus (1079–1142) Person, Werk und Wirkung* (Trier, 1980). E. Bertola, 'Le Critiche di Abelard ad Anselmo di Laon ed a Guglielmo di Champeaux', *Rivista di Filosofia Neo-Scolastica*, LII (1960), 495–522 (discussing the historical value of Abelard's criticisms of his masters). A. M. Landgraf, *Introduction à l'Histoire de la Littérature Théologique de la Scolastique Naissante* (Montreal; Paris, 1973), is a translation with revision of Landgraf, *Einführung in die Geschichte der theologischen Literatur der Frühscholastik* (Regensburg, 1948). M.-D. Chenu, *La Théologie au Douzième Siècle* (Paris, 1957) (collected studies on the theme). R. Blomme, *La Doctrine du Péché dans les Ecoles Théologiques de la Première Moitié du XIIe Siècle* (Louvain, 1958), on a theological theme which has an interest for Abelard's views. A. Lang, *Die theologische Prinzipienlehre der mittelalterlichen Scholastik* (Freiburg im Breisgau, 1964), studies the development of theological method. J. de Ghellinck, *Le Mouvement Théologique du XIIe Siècle* (2nd edn; Bruges; Paris, 1948), especially for the context of Peter Lombard. P. Delhaye, *Pierre Lombard, sa Vie, ses Oeuvres, sa Morale* (Montreal; Paris, 1961). Several studies helpfully focus on aspects of the influence of the liberal arts programme on the philosophical-theological movement; see: M.-D. Chenu, 'Grammaire et Théologie aux XIIe et XIIIe Siècles', *AHDLMA*, x (1936), 5–28; J. Jolivet, 'Elements pour une Etude des Rapports entre la Grammaire et l'Ontologie au Moyen Age', in J. P. Beckmann *et al.*, eds, *Sprache und Erkenntnis im Mittelalter*, 2 vols (Berlin; New York, 1981), I, 135–64; P. Delhaye, 'L'Enseignement de la Philosophie Morale au XIIe Siecle', *Mediaeval Studies*, XI (1949), 77–99: cf. Delhaye, ' "Grammatica" et "Ethica" au XIIe Siècle', *Recherches de Théologie Ancienne et Médiévale*, XXV (1958), 59–110.

Gilbert of Poitiers: H. C. van Elswijk, *Gilbert Porreta, sa Vie, son Oeuvre, sa Pensée* (Louvain, 1966), and particularly on the controversy surrounding him, A. Hayen, 'Le Concile de Reims et l'Erreur Théologique de Gilbert de la Porrée', *AHDLMA*, x (1935–6), 29–102.

M.-D. Chenu, 'Platon à Cîteaux', *AHDLMA*, XXI (1954), 99–106, criticises the tendency to distinguish too sharply between a theology hostile to the philosophical strand and the intellectualist approach.

Hugh of St Victor: R. Baron, *Science et Sagesse chez Hugues de Saint-Victor* (Paris, 1957) and *Etudes sur Hugues de Saint-Victor* (Desclée de Brouwer, [Paris], 1963); D. van den Eynde, *Essai sur la Succession et la Date des Ecrits de Hugues de St-Victor* (Rome, 1960).

T. Gregory, *Platonismo Medievale Studi e Ricerche* (Rome, 1958) and E. Garin, *Studi sul Platonismo Medievale* (Florence, 1958), are important for this strand. For brief and specific treatment see E. Jeauneau, 'L'Héritage de la Philosophie Antique durant le Haut Moyen Age', in *Settimana di Studio del Centro Italiano di Studi sull' Alto Medioevo*, XXII (Spoleto, 1975), 17–54.

Much of the literature on the cosmology of the period centres on the concept of the 'school of Chartres', for criticism of which see the bibliography in section A. However one regards the strand of thought in question, the traditional approach to describing it has contributed much of lasting importance and has a historiographical interest of its own. A. Clerval, *Les Ecoles de Chartres au Moyen Age* (Paris, 1895), was the pioneering study. On individual figures, see: E. Jeauneau, ' "Nani gigantum humeris insidentes", Essai d'Interpretation de Bernard de Chartres', *Vivarium*, v (1967), 79–99, and 'Le Prologue in Eptatheucon de Thierry de Chartres', *Mediaeval Studies*, xvi (1954), 171–5; T. Gregory, *Anima Mundi La Filosofia di Guglielmo di Conches e la Scuola di Chartres* (Florence, 1955). On the 'school': E. Jeauneau, 'Note sur l'Ecole de Chartres', *Studi Medievali*, 3rd series, v (1964) 821–65, and 'Macrobe, source du Platonisme Chartrain', *Studi Medievali*, 3rd series, I (1960), 3–24; J. M. Parent, *La Doctrine de la Création dans l'Ecole de Chartres* (Paris; Ottawa, 1938). M.-T. d'Alverny, 'Le Cosmos Symbolique du XIIe Siècle', *AHDLMA*, xx (1953), 69–81. On the influence of medical theory: A. Birkenmajer, *Le Role Joué par les Médecins et les Naturalistes dans la Réception d'Aristote aux XIIe et XIIIe Siècles* (La Pologne au VIe Congrès International des Sciences Historiques; Warsaw, 1930); H. Schipperges, 'Einflüsse arabischer Medezin auf die Mikrokosmosliteratur des 12. Jahrhunderts', in *Antike und Orient im Mittelalter: Vorträge der Kölner Mediaevistenangung 1956–1959*, ed. P. Wilpert (Berlin, 1962; Miscellanea Mediaevalia, I), pp. 129–53.

4. NEW SOURCES AND NEW INSTITUTIONS

Arabic thought and its influence: G. Quadri, *La Philosophie Arabe dans l'Europe Médiévale des Origines à Averroès* (Paris, 1947) (translated from the Italian), is valuable. On Islamic theology: L. Gardet and M. M. Anawati, *Introduction à la théologie Musulmane* (Paris, 1948). G. C. Anawati, 'Le Néoplatonisme dans la Pensée Musulmane: Etat Actuel des Recherches', in *Plotino e il Neoplatonismo in Oriente e in Occidente* (Accademia Nazionale dei Lincei; Rome, 1974), pp. 339–405, is a good statement. *L'Occidente e l'Islam nell' Alto Medioevo* (Settimane di Studio del Centro Italiano di Studi sull' Alto Medioevo, xII; Spoleto, 1965), has pertinent studies. For individual figures, see: A.-M. Goichon, *La Philosophie d'Avicenne et son Influence en Europe Médiévale* (2nd edn; Paris, 1979); E. Gilson, 'Avicenne en Occident au Moyen Age', *AHDLMA*, xxxvi (1969), 89–121; L. Gauthier, *Ibn Rochd* (Paris, 1948); J. Schlanger, *La Philosophie de Salomon ibn Gabirol Etude d'un Néoplatonisme* (Leiden, 1968); H. Serouya, *Maimonides, sa Vie, son Oeuvre, avec un Exposé de sa Philosophie* (Paris, 1951). On the intellect there is extensive coverage: O. Hamelin, *La Théorie de l'Intellect d'après Aristote et ses Commentaires* (ed. E. Barbotin; Paris, 1953); E. Barbotin, *La Théorie Aristotélicienne de l'Intellect d'après Théophraste* (Louvain; Paris, 1954); P. Moraux, *Alexandre d'Aphrodise Exégète de la Noétique d'Aristote* (Liege; Paris, 1942). The introductions to G. Verbeke, ed., *Themistius, Commentaire sur le Traité de l'Ame d'Aristote, Traduction de Guillaume de Moerbeke* (Louvain; Paris, 1957), and Verbeke, ed., *Jean Philopon, Commentaire sur le De Anima d'Aristote, Traduction de Guillaume de Moerbeke* (Louvain; Paris, 1966), are important. See also, G. Verbeke, 'Introduction sur la Doctrine Psychologique d'Avicenne', in S. van Riet, ed., *Avicenna Latinus, Liber de Anima seu Sextus de naturalibus IV–V* (Louvain; Leiden, 1968). The influence of the Arabic theories on the Latin tradition is studied in E. Gilson, 'Les Sources Greco-Arabes de l'Augustinisme Avicennisant', *AHDLMA*, IV (1929–30), 5–149, though the term 'augustinisme avicennisant' is not helpful. A. Rohner, *Das Schöpfungsproblem bei Moses Maimonides, Albertus Magnus und Thomas von Aquin* (*BGPMA*, vol. xI, Part 5; Münster, 1913), on a sensitive and central question.

Translations: M. Steinschneider, *Die Europäischen Übersetzungen aus dem Arabischen bis Mitte des 17. Jahrhunderts* (Vienna, 1904–5; reprinted, Graz, 1956), is the basic catalogue of western translations but is outdated on many points, especially of attribution. L.

Minio-Paluello, 'Aristotele dal Mondo Arabo a quello Latino', in *L'Occidente e l'Islam nell' Alto Medioevo*, is important for calling attention to several misinterpretations. M. Grabmann, 'Aristoteles im Zwoelften Jahrhundert', *Mediaeval Studies*, XII (1950), 123–62, is a useful review of the scene and of scholarly activity in it. For individual authors and translators, see: M. T. d'Alverny, 'Notes sur les Traductions Médiévales des Oeuvres Philosophiques d'Avicenne', *AHDLMA*, XIX (1952), 337–58; d'Alverny, 'Les Traductions d'Avicenne (Moyen Age et Renaissance)', in *Avicenna nella Storia della Cultura Medievale* (Accademia Nazionale dei Lincei; Rome, 1957), pp. 71–87 and a series of articles by her, entitled 'Avicenna Latinus' in *AHDLMA*, XXVIII–XXXIX (1961–72); H. Bedoret, 'Les Premières Traductions Tolédanes de Philosophie, Oeuvres d'Alfarabi', *Revue Néo-Scolastique de Philosophie*, XLI (1938), 80–97; M. Alonso Alonso, 'Traducciones del Arcediano Gundisalvo', *Al-Andalus*, XII (1947), 295–338; M. T. d'Alverny, 'Avendauth?', *Homenaje a Millás-Vallicrosa*, I (Barcelona, 1954), 19–43, which cleared cluttered ground. R. Lemay, 'Dans l'Espagne du XIIe Siècle. Les Traductions de l'Arabe au Latin', *Annales, Economies, Sociétés, Civilisations*, XVIII (1963), 639–65, is a useful survey of translators and of the geography of the process.

Universities: J. Verger, *Les Universités au Moyen Age* (Paris, 1973); S. d'Irsay, *Histoire des Universités Françaises et Etrangères*, I (Paris, 1933); but see principally section A, above. J. Destrez, *La Pecia dans les Manuscrits Universitaires du XIIIe et du XIVe Siècle* (Paris, 1935), on an aspect of book production. P. Glorieux, *La Faculté des Arts et ses Maîtres au XIIIe Siècle* (Paris, 1971), is mainly a listing but has a short introduction. Glorieux, *La Littérature Quodlibétique*, 2 vols (Paris, 1925–35), is the fundamental work on this subject. The collection *Arts Libéraux et Philosophie au Moyen Age* (Actes du IVe Congrès International de Philosophie Médiévale, Montréal, 1967; Montreal: Paris, 1969) has a section on the arts in the university.

5. ARISTOTELIAN PHILOSOPHY IN THE UNIVERSITY – THE FIRST PHASE OF ASSIMILATION

and

6. ARISTOTELIAN PHILOSOPHY AND CHRISTIAN THEOLOGY – SYSTEM BUILDING AND CONTROVERSY

F. van Steenberghen, *La Philosophie au XIIIe Siècle* (Louvain; Paris, 1966), is an indispensable survey which provides extensive bibliography. His 'L'Organisation des Etudes au Moyen Age et ses Répercussions sur le Mouvement Philosophique', *Revue Philosophique de Louvain*, LII (1954), 572–92, is a useful statement on the programme of studies; cf. P. Glorieux, 'L'Enseignement au Moyen Age. Techniques et Méthodes en Usage à la Faculté de Théologie de Paris au XIIIe Siècle', *AHDLMA*, XXXV (1968), 65–186.

On the 1210 condemnation there is a series of studies: G. Théry, *Autour du Décret de 1210: I. David de Dinant* (Bibliothèque Thomiste, VI; Paris, 1925), and *Autour du Décret de 1210: II. Alexandre d'Aphrodise* (Bibliothèque Thomiste, VII; Paris 1926); G. C. Capelle, *Autour du Décret de 1210: III. Amaury de Bène. Essai sur son Panthéisme Formel* (Bibliothèque Thomiste, XVI; Paris, 1932).

K. Jacobi, *Die Modalbegriffe in den logischen Schriften des Wilhelm von Shyreswood und in anderen Kompendien des 12 und 13 Jahrhunderts: Funktionbestimmung und Gebrauch in der logischen Analyse* (Leiden, 1980), is for the specialist in this area.

A. Masnovo, *Da Guglielmo d'Auvergne a San Tomaso d'Aquino* 3 vols (Milan, 1930–45), provides useful coverage of a period which is rather neglected. C. Ottaviano, *Guglielmo d'Auxerre († 1231). La Vita, le Opere, il Pensiero* (Rome, [1929]). M. Baumgartner, *Die Erkenntnislehre des Wilhelm von Auvergne*, (*BGPMA*, vol. II, Part 1; Münster, 1893). A.

Quentin, *Naturkenntnisse und Naturanschauungen bei Wilhelm von Auvergne* (Hildesheim, 1976). A. Forest, 'Guillaume d'Auvergne, Critique d'Aristote', in *Etudes Médiévales Offertes à M. le Doyen Augustin Fliche de l'Institut* (Montpellier, 1952), pp. 67–79. E. Gilson, 'La Notion d'Existence chez Guillaume d'Auvergne', *AHDLMA*, xv (1946), 55–91. On the developing character of thought: R. de Vaux, *Notes et Textes sur l'Avicennisme Latin aux Confins des XIIe et XIIIe Siècles* (Bibliothèque Thomiste, xx; Paris, 1934); E. Gilson, 'Les Sources Gréco-Arabes de l'Augustinisme Avicennisant', *AHDLMA*, iv (1929–30), 5–149; E. Bertola, 'E Esistito un Avicennismo Latino nel Medioevo?' *Sophia*, xxxv (1967), 318–34; xxxix (1971), 278–320; R. de Vaux, 'La Première Entrée d'Averroës chez les Latins', *Revue des Sciences Philosophiques et Théologiques*, xxii (1933), 193–245. P. Glorieux, 'Les Années 1242–1247 à la Faculté de Théologie de Paris', *Recherches de Théologie Ancienne et Médiévale*, xxix (1962), 234–49. F. Pelster, 'Adam von Bocfeld (Bockingfold), ein Oxforder Erklärer des Aristoteles um die Mitte des xiii Jahrhunderts, sein Leben und seine Schriften', *Scholastik*, xi (1936), 196–224. O. Lottin, 'La Pluralité des Formes Substantielles avant Saint Thomas d'Aquin. Quelques documents nouveaux' *Revue Néoscolastique de Philosophie*, xxxiv (1932), 449–67.

F. van Steenberghen, 'Albert le Grand et l'Aristotélisme', *Revue Internationale de Philosophie*, xxxiv (1980), no. 133–134, 566–74, is a useful general statement. B. Geyer, 'Albertus Magnus und die Entwicklung der Scholastischen Metaphysik', in P. Wilpert, ed., *Die Metaphysik im Mittelalter* (Miscellanea Mediaevalia, ii; Berlin, 1963), pp. 3–13 (a conference paper from a useful collection). G. Wieland, *Untersuchungen zum Seinsbegriff im Metaphysikkommentar Alberts des Grossen* (*BGPMA*, Neue Folge, vol. vii; Münster, 1971), on Albert's treatment of a central concept. A. Zimmermann, ed., *Albert der Grosse, seine Zeit, sein Werk, seine Wirkung* (Miscellanea Mediaevalia, xiv; Berlin; New York, 1981), is a valuable collection treating Albert's philosophical and scientific work and his influence. H. Ostlender, ed., *Studia Albertina. Festschrift für Bernhard Geyer* (*BGPMA*, Supplementary vol. iv; Münster, 1952), is largely devoted to theological aspects of Albert's work; among the aspects of philosophical interest covered, note A. J. Backes, 'Der Geist als höherer Teil der Seele nach Albert dem Grossen', pp. 52–67, J. Hansen, 'Zur Frage der anfangslosen und zeitlichen Schöpfung bei Albert dem Grossen', pp. 167–88; A. Hufnagel, 'Das Person-Problem bei Albertus Magnus', pp. 202–33 (on an aspect which was a topic also in the twelfth century). F. Ruello, *La Notion de Vérité chez Saint Albert le Grand et chez Thomas d'Aquin de 1243 à 1254* (Louvain; Paris, 1969), is a detailed and interesting study of this aspect in the early thought of both figures. See also, on another aspect, G. de Mattos, 'L'Intellect Agent Personnel dans les Premiers Ecrits d'Albert le Grand et de Thomas d'Aquin', *Revue Néoscolastique de Philosophie*, xliii (1940), 145–61.

Controversy and condemnations: E.-H. Wéber, *La Controverse de 1270 à l'Université de Paris et son Rétentissement sur la Pensée de S. Thomas d'Aquin* (Paris, 1970), has been challenged by B. Bazán, 'La Dialogue Philosophique entre Siger de Brabant et Thomas d'Aquin. A propos d'un Ouvrage Récent de E. H. Wéber, O.P.', *Revue Philosophique de Louvain*, lxxii (1974), 53–155. Wéber maintained his position in the course of his *Dialogue et Dissensions entre Saint Bonaventure et Saint Thomas d'Aquin à Paris (1252–1273)* (Paris, 1974), and in 'Les Discussions de 1270 à l'Université de Paris et leur Influence sur la Pensée Philosophique de S. Thomas d'Aquin', in A. Zimmermann, ed., *Die Auseinandersetzungen an der Pariser Universität im XIII Jahrhundert* (Miscellanea Mediaevalia, x; Berlin, 1976). F. van Steenberghen, *Maître Siger de Brabant* (Louvain; Paris, 1977), is now the standard account of this figure. R. Hissette, *Enquête sur les 219 Articles Condamnés à Paris le 7 mars 1277* (Louvain; Paris, 1977), is an indispensable and judicious analysis.

Supplementary Bibliography

1. GENERAL REVIEWS AND BIBLIOGRAPHICAL AIDS

L. M. de Rijk, *La Philosophie au Moyen Age* (Leiden, 1985).
J. Marenbon, *Later Medieval Philosophy (1150–1350). An Introduction* (London, 1987).
M. T. Fumagalli Beonio Brocchieri and M. Parodi, *Storia della Filosofia Medievale da Boezio a Wyclif* (Rome/Bari, 1989).
Augustinus-Lexikon, ed. C. Mayer (Basel/Stuttgart, 1986–).
   M. Brennan, *Guide des Etudes Erigéniennes Bibliographie Commentée des Publications 1930–1987/A Guide to Eriugenian Studies: a Survey of Publications 1930–1987* (Fribourg/Paris, 1989).
   C. B. Schmitt and D. Knox, *Pseudo-Aristoteles Latinus: a Guide to Latin Works Falsely Attributed to Aristotle before 1500* (London, 1985); J. Kraye, W. F. Ryan and C. B. Schmitt, eds, *Pseudo-Aristotle in the Middle Ages: the 'Theology' and other Texts* (London, 1986).
   C. H. Lohr, *Commentateurs d'Aristote Médiéval Latin/Aristotle Commentators: A Bibliography of Recent Secondary Literature* (Fribourg/Paris, 1988).
   'Medieval Islamic Philosophy and Theology. Bibliographical Guide (1986–1989)', *Bulletin de Philosophie Médiévale*, xxxii (1990), 106–35.
   E. W. Crosby, C. J. Bishko and R. L. Kellogg, *Medieval Studies: a Bibliographical Guide* (New York/London, 1983).
   J. A. Alford and D. P. Seniff, *Literature and Law in the Middle Ages: A Bibliography of Scholarship* (New York/London, 1984).
   L. D. Reynolds, ed., *Texts and Transmission: a Survey of the Latin Classics* (Oxford, 1983). N. G. Wilson, *Scholars of Byzantium* (London, 1983).

Miscellaneous Collected Papers (some collections will be found under individual chapter divisions and thematically organised below)
L. Bieler (ed. R. Sharpe), *Ireland and the Culture of Early Medieval Europe* (London, 1987). M Esposito (ed. M. Lapidge), *Latin Learning in Mediaeval Ireland* (London, 1988). J. Chatillon, *D'Isidore de Séville à Saint Thomas d'Aquin, Etudes d'Histoire et de Théologie* (London, 1985). *Culture et Travail Intellectuel dans l'Occident Médiéval*, eds G. Hasenohr and J. Longère (Paris, 1981). *Philosophie im Mittelalter. Entwicklungslinien und Paradigmen*, eds J. P. Beckmann, L. Honnefelder, G. Schrimpf and G. Wieland (Hamburg, 1987). J. Pinborg, *Medieval Semantics: Selected Studies on Medieval Logic and Grammar* (London, 1984). W. J. Courtenay, *Covenant and Causality in Medieval Thought* (London, 1984). C. Wenin, ed., *L'Homme et son Univers au Moyen Age, Actes du Septième Congrès International de Philosophie Médiévale (30 août-4 septembre 1982)*, 2 vols; (Louvain-la-Neuve, 1986).

Science and Cosmology
P. Duhem (tr. R. Ariew), *Medieval Cosmology: Theories of Infinity, Place, Time, Void and the Plurality of Worlds* (translation and abridgement of *Le Système du Monde*). D. Buschinger and A. Crépin, eds, *Les Quatre Eléments dans la Culture Médiévale* (Göppinger, 1983) (papers on various aspects of the elemental theory). L. D. Roberts, ed., *Approaches to Nature in the Middle Ages* (Binghampton, N.Y., 1982); J. Weisheipl (ed. W. E. Carroll), *Nature and Motion in the Middle Ages* (Washington, D.C., 1985). S. Bemrose, *Dante's Angelic Intelligences: their Importance in the Cosmos and in Pre-Christian Religion* (Rome, 1983). E. Grant, 'Medieval and Renaissance Scholastic Conceptions

291

of the Influence of the Celestial Region on the Terrestrial', *Journal of Medieval and Renaissance Studies*, xvii (1987), 1–23. R. Sorabji, *Time, Creation and the Continuum Theories in Antiquity and the Early Middle Ages* (London, 1983). J. E. Murdoch, *Antiquity and the Middle Ages* (Album of Science, 3; New York, 1984), is devoted to scientific illustration. E. Grant and J. E. Murdoch, eds, *Mathematics and its Applications to Science and Natural Philosophy in the Middle Ages: Essays in Honour of Marshall Clagett* (Cambridge, 1987), traces the impact of a technical subject on more general intellectual culture.

Society

O. Langholm, *Wealth and Money in the Aristotelian Tradition: A Study in Scholastic Economic Sources* (Bergen, 1983). J. Le Goff, *Your Money or Your Life: Economy and Religion in the Middle Ages* (New York, 1985). W. Stürner, *Peccatum und Potestas Der Sündenfall und die Entstehung der herrscherlichen Gewalt im mittelalterlichen Staatsdenken* (Sigmaringen, 1987), traces the application to political thought of a theological premiss from the patristic period. J. H. Burns, ed., *The Cambridge History of Political Thought c.350 – c.1450* (Cambridge, 1988). M. Mostert, *The Political Theology of Abbo of Fleury* (Hilversum, 1987). A. Black, *Guilds and Civil Society in European Political Thought from the Twelfth Century to the Present* (London, 1984) and S. Reynolds, *Kingdoms and Communities in Western Europe 900–1300* (Oxford, 1984) focus on the ideas implicit in collective organization. J. R. Sweeney and S. Chodorow, eds (foreword by S. Kuttner), *Popes, Teachers and Canon Law in the Middle Ages* (Ithaca/London, 1989). S. Kuttner, *Gratian and the Schools of Law, 1140–1234* (London, 1983). S. Kuttner and K. Pennington, eds, *Proceedings of the Sixth International Congress of Medieval Canon Law* (Vatican City, 1985), includes among its numerous studies important relevant contributions under the heading 'Schools: Italy and France'. A. Gouron, *Etudes sur la Diffusion des Doctrines Juridiques Médiévales* (London, 1987). F. Elsener, *Studien zur Rezeption des gelehrten Rechts: ausgewählte Aufsätze*, ed. F. Ebel and D. Willoweit (Sigmaringen, 1989).

Themes of General, Contextual and Special Interest

G. Verbeke, *The Presence of Stoicism in Medieval Thought* (Washington, 1983) and M. L. Colish, *The Stoic Tradition from Antiquity to the Early Middle Ages* (2 vols; Leiden, 1985). Colish, *The Mirror of Language: a Study in the Medieval Theory of Knowledge* (2nd edn; London, 1984). M. Amsler, *Etymology and Grammatical Discourse in Late Antiquity and the Early Middle Ages* (Amsterdam/Philadelphia, 1989). F. M. Clover and R. S. Humphreys, eds, *Tradition and Innovation in Late Antiquity* (Madison, 1989). G. Wieland, 'Plato or Aristotle – a Real Alternative in Medieval Philosophy?', in J. F. Wippel, ed., *Studies in Medieval Philosophy* (Washington, D.C., 1987); C. J. de Vogel, 'Platonism and Christianity: a Mere Antagonism or Profound Common Ground?', *Vigiliae Christianae*, xxxix (1985), 1–62 (a discursive examination of the two outlooks, mainly but not exclusively in the early Christian period); H. G. Senger, 'Aristotelismus vs. Platonismus. Zur Konkurrenz von zwei Archetypen der Philosophie im Spätmittelalter', in A. Zimmermann, ed., *Aristotelisches Erbe im arabisch-lateinischen Mittelalter* (Berlin/New York, 1986; Miscellanea Medievalia). *La Notion de Liberté au Moyen Age: Islam. Byzance, Occident* (Paris, 1985). A. Funkenstein, *Theology and the Scientific Imagination from the Middle Ages to the Seventeenth Century* (Princeton, 1986). B. P. Gaybba, *Aspects of the Medieval History of Theology: Twelfth to Fourteenth Centuries* (Pretoria, 1988). J. J. E. Gracia, *Introduction to the Problem of Individuation in the Early Middle Ages*, (Munich/Vienna/Washington, 1984). P. Allen, *The Concept of Woman: the Aristotelian Revolution 750 BC–AD 1250* (Montreal/London, 1985) (and see also on this subject, E. Ennen, *Frauen im Mittelalter* (Munich, 1984)). *Sewanee Mediaeval Colloquium: Occasional Papers 2* (Sewanee, Tenn., 1985), includes J. McEvoy, '*Philia* and *Amicitia*: the Philosophy of Friendship from Plato to Aquinas'. F. Oakley,

Omnipotence, Covenant and Order: An Excursion in the History of Ideas from Abelard to Leibniz (Ithaca/London, 1984), examines the concept of divine power, absolute and ordained, and see also on the theme, T. Rudavsky, ed., *Divine Omniscience and Omnipotence in Medieval Philosophy: Islamic, Jewish and Christian Perspectives* (Dordrecht/Boston/Lancaster, 1985).

2. SOURCES

Some source material will also be found interspersed with the bibliographies of secondary literature.

Early
M. Masi, tr., *Boethian Number Theory: A Translation of the 'De Institutione Arithmetica'* (Amsterdam, 1983). *Boethius's 'In Ciceronis Topica'*, tr. E. Stump (New York/London, 1988).

Carolingian
Eriugena: G. H. Allard, comp., *Johannis Scoti Eriugenae, Periphyseon: Indices Générales* (Montreal/Paris, 1983); *Periphyseon*, tr. I. P. Sheldon-Williams (revised by J.J. O'Meara) (Montreal/Paris, 1987); E. Jeauneau, ed., *Ambigua ad Iohannem iuxta Iohannis Scotti Eriugenae Latinam Interpretationem* (Turnhout/Leuven, 1988).
    Jonas of Orleans, *The 'De institutione regia' A Ninth-century Political Tract*, tr. R. W. Dyson (Smithtown, N. J., 1983).

Tenth Century
Abbo of Fleury, *Quaestiones Grammaticales*, ed. and tr. A. Guerreau-Jalabert (Paris, 1982).

Eleventh-century
R. B. C. Huygens, ed., *Beringerius Turonensis Rescriptum contra Lanfrannum* (Corpus Christianorum, Continuatio Medievalis, lxxxiv–lxxxivA; Turnhout, 1988).
    J-C. Didier, 'Hugues de Breteuil, Evêque de Langres († 1050), Lettre à Bérenger de Tours sur la Présence Réelle', *Recherches Augustiniennes*, xvi (1981), 289–331.
    J. Hopkins, ed. and tr., *A New Interpretative Translation of St Anselm's 'Monologion' and 'Proslogion'* (Minneapolis, 1986).
    G. R. Evans, *A Concordance of the Works of St Anselm* (4 vols.; New York, 1984).
    G. R. Evans and A. S. Abulafia, eds, *The Works of Gilbert Crispin Abbot of Westminster* (Oxford, 1986).
    Pseudo-Bede, De mundi celestis terrestrisque constitutione: A Treatise on the Universe and Soul, ed. and tr. C. Burnett (London, 1985).

Twelfth-century
J. Barrow, C. Burnett and D. Luscombe, 'A Checklist of the Manuscripts Containing the Writings of Peter Abelard and Heloise and Other Works Closely Associated with Abelard and his School', *Revue d'Histoire des Textes*, xiv–xv (1984–1985), 183–302. S. Buzzetti, ed., *Sententie Magistri Petri Abelard (Sententie Hermanni))* (Florence, 1983). E. R. Smits, ed., *Peter Abelard Letters IX–XIV: An Edition with an Introduction* (Groningen, 1983). C. Burnett, 'Peter Abelard *Soliloquium*. A Critical Edition', *Studi Medievali*, 3rd ser., xxv (1984), 857–94. *Petri Abaelardi Opera Theologica*, vol. 3: *Theologia 'Summi Boni' Theologia 'Scholarium'*, eds E. M. Buytaert and C. J. Mews (Turnhout, 1987).

P. Gautier Dalché, *La 'Descriptio Mappe Mundi' de Hugues de Saint-Victor: Texte Inédit avec Introduction et Commentaire* (Paris, 1988). J. Chatillon, ed., *Trois Opuscules Spirituels de Richard de Saint-Victor* (Paris, 1986). E. Martineau, ed. and tr., *Achard de Saint-Victor. L'Unité de Dieu et la Pluralité des Créatures/De Unitate Dei et Pluralitate Creaturarum* (accompanied by a lesser text) (Saint-Lambert des Bois, 1987).

G. Maurach, ed., *Wilhelm von Conches, Philosophia* (Pretoria, 1980).

The Latin Rhetorical Commentaries by Thierry of Chartres, ed. K. M. Fredborg (Toronto, 1988). H. J. Westra, ed., *The Commentary on Martianus Capella's 'De Nuptiis Philologiae et Mercurii' attributed to Bernardus Silvestris* (Toronto, 1986). *John of Salisbury's 'Entheticus Maior et Minor'*, ed. and tr., J. van Laarhoven (Leiden, 1987).

Wilhelmus Lucensis, *Commentum in Tertiam Ierarchiam Dionisii Que Est de Divinis Nominibus*, ed. F. Gastaldelli (Florence, 1983).

William of St Thierry, *De Natura Corporis et Animae*, ed. and tr. (into French), M. Lemoine (Paris, 1990).

Hermann of Carinthia, *De Essentiis*, ed. and tr. C. Burnett (STGM, Band 15; Leiden/Cologne, 1982).

Alexander Nequam, *Speculum Speculationum*, ed. R. M. Thomson (Auctores Britannici Medii Aevi; Oxford, 1988).

S. Ebbesen and L. B. Mortensen, eds, *Andreae Sunonis Filii Hexaemeron* (2 vols, Copenhagen, 1985–8) (a late twelfth-century metrical poem reflecting contemporary Parisian theology of which Andrew was a master *c.* 1180).

The transmission of ancient texts and Arabic thought

R. J. Long, 'Alfred of Sareshel's Commentary on the Pseudo-Aristotelian *De Plantis*. A Critical Edition', *MS*, xlvii (1985), 125–67. Adelard of Bath, *The First Latin Translations of Euclid's 'Elements' commonly ascribed to Adelard of Bath, Books I–VIII and Books X.36–XV.2*, ed. H. L. L. Busard (Toronto, 1983). F. M. Schroeder and R. B. Todd, ed. & tr., *Two Greek Aristotelian Commentators on the Intellect: the 'De intellectu' attributed to Alexander of Aphrodisias and Themistius' Paraphrase of Aristotle 'De anima' 3.4–8* (Medieval Sources in Translation; Toronto, 1990) (See for this whole subject, R. Sorabji, ed., *Aristotle Transformed: the Ancient Commentators and their Influence* (Ithaca, 1990)). *Al-Farabi's Commentary and Short Treatise on Aristotle's De Interpretatione*, translated with an Introduction and Notes by F. W. Zimmermann (London, 1981). Ibn Sina, *Remarks and Admonitions, Part One: Logic*, tr. S. C. Inati (Toronto, 1984); Avicenna Latinus: *Liber de Philosophia Prima sive Scientia Divina V–X*, ed. S. van Riet (Introduction Doctrinale par G. Verbeke) (Louvain/Leiden, 1980); *Liber de Philosophia Prima sive Scientia Divina I–X Lexiques*, by S. van Riet (Louvain-la-Neuve/Leiden, 1983); *Liber Tertius Naturalium De Generatione et Corruptione*, ed. S. van Riet (Introduction Doctrinale par G. Verbeke) (Louvain-la-Neuve/Leiden, 1987); Avicenna Latinus, *Liber Quartus Naturalium De Actionibus et Passionibus Qualitatum Primarum*, ed. S. van Riet (Introduction Doctrinale par G. Verbeke) (Leiden, 1989). *Averroes, Middle Commentaries on Aristotle's 'Categories' and 'De Interpretatione'*, tr. C. E. Butterworth (Princeton, 1983). An important extract of the 'Metaphysics' is presented in A. Martin, tr., *Averroes Grand Commentaire de la Métaphysique d'Aristote[...]Livre Lam-Lamda* (Paris, 1984) and C. Genequand, *Ibn Rushd's Metaphysics: A Translation with Introduction of Ibn Rushd's Commentary on Aristotle's 'Metaphysics' Book Lam* (2nd edn; Leiden, 1986). *Alfred of Sareshel's Commentary on the Metheora of Aristotle: Critical Edition, Introduction and Notes*, ed. J. K. Otte (STGM, Band 19; Leiden, etc., 1988). P. Lucentini, ed., *Liber Alcidi De Immortalitate Animae: Studio e Edizione Critica* (Naples, 1984) (argues that this anonymous work which is difficult to date was written in twelfth-century Norman Italy). Proclus, *Commentaire sur le Parménide de Platon Traduction de Guillaume de Moerbeke, 1: Livres I–IV* and *2: Livres V–VII et Notes Marginales de Nicolas de Cues*, ed. C. Steel (Louvain, 1982–4). Constantine the African, *Liber de Coitu El Tratado de Andrologia*

Estudio y Edición Crítica, ed. and tr. (into Spanish), E. M. Cartelle (Santiago de Compostela, 1983).

Jewish
Abraham ibn Daud, *The Exalted Faith*, tr. N. M. Samuelson (ed. G. Weiss) (London/ Toronto, 1986), on the theme of the congruence of Judaism and philosophy.

Thirteenth-century
C. Lafleur, *Quatre Introductions à la Philosophie au XIIIe Siècle: Textes Critiques et Etude Historique* (Montreal/Paris, 1988). F. Hudry, ed. and tr., *Le Livre des XXIV Philosophes* (Grenoble, 1989) (an anonymous treatise of the early thirteenth century, which had an important influence especially on the late medieval mystical tradition). William of Auvergne, *The Trinity or the First Principle*, tr. R. J. Teske and F. C. Wade (Milwaukee, 1989). *Philippi Cancellarii Parisiensis Summa de Bono*, ed. N. Wicki (2 vols; Berne, 1985). *Guillelmus de Morbecca, Proclus: Elementatio Theologica*, ed. H. Boese (Louvain, 1987). Roger Bacon, *Compendium of the Study of Theology Edition and Translation with Introduction and Notes*, ed. T. S. Maloney (STGM, Band 20; Leiden etc., 1988). *Alberti Magni Opera*, tom. IV, vol. i: *Physica Libri 1–4*, ed. P. Hossfeld (Münster, 1987). J. J. Scanlan, tr., *Albert the Great. Man and the Beasts. De Animalibus (Books 22–26)* (Binghampton, 1987). The Leonine edition of Aquinas' works is extended with *Quaestiones Disputatae de Malo* (Rome/Paris, 1982), *Sentencia Libri de Anima* (Rome/Paris, 1984) and *Sentencia Libri de Sensu et Sensato cuius secundus tractatus est De Memoria et Reminiscentia* (Paris, 1985). S. Tugwell, ed. and tr., *Albert and Thomas: Selected Writings* (New York/Mahwah, N. J., 1988), presents writings bearing on the spirituality of these figures. R. A. Gauthier, ed., *Anonymi Magistri Artium (c. 1245–1250) Lectura in Librum de Anima a Quodam Discipulo Reportata (Ms. Roma Naz. V. E. 828)* (Grottaferrata, 1985), presents an outstanding text for the history both of teaching in the arts faculty and of the reception of Aristotle, confirming earlier observations on the theological perspective adopted in the first phase. L. M. de Rijk, *Some Earlier Parisian Tracts on the Distinctiones Sophismatum* (Nijmegen, 1988), edits representatives of teaching in the thirteenth century. T. S. Maloney, tr., *Three Treatments of Universals by Roger Bacon* (Binghampton, N.Y., 1989). On topics of most philosophical concern in Kilwardby's Sentence commentary: Robert Kilwardby, *Quaestiones in librum primum Sententiarum* ed. J. Schneider (Munich, 1986); Robert Kilwardby, *Quaestiones in librum tertium Sententiarum, 2: Tugendlehre* ed. G. Leibold (Munich, 1985). On other sources of his thought: Robert Kilwardby, *On Time and Imagination: 'De tempore' 'De spiritu fantastico'*, ed. P. O. Lewry (Auctores Britannici Medii Aevi; Oxford, 1987); Robert Kilwardby, *De Natura Relationis* and *In Donati Artem Maiorem III*, ed. L. Schmücker (Brixen, 1984). Iohannes Pecham, *Quodlibeta quatuor: Quodlibeta I–III*, ed. G. J. Etzkorn; *Quodlibeta IV (Romanum)*, ed. F. Delormé (rev. G. J. Etzkorn) (Grottaferrata, 1989). The text of Siger de Brabant, *Quaestiones in Metaphysicam* is reviewed by W. Dunphy and A. Maurer from the Munich and Cambridge manuscripts (Philosophes Médiévaux, 24–5; Louvain-la-Neuve, 1981–3). *Boethii Daci Quaestiones super IVm Meteorologicorum*, ed. G. Fioravanti (Copenhagen, 1979); Boethius of Dacia, *On the Supreme Good, On the Eternity of the World, On Dreams*, tr. J. F. Wippel (Toronto, 1987). Guilelmus de la Mare, *Scriptum in Primum Librum Sententiarum*, ed. H. Kraml (Munich, 1989). A. J. Celano, 'Peter of Auvergne's Questions on Books I and II of the *Ethica Nicomachea*. A Study and Critical Edition', *MS*, xlviii (1986), 1–110. The *Corpus Philosophorum Teutonicorum Medii Aevi* is publishing the important work, *De summo bono*, of Albert's pupil, Ulrich von Strassburg, of which have appeared to date Liber 2, Tractatus i–4, ed. A. de Libera (Hamburg, 1987), Liber 4, Tractatus 1–2.7, ed. S. Pieperhoff (Hamburg, 1987). R. C. Dales and O. Argerami, eds, *Medieval Latin Texts on the Eternity of the World* (Leiden, 1991).

3. SECONDARY WORKS (LISTED BY CHAPTER DIVISIONS, OMITTING CH. 1)

CHAPTER 2. FROM ANCIENT WORLD TO MIDDLE AGES: ADAPTATION AND TRANSMISSION

1. St Augustine

H. Chadwick, *Augustine* (Oxford, 1986). C. Kirwan, *Augustine* (The Arguments of the Philosophers; London, 1989); J. J. O'Donnell, *Augustine* (Boston, 1985); P. G. Kuntz, 'Augustine: from *Homo erro* to *Homo viator*', in L. J. Bowman, ed., *Itinerarium: the Idea of a Journey* (Salzburg, 1983). G. Reale, *L'Opera Letteraria di Agostino tra Cassiciacum e Milano: Agostino nelle Terre di Ambrogio* (Palermo, 1987) (conference papers; includes articles on *Contra academicos, De beata vita, De ordine*). L. C. Ferrari, *The Conversions of St Augustine* (Villanova, Pa., 1984). R. McMahon, *Augustine's Prayerful Ascent: An Essay on the Literary Form of the 'Confessions'* (Athens, Ga/London, 1989). R. J. O'Connell, *The Origin of the Soul in St Augustine's Later Works* (New York, 1987). G. O'Daly, *Augustine's Philosophy of the Mind* (London, 1987). L. Hoelscher, *The Reality of the Mind. St Augustine's Arguments for the Human Soul as a Spiritual Substance* (London, 1986). M. Smalbrugge, *La Nature Trinitaire de l'Intelligence Augustinienne de la Foi* (Amsterdam, 1988), though theological has much of importance on Augustine's epistemology. E. B. King and J. T. Schaefer, eds., *St Augustine and his Influence in the Middle Ages* (Sewanee, Tenn., 1988) is an important group of studies. R. A. Markus, 'Augustine's Confessions and the Controversy with Julian of Eclanum. Manicheism revisited', *Augustiniana*, xli (1991), 913–25. P. F. Fransen, 'Augustine, Pelagius and the Controversy on the Doctrine of Grace', *Louvain Studies*, xii (1987), 172–81. J. Wetzel, 'The Recovery of Free Agency in the Theology of St Augustine', *Harvard Theological Review*, lxxx (1987), 101–25. On Augustine's Platonism, specifically, see G. Madec, 'Le Néoplatonisme dans la Conversion d'Augustin. Etat d'une question centenaire', in C. Mayer and K. H. Chelius, eds, *Internationales Symposium über den Stand der Augustinus-Forschung vom 12. bis 16. April 1987* (Giessener Augustinus-Studien, I; Würzburg, 1989), pp. 9–25 and P. F. Beatrice, 'Quosdam Platonicorum Libros. The Platonic Readings of Augustine in Milan', *Vigiliae Christianae*, xliii (1989), 248–81. A. J. Stoclet, 'Le *De Civitate Dei* de S. Augustin Sa Diffusion avant 900', *Recherches Augustiniennes*, xix (1984), 185–209 and M. M. Gorman, 'The Diffusion of the Manuscripts of St Augustine's *De Doctrina Christiana* in the Early Middle Ages', *RB*, xcv (1985), 11–24, on the history of two important texts, and less centrally, E. Dekkers, 'Sur la diffusion au moyen âge des oeuvres moins connues de S. Augustin', in *Homo Spiritalis. Festgabe für Luc Verheijen, OSA*, ed. C. Mayer (Würzburg, 1987), 446–59. G. R. Evans, 'Augustine on the Soul. The Legacy of the Unanswered Questions', *Augustinianum*, xxv (1985), 283–94.

2. Boethius, his Context, Aftermath, the Liberal Arts tradition and Pre-Carolingian

E. Reiss, *Boethius* (Boston, 1982). S. Lerer, *Boethius and Dialogue. Literary Method in 'The Consolation of Philosophy'* (Princeton, 1985). R. Andrews, 'Boethius on Relation in *De Trinitate*' in M. Asztalos, ed., *The Editing of Theological and Philosophical Texts from the Middle Ages* (Acta Universitatis Stockholmiensis, Studia Latina 30; Stockholm, 1986). E. Stump, '*Hamartia* in Christian Belief: Boethius on the Trinity', in D. V. Stump, J. A. Arieti, L. Gerson and E. Stump, eds, *Hamartia: the Concept of Error in the Western Tradition* (New York/Toronto, 1983). G. d'Onofrio, 'Dialectic and theology. Boethius' *Opuscula Sacra* and their early medieval readers', *SM*, 3rd ser., xxvii (1986), 45–67.

S. Krautschick, *Cassiodor und die Politik seiner Zeit* (Bonn, 1983); S. Leanza, ed., *Atti della Settimana di Studi su Flavio Magno Aurelio Cassiodoro. Cosenza-Squillace, 19–24 settembre 1983* (Soveria Mannelli, 1986). L. Viscido, *Studi sulle 'Variae' di Cassiodoro* (Soveria

Mannelli, 1987). S. J. B. Barnish, 'The Work of Cassiodorus after his Conversion', *Latomus*, xlviii (1989), 157–87.

J. M. Petersen, *The Dialogues of Gregory the Great in their Late Antique Cultural Background* (Toronto, 1984). G. R. Evans, *The Thought of Gregory the Great* (Cambridge, 1986). J. M. Petersen, '"Homo omnino Latinus?" The Theological and Cultural Background of Pope Gregory the Great', *Speculum*, lxii (1987), 529–51.

D. L. Wagner, ed., *The Seven Liberal Arts in the Middle Ages* (Bloomington, Ind., 1983), is an important collection on this tradition, for background of which see I. Hadot, *Arts Libéraux et Philosophie dans la Pensée Antique* (Paris, 1984). J. J. Contreni, *Codex Laudunensis 468: A Ninth-century Guide to Virgil, Sedulius and the Liberal Arts* (Turnhout, 1984), studies a school-text. D. Shanzer, *A Philosophical and Literary Commentary on Martianus Capella's 'De Nuptiis Philologiae et Mercurii', Book I* (New York/London, 1986). M. Bernhard, 'Glossen zur Arithmetik des Boethius' in S. Krämer and M. Bernhard, eds, *Scire Litteras Forschungen zum mittelalterlichen Geistesleben* (Munich, 1988). N. J. Green-Pedersen, *The Tradition of the Topics in the Middle Ages. The Commentaries on Aristotle's and Boethius' Topics* (Munich, 1984). F. Troncarelli, *Tradizioni Perdute. La Consolatio Philosophiae nell' Alto Medioevo* (Padua, 1980); Troncarelli, *Boethiana Aetas. Modelli Grafici e Fortuna Manoscritta della Consolatio Philosophiae tra IX e XII Secolo* (Alessandria, 1987); Troncarelli, 'Boezio nel circolo d'Alcuino. Le più antiche glosse carolinge alla *Consolatio Philosophiae*', *Recherches Augustiniennes*, xxii (1987), 223–41. Troncarelli, 'La Più Antica Interpretazione della *Consolatio Philosophica*', *Nuova Rivista Storica*, lxxii (1988), 501–50. J. C. Frakes, *The Fate of Fortune in the Early Middle Ages. The Boethian Tradition* (STGM, Band 23; Leiden etc., 1988). A. J. Minnis, ed., *The Medieval Boethius, Studies in the Vernacular Translations of the De Consolatione Philosophiae* (Cambridge, 1987).

J. Fontaine, *Tradition et Actualité chez Isidore de Séville* (London, 1988) (collected studies).

G. H. Brown, *Bede the Venerable* (Boston, 1987); G. Bonner et al., eds, *St Cuthbert, his Cult and his Community to AD 1200* (Woodbridge, 1989).

3. CAROLINGIAN

R. McKitterick, *The Carolingians and the Written Word* (Cambridge, 1989). J. J. Contreni, 'The Carolingian Renaissance' in W. Treadgold, eds., *Renaissances Before the Renaissance: Cultural Revivals of Late Antiquity and the Middle Ages* (Stanford, 1984); M. L. Colish, 'Carolingian Debates over *Nihil* and *Tenebrae*: a Study in Theological Method', *Speculum*, lxix (1984), 757–95; R. E. Sullivan, 'The Carolingian Age: Reflections on its Place in the History of the Middle Ages', *Speculum*, lxiv (1989), 267–306, is an excellent review of the state of Carolingian studies, including the intellectual scene. B. M. Kaczynski, *Greek in the Carolingian Age: The St Gall Manuscripts* (Cambridge, Mass., 1989), focuses on this important topic through consideration of one centre. See also M. Herren, *The Sacred Nectar of the Greeks: the Study of Greek in the West in the Early Middle Ages* (London, 1989).

John Scotus Eriugena
J. J. O'Meara, *Eriugena* (Oxford, 1988) and D. Moran, *The Philosophy of John Scottus Eriugena: A Study of Idealism in the Middle Ages* (Cambridge, 1989) review and extend the scholarship on this figure, of whom Moran offers a major reinterpretation. *Jean Scot Ecrivain*, ed. G.-H. Allard (Montreal/Paris, 1986) (conference proceedings). *Eriugena Redivivus. Zur Wirkungsgeschichte seines Denkens im Mittelalter und im Ubergang zur Neuzeit*, ed. W. Beierwaltes (Heidelberg, 1986) (conference proceedings). E. Jeaneau, *Etudes Erigéniennes* (Paris, 1987), consists largely though not exclusively of previously printed studies. G. Madec, *Jean Scot et ses Auteurs: Annotations Erigéniennes* (Paris, 1988).

A. Wohlmann, *L'Homme, le Monde Sensible et le Péché dans la Philosophie de Jean Scot Erigène* (Paris, 1987). W. Lourdaux and D. Verhelst, eds, *Benedictine Culture 750–1050* (Louvain, 1983), contains C. Steel, '*Nobis ratio sequenda est*: Réflexions sur le rationalisme de Jean Scot Erigène'. G. A. Piemonte, '*Vita in Omnia Pervenit*'. El Vitalismo *Eriugeniano y la Influencia de Mario Victorino* (Buenos Aires, 1988). E. Porcelloni, 'Il problema della derivazione del mondo da Dio in Giovanni Scoto Eriugena', *Euntes Docete*, xl (1987), 463–88. G. d'Onofrio, 'Giovanni Scoto e Remigio di Auxerre. A proposito di alcuni commenti altomedievali a Boezio', *SM*, 3rd ser., xxii (1981), 587–693. P. Rossi, 'Giovanni Scoto nel suo tempo. L'organizzazione del sapere in età carolingia', *SM*, 3rd ser., xxix (1988), 445–55. W. Otten, 'The Interplay of Nature and Man in the *Periphyseon* of Johannes Scottus Eriugena', *Vivarium*, xxviii (1990), 1–16.

G. Schrimpf, 'Die ethischen Implikationen der Auseinandersetzung zwischen Hraban und Gottschalk um die Prädestinationslehre', *Archiv für Geschichte der Philosophie*, lxviii (1986), 153–73. D. E. Nineham, 'Gottschalk of Orbais, Reactionary or Precursor of the Reformation?', *Journal of Ecclesiastical History*, xl (1989), 1–18.

CHAPTER 3. THE CENTRAL MIDDLE AGES – LOGIC, THEOLOGY AND COSMOLOGY

Lourdaux and Verhelst, *Benedictine Culture*: see especially, P. Riché, 'Les moines bénédictins, maîtres d'école (VIIIe–XIe siècles)' and M. L. Arduini, '*Magistra Ratione: Auctoritas, Traditio, Ratio* von Anselm bis Adelard von Bath'. B. M. Olsen, *L'Etude des Auteurs Classiques Latins aux XIe et XIIe Siècles* (3 vols; Paris, 1982–9). E. Rozanne Elder, ed., *From Cloister to Classroom: Monastic and Scholastic Approaches to Truth* (Kalamazoo, 1986) has several studies of particular interest and relevance. D. Nebbiai-Dalla Guarda, *La Bibliothèque de l'Abbaye de Saint-Denis en France du IXe au XVIIIe Siècle* (Paris, 1985) is a reconstruction of the monastic library of the abbey over the centuries. P. Riché, *Ecoles et Enseignement dans le Haut Moyen Age: Fin du Ve Siècle–Milieu du XIe Siècle* (2nd edn, Paris, 1989) (originally published as *Les Ecoles et l'Enseignement dans l'Occident Chrétien*). C. M. Radding, *The Origins of Medieval Jurisprudence, Pavia and Bologna 850–1150* (New Haven/London, 1988). V. I. Flint, *Ideas in the Medieval West: Texts and their Contexts* (London, 1988) is a stimulating collection concentrating on the central period.

P. Riché, *Gerbert d'Aurillac Le Pape de L'An Mil* (Paris, 1987).

Th. G. Bucher, 'Petrus Damiani, ein Freund der Logik?', *Freiburger Zeitschrift für Philosophie und Theologie*, xxxvi (1989), 267–310.

Anselm

R. W. Southern, *Saint Anselm, A Portrait in a Landscape* (Cambridge, 1990). S. Vanni Rovighi, *Introduzione a Anselmo d'Aosta* (Bari, 1987). G. R. Evans, *Anselm* (Wilton, Conn., 1989). Y. Cattin, *La Preuve de Dieu. Introduction à la Lecture du Proslogion d'Anselme de Canterbury* (Paris, 1986). H. Külling, *Wahrheit als Richtigkeit, Eine Untersuchung zur Schrift De Veritate von Anselm von Canterbury* (Berne, 1984). P. Gilbert, *Dire l'Ineffable. Lecture du Monologion de S. Anselme* (Paris, 1984); Gilbert, *Le Proslogion de S. Anselme. Silence de Dieu et Joie de l'Homme* (Rome, 1990). M. Parodi, *Il Conflitto dei Pensieri Studio su Anselmo d'Aosta* (Bergamo, 1988). E. Bertola, 'I precedenti del metodo di Anselmo di Canterbury nella storia dottrinale cristiana', *RTAM*, 1 (1983), 99–144. W. Christe, '*Sola ratione*. Zur Begründung der Methode des *intellectus fidei* bei Anselm von Canterbury', *Theologie und Philosophie*, lx (1985), 341–75. R. Schönberger, 'Responsio Anselmi. Anselms Selbstinterpretation in seiner Replik auf Gaunilo', *Freiburger Zeitschrift für Philosophie und Theologie*, xxxvi (1989), 3–46. *Les Mutations Socio-Culturelles au tournant des XIe–XIIe Siècles Etudes Anselmiennes. Colloque Organisé par le CNRS sous la présidence de M. Jean Pouilloux membre de l'Institut. Abbaye Nôtre-Dame du Bec Le*

Bec-Hellouin 11-16 juillet 1982 (Colloques Internationaux du Centre National de la Recherche Scientifique; Paris, 1984), is an excellent collection on the context, character and method of Anselm's thought.

A. Sapir Abulafia, 'An Attempt by Gilbert Crispin, Abbot of Westminster, at Rational Argument in the Jewish-Christian Debate', *Studia Monastica*, xxvi (1984), 55–74. Abulafia, 'The *Ars Disputandi* of Gilbert Crispin, Abbot of Westminster (1085–1117)', in *Ad Fontes Opstellen aangeboden aan Prof. Dr C. van de Kieft*, ed. C. M. Cappon *et al.* (Amsterdam, 1984).

C. Burnett, ed., *Adelard of Bath: An English Scientist and Arabist of the Early Twelfth Century* (London, 1987).

P. Dronke, ed., *A History of Twelfth-century Western Philosophy* (Cambridge, 1988).

Ph. Delhaye, *Enseignement et Morale au XIIe Siècle* (Fribourg/Paris, 1988), collects three previously published studies.

S. C. Ferruolo, 'The Twelfth-century Renaissance', in Treadgold, ed., *Renaissances before the Renaissance* [see above, 3.2.3].

G. H. Allard and S. Lusignan, eds, *Les Arts Mécaniques au Moyen Age* (Montreal/Paris, 1982), includes discussion of aspects of this topic as perceived by Hugh of St Victor.

E. Dutton, 'The Uncovering of the *Glosae super Platonem* of Bernard of Chartres', *MS*, xlvi (1984), 192–221, argues for this ascription of a *Timaeus* commentary. G. R. Evans, 'The Uncompleted "Heptateuchon" of Thierry of Chartres', *History of Universities*, iii (1983), 1–13. J.-Ch. Payen, 'L'Utopie chez les Chartrains', *Le Moyen Âge*, xc (1984), 25–41. J. Newell, 'Rationalism at the School of Chartres', *Vivarium*, xxi (1983), 108–26. T. Gregory, 'Le Platonisme du XIIe Siècle', *RSPT*, lxxi (1987), 243–59.

F. Giusberti, *Materials for a Study of Twelfth-century Scholasticism* (History of Logic, 2; Naples, 1982), deals with the influence of logic on theology. See also, *Gilbert de Poitiers et ses Contemporains. Aux Origines de la Logica Modernorum*, eds J. Jolivet and A. de Libera (Naples, 1987).

J. H. van Engen, *Rupert of Deutz* (Berkeley, 1983) promotes revision of the thought of a theologian who was for long regarded as conservative but whose work is becoming appreciated for its innovative content. Van Engen, 'Rupert of Deutz and William of Saint-Thierry', *RB*, xciii (1983), 327–36. M. L. Arduini, *Neue Studien über Rupert von Deutz. Sieben Beiträge* (Siegburg, 1985). See also A. M. Piazzoni (as noted below).

M. L. Arduini, '"Rerum mutabilitas". Welt, Zeit, Menschenbild und "Corpus Ecclesiae-Christianitatis" bei Honorius von Regensburg (Augustodunensis). Zum Verständnis eines politischen Rationalismus im XII. Jahrhundert', *RTAM*, lii (1985), 78–108; on Honorius Augustodunensis more generally, see Flint, *Ideas in the Medieval West* (above), which includes further bibliographical guidance on this thinker, and in relation to one important aspect, S. Gersh, 'Honorius Augustodunensis and Eriugena. Remarks on the Method and Content of the *Clavis Physicae*', in *Eriugena Redivivus*, ed. Beierwaltes [see under 3.2.3 above].

M. T. Clanchy, 'Abelard's Mockery of St Anselm', *JEH*, xli (1990), 1–23 (cf. D. E. Luscombe, 'St Anselm and Abelard', *Anselm Studies*, i (1983), 207–29). C. J. Mews, 'On Dating the Works of Peter Abelard', *AHDLMA*, lii (1985), 73–134. L. Moonan, 'Abelard's Use of the *Timaeus*', *AHDLMA*, lvi (1989), 7–90. C. Mews, 'Peter Abelard's *Theologia Christiana* and *Theologia Scholarium* Re-examined', *RTAM*, lii (1985), 109–58; Mews, 'The *Sententie* of Peter Abelard', *RTAM*, liii (1986); Mews, 'The Lists of Heresies imputed to Peter Abelard', *RB*, xcv (1985), 73–110 (see too C. S. F. Burnett, 'Peter Abelard, *Confessio Fidei "Universis"*. A Critical Edition of Abelard's Reply to Accusations of Heresy', *MS*, xlviii (1986), 111–38; Mews, 'A Neglected Gloss on the "Isagoge" by Peter Abelard', *Freiburger Zeitschrift für*

Philosophie und Theologie, xxxi (1984), 35–55; Mews, 'Un Lecteur de Jérôme au XIIe Siècle, Pierre Abélard' in *Jérôme entre l'Occident et l'Orient Actes du Colloque de Chantilly (septembre 1986)*, publiés par Y.-M. Duval (Paris, 1988). E. Bertola, 'La dottrina morale di Pietro Abelardo', *RTAM*, lv (1988), 53–71. G. Boss, 'Le combat d'Abélard', *Cahiers de Civilisation Médiévale*, xxxi (1988), 17–27. *Abélard en son Temps. Actes du Colloque International organisé a l'Occasion du 9e Centenaire de la Naissance de Pierre Abélard (14–19 mai 1979)* (Paris, 1981), has important contributions on Abelard's context, the contemporary schools scene and his teaching. J. Jolivet, *Aspects de la Pensée Médiévale Abélard Doctrines du Langage* (Paris, 1987). L. M. de Rijk, 'Peter Abelard's semantics and his doctrine of Being', *Vivarium*, xxiv (1986), 85–127. L. Moonan, 'Abelard's use of the *Timaeus*', *Archives d'Histoire Doctrinale et Littéraire du Moyen Age*, lvi (1989), 7–90. F. Vergani, '"Sententiam vocum seu nominum non caute theologiae admiscuit", Ottone di Frisinga di fronte ad Abelardo', *Aevum*, lxiii (1989), 193–224. W. Eberhard, 'Ansätze zur Bewältigung ideologischer Pluralität im XII. Jahrhundert. Pierre Abélard und Anselm von Havelberg', *Historisches Jahrbuch*, cv (1985), 353–87. J. Verger and J. Jolivet, *Bernard-Abelard, ou le Cloître et l'Ecole* (Paris, 1982) is a very useful presentation of both figures. G. R. Evans, *The Mind of St Bernard of Clairvaux* (Oxford, 1983). J. Leclercq, *Recueil d'Etudes sur S. Bernard et ses Ecrits*, iv (Rome, 1987). Leclerq, *Bernard de Clairvaux* (Paris, 1989). E. Bertola, 'Libertà e grazia nel pensiero di Agostino e di Bernardo di Chiaravalle', *Doctor Communis*, xxxix (1986), 339–50. J.-P. Torrell and D. Bouthillier, *Pierre le Vénérable et sa Vision du Monde, sa Vie son Oeuvre. L'Homme et le Démon* (Louvain, 1986); Torrell and Bouthillier, *Pierre le Vénérable Abbé de Cluny, Le Courage de la Mesure* (Chambray-lès-Tours, 1988). A. M. Piazzoni, *Guglielmo di Saint-Thierry Il Declino dell' Ideale Monastico nel Secolo XII* (Rome, 1988), despite its restricted title has much of general interest to the context; see also A. M. Piazzoni, '"Monachus licet scholasticus". Guglielmo di Saint Thierry e Ruperto di Deutz', *SM*, 3rd ser., xxv (1985), 611–39. S. Ernst, *Gewissheit des Glaubens. Das Glaubenstraktat Hugos von St Viktor als Zugang zu seiner theologischen Systematik* (Münster, 1987; *BGPTMA*); Ernst, 'Der autonomer Ethik innerhalb des christlichen Glaubens. Moraltheologische Prinzipien nach Hugo von St Viktor', *Theologie und Philosophie*, lxii (1987), 216–42. F. Gasparri, 'Godefroid de Saint-Victor. Une personnalité peu connue du monde intellectuel et artistique parisien au XIIe siècle', *Scriptorium*, xxxix (1985), 57–69. L. M. de Rijk, 'Semantics and Metaphysics in Gilbert of Poitiers. A Chapter of Twelfth-century Platonism', *Vivarium*, xxvi (1988), 73–112, xxvii (1989), 1–35. W. J. Courtenay, 'Nature and the Natural in Twelfth-century Thought', is a previously unpublished study contained in his collection *Covenant and Causality* [see 1.1, above].

M. Wilks, ed., *The World of John of Salisbury* (Oxford, 1984). G. Dotto, *Giovanni di Salisbury: La Filosofia come Sapienza* (Assisi, 1986). E. Jeauneau, 'Jean de Salisbury et la Lecture des Philosophes', *Revue des Etudes Augustiniennes*, xxix (1983), 145–74. K. S. B. Keats-Rohan, 'John of Salisbury and Education in Twelfth-century Paris from the Account of his *Metalogicon*', *History of Universities*, vi (1986–7), 1–45. Keats-Rohan, 'The Chronology of John of Salisbury's Studies in France. A Reading of *Metalogicon* II. 10', *SM*, 3rd ser., xxviii (1987), 193–203. C. J. Nederman and J. Brückmann, 'Aristotelianism in John of Salisbury's *Policraticus*', *Journal of the History of Philosophy*, xxi (1983), 203–29. C. J. Nederman, 'Knowledge Virtue and the Path to Wisdom. The unexamined Aristotelianism of John of Salisbury's *Metalogicon*', *MS*, li (1989), 268–86. Nederman, 'The Aristotelian Doctrine of the Mean and John of Salisbury's Concept of Liberty', *Vivarium*, xxiv (1986), 128–42.

R. W. Hunt (ed. M. Gibson), *The Schools and the Cloister. The Life and Writings of Alexander Nequam (1157–1217)* (Oxford, 1984).

Among theological studies which bear on the themes reviewed may be noted M. Aliotta, *La Teologia del Peccato in Alano di Lille* (Palermo, 1986); G. Macy, *The Theologies of the Eucharist in the Early Scholastic Period. A Study of the Salvific Function of the Sacrament According to the Theologians, c. 1080–c. 1220* (Oxford, 1984); J. Bougerol, *La Théologie de l'Espérance aux XIIe et XIIIe Siècles*, 2 volumes (Paris, 1985).

S. Ebbesen, '*Corpus Philosophorum Danicorum Medii Aevi*, Archbishop Andrew (†1228) and Twelfth-century Techniques of Argumentation', in Asztalos, ed., *The Editing of Theological and Philosophical Texts* [see 3.2.2, above].

T. Stiefel, *The Intellectual Revolution in Twelfth-century Europe* (New York, 1985).

B. McGinn, *The Calabrian Abbot Joachim of Fiore in the History of Western Thought* (New York/London, 1985).

The Bible

C. F. R. De Hamel, *Glossed Books of the Bible and the Origins of the Paris Booktrade* (Woodbridge, 1984), considers the physical aspects of glossing. G. R. Evans, *The Language and Logic of the Bible: the Earlier Middle Ages* (Cambridge, 1984). P. Riché and G. Lobrichon, eds, *Le Moyen Age et la Bible* (Paris, 1984). B. Smalley, *The Gospels in the Schools c. 1100–c.1280* (London, 1985).

A. S. Abulafia, 'Jewish–Christian Disputations and the Twelfth-century Renaissance', *Journal of Medieval History*, xv (1989), 105–25. See also, V. I. J. Flint, 'Anti-Jewish Literature and Attitudes in the Twelfth Century' in Flint, *Ideas in the Medieval West* [above].

J. Fried, ed., *Schulen und Studium in sozialen Wandel des hohen und späten Mittelalters* (Sigmaringen, 1986), has among other studies the following of general interest to this and the later period: A. Wendehorst, 'Wer konnte im Mittelalter lesen und schreiben?'; P. Johanek, 'Klosterstudien im 12. Jahrhundert'; J. Verger, 'A propos de la Naissance de l'Université de Paris: Contexte Social, Enjeu Politique, Portée Intellectuelle'; H. G. Walther, 'Die Anfänge des Rechtstudiums und die kommunale Welt Italiens im Hochmittelalter'; J. Miethke, 'Die Kirche und die Universitäten im 13. Jahrhundert'; R. Schneider, 'Studium und Zisterzienserorden'.

CHAPTER 4. NEW SOURCES AND NEW INSTITUTIONS

Arabic Thought and the Translations

O. Leaman, *An Introduction to Medieval Islamic Philosophy* (Cambridge, 1985). C. Sirat, *A History of Jewish Philosophy in the Middle Ages* (Cambridge, 1985). Sirat, *La Philosophie Juive Médiévale en Terre d'Islam* (Paris, 1988); *La Philosophie Juive Médiévale en Pays de Chrétienté* (Paris, 1988). Sirat, 'Les philosophes juifs d'Espagne au moyen âge et leurs rapports avec la philosophie arabe et chrétienne', *Revue des Etudes Juives*, cxliv (1985), 39–56.

A. Zimmermann, ed., *Aristotelisches Erbe im arabisch-lateinischen Mittelalter* (Berlin/New York, 1986; Miscellanea Medievalia), has a number of specialist studies of texts of Averroes and of the translating work of William of Moerbeke.

G. Verbeke, *Avicenna Grundleger einer neuen Metaphysik* (Wiesbaden, 1983). J. R. Michot, *La Destinée de l'Homme selon Avicenne* (Louvain, 1986).

B. S. Kogan, *Averroes and the Metaphysics of Causation* (Albany, N.Y., 1985); O. Leaman, *Averroes and his Philosophy* (Oxford, 1988). H. A. Davidson, 'Averroes on the Material Intellect', *Viator*, xvii (1986), 91–137. Davidson, 'Averroes on the Active Intellect as a Cause of Existence', *Viator*, xviii (1987), 191–225.

N. Roth, *Maimonides: Essays and Texts, 850th Anniversary* (Madison, Wisc., 1985). O. Leaman, *Moses Maimonides* (Arabic Thought and Culture; London, 1990). J. A. Buijs, ed., *Maimonides, A Collection of Critical Essays* (Notre Dame, Ind., 1988). F. Niewöhner, *Maimonides Aufklärung und Toleranz im Mittelalter* (Heidelberg, 1988). M. Kellner, *Dogma in Medieval Jewish Thought from Maimonides to Abravanel* (Oxford, 1986).

H. A. Davidson, *Proofs for Eternity, Creation and the Existence of God in Medieval Islamic and Jewish Philosophy* (Oxford, 1987): an authoritative account of discussion of these topics and influence on it of classical ideas.

M. E. Marmura, ed., *Islamic Theology and Philosophy: Studies in Honor of George F. Hourani* (Albany, N.Y., 1984).

J. Beer, ed., *Medieval Translators and their Craft* (Kalamazoo, 1989).

Universities

J. I. Catto, ed., *The Early Oxford Schools* (The History of Oxford University, 1; Oxford, 1984). S. C. Ferruolo, *The Origins of the University: The Schools of Paris and their Critics 1100–1215* (Stanford, 1985). A. B. Cobban, *The Medieval English Universities: Oxford and Cambridge to c. 1500* (Aldershot, 1988). D. R. Leader, *The University to 1546* (A History of Cambridge University, vol. 1; Cambridge, 1988). B. Andenmatten, *et al.*, eds., *Ecoles et Vie Intellectuelle à Lausanne au Moyen Age* (Lausanne, 1987). R. W. Southern, 'The Changing Role of Universities in Medieval Europe', *Historical Research* lx (1987), 133–146.

CHAPTER 5. ARISTOTELIAN PHILOSOPHY IN THE UNIVERSITY

and

CHAPTER 6. ARISTOTELIAN PHILOSOPHY AND CHRISTIAN THEOLOGY – SYSTEM BUILD-
ING AND CONTROVERSY

The argument of R. A. Gauthier, in 'Notes sur les débuts (1225–1240) du premier "averroisme"', *RSPT*, lxvi (1982), 321–74, and 'Le traité *De Anima et De Potenciis Eius* d'un Maître ès Arts (vers 1225)', *RSPT*, lxvi (1982), 3–56, has been endorsed and advanced by the dating proposed by N. Wicki for the *Summa de Bono* of Philip the Chancellor (see under 1.2, 'Sources', above), with the result that the terminus of 1230, long established for the first influence of Averroism at Paris, has now to be shifted back significantly.

J. Rohls, *Wilhelm von Auvergne und der mittelalterliche Aristotelismus* (Munich, 1980).

L. Hödl, 'Das "intelligibile" in der scholastischen Erkenntnislehre des XIII. Jahrhunderts', *Freiburger Zeitschrift für Philosophie und Theologie*, xxx (1983), 345–72.

J. G. Bougerol, 'La Glose sur les Sentences du Manuscrit Vat. Lat. 691', *Antonianum*, lv (1980), 108–73, throws interesting light on the Franciscan studium at Paris in the period 1236–1245.

R. W. Southern, *Robert Grosseteste. The Growth of an English Mind in Medieval Europe* (Oxford, 1986), a powerfully argued reinterpretation of Grosseteste's intellectual development. P. Raedts, *Richard Rufus of Cornwall and the Tradition of Oxford Theology* (Oxford, 1987), studies the first Franciscan theologian at Oxford whose works have survived. On the whole period, see also Catto, *Early Oxford Schools* [under 3.4, above]. M. Huber-Legnani, *Roger Bacon Lehrer der Anschaulichkeit. Der franziskanische Gedanke und die Philosophie des Einzelnen* (Freiburg i. B., 1984). F. Alessio, *Introduzione a Roggero Bacone* (Rome, 1985). D. C. Lindberg, 'Roger Bacon and the Origins of *Perspectiva* in the West', in E. Grant and J. E. Murdoch, eds, *Mathematics and its Applications to Science and Natural Philosophy in the Middle Ages* (Cambridge, 1987). Lindberg, 'Science as Handmaiden. Roger Bacon and the Patristic Tradition', *Isis*, lxxviii (1987), 518–36.

J. Brams and W. Vanhamel, eds, *Guillaume de Moerbeke. Recueil d'Etudes à l'Occasion du 700e Anniversaire de sa Mort (1286)* (Louvain, 1989), has among the contributions of most general interest: G. Verbeke, 'Moerbeke, traducteur et interprète; un texte et une pensée', A. P. Bagliani, 'Guillaume de Moerbeke et la cour pontificale'; C. Steel,

'Guillaume de Moerbeke et saint Thomas'. See also, R. Wielockx, 'Guillaume de Moerbeke réviseur de sa révision du *De Anima*', *RTAM*, liv (1987), 113–85.

Asztalos, ed., *The Editing of Theological and Philosophical Texts* [see 3.2.2, above], contains a number of studies of general interest to the historian of thought in the period: J. Hamesse, '"Reportatio" et Transmission de Textes'; N. Wicki, 'La *Pecia* dans la Tradition Manuscrite de la *Summa de Bono* de Philippe le Chancelier'; A. de Libera, 'La Littérature des *Sophismata* dans la Tradition Terministe Parisienne de la Seconde Moitié du XIIIe Siècle'.

R. Sorabji, ed., *Aristotle Transformed: the Ancient Commentators and their Influence* (Ithaca, 1990).

G. Meyer and A. Zimmermann, eds, *Albertus Magnus Doctor Universalis 1280/1980* (Mainz, 1980) contains important essays on the context and character of Albert's thought. I. Craemer-Ruegenberg, *Albertus Magnus* (Munich, 1980). A. de Libera, *Albert le Grand et la Philosophie* (Paris, 1990). P. Hossfeld, 'Die eigenen Beobachtungen des Albertus Magnus', *Archivum Fratrum Praedicatorum*, liii (1983), 147–74. P. Hossfeld, 'Die Physik des Albertus Magnus (Teil I, die Bücher 1–4), Quellen und Charakter', *Archivum Fratrum Praedicatorum*, lv (1985), 49–65. Hossfeld, 'Albertus Magnus über die Ewigkeit aus philosophischer Sicht', *Archivum Fratrum Praedicatorum*, lvi (1986), 31–48. R. Wisser, 'Albertus Magnus, ein Mensch auf dem Weg durch die Wirklichkeit', *Zeitschrift für Religions- und Geistesgeschichte*, xxxviii (1986), 311–44. R. Imbach and C. Flüeler, eds, 'Albert der Grose und die deutsche Dominkanerschule. Philosophische Perspektiven', *Freiburger Zeitschrift für Philosophie und Theologie*, Band 32 (1985), Heft 1/2), is mainly devoted to Albert's influence but note as bearing directly on his thought: B. Mojsisch, 'Grundlinien der Philosophie Alberts des Grossen' (pp. 27–44) and C. Wagner, 'Alberts Naturphilosophie im Licht der neueren Forschung (1979–1983)' (pp.65–104); and on Albert's pupil, Ulrich of Strassburg: A. de Libera, 'Ulrich de Strasbourg, lecteur d'Albert le Grand' (pp. 105–36). See also, A. de Libera, 'Philosophie et Théologie chez Albert le Grand et dans l'Ecole Dominicaine Allemande', in A. Zimmermann and G. Vuillemin-Diem, eds, *Die Kölner Universität im Mittelalter, geistige Wurzeln und soziale Wirklichkeit* (Miscellanea Mediaevalia, 20; Berlin, 1989). A. Fries, 'Zur Problematik der *Summa Theologiae* unter dem Namen des Albertus Magnus', *Franziskanische Studien*, lxx (1988), 68–91 and Fries, 'Zum Verhältnis des Albertus Magnus zur *Summa Theologiae* unter seinem Namen', *Franziskanische Studien*, lxxi (1989), 123–37. R. Wielockx, 'Zur *Summa Theologiae* des Albertus Magnus', *Ephemerides Theologicae Lovanienses*, lxvi (1990), 78–110.

R. Link-Salinger, *et al.*, eds, *A Straight Path: Studies in Medieval Philosophy and Culture. Essays in Honour of Arthur Hyman* (Washington, D. C., 1988), has important contributions on the period; see especially, D. B. Burrell, 'Aquinas's Debt to Maimonides'; M. T. Clark, 'Willing Freely According to Thomas Aquinas'; J. Hackett, 'Averroes and Roger Bacon on the Harmony of Religion and Philosophy'; A. L. Ivry, 'Averroes and the West: the First Encounter/Non-encounter'; B. S. Kogan, 'The Problem of Creation in Late Medieval Jewish Philosophy'; J. F. Wippel, 'Thomas Aquinas and the Axiom "What is Received is Received according to the Mode of the Receiver"'.

F. Corvino, *Bonaventura da Bagnoregio Francescano e Pensatore* (Bari, 1980). V. Ch. Bigi, *Studi sul Pensiero di S. Bonaventura* (Assisi, 1988). L. J. Bowman, 'What Kind of Journey is Bonaventura's *Itinerarium*?', in Bowman, ed., *Itinerarium* (see Chapter 2:1 above). R. Russo, *La Metodologia del Sapere nel Sermone di S. Bonaventura 'Unus est magister vester Christus'* (Rome 1982), considers the epistemology, as does T. Overton, 'Saint Bonaventure's Illumination Theory of Knowledge. The Reconciliation of Aristotle, Pseudo-Dionysius and Augustine', *Miscellanea Franciscana*, lxxxviii (1988), 108–21. A. Di Maio, 'La Dottrina Bonaventuriana della Natura', *Miscellanea Francescana*, lxxxix (1989), 335–92. A. Speer, 'Metaphysica reducens. Metaphysik als erste Wissenschaft im Verständnis Bonaventuras', *RTAM*, lvii (1990), 142–82, contributes, through consideration of a particular point, to the continuing revision of his significance. A. Speer, *Triplex Veritas. Wahrheitsverständnis und philosophische Denkform Bonaventuras* (Werl/Westfalen, 1987).

L. P. Gerson, ed., *Graceful Reason: Essays in Ancient and Medieval Philosophy Presented to Joseph Owens, CSSR* (Toronto, 1983), includes most pertinently: L. Sweeney, 'Are Plotinus and Albertus Magnus Neoplatonists?'; C. J. de Vogel, '*Deus Creator Omnium*: Plato and Aristotle in Aquinas' Doctrine of God'; J. A. Weisheipl, 'The Date and Context of Aquinas' *De aeternitate mundi*' (which places that treatise slightly later than was previously thought); J. F. Wippel, 'Quidditative Knowledge of God According to Thomas Aquinas'; W. Dunphy, 'Maimonides and Aquinas on Creation: a Critique of their Historians'; F. van Steenberghen, 'Thomas d'Aquin et Siger de Brabant en quête d'arguments pour le monothéisme'.

M. F. Johnson, '"Alia lectura fratris thome": A List of the New Texts of St Thomas Aquinas Found in Lincoln College Oxford, Ms. Lat. 95', *RTAM*, lvii (1990), 34–61, surveys the question of Thomas' second (Roman) Commentary on Book I of the Sentences (cf. L. E. Boyle, in *MS*, xlv (1983), 418–29).

R. Hissette, 'Albert le Grand et Thomas d'Aquin dans la Censure Parisienne du 7 mars 1277', in A. Zimmermann, ed., *Studien zur mittelalterlichen Geistesgeschichte und ihren Quellen* (Miscellanea Mediaevalia, 15; Berlin/New York, 1982). J. F. Wippel, *Metaphysical Themes in Thomas Aquinas* (Washington, D.C., 1984) (collected studies on specialist topics). R. Padellaro De Angelis, *L'Influenza del Pensiero Neoplatonico sulla Metafisica di S. Tommaso d'Aquino* (Rome, 1981). A. Zimmermann and C. Kopp, *Thomas von Aquin. Werk und Wirkung im Licht neuerer Forschungen* (Berlin/New York, 1988). R. Schenck, 'Perplexus supposito quodam. Notizen zu einem vergessenen Schlüsselbegriff thomanischer Gewissenslehre', *RTAM*, lvii (1990), 62–95.

W. Kühn, *Das Prinzipienproblem in der Philosophie des Thomas von Aquin* (Amsterdam, 1982). U. Eco, (tr. H. Bredin), *The Aesthetics of Thomas Aquinas* (Cambridge, Mass., 1988). Y. Congar, *Thomas d'Aquin, Sa Vision de la Théologie et de l'Eglise* (London, 1984; collected essays). L. Elders, *Autour de S. Thomas d'Aquin. Recueil d'Etudes sur sa Pensée Philosophique et Théoligique* (2 vols; Paris, 1987).

W. J. Hankey, *God in Himself. Aquinas' Doctrine of God as Expounded in the 'Summa Theologiae'* (Oxford, 1987). C. Hughes, *On a Complex Theory of a Simple God. An Investigation in Aquinas' Philosophical Theology* (Ithaca/London, 1989). D. J. Merriell, *To the Image of the Trinity A Study in the Development of Aquinas' Teaching* (Toronto, 1990).

W. Schmidl, *Homo Discens. Studien zur pädagogischen Anthropologie bei Thomas von Aquin* (Vienna, 1987), on an aspect of wide epistemological and psychological interest.

J. Aertsen, *Nature and Creature. Thomas Aquinas's Way of Thought* (STGM, Band 21; Leiden etc., 1988). *La Philosophie de la Nature de S. Thomas d'Aquin* (Studi tomistici, 18; Vatican City, 1982) (conference proceedings).

R. A. Gauthier, 'Notes sur Siger de Brabant. I. Siger en 1265', *RSPT*, lxvii (1983), 201–32, and Gauthier, 'Note sur Siger de Brabant (fin). II. Siger en 1272–1275. Aubry de Reims et la Scission des Normands', *RSPT*, lxviii (1984), 3–49, offer interesting sidelights on Siger's development and the university context. R. C. Dales, 'The Origin of the Doctrine of the Double Truth', *Viator*, xv (1984), 169–79. A. Maurer, 'Siger of Brabant and Theology', *MS*, l (1988), 257–78. T. P. Bukowski, 'Siger of Brabant vs. Thomas Aquinas on Theology', *The New Scholasticism*, lxi (1987), 25–32. C. J. Ryan, 'Man's Free Will in the Works of Siger of Brabant', *MS* xlv (1983), 155–99. A. Caparello, *La 'Perspectiva' in Sigieri di Brabante* (Vatican City, 1987; Studi Tomistici, 31). A. J. Celano, 'Boethius of Dacia *On the Highest Good*', *Traditio*, xliii (1987), 199–214, offers a detailed reading.

G. Wieland, *Ethica-scientia practica Die Anfänge der philosophischen Ethik im 13. Jahrhundert* (Münster W., 1981), on a topic which was both central and sensitive; on a specific phase, see also H. Borok, *Der Tugendbegriff des Wilhelm von Auvergne (1180–1249). Eine moralhistorische Untersuchung zur ideengeschichtlichen Rezeption der aristotelischen Ethik* (Düsseldorf, 1979).

L. Bianchi, *L'Errore di Aristotele La Polemica contro l'Eternità del Mondo nel XIII Secolo* (Florence, 1984) considers an important topic of controversy, as does R. C. Dales, *Medieval Discussions of the Eternity of the World* (Leiden, 1990). See also, specifically, C. Stroick, 'Die Ewigkeit der Welt in den Aristoteleskommentaren des Thomas von Aquin', *RTAM*, li (1984), 43–68. E. Grant, 'Issues in Natural Philosophy at Paris in the Late Thirteenth Century', *Medievalia et Humanistica*, n.s. xiii (1985), 75–94.

R. Hissette, 'Trois Articles de la Seconde Rédaction du *Correctorium* de Guillaume de la Mare', *RTAM*, li (1984), 230–41. L. Lunetta, 'La Pluralità delle Forme nel *Correctorium Fratris Thomae* di Guglielmo de la Mare', *SM*, 3rd ser, xxviii (1987), 729–49.

A. Maurer, *Being and Knowing: Studies in Thomas Aquinas and Later Medieval Philosophers* (Toronto, 1990).

D. Burr, *Eucharistic Presence and Conversion in Late Thirteenth-century Franciscan Thought* (Philadelphia, 1984).

S. P. Marrone, *Truth and Scientific Knowledge in the Thought of Henry of Ghent* (Cambridge, 1985), complements the same author's work on epistemology in the earlier part of the century.

Index